The Social Life of Books

ƆWƐ

THE LEWIS WALPOLE SERIES
IN EIGHTEENTH-CENTURY CULTURE AND HISTORY

The Lewis Walpole Series, published by Yale University
Press with the aid of the Annie Burr Lewis Fund, is dedicated
to the culture and history of the long eighteenth century (from
the Glorious Revolution to the accession of Queen Victoria). It
welcomes work in a variety of fields, including literature and
history, the visual arts, political philosophy, music, legal history,
and the history of science. In addition to original scholarly work,
the series publishes new editions and translations of writing from
the period, as well as reprints of major books that are currently
unavailable. Though the majority of books in the series will
probably concentrate on Great Britain and the Continent, the
range of our geographical interests is as wide as
Horace Walpole's.

The Social Life of Books

Reading Together in the Eighteenth-Century Home

Abigail Williams

Yale
UNIVERSITY PRESS

NEW HAVEN AND LONDON

Published with assistance from the Annie Burr Lewis Fund.

Yale University Press books may be purchased in quantity for educational, business, or promotional use. For information, please e-mail sales.press@yale.edu (U.S. office) or sales@yaleup.co.uk (U.K. office).

Set in Fournier type by IDS Infotech Ltd., Chandigarh, India.
Printed in the United States of America by

ISBN 978-0-300-20829-0
Library of Congress Control Number 2016958764
A catalogue record for this book is available from the British Library.

This paper meets the requirements of ANSI/NISO Z39.48-1992 (Permanence of Paper).

10 9 8 7 6 5 4 3 2 1

Contents

Acknowledgments

I wish I could say I had written this book at the kitchen table, surrounded by the crumbs and chaos of family life. But projects like this one are really born of solitary hours in underfunded local record offices, or in scholarly research libraries. I am enormously grateful to all the archivists who helped me find and understand the materials in their collections, and especially those in the record offices in Sheffield, Warwick, Somerset, West Devon, Edinburgh, and Gloucester. In rare book libraries, I thank in particular, Clive Hurst, Sarah Wheale, Andrew Honey, and the staff at the Bodleian library, Geoff Day and the library of Winchester College, and Ralph McLean at the National Library of Scotland. I have learnt a lot too from working with colleagues in museums. My understanding of material culture has been energized by the work I have done with Giovanna Vitelli and the university engagement programme at the Ashmolean Museum, and also by my valuable collaboration with Hannah Fleming, Elyse Bell, and others at the Geffrye Museum in London. My research time was funded by the British Academy and the Leverhulme Trust, and without it I couldn't have written the book. St. Peter's College and the Faculty of English have been generous and supportive employers.

One of the most enjoyable parts of doing this project has been my time with the friends and family who hosted me on my research trips, and made my evenings such fun: Penny and Tony Cronin, Robert and Marion Hadaway, Eleanor Collins and Fraser Macdonald, Rob Wyke, Bridget Thornborrow and Mark Heap. I have also been part of two stimulating AHRC research groups, the "Voices and Books" network led by Jenny Richards and Richard Wistreich, and "Uses of Poetry" led by Kate Rumbold. Both have fed my thinking in significant ways, and given full meaning to the social acquisition of knowledge. My friends and my former students in my two book groups in Oxford and London have reminded me repeatedly how enjoyable it is to talk about books as well as read them. Other friends and colleagues have reviewed chapters or drafts for me, and I am indebted here to Adam Smyth, Ros Ballaster, Alex Harris, Stacey McDowell, Ros Powell, and Christy Ford, as well as to the anonymous Yale readers and my editors, Chris Rogers and Sarah Miller. Many of my mistakes and most annoying verbal tics have been gently ironed out by the copyediting of Hilary Hammond and Paul Betz. I have had brilliant research assistants, who have read, corrected and shown me things I couldn't have found for myself: Elyse Bell, Adam Bridgen, Christy Ford, Peter Huhne, and Rebekah King. Much of what I have learnt about eighteenth-century reading has been built on the rich scholarship of the late Stephen Colclough, to whom I owe a huge debt. Thank you to Linda Bree, Antony Buxton, Bridget Clarke, Barbara Crosbie, Matthew Grenby, Emma Walshe, and Charlie Withers, amongst others, for sharing your research treasures.

One of my readers' criticisms about an early draft of the book was that it didn't adequately recognize unhappiness and discord in the home. Thank you to Giles, Eliza, William, Mum, and Laura for enabling me to make that elementary error.

The Social Life of Books

Introduction

Home Improvements

On 15 April 1802, Dorothy and William Wordsworth took one of the most significant walks in literary history. They set out in blustery weather, across the fells near Ullswater in the Lake District. It was misty and mild, with a strong wind, and the first signs of spring were emerging in the hedgerows. Passing Gowbarrow Park, they saw a few wild daffodils, and then as they walked along, they discovered a whole belt of them, almost as broad as a road. Dorothy's journal entry reads:

> I never saw daffodils so beautiful they grew among the mossy stones
> about & about them, some rested their heads upon these stones as on
> a pillow for weariness & the rest tossed & reeled & danced & seemed
> as if they verily laughed with the wind that blew upon them over the
> Lake, they looked so gay ever glancing ever changing.

Brother and sister continued their walk and later found refuge in a tavern, where they enjoyed a robust meal of ham and potatoes. After supper, Dorothy recounts: "William was sitting by a bright fire when I came downstairs. He soon made his way to the Library piled up in a corner of the window. He brought out a volume of Enfield's Speaker, another miscellany, & an odd volume of Congreve's plays. We had a glass of warm rum & water—we enjoyed ourselves & wished for Mary."[1]

There is much to say about this record of a day. Dorothy's diary entry, fuller than the extract quoted here, was to provide the basis for her brother's more celebrated poem "I wandered lonely as a cloud," written two years later, in which he describes the daffodils as joyful companions to a solitary poet-walker. The poem became perhaps the most famous lyric in English literature, the embodiment of the romantic celebration of imagination and nature. Dorothy's diary, on the other hand, is less known outside academic circles. What is also striking is that the poem and the diary represent two very different kinds of literary activity. In writing about the daffodils, Wordsworth emphasised the solipsistic aspect of his experience: the solitary, absorptive, silent nature of imagination, and the images that "flash upon the inward eye." But his sister's journal entry, behind that poem, records the mutual enjoyment of the walk and its daffodils, and it ends, significantly, with communal domestic entertainment. Brother and sister sit by the fire in a tavern after a long day out, taking down random popular collections of verse and drama from the shelves, and reading them aloud together over a glass of rum before bed. Dorothy's version, written in a diary that she often read aloud to her brother, is a story about shared experience.

William Wordsworth and other romantic writers were hugely influential in shaping a model of poetry and literature as a form of individual self-expression, and reading as a source of personal inspiration and self-discovery. For centuries before and since them, poets, artists, and philosophers have, in one historian's words, "limned their aloneness," emphasizing the role of solitude in the creation of culture and knowledge.[2] But communal reading and literary activity have been an equally important part of our cultural history. What might we learn if we dwelt a bit longer on Dorothy Wordsworth's account of her day of walking and reading? Was their experience shared or singular? Was enjoying a book together the same as doing it alone? These questions reverberate throughout the history of sociable reading. The episode illuminates how the appreciation of a work could be shaped by the practical settings within which it was enjoyed—in this case, the valuing of "an odd volume" of Congreve's plays is less about its content, and more about the circumstances in which it is read, over a glass of warm rum, with a loved one, after a memorable day out. We see the whimsical, happenstance nature of literary choices: the Wordsworths take down whatever they find on the shelves of the tavern, and it serves an end, for an evening—it is not a carefully thought out programme of intellectual improvement. What is read is less important than how. The story also illustrates the role of compilations: the other book that Dorothy names, William Enfield's *The Speaker*, was one of the most popular collections of the time, a selection of verse and prose originally aimed at the moral and social improvement of the young, but which came to be used in many homes as a familiar assortment of readable extracts to while away an afternoon or evening in company. Dorothy's example of shared reading offers us a literary experience in which place, company, food, drink, and accessibility all play an important part.

A history of sociable reading puts books back into lives and homes, enabling us to see literature in the round. Hairdressing, carriage rides, and stuttering children all play a part in its story. We can see the way readers' hopes, choices, constraints, and concerns form part of the history of meanings of the book we hold before us three centuries later. It highlights how certain practical and cultural contexts—limited lighting, rudimentary ophthalmology, increased leisure time, desire for the display of polite knowledge—affected the ways in which books were consumed. It also enables us to understand better some of the particularities of the literary history of the era. Sometimes reading together was a preventative measure—particularly in the case of newly fashionable prose fiction, which was widely represented as dangerously titillating. The eroticised solitary female reader depicted in Auguste Bernard d'Agesci's painting *Lady Reading the Letters of Heloise and Abelard* evokes powerfully the perceived seductions of fiction that accompanied the heated debates over the rise of the novel (fig. 1). In fact, she is probably not a reliable representation of the average eighteenth-century novel reader, who, according to some recent book historians, was more likely to have been a respectable middle-aged man. But we can see in her an image of the moral laxity that could stem from ungoverned fiction reading. Sociable reading could be a corrective to such habits, enabling parents to regain some control over the reading lives of their household, and to guide the young and morally vulnerable towards more appropriate forms of literature.

By considering the life of books read out loud, we can also start to see and hear the orality in the history of the book. The sharing of reading is evident both in the material form of books and in their reception history. Print sizes, book formats, and genres of writing were shaped by their suitability for performance. Large text, small books, short extracts, episodic structure, epigrammatic snippets: all made text more portable or more adaptable for use in company. Focussing on the performed and spoken nature of printed text gives us new insights into the way eighteenth-century literature was valued by its readers, forcing us to think about texts with audiences rather

Fig. 1. Auguste Bernard d'Agesci, *Lady Reading the Letters of Heloise and Abelard*, c. 1780, oil on canvas (Charles H. and Mary F. S. Worcester Collections, 1994.430, The Art Institute of Chicago; photography © The Art Institute of Chicago)

than readers, texts that were, as the great cultural historian Robert Darnton puts it, "better heard than seen."[3] Miss Elizabeth Hamilton, a young woman growing up in a gentry family in Stirlingshire in the 1780s, voiced a common opinion when she remarked that the best prose style was "always that which could be longest read without exhausting the breath."[4] The relationship between sentence structure and speech probably played an important part in readerly choices, yet it is not something that commonly features in a history of the literature of the period. Orality is also strongly linked to affect, and the popularity of sentimental literature. Harriet Martineau recounts the transformative impact of reading aloud: "I remember my mother and sister coming home with swollen eyes and tender spirits after spending an evening with Mrs. Opie, to hear 'Temper,' which she read in a most overpowering way. When they saw it in print, they could scarcely believe it was the same story."[5] These factors might help us to understand some of the anomalies of eighteenth-century literature. Was it profound intonation and splendid declamation that secured the now improbable success of James Macpherson's Ossian poetry? Was the popularity of sentimental fiction based on its appeal as the tearful centrepiece of an eighteenth-century social gathering?

This book explores the lesser known world of the everyday uses of books and reading in company, in the homes of the middling sort and lesser gentry.[6] Although the schoolroom, the parish church, the tavern, the coffee-house, and the university all provided important locations for reading aloud, the home was a space distinct in itself, a place that was both public and private, a site of intimacy and also of social display. It was a place of leisure and also of work: a way in which to retreat from the world, but also to prepare oneself for it. Revisiting the busy world of domestic reading offers us the chance to explore the many ways in which books have knitted people together. In exploring the reading life of the home, we get a sense of the complex mix of piety, control, self-improvement, irreverence, and social exchange that shaped eighteenth-century society. People enjoyed their literature in an array of popular, and now unfamiliar, formats, from commonplace books to "spouting collections," as well as in the conventional editions that we are familiar with. They were as likely to read aloud nonfictional texts, particularly histories and religious works, as fictional ones—but the literature telling them how to read, in the home, was primarily focussed on literary works. They studied books on how to improve their elocution skills, learning to assume postures of passion or pathos as they read aloud in company. They copied down and shared their favourite poems, read out dialogues from popular novels, orated moving or comic fragments of plays, lent one another volumes of sermons, and discussed them afterwards. They used tattered old books that had been knocking around a whole village or a family, and they also bought the newly accessible compilations designed for home consumption. They invested in sofas in their libraries, or put bookcases round the fire to enable the sociable enjoyment of books.

Contexts of Reading: Print and Home

To understand fully how books were used, we need to recognise the profound shifts in print culture occurring at this time. It is widely accepted that the eighteenth century saw the birth and evolution of a commercial literary culture, the rise of the professional writer, and the expansion of popular literacy.[7] Recent decades have seen a surge of interest in the history of reading, and a commitment to the idea that how books were used is as important as what's in them.[8] Some literary and cultural historians have identified alongside, and related to, the social changes of the eighteenth century a "reading revolution."[9] They have argued that improving literacy and increased access to a broader range of secular works brought about a move from the intensive oral reading of a few books to the extensive silent reading of a wide range of more secular works.[10] Others have traced a shift from oral to silent reading in changing prose style and sentence structure, in which the greater use of pauses, for example, reflects a diminishing concern for the needs of the listener.[11] But while there is much to be said for the increasing practice of silent reading, pleasure and sociability were also important. Lots of people continued to read aloud because they enjoyed it, like poor Betsy Sheridan, who was banned by her father from family readings of poetry. Longing to read Cowper's poems in company, she said that "this sort of solitary pleasure is like sitting down to a feast alone, when certainly the humblest fare will give more satisfaction if we partook of it with a social, friendly, being."[12] Reading together enabled others to benefit from the book in hand, as the poet William Cowper observed in his rosy picture of the man in rural retirement. In his "warm but simple home"

> he enjoys
> With her who shares his pleasures and his heart,
> Sweet converse, sipping calm the fragrant lymph
> Which neatly she prepares; then to his book
> Well chosen, and not sullenly perused
> In selfish silence, but imparted oft
> As aught occurs that she may smile to hear,
> Or turn to nourishment digested well.[13]

The continuing importance of shared reading is evident in the increasing output of recital books and evening entertainers, embellished with images of reading groups, their titles invoking merry evenings round the fire. These books, like domestic editions of Shakespeare's plays, or magazine abridgements of novels, were aimed at the middling sort, who provide the focus, but not the exclusive source, for the reading habits examined here. They were people who wanted to improve themselves, or their families, who hoped to entertain one another, and didn't necessarily have extensive formal and classical education, or the resources of a vast library. There is widespread anecdotal evidence of readers who describe reading aloud or performing literary texts in the home, and contemporary paintings and engravings depict scenes of performed reading in groups. Conversation-piece portraits of the era commonly depict books as part of the proudly displayed cultural capital of the sitters, as in the portrait of the Huguenot jeweler Charles Moyse-Roubel and his family (fig. 2). *The Social Life of*

Fig. 2. Portrait of a family in an interior, thought to be the Roubel family, by an unknown artist, 1750s, oil on canvas (Geffrye Museum, 148/2010, © The Geffrye, Museum of the Home, London)

Books challenges the idea of the public to private "reading revolution" by showing the ways in which eager readers and canny printers and publishers celebrated the social and educative role of books out loud and in company.

Reading aloud could mean sitting on a bench and reading cheap printed versions of folk tales to an illiterate artisan audience, or gathering the family around for a sermon on Sunday evening. It could mean sitting alone and enjoying the sound of a text. It could also, increasingly, mean standing up in a newly furnished parlour and clutching one's breast in delivery of the sentimental apogee of a recent novel to a group of polite acquaintances. With new formats and new forms of access, readers engaged with books in multiple ways, and the fates of individual works offer glimpses of how texts circulated in ways sometimes unimagined by their original authors. Alain-René Lesage's *The Devil Upon Two Sticks* (*Le Diable Boiteux*) was a comic novel first published in French in 1707, and translated into English the following year. It is seldom read now. But for a century after its first publication, it was reprinted nearly forty times, enjoying a consistent success. With its energetic picaresque narrative, it appealed to all sorts of people. The unhappy Nottinghamshire spinster Gertrude Savile sitting alone in her room read it from supper till midnight in October 1729.[14] George Sandy, a fifteen-year-old apprentice in Edinburgh, who founded a reading group with two of his teenage friends, noted in March 1788 that *The Devil Upon Two Sticks* had been added to their small library of shared books.[15] The Wye book club in Herefordshire were taking turns reading it in 1814.[16] During the 1780s and '90s it was bought by reading associations in Manchester, Halifax, and Macclesfield, and offered to subscribers by circulating libraries in Newcastle, Oxford, London, and Bath.[17] Settled in their Norfolk vicarage, Nancy Woodforde and her uncle enjoyed William Combe's six-volume continuation of the novel, published in 1790–91, and noted on 16 February that "Mrs Custance sent me The Devil upon two Sticks in England to read, which is a very clever entertaining thing indeed and gives you an idea of many wonderful characters in the present age." A couple of days later she remarked: "A dreadful Cold Day with Frost and Snow. Entertained ourselves with reading the Devil upon two Sticks, sometimes I read and sometimes my Uncle." Nancy complains that the freezing weather continues to prevent her from going out; "However I have been much entertained with hearing my Uncle read the Devil upon two Sticks and with sometimes reading part of it to him." By 25 February, they had reached volume 5, and she declared it "the cleverest Book I ever read."[18]

As Nancy's experience suggests, the afterlife of Lesage's book was at least as vigorous as its primary reception. It was read in the original, in translation, and in continuation. It could be read in parts, in magazines, and in an abridged version. It also existed in the form of a coloured harlequinade, a folded pamphlet of four panels, which sold for sixpence plain, or a shilling coloured, and enabled readers to "discover" the story by lifting flaps to reveal different elements of the plot.[19] You didn't actually have to read the novel to know the story. In 1776 the actor and producer Samuel Foote staged his own theatrical adaptation of the novel, casting himself as the hero. And *The Devil Upon Two Sticks* also lived on in popular musical culture, used as the basis for a satirical ballad print on Robert Walpole's administration in the 1740s. These piecemeal sources remind us of some important aspects of book circulation at this time: that some of the most loved works are now little known; that readers had access to their books in many ways, through borrowing, informal book groups, and organised literary societies; that their knowledge of a book might come from a number of forms—stage adaptation, pop-up book, abridgement, or satirical print.

The book trade was not the only thing that was changing during the eighteenth century. The home also evolved, and came to play an increasingly prominent role as a space for leisure and hospitality. Joseph Addison famously pronounced in his introduction to the *Spectator* that he would bring culture "out of Closets and Libraries, Schools and Colleges, to dwell in Clubs and Assemblies, at Tea-Tables, and in Coffee-Houses."[20] The coffeehouses he described have come to dominate academic accounts of bourgeois sociability at this time. But (as we can see from the quotation) Addison saw the home and the tea table as part of the new informal world of knowledge and culture. The design and social history of the home in this period corroborates this sense of the domestic house as a location that confounds the distinction between public and private.[21] This is the era in which polite visiting—the notion of the home as a socialised cultural space—takes off, and this is reflected in the social history of the physical home. *The Social Life of Books* will tell us something about what people were actually *doing* in those newly wallpapered rooms.

While the home operated as a semipublic reception space, it was also lauded as a secluded, virtuous environment, distinct from the distractions of the wider world. In an age of more and more public entertainment, from concerts to pleasure gardens to circulating libraries, domestic space seemed to some to represent a less challenging, more controllable venue in which to spend time. The home, as an embodiment of the family, offered an emblem of moral rectitude. As Cowper wrote in *The Task* in 1785: "Domestic happiness, thou only bliss / Of Paradise that has survived the Fall / . . . Thou art the nurse of virtue."[22] The reality was that every home was different, that houses contained excess and transgression as much as anywhere else. But the idea of home and the wholesome domesticity within it acquired an increasingly privileged status in the ethical vocabulary of the later eighteenth century.[23]

People shared their literature in very different ways: reading books together as a sedative, a performance, an accompaniment to handiwork, a means of whiling away a journey or a long dark evening. They saw reading as a pick-me-up and a dangerous influence, a source of improvement, a way to stave off boredom, and even as a health-giving substitute for the benefits of a walk in the open air. Reading could be about isolation and retreat, or it could be the foundation of sociable interaction. A history of the social life of books is necessarily a work born of myriad sources. It involves reading between the lines and joining dots that may not always be entirely visible. But once we start to do so, we can start to understand more fully what books have meant to readers of the past.

1. How to Read

Went into the Church, heard the Vicar by his snuffling, Lisping,
and Vile reading spoil the most awful and Solemn Service.
—Diary of Lady Eleanor Butler, 29 September 1785

Two contradictory things happen in the history of eighteenth-century reading.
One is the birth of a generation of silent readers. By the end of the century,
some books were cheap enough, and literacy widespread enough, that for the
first time many people could read on their own, silently. But at the same time
there was a near obsession with learning to read out loud: this was the great age
of elocution. Of course, rhetoric, the art of speech, had a long and well-
documented history, and was the subject of numerous treatises, from the
Sophists onwards. As historians have shown, rhetorical culture shaped the early
modern period, and is key to understanding education, intellectual history,
political culture, and literary form, the ways in which men and women thought,
wrote, and acted—but most importantly, sounded. Ben Jonson's claim that "no
glasse renders a mans forme, or likenesse, so true as his speech" offers a powerful
endorsement of the idea of speech—rather than writing—as the image of the
mind.[1] Sixteenth-century theory and handbooks on rhetoric assumed oral
performance was the main aim of those studying rhetoric.[2] Over the eighteenth
century, ideas about delivery and linguistic effect were repackaged in more
plentiful and accessible forms for aspirational audiences eager to acquire skills
of self-improvement.[3] We see a tension between nostalgia for ancient eloquence,
so privileged in the early modern period, and a new emphasis on polite style and
genteel social accomplishment.[4] Reading out a written text becomes a popular
art form, hobby, spectator sport, subject of academic enquiry, and topic of
satire. This chapter explores the culture of learning to read well, and considers
what it was that the good reader was supposed to be doing.

Learning to Read: The Sermon as Example

Eighteenth-century readers had discerning ears. Their understanding of the ways texts could be transfigured (or disfigured) in performance had long been honed through regular consumption of church sermons.[5] Both the experience of listening to sermons and the mass of printed discussion of what made sermon delivery *good* are crucial to reconstructing the history of domestic reading practice in the eighteenth century. In a culture in which the reading of a Sunday sermon was the main performance of the week, each speaker's efforts were judged in terms of both content and delivery. Audiences were also alert to the differences between spoken and written performance. At home one Sunday in 1727, Gertrude Savile spent her afternoon reading the latitudinarian divine George Stanhope's published sermon "Death and Judgment," and pronounced at the end: "I think he is a better orator than Casuist: his Argument is not in so clear a Stile."[6] It seems unlikely that she had heard him reading this sermon, which was first published over thirty years earlier, but she is clear that his style suits oral performance better than written. Perhaps the rhetorical force of his performance in the pulpit obscured contortions in the logic of his argument more manifest on paper. This contemporary awareness of the gap between silent reading and speaking of a text is fundamental to the history of reading aloud. It is evident from Savile's other observations on preaching; having spent a quiet evening at needlework and her harpsichord, she picked up after supper Edward Young's recently published sermon "A True Estimate of Human Life," and enthused: "Extreordinary stile. Poeticall, exceeding entertaining."[7] A few months later she went to a Sunday service at St. James's church, and was quite shocked by what she heard: "Extreordinary Sermon. Blunders in the delivery and a perticularity in the Stile made the Congregation merry and prejudiced them against the goodness of it. I thought it something of Dr. Young's Stile, and after found it *was* him."[8] Poor Dr. Young. This account reminds us of the pressure the clergyman must have been under, in a performative church culture where critical congregations were not the docile reverent sheep we are apt to imagine.[9] His poor delivery clearly undercut the "Extreordinary stile" that had so pleased Gertrude Savile on paper.

Gertrude was not the only listener who regularly recorded her views. Dudley Ryder, a young single lawyer and son of a Dissenting draper, usually went to two sermons on a Sunday, and typically had something to say about both as he shopped around the churches of London.[10] A visit to see the poet Joseph Trapp preaching one afternoon in June 1715 prompted a conversation with his cousin about competent preaching: "We talked together about the great advantage of a proper pronunciation and of that natural way of delivering a discourse which is scarce ever to be met with when men talk in the pulpit in the same tone of voice as they do in common conversation."[11] Ryder and his cousin here struck on one of the ironies of reading in performance, then and now: in order to sound authentic, to have "proper" pronunciation and "natural" delivery, one has to learn a way of speaking that is different from normal, common conversation. Informality is an art. Ryder went on to specify his grievances about Parson Trapp's performance that Sunday: "He . . . behaves very strangely in the pulpit, full of uncouth gestures and postures. His sermon was not very extraordinary, not what one would have expected from a good poet."[12]

It's interesting that both Savile and Ryder desired the same thing of their preachers—something "extraordinary"—and were subsequently disappointed when they found an admired poet distinctly below par in the pulpit. One notable feature of Ryder's running commentary on sermon-giving is that his taste in delivery is quite eclectic. He likes plainness, but he also likes theatricality. On one hand, therefore, he went to hear the preacher Jeremiah Hunt at the independent congregation at Pinners Hall, and applauded his "plain familiar style and manner," stating: "He is not a man of very fluent way of speaking and therefore will never be a very popular man, but is very much liked by men of judgement that prefer good sense before a good style."[13] But he also went to hear a Mr. Smith at Dr. Williams's, and commended the way in which he "makes use of a certain vehemence in his delivery that is very proper. He seems to imitate a little Booth, the actor."[14] Liveliness was also important. A Mr. Briscoe was castigated for his "very dull manner of delivery" and "simple air," which led Ryder to reflect on "what a vast advantage it is to appear lively and brisk in what a man does. I find this fault in myself at home."[15] Ryder knew that a good show was about vocal mechanics as well as style, as in the case of the unlucky Mr. Mayo, who suffered from the "misfortune that his voice tires before he gets to the end of his sermons."[16] It seems that there was a place in church oratory both for theatricality and for plain speaking. But before a critical congregation in the early eighteenth century, there was no room for incompetence (fig. 3).

Fig. 3. William Hogarth, *The Sleeping Congregation*,
London, 26 October 1736, engraving with etching
(Wellcome Library, London)

Reading and the Elocution Industry

Eighteenth-century churchgoing created a body of judicious listeners
informed by the soundscape of worship. Their enjoyment of the spoken
word was determined by the vagaries of performance: pronunciation, style,
theatricality, accessibility, gesture, posture, and appearance. Ryder and
Savile's accounts come from the first quarter of the century, at the start of
what has become known as the great age of elocution. The art of delivering
a sermon was a topic of considerable concern in early modern England. But
the mid–eighteenth century saw the birth of an elocution movement that
came to dominate debates about language, performance, and every aspect of
public speaking: while a vast number of books aimed at teaching good
delivery were published, the essay on how to read aloud became a genre in
itself.[17] Ideas about language and grammar were also influenced by the vogue

for speaking as elocution. Whereas in the seventeenth century writings on language focussed on ideas, during the eighteenth century linguists become preoccupied with the ability to communicate through speech and with the social context of speaking.

The most famous elocutionists of the mid–eighteenth century were Thomas Sheridan and John Walker, both of whom evangelised about the power of good oratory in print and in public lectures. A common emphasis of their and other elocution works of the time is conveyed feeling over textual content. It is not the words that persuade, but the sincere expression of emotion. Consequently, much of the practical theory of how to speak well focusses on the means of infusing feeling into the text. As Francis Gentleman, author of a short introduction to elocution, put it: "What we read or speak *unfelt*, must be like painting without light or shade."[18]

The primary market for a good proportion of these primers on elocution was clergymen, who must have hoped that with some assistance they could become charismatic leaders of their flocks. The kind of printed guidance available ranged from the short and anonymous *Some Rules for Speaking and Action* (1716) to the two-volume *A System of Oratory* (1759) by John Ward, a handsomely produced octavo version of a series of lectures originally given at Gresham College, in London, published with an inaugural oration spoken in Latin. At both ends of the market, reference was made to classical models of rhetoric, and some, like Thomas Sheridan, went so far as to argue that good public speaking would revive the glory of ancient Greece and Rome in modern Britain. However, in the case of *Some Rules for Speaking and Action* and other cheap guides, the emphasis was on the rudiments: variation in tone and speed, use of pacing, and body control: "The *Mouth* should not be *writh'd*, the *Lips bit* or *lick'd*, the *Shoulders shrugg'd*, nor the *Belly thrust out*."[19]

Not everyone approved of the new vogue for taught speaking. James Boswell records an encounter between Samuel Johnson and the elocutionist John Walker.

> Mr. Walker, the celebrated master of elocution, came in, and then we went up stairs into the study. I asked him if he had taught many clergymen. Johnson. "I hope not." Walker. "I have taught only one, and he is the best reader I ever heard, not by my teaching, but his own natural talents." Johnson. "Were he the best reader in the world, I would not have it told that he was taught." Here was one of his

peculiar prejudices. Could it be any disadvantage to the clergyman to have it known that he was taught an easy and graceful delivery? Boswell. "Will you not allow, Sir, that a man may be taught to read well?" Johnson. "Why, Sir, so far as to read better than he might do without being taught, yes. Formerly it was supposed that there was no difference in reading, but that one read as well as another."[20]

Johnson's distaste for elocution seems to rest on his conviction that great delivery should seem innate, rather than taught. It is not clear whether he disapproved altogether of the idea of elocution training, or just thought that one shouldn't own up to it in public. His comments register the relative novelty of the elocution movement, and increasing aspirations for reading aloud.

Johnson and Walker's discussion of tuition versus natural talent goes to the heart of eighteenth-century debates on how to read well. Dudley Ryder and his cousin's conversation about good preaching, cited earlier, turned on the question of how to *simulate* informality within performed reading, because simply *being* informal wasn't enough for public performance. Nature, informality, and ease are key terms in elocution writings. Mannered and stiff delivery was frowned upon. But naturalism needed to be learnt. All the guides of the period stress that the key to effective (and affective) reading was the exaggerated mimicry of a form of natural speech. Readers had to find a way of channelling into public performance the intonation and expression used when they genuinely felt something. James Fordyce, one of the most prolific and widely read conduct writers of the age, urged his readers to imagine their friends telling them a story, and how their emotions would play out in their faces: "the various turns of their Features, the various Radiations of their Hearts, in their Eyes; to observe these glancing with all the bland Lightening of an Animated Tenderness, or melting into the mild Suffusions of Sympathy, or beaming with the cordial Smiles of Congratulation, or darting Forth the very Flame of Virtue."[21] If a speaker could learn to project some of these effects in the pulpit, the result would be transformative: the preacher's face would become "a sort of bright *Mirrour* to his *Mind*, in which we discern the successive Images of Truth and Virtue, that rise up there."[22]

A primary audience for works on elocution was indeed the clergyman hoping to acquire more powerful pulpit skills. The upsurge of interest in public speaking and powerful delivery was partly related to changing trends in Anglican theology, along with developing ideas of innate human sympathy.[23] The latitudinarian movement of the late seventeenth century had emphasised the sociability of religion, with a consequent emphasis on the role of emotional appeal and affectivity within the sermon. And if affectivity was the key to modern Christianity, preachers needed to learn how to create it. Perhaps the reason why so many preachers were seen as, or believed themselves to be, rhetorically ineffective lay in circumstances beyond their control: namely, their nationality. There was at this time a widespread belief that the British were just too physically undemonstrative to be good communicators. The moral and economic philosopher Adam Smith noted the Englishman's reluctance to gesticulate: "A Frenchman, in telling a story that was not of the least consequence to him or anyone else, will use a thousand gestures and contortions of his face, whereas a well-bred Englishman will tell you one in which his life and fortune are concerned, without altering a muscle in his face."[24]

Smith's comic national stereotyping was a problem for a religious culture aiming for powerful verbal communication. Inhibited by their innate national reserve, Britons would have to be taught how to emote and to project feeling more visibly, because, as Gilbert Austin later observed in 1806, "the speakers of our islands cannot depend solely on nature."[25] One of the figures they were encouraged to learn from was, perhaps not surprisingly, a Frenchman, whose writings were mined for advice on how to convey the passions.[26] Charles Le Brun's *A Method to Learn to Design the Passions* was first published in English in 1734 (fig. 4). Le Brun, chief painter to the French king, wrote primarily about the visual depiction of emotion, and his descriptions and illustrations of the passions became the backbone of eighteenth-century elocution theory. Different arrangements of the face and body denoted particular emotions. He was especially interested in the expressive role of the eyebrow: "the only Part of the whole Face, where the Passions best make themselves known" (he also discussed ways of disporting the nose, mouth, and neck).[27] Here is his description of the presentation of horror:

> the Eye-brow will be still more knit than in the former Action; the Pupil, instead of appearing situate[d] in the middle of the Eye, will be sunk low; the Mouth will be half open, but more compressed in the middle than at the corners, which will seem drawn back. By this Action will be form'd wrinkles in the Cheek; the face will appear of

HORROUR.

An object despis'd sometimes causes horrour, & then the eye-brow knits, & sinks a great deal more. The eye-ball placed at the bottom of the eye is half cover'd by the lower eye-lid; the mouth is half open, but closer in the middle than the sides, which being drawn back, make wrinkles in the cheeks; the face grows pale, & the eyes become livid; the muscles & the veins are marked.

Fig. 4. A representation of the emotion of horror from Charles Le Brun, *Heads, representing the various passions of the soul; as they are expressed in human countenance,* published by Robert Sayer, London, c. 1760 (Wellcome Library, London)

a pale colour; the Lips and Eyes a little upon the livid: in which this Passion has some resemblance of Fright.[28]

Eighteenth-century portraiture was greatly influenced by Le Brun. William Hogarth's celebrated portrait from the 1740s of David Garrick acting the part of Shakespeare's Richard III shows some of Le Brun's theories in practice (fig. 5). The image, which depicts King Richard haunted by the ghosts of his victims before the battle of Bosworth, presents Garrick's face in the pose of horror and amazement described by Le Brun.[29]

Le Brun's writings provided a way of categorizing particular passions and their corresponding expression in performance, and he became an influential source for later essays on affective delivery. The emphasis on the embodied nature of emotion, and the notion that feeling was translated through an established vocabulary of gesture and pose, reinforced the connection between speech and formalised physical gesture that was characteristic of much early modern dramatic practice.[30] It also reflected the

Fig. 5. William Hogarth, *Mr Garrick in the Character of Richard the 3d*, London, 20 June 1746, etching (Wellcome Library, London)

elocutionists' belief that the communication of emotions often exceeded the bounds of language. Thomas Sheridan observed that "whenever the force of these passions is extreme, words give place to inarticulate sounds: sighs, murmurings, in love; sobs, groans, and cries in grief; half choaked sounds in rage; and shrieks in terrour, are then the only language heard."[31] Sheridan insisted that these sounds and tones could have "more power in exciting sympathy, than any thing that can be done by mere words."

These ideas about conveying the passions through rapturous gesture and choking grief were influential in placing the emphasis on the nonverbal aspects of delivery, but they were not always helpful models for women learning recitation skills. The emphasis on the passions sat awkwardly in a culture in which women were not supposed to show feelings—or at least, not all of them.[32] Le Brun's illustrations depict men displaying the strong passions of horror, hatred, rage, despair, and contempt, but women are only drawn in states of pure love, desire, hope, and sadness. Acting manuals reflected this caution about the limited range of passions appropriate for women: "Female performers, in particular, should be careful how they go beyond the limits which nature has set them . . . as few of them having the compass of a man's abilities, they often, by great pains, render themselves peculiarly disagreeable."[33]

Emphasizing the communication of feelings, rather than just words or ideas, also permeated eighteenth-century writings on linguistics. Good reading aloud would project emotion and evoke audience response. Thus elocutionary ideals come to dominate theoretical works of this period, and indicate a marked shift from the seventeenth-century understanding of words as real objects or logical ideas to words as the vehicles of expressed emotions and feelings.[34] The primary function of language was not to clarify ideas but to speak, meaningfully, to others. Consequently, textbooks on language emphasise speech as social action, and their grammatical analysis of written language is dependent upon language as spoken. One introduction to grammar explains:

> As in Speech or Discourse there are several Motions made by different Parts of the Body . . . in order to excite Attention and transmit a more clear and perfect Idea to the Hearer, of the Meaning and Intention of the Speaker: So Writing being the very Image of Speech, there are several Points or Marks made use of in it, not only to mark the Distance of Time in Reading, and to prevent any Obscurity or Confusion in the Sense; but also, that the various Affections and Emotions of the Soul, described by the Writer, may be more clearly distinguished and comprehended by the Reader.[35]

In this account of language, not only are writing and speech the same thing; but the marks on the page are the equivalent of physical gestures, intended to intensify the meaning of the words spoken.

One of the results of this thinking was that punctuation was primarily elocutionary, determining a speaker's pauses, speed, and intonation: the "Distance of Time in reading."[36] So, Henry Care, writing in 1687, defines a comma both in terms of syntax and performance: "A comma . . . is a note of a short stay, or distinction between words in the same sentence, when yet the Sense is imperfect, to supply which, something follows depending on what went before: And therefore in Reading, the Voice must there be a very little stopt, but the tenor of it still kept up."[37]

Eighteenth-century linguists' preoccupation with oral delivery meant that punctuation came increasingly to be seen as a sort of notation. Theorists were fascinated by the parallels between musical notation and instructions for pronunciation.[38] Thomas Sheridan declared his intention to reduce "the pronunciation of each word to a certainty by fixed and visible marks," as in music.[39] Perhaps the most elaborate attempt to establish the connection between music and spoken language was Joshua Steele's *Prosodia Rationalis; or, an Essay Towards Establishing the Melody and Measure of Speech*, from the 1770s (fig. 6). Steele created a scheme of marks for timing which would reflect accent and cadence, rests and pauses. Whether many people ever actually used such a method to help their performance seems doubtful, but both John Walker and Thomas Sheridan, the most prominent elocutionists of the era, recommended that students use marked-up copies of texts for practice in

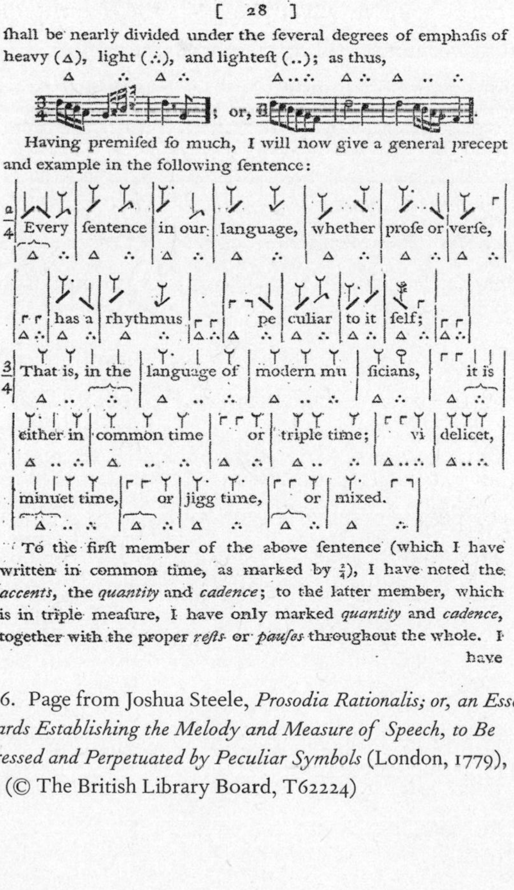

[28]

shall be nearly divided under the several degrees of emphasis of heavy (△), light (∴), and lightest (..); as thus,

(musical notation) ; or, *(musical notation)*

Having premised so much, I will now give a general precept and example in the following sentence:

(notated example) Every | sentence | in our | language, | whether | prose or | verse, |

has a | rhythmus | pe | culiar | to it | self; |

That is, in the | language of | modern mu | sicians, | it is |

either in | common time | or | triple time; | vi | delicet, |

minuet time, | or | jigg time, | or | mixed. |

To the first member of the above sentence (which I have written in common time, as marked by ¾), I have noted the accents, the *quantity* and *cadence*; to the latter member, which is in triple measure, I have only marked *quantity* and *cadence*, together with the proper *rests* or *pauses* throughout the whole. I have

Fig. 6. Page from Joshua Steele, *Prosodia Rationalis; or, an Essay Towards Establishing the Melody and Measure of Speech, to Be Expressed and Perpetuated by Peculiar Symbols* (London, 1779), p. 28 (© The British Library Board, T62224).

delivery. This involved printing sentences in separate portions for correct emphasis, and adding hyphens between accented and unaccented words.

Secular Oratory

The preoccupation with how to read well played a significant part in the public understanding of pulpit oratory in the eighteenth century, while the emphasis on the passions clearly spoke to the modern preacher. But elocution had secular as well as spiritual uses. There were those who relied on public speaking in their professional roles, such as lawyers and politicians, and many of the guides to public speaking name them as potential readers. It was also a way of rising socially. In the 1750s oratory emerged as a craze for tradesmen and apprentices, who formed amateur debating and recitation societies that became known as "spouting clubs."[40] The spouting club, dedicated to the practice and performance of public speaking, provided a responsive audience to aid the aspiring speaker. The clubs were often located in the City of London, or on the edge of it, which suggests the makeup of their member-ship: tradesmen, merchants, and apprentices, eager to learn to read well— with all the potential for social mobility that brought. Printed collections of verse and prose were issued to provide material for these meetings, or perhaps more informal gatherings: you could choose between *The Spouter's Companion* (1770), *The Sentimental Spouter* (1774), *The New Spouter's Companion: or, Complete Theatrical Remembrancer and universal key to theatrical knowledge* (1781), *The Spouter's New Guide* (1796), and *The Juvenile Roscius: or Spouter's Amusement* (1770).

Most of the contemporary references to the spouting clubs seem to be satirical, mocking the lack of education of the speakers, and their religious and political heterodoxy. The London-based trainee lawyer Sylas Neville complained about his visit to the Robin Hood Club in November 1768: "where all sorts of people may harangue on moral & political subjects which few of them understand. In such clubs young men whose passions are strong & their reason weak are furnished with arguments against the sacred obliga-tions of virtue, the sophistry of which too many are neither willing nor able to see."[41]

By the 1760s the ordinary man's desire to train his speaking skills had become a topic of both amusement and concern. One contributor to the *St James's Chronicle* took note of the popular stereotype of the English being awkwardly at a loss for words: they "are so very backward in speaking that their Tongues seem to be frozen, as it were, and their Mouths closed up, by the Coldness of their Northern Climate." But of late, he observed with some alarm, the combination of rhetorical academies, lecturers on elocution, and seminaries of rhetoric for religious oratory have removed national taciturnity, "untying the Tongues and removing the Impediments of Speech in their hitherto-silent Countrymen."[42]

By the mid–eighteenth century, oratory was both a hobby for aspirant tradesmen and a spectator sport. Certain spouting clubs evidently attracted a public audience, and included theatrical performance—sometimes with unfortunate consequences. The *Public Advertiser* of 5 September 1764 recorded some messy spouting:

> One Day last Week, while some Members of a Spouting Club, not far from Temple Bar, were exhibiting their talents to a large Audience, a Top Genius, in the last Scene of Barbarossa, had like to have concluded his Part rather too tragically, for, transported with all the Fire of the Person represented, he could not wait to be harmlessly assassinated, but threw himself upon his Antagonist's Dagger, which being a real one, and very sharp, penetrated thro' his Waistcoat and Shirt, and drew Blood; the sight of which, in an Instant, dispell'd the fumes of Enthusiasm, and from an Indian Prince he sunk into his original Character, that of a Journeyman Barber.[43]

However, much of the public speaking on display was more professional, and was led by the celebrity orators of the day. Thomas Sheridan wrote a series of books on reading aloud, gave lecture tours, and organised events that blended acting, reading, and speech. Called "Attic evenings" in allusion to ancient Greek entertainments, they combined instrumental music, song, and readings, and sometimes a lecture on elocution. They were not to everyone's taste. One disgruntled audience member complained that he "introduced too much of his dissertation on elocution, which was by no means suited to the taste of a mixed audience . . . his voice was, as Churchill describes it, 'irregular, deep, and shrill by fits.'"[44] William Henley, later known as "orator Henley," had a promising pedigree as a commercial orator, with a joint career as a clergyman and Grub Street author. In 1726 he founded the Oratory, an independent academy for the delivery of sermons and lectures, with the prime purpose of improving the state of public speaking.[45]

By the 1760s there was a booming trade in comic versions of public oratory. The actor Samuel Foote put on burlesque oratories at the Haymarket, and Alexander Stevens joined in with his own parody of eloquence, advertised as "A Comic Lecture on the Pilgrims Progress, a Disquisition on the Inquisition, and Orators Oratorised . . . The Question, in which Specimens of true and false Eloquence will be given by the Rostrator, is How far the Parabola of a Comet affects the Vegetation of a Cucumber."[46] Undercutting the solemnity of tone and content of public oratory, evenings such as this were a precursor to Stevens's later, phenomenally successful entertainment, "The Lecture on Heads."[47]

Domestic Oratory

The fact that reading well out loud had become by the latter half of the eighteenth century a social activity and a thriving spectator sport reminds us again of the pleasure that listeners derived from hearing someone else reading. It was a pleasure they were keen to take home with them. Although many of the elocution guides are directed towards the uses of reading aloud in public contexts, they were also aimed at the domestic sphere. In *The Art of Speaking*, first published in 1761, James Burgh told his readers:

> Suppose a youth to have no prospect either of sitting in parliament, of pleading at the *bar*, of appearing in the *pulpit;* does it follow, that he need bestow *no pains* in learning to speak properly his *native language?* Will he never have occasion to read in a company of his friends, a copy of *verses*, a *passage* of a *book*, or *newspaper?* Must he never read a discourse of Tillotson, or a chapter of the Whole Duty of Man, for the instruction of his children and servants? Cicero justly observes, that address in speaking *is highly ornamental, as well as useful, even in private life*. The *limbs* are parts of the body much less noble than the *tongue*. Yet no gentleman grudges a considerable expence of time and money to have his son taught to use *them* properly.[48]

No young man could afford to let slip a skill that would serve him so well in the public or private contexts suggested here: reading verses, passages of books, or newspapers with friends; reading improving theological works to his family and children. Domestic oratory was part of the role of the well-bred young man in the eighteenth century, and it took different forms. It needed to be learnt.

It is hard to know exactly how to interpret Burgh's preface, or precisely who this kind of collection was aimed at and used by. The popular elocution movement was inextricably linked to social aspiration, the standardization of pronunciation, and the elimination of regional accents.[49] In putting his instruction on a par with the rhetorical training of vicars, barristers, and politicians, Burgh offered aspiring tradesmen and professionals a glimpse of cultural capital within their grasp. The appeal of elocution for this kind of lower-middle-class readership is made explicit by James Fordyce in his *Sermons to Young Women*. Fordyce is very clear about the sorts of women he hopes will acquire elocutionary skills. Mindful of the daughters of aspirational tradesmen, he observes: "what can be more ridiculous than to see our city girls, not excepting the daughters of plain tradesmen and honest mechanics, taught for years together, at great expence, a smattering of that [foreign languages] which soon after they leave the Boarding-school is generally forgotten; while they are left ignorant of the superior beauties and just pronunciation of their mother-tongue?"[50] Learning to read well, one could acquire important presentational skills, as John Drummond explains in his *Collection of Poems for Reading and Repetition* (1762): "It will [enable young people] to conquer that hesitation of speech, very common to young people; to remove that simple downcast look, which is often interpreted as meanness of spirit, want of education, or of proper encouragement; and may assist them in attaining that unaffected address, which is equally remote from impudent effrontery, and clownish bashfulness."[51]

There is some evidence to suggest that tuition in how to read literature aloud extended further down the social scale. A much-used copy of *A Key to Spelling and Introduction to the English Grammar, Designed for the Use of Charity and Sunday-Schools* (1788), a book designed to teach pronunciation and grammar to the children of the poor, shows that these children, who might not actually have learned to write themselves, were nonetheless urged to read well. The copy in the British Library is interleaved with a teacher's marginal notes, one of which states: "When you speak in public, or in any Oration, do not clip your Words, but express every Syllable, except in Poetry where the Measure being confined may require it. As, say not, Should'st for Shouldest, Could'st for Couldest."[52]

Within the home, the craze for elocution could encompass those unlikely to speak in public. Many of the public contexts for oratory—not only the professional ones, like law, politics, and the church, but also the social spouting clubs or theatrical performances—excluded women. Although there were some female debating societies, the oratory movement was primarily a male activity within which speaking women were lampooned:[53]

> Fair *Celia* may prattle as much as she will,
> And by *public harangue,* give a hint of her skill;
> In the mind of her swain this reflection must come,
> "If thus noisy *abroad,* she'll be much worse at *home.*"[54]

The domestic household, with its selective sociability, offered an opportunity for women to read aloud in a more acceptable way, and the large numbers of domestic instructors and collections of extracts available supplied ready-made guides.[55]

However folksy and nostalgic reading aloud in the home may seem to us now, it was done within a culture of keen interest in the arts of elocution and verbal self-improvement. Some women and children evidently trained with their own visiting elocutionary tutors: the contributor to the *St James's Chronicle* blames the rise in British loquacity both on the public rhetorical academies and on the likes of "Mr. *Farro,* who undertakes to teach the Rudiments of Eloquence to all good little Boys and Girls, and their Mammas into the Bargain."[56] Reading well would add polish to young women, and give them skills that they could demonstrate to their advantage. Many images of idealised reading together show young women and men attractively joined in their leisure pursuits.

The slightly predatory vicar William Jones certainly enjoyed the intimacy of shared reading—Jones had a predilection for his young female students, and at one point in his diary he breaks out into an encomium on the joys of reading together with a blossoming pupil:

> Miss Joachim is come! . . . Now for all the beauties in poetry, &c, which
> I have selected since I saw her last at my cottage. It fares, with me at
> least, when I remark strikingly beautiful & pathetic passages, whether
> in prose or poetry . . . the pleasure is scarcely half-felt, or enjoyed,
> unless I have some one, near me,—with whom I may, as it were, inter-
> change my ideas, & communicate my pleasurable feelings![57]

James Burgh's book *The Art of Speaking* is typical of many of the home guides on reading. Its contents are largely secular, and it includes entertaining, moving, or dramatic extracts from a range of authors, that are marked up with pointers to aid the reader's speaking. So we have the "emphatical Words printed in Italics," and there are notes referring back to the "Essay" on reading at the beginning of the volume.[58] In keeping with the contemporary enthusiasm for the passions, the examples Burgh gives are divided up by emotional theme—indignation, pity, anger—and the authors range from Aristotle to Milton and Addison. The book told you how to read, and then talked through examples of good reading and speaking practice. A similar volume is John Drummond's *The Art of Speaking and Reading in Public* (1780), with the subtitle *For the Use of Schools and Private Perusal*.[59] The texts included here are predominantly literary, and from a range of genres. Some are dramatic and stirring orations: the story of Damocles, Cassius's speech exhorting Brutus to oppose Caesar, and Queen Elizabeth's speech to the army at Tilbury. Others are sentimental, such as the death of Le Fever in Sterne's *Tristram Shandy*, or lyrical, such as Milton's *Morning Hymn*, or dramatic dialogues from Molière, or comic pieces such as "The Humourous Scene of cramming Sir John Falstaff into a Basket."[60] Each is accompanied by marginal notes indicating the relevant passion or genre of delivery, the various kinds of which had been described in their verbal and physical manifestations in the introduction.

Collections such as these serve a dual function: they are both guides on how to read and literary anthologies or miscellanies. The way in which they assembled gobbets of texts, specifically for sociable delivery, suggests that many of the numerous miscellanies of the period were probably used for this purpose, as we shall see later. To be read aloud, texts needed to be manageably short, and it is partly for this reason that so many of the verse and prose collections of the eighteenth century privilege small portions of poems and novels. How writing was categorised and marked up according to the appropriate passion and effect also sheds light on forms of writing and reading. If much literature was consumed in performance, and performance was understood to be the projection of distinctly codified emotions, this might help us to understand why eighteenth-century prose fiction takes the forms it does, as we shall see in Chapter 7.

Guides to domestic reading did not just deal with enunciation—gesture and the physical articulation of passion were also part of the performance. The elocutionist John Walker addresses the matter of how to stand and deliver:

> When we read to a few persons only in private, . . . we should
> accustom ourselves to read standing; that the book should be held in
> the left hand; that we should take our eyes as often as possible from
> the book, and direct them to those that hear us . . . When any thing
> sublime, lofty, or heavenly, is expressed, the eye and the right hand
> may be very properly elevated; and when any thing low, inferior, or
> grovelling is referred to, the eye and hand may be directed down-
> wards: when any thing distant or extensive is mentioned, the hand
> may naturally describe the distance or extent; and when conscious
> virtue, or any heart-felt emotion, or tender sentiment occurs, we
> may as naturally clap the hand on the breast.[61]

To a modern reader Walker's instructions sound impossibly stagey
and artificial. Did readers really clap a hand over the heart at every tender
moment? Did they remember to look up and down at the appropriate
times? His instructions remind us that informality is a relative concept.
The elocutionary movement privileged ease and naturalism, but that
took the form of what now seems to us very artificial manifestations of
feeling.

For those who found the approach of reading by classified passion
overly schematic, later reading primers provided more practical guides. These
afforded a greater sense of elocutionary hand-holding than previous works
had, by including running commentaries on how to read aloud particular
sections of a work. Reading primers combine two forms of instruction: they
tell the reader how to deliver a piece, and also indicate what is moving, significant, or affecting about it. They were likely aimed at a readership with little
formal literary education, since they set about to tackle the basics of literary
appreciation in their instructions.[62] *The Reader or Reciter* (1799), a work "by
the Assistance of Which any Person may Teach Himself to Read or Recite
English Prose with the Utmost Elegance and Effect," was devoted to prose,
with a smattering of drama. In the advertisement the anonymous author takes
issue with Thomas Sheridan's prescriptive emphasis on accuracy, which, it is
claimed, is liable to become "frigidly inanimate."[63] His more practical instruction takes the form of italicised passages of commentary in the text, interspersed with passages of explication and encouragement, urging users to
overcome their self-consciousness and be "unembarrassed."[64] Here is his
version of a passage from the *Rambler*:

OBIDAH, the son of Abensina, left the caravansera early in the morning, and pursued his journey through the plains of Indostan. (*Be now a little warm and animated in your expression.*) He was fresh and vigorous with rest; he was animated with hope; he was incited by desire. (*Now look as if you were viewing the scene described.*) He walked swiftly over the vallies, and saw the hills gradually rising before him. (*You must glow with the writer, in your expression, as you proceed with this enchanting description.*)[65]

It's not entirely clear how one learnt to "glow," but as this extract shows, careful treatment was required if one was to do justice to one's author. One of the ironies of *The Reader* is that while many of its passages for imitation are taken from Samuel Johnson and Laurence Sterne, both authors had mocked the idea of taught delivery.[66] It is also significant that the literary content of both *The Reader* and *Sheridan and Henderson's Practical Method* is not contemporary. Almost all the texts reproduced are from at least thirty and often fifty or more years previously. As remains the case today, old favourites, the kinds of stories and poems that middle-class and lower-middle-class domestic audiences wanted to hear, were far from the cutting edge of literary fashion.[67]

One of the features of the elocution movement was its common insistence that there was a right way to do things—and many wrong ways. According to the experts, close textual analysis would lead to the correct delivery of a passage, and so a lot of the teaching involved explaining what texts actually meant, before they could be delivered effectively. Here is a snippet of Thomas Sheridan's eight-page treatment of the Lord's Prayer:

In the first words of it, "Our Father which art in Heaven"—that false emphasis on the word, *art*, has almost universally prevailed. This strong stress upon the affirmative, *art*, looks as if there might be a doubt, whether the residence of God were in Heaven, or not; and the impropriety of the emphasis will immediately appear, upon changing the word we are accustomed to, to another of the same import.[68]

Sheridan's writings and lectures painstakingly covered the various aspects of delivery—emphasis, pauses, tone, and gesture. These things could be learned through practice and close reading, but some of the obstacles to good reading were an accident of birth. Class and gender were often at the heart of elocution, even if they weren't always explicitly discussed.[69] A few guides addressed the "correct" form of pronunciation, which was cleansed of provincial taint. The introduction to *Beauties of Eminent Writers,* published in Edinburgh in 1794, gave as its first lesson examples of the sounds of the vowels, explaining that "the exercises annexed to this rule will tend to give foreigners and provincials (particularly North Britons) the proper sounding of the vowels, which is the principal difficulty in English pronunciation."[70] Such observations expose the close connection between elocution and social mobility, and the extent to which those learning to read aloud would need to compensate for their own regionality before they could become truly polite. Readers might also have to address their own gender: women were accused of being particularly prone to the sing-song intonation so frowned upon in eighteenth-century advice manuals.[71] Fordyce criticised women for "running too commonly into a monotony, which their teachers have not taken sufficient pains to correct."[72] But as he was berating his young women for not being better coached, Fordyce also worried about whether it was suitable for them to be reading aloud at all: "I mentioned the exercise of Reciting verses. With relation to this, I would only say, that I do not wish a young woman to indulge it in any company, that is not very private and chosen indeed; how much soever it is to be desired, that she should store her memory with some of the most select sentiments, and striking descriptions, from the best writers both in verse and prose."[73]

Fordyce was nervous about women reciting willy-nilly because it smacked too much of performance. Here we see one of the core tensions within the elocutionary movement, and in particular the history of reading aloud: the difference between theatrical and domestic recital. This was an important distinction for both men and women to grasp. While the author of *The Reader* recommends Shakespeare for readings, as fine displays of the human passions, he also states: "It will not be expected in the reader that he should enter into a theatrical exhibition of them, and give them that personation which we are used to see displayed on the stage."[74] The author of the *Sheridan and Henderson* collection is in the same position, urging his pupils to be more expressive in their reading, yet not overly dramatic. He tries to find a middle way between "the cold inanimated manner usually adopted by readers in common [and] the theatrical cant frequently practiced by most of our public performers."[75] Many elocutionists and educationalists stress the difference between a conversational and a theatrical style of reading. It is hard to be sure of exactly which elements of dramatic practice were included in this "theatrical cant," but teaching manuals concur in the things they disapprove of: strongly marked contrasts of emotion; high volume; slow tempo; a sing-song style, and a heavy rhythmic pattern or "chant."[76] The sing-song or chant-like styles of reading were good for attracting attention on stage, but less useful for polite, conversational settings.

Theatrical performance occupies a curious space in the history of domestic reading aloud. Just as in the wider elocutionary teaching of the time, there is a clear emphasis on naturalism over theatricality. Even in the theatre itself this charge against artificial delivery was made, particularly in relation to tragedy. The young London lawyer Dudley Ryder states: "I observed in the general that the manner of speaking in our theatres in tragedy is not natural. There is something that would be very shocking and disagreeable and very unnatural in real life. Persons would call it theatrical, meaning by that something stiff and affected."[77] Similarly, James Fordyce urges readers to speak "as near the ordinary Way of speaking in common Conversation as possible. Let them not declaim, not imitate the *Theatrical* Manner, which over-does, or leads out of Nature, but speak easily."[78] At the same time, however, prominent performers on the stage were seen as good models for imitation and authorities on delivery. The anonymous author of *The Art of Delivering Written Language* (London, 1775) dedicated his work to David Garrick, the most celebrated actor of the day, because he was, he claimed, "so conspicuous in the world of elegant learning, and so universally allowed one of the first judges of propriety in every branch of oral delivery."[79] However, too much theatrical influence made a reading too artificial. Too mannered, too frigid, too inanimate, too flippant, not flippant enough, unsentimental, or just plain boring—these were the potential obstacles for budding speakers of the period. Reading well in the eighteenth century was harder than it sounded.

There is very little surviving evidence of individuals' experiences of learning to read aloud, and most of what we know comes from printed guides and treatises on elocution and delivery. It is hard to gauge how far actual performance correlated with the theory, and more or less impossible to know what reading really sounded like. And there were many readers who happily continued to read away to one another utterly heedless of the changing intellectual contexts of theories of reading and delivery. So it is important not to assume that all the shared reading described later in this book adhered to the prescriptive models offered by Sheridan and others. What is significant is that both in printed advice and in actual practice, the social uses of books were commonly linked to the idea of politeness and accomplishment—and of appearing at ease.

The commonplace books and correspondence of the Chubb family in Somerset, in southwest England, offer some insight into the link between reading, cultural attainment, and refinement. Jonathan Chubb (born 1715) was a timber and wine merchant in the thriving market town of Bridgwater. Little is known of his family. He was said to be, according to a later family memorandum, "a man of very peculiar character, of very strong will, and very reserved."[80] Jonathan Chubb kept a commonplace book, in which he recorded information about his trade, weights and measures, the movements of the planets, and an alphabetised series of verse commonplaces on themes such as "Affliction" and "Chastity." He also made notes on his young children's progress. He took a particular pride in the achievements of his son and heir, John, or Jack, Chubb (in regard to his two daughters, Kitty and Sophia, he notes only measles and marriages). John was born in May 1746, and by the time he was a little over three, his father wrote: "Can tell most Words; & read properly, almost any of Gays Fables; & can write ye Alphabet, but not words." It's hard to imagine any contemporary three-year-old reading or reciting John Gay's *Fables*. By the time he was four and a half, John "Can write almost as well as this, can read English, especially Verse, better than one half of the Parsons & other men who are supposed able to read. Knows a great many Latin Words & can read Greek with but little hesitation." In 1751 "Jack is now five years old, & can construe & parse the 1st Georgick of Virgil, with very few Blunders."[81] As a small boy, John was already being encouraged to read adult literary texts aloud, including those in Latin and Greek, and his father took pleasure in his ability to do so well. Jonathan Chubb was to continue to try to shape his son for the world, and to guide him in more intangible social skills—perhaps because as a reserved man, he found this difficult himself. When he was thirteen, John spent some time in London staying with an uncle in Cheapside—in theory, he was deciding what to do with his life. The series of letters between him and his father from October 1759 to March 1760 illustrate the ambitions of both men, which are at times in conflict. Once John is installed in London, his father writes to him with some important advice:

Dear Jack

    Among other things learn Politeness. The Essence of which is
Freedom & Ease. Its Reverse is Affectation more than Awkwardness.
The having Pride sufficient to lift you above Vanity (any kind of
which makes the Coxcomb) is the best Gaurd [sic] against Affectation.
But you must also beware of immitating even the Character that you
approve the most. A Copier is a Mimick. You should be as free &c as
that Person is free &c; but not in the same manner. We should learn
from the ancient good Authours to give proper Rules to our Works,
not their Rules; *such* as, as naturally suit Ours, as *theirs* Theirs. To do
other-wise is to act the Daw in borrowed Plumes. And not to be
Original is not to be a Self. . . . The Difficulty of learning Politeness
consists in its Ease. It ought to be so simple and natural that it should
not be, must not appear to be, acquired. To learn is to use art, inconsistent with simplicity.[82]

Learning to be polite was just like learning to read aloud—it had to
look unlearnt, natural, and easy. Jonathan Chubb decided that a good way to
teach his son sociability was to send him passages of Horace, urging him to
"if possible pass your Evenings like the Companions of Horace," before
quoting from the sixth satire, which spoke of the value of virtuous, serious
conversation. Jack had slightly different ideas from his father about how he
wanted to succeed in the world. His father advised him not to play cards,
but John argued that to avoid them was to cut oneself off from making
friendships—something Jonathan Chubb had told him was very important.
He also wanted to stay in London: "If it was not to see you, my dr Mama, &
Sisters, I should never wish to see Bridgewater more. I cannot perceive how
a Person that has any Spirit, any desire of Pushing forward in the World, or
any desire for Company can live in the country."[83] The problem was that
young John Chubb, who had been sent to London to fix on a profession,
chose an unsuitable one. In a letter of December 1759 he declared he wanted
to become "A Limner," or a painter. He listed six reasons why, the last of
which was "6thly Bec: one has the Pleasure of looking at Pretty Ladies &c."[84]

As one might imagine, for a prosperous provincial businessman who
wanted his son to acquire a useful skill and come home, this seemed like a
terrible idea. The correspondence shows father and son politely trying to
reconcile two different versions of John's future: one of a life of provincial
professional ease in Bridgwater, and one of a sketchily imagined artistic

endeavour in London. The artist plan came to nothing, and John Chubb returned to his hometown, where he eventually became mayor. He carried on painting, and his pictures and sketches have become a rich visual resource describing the contemporary local world he lived in.[85] He continued to develop the sociable literary pursuits his father had been so proud of when he was four or five, and his commonplace books, discussed later on, are full of impromptu verses, imitations of Horace, poems addressed to friends, bon mots, and political ballads. Some of them are marked up for oral delivery.[86] And he was to pass on the same emphasis on reading well that he had gained from his father. In 1798 he wrote to his young son, Morley Chubb, who was at a local school, enclosing lines of a speech he had written for Morley to recite at the school's Christmas exhibition: "If you do learn them, take care to pronounce them slowly & distinctly, & notice the pauses, and the emphasis on the words, that are marked: & don't give a copy of them to any body, for tho they may pass off in speaking, they will not bear the eye. Perhaps I may see you by the time you have learned to repeat them, & then I shall hear how you are likely to come off" (fig. 7).[87]

⁂

John Chubb's story is a modest one, but it gives us some sense of the aspiration and the steady acquisition of cultural sophistication that underwrote much of reading practice in the eighteenth century. Far from being a dying custom of preliterate communities, reading out loud *well* was at the very centre of polite accomplishment. This is probably because it was increasingly a matter of social preference rather than the only way a book could be consumed. Teachings on how to read aloud had a very visible public dimension, as well as a private one. In a world in which everyone from the Prince of Wales's children down to bakers and barbers' apprentices in Middle Temple was furiously working away at reading out loud with style, it is unthinkable that these ambitions and skills were not extended to the home. The proliferation of guides and primers not only showed readers how to achieve affect; they also gave them collections of great and favourite literature to appreciate. The elocution movement shaped not only *how* words were spoken, but also *what* was spoken.

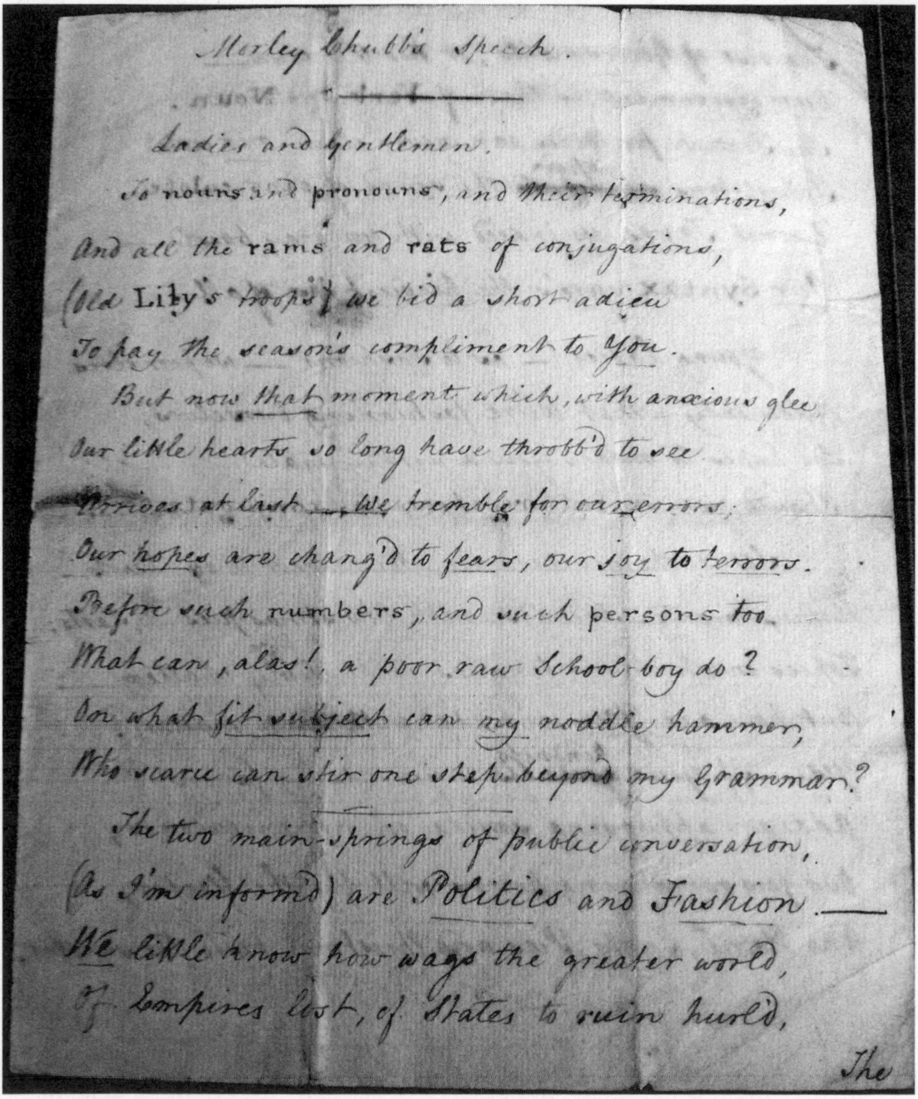

Morley Chubb's Speech.

Ladies and Gentlemen,

To nouns and pronouns, and their terminations,
And all the rams and rats of conjugations,
(Old Lily's troops) we bid a short adieu
To pay the season's compliment to You.

But now that moment which, with anxious glee
Our little hearts so long have throbb'd to see
Arrives at last — We tremble for our errors;
Our hopes are chang'd to fears, our joy to terrors.
Before such numbers, and such persons too
What can, alas! a poor raw School-boy do?
On what fit subject can my noddle hammer,
Who scarce can stir one step beyond my Grammar?

The two main-springs of public conversation,
(As I'm inform'd) are Politics and Fashion —
We little know how wags the greater world,
Of Empires lost, of States to ruin hurl'd,

The

Fig. 7. Marked-up speech in a letter from John Chubb to his son Morley Chubb, 1798 (South West Heritage Trust, Somerset Archives and Local Studies, A/CSC 2/4; reproduced by permission of Bridgwater Town Council)

2. Reading and Sociability

Bo & me dined at G.P. [grandfather's house] we took a walk to
Kilburn after dinner Mrs Cary drank at G.P. Bo & me Read to G.P.
—Diary of William Burgess, 19 March 1790

Home or Abroad?

In 1785 the thirty-five-year-old Elizabeth Brain proudly put the final stitches
into the embroidered sampler she had been working on for several weeks
(fig. 8). A stretch of woolen canvas, the size of an A4 piece of paper, it was a
bold and confidently executed piece, embellished in fine detail with coloured
silks. Its subject, like many of its kind, was the life of the home. It depicts a
four-square house finely set in a landscaped garden, a sinuous drive twisting
through carefully placed fruit trees and deer. A curved bench beside a lake
offers a place for contemplation of the ordered idyll. Right at the heart of the
composition, Elizabeth Brain has embroidered some text, which reads:
"Conversation speak with ease, / Shun Barbarous words / as Rocks in seas."

This sampler is an object that says much about domesticity in the eighteenth century. Shunning religious themes in favour of the robustly secular,
Elizabeth Brain chose to embroider a piece that celebrated both the material
joys of a home and the social values associated with this idyll—easy conversation, a world free of jarring discord. Her act of needlework was also a testament to her own domestic virtue, a vision of a home as a place of respite, yet
one in which hands were never idle. With its twinnings of home and sociability, leisure and virtuous productivity, her work embodies many of the fundamental concepts that inform shared reading in the eighteenth-century home.

By the end of the eighteenth century there were numerous newly available places in which to spend leisure time and money in company—pleasure

36

Fig. 8. Sampler by Elizabeth Brain, 1785, woolen canvas embroidered with silks (Victoria and Albert Museum, T.750-1974; © Victoria and Albert Museum, London)

gardens, coffeehouses, museums, and concerts were a novelty, and the cause of much comment and excitement.[1] It is undoubtedly true that many people took full advantage of these innovations in external leisure activity. But diaries and inventories show us that the home remained an essential place of recreation for women—and men—of property.[2] Our forebears supped, they dined, they played cards, read, gossiped, argued, and performed music together in their homes throughout the eighteenth century. The choice of home over away would have been in part determined by economics and geography. For those living in the countryside, socializing in the home would have been the norm. Nicholas Blundell, a Catholic landowner living in Little Crosby, an estate just south of Liverpool, notes many occasions for spontaneous and extensive hospitality of family and neighbours:

> Whilst I was out I was sent for home, being my brother Langdale
> was come to lodg here . . . Lord Molineaux sent a Servant to let us

know he intended to dine here on Thursday . . . Coz. Scarisbrick
sent to let me know his famoly and Croston famoly design to lodge
here on Monday Next . . . William Ainsworth came here betymes in
ye Morning. He brought a Present of Fish. He went a-Coursing
with me. He lodged here.[3]

Blundell's roll call of his guests is interesting for what it tells us about
the range of people he hosted—in this case, his guests run from the local
aristocracy (Molineaux), to his tenant farmer (Ainsworth), to his extended
family. It is also clear that this hospitality was often impromptu, and could
stretch out for a considerable period of time. It would have demanded a capacious larder and the ability to provide meals for large groups at short notice—
Blundell's "Disbursement Book" shows that food and drinks were laid on in
quantities that reflect continual and large-scale entertaining.[4] One of the
interesting features of Blundell's diary is that he records his life in relation to
social exchanges. Each volume of the diary is prefaced by an index that
includes the following categories:

I.   We lodged abroad or came home. Servants or others went hence or came
      to live here.
II.   We dined abroad or were abroad at Noone.
III. We made Visets after Diner
IV.   At Diversions at Home or Abroad . . .
IX.   Persons dined or suped here or came after Diner.
XV.   Relating to Licker. Commicall Passages or pleasant . . . dis-cours.[5]

That this is the primary way in which he categorises his time and marks out
the year is significant. Blundell's access to public entertainments would have
been limited by the fact that he lived in a small rural village in Lancashire.
Domestic entertainment wasn't just the fate of those living outside London,
or those with families, however. Even unmarried bachelors spent evenings at
home entertaining their friends rather than out at the inn or coffeehouse.
Dudley Ryder spends a large part of his time entertaining his friends in his
rooms, or visiting them. The same is true for many seemingly clubbable men
of the eighteenth century who, like James Boswell, embraced home entertainment with enthusiasm—and not just because it was cheaper. The inventories of middle-class domestic houses show that the prime location for the
entertainment of others—the parlour—frequently included a card table, a

harpsichord, game boards, and tea tables.[6] They also seem often to have contained objects to interest others, and diarists of the period mention showing collections of fossils, prints, or drawings to their friends. The Norfolk parson James Woodforde describes being shown (at some length) the coin collection of a clerical friend; London lawyer Sylas Neville collects shells, fossils, and semiprecious stones and entertains in his "best parlor";[7] Henry Prescott, a clerical official from Chester, spends evenings with local male friends discussing ideas, books, and antiquities over a "domestic pint."[8]

The Advantages of Home Entertainment

Staying at home was often more practical and cheaper than going out. But it also had moral benefits, particularly for women. Was it really wholesome to spend one's time amongst relative strangers? James Fordyce counsels his female readers to be cautious of the giddy world of public sociability: "Are these the scenes of true enjoyment? What, where the heart cannot be unfolded; where the understanding has little or no play; where all is reserve, ceremony, show?"[9] Public gatherings and entertainments were all surface, he argued, and because of that they could provide no lasting enjoyment. Those who had to turn to such follies to amuse themselves were to be pitied, because they were unable to find enjoyment closer to home: in themselves, in reading, in rational conversation, amongst their family, or in "real friendship." Fordyce's emphasis on the home reminds us that the house was not necessarily a place of retreat from social exchange. As he saw it, it was within the home that one found the lasting and beneficial pleasures of friendship and conversation. We find similar arguments made by the anonymous editor of a collection of popular poetry published in 1750, entitled *A New Tea-Table Miscellany: or, Bagatelles for the Amusement of the Fair Sex*. Like Fordyce's sermons, this collection was aimed at female readers, and the pleasures of conversation at home, around the tea table, are gendered. Conversation, we are told,

> is no where to be found so perfect, and free from the views of
> interest, the stings of rancor, or the pangs of revenge, as at the
> TEA–TABLE; for if the merchant transacts business with his
> brother-merchant, the sweets of the conversation are lost, and as it
> were swallow'd up in the diffidence they have of each other, the

dread they have of being over-reach'd, and the gloomy imaginations of losing some of that fortune, the encrease of which is their
daily care. Hence arises the unmanly habit of dissimulation, of
keeping ourselves upon the reserve, and lying in wait to take advantage of the slips and weaknesses of each other.

But at the social and grief-removing tea table, all selfish views are
lost, all restraint is laid aside, all ceremony discarded, all the company
is entitled to the same freedom, and all glad to bless and be bless'd, in
the mutual reception and diffusion of happiness and pleasure.[10]

This author, like Fordyce, emphasises the potential for deception and
dissimulation within more public arenas. He also stresses the improving
potential of mixed company within the home—the company around the table
consists, he says, of "parents and their children, brothers and sisters, friends,
relations and strangers."[11] This is in sharp contrast to the competitive all-male
environment he associates with socializing outside the home—which,
perversely, can foster the "unmanly" habit of dissimulation.[12] Sociability in
mixed company was increasingly perceived to be more polite than all-male
gatherings.[13] The paradigm of the mixed group was an emblem of virtue and
prosperity, as the many conversation-piece portraits of the period amply
illustrate.[14]

Within the world of domestic hospitality there were very different ways
of seeing others at home. In London, a typical pattern might involve several
short visits in one day. But in the country, with longer distances, visiting was
more likely to take the form of a prolonged period staying with a host.[15] In
fact, we can see contemporaries disputing the merits of these different kinds
of social occasions. Was a house party more beneficial than a visit? How long
was long enough in the company of others? Surviving diaries of the period
reveal a bewildering number of visits made and received during the course of
each day.[16] A sample entry from the diary of Elizabeth Tyrrell, a middle-aged
mother from a professional merchant family living just outside London, lists
many instances of impromptu hospitality, in which friends and family would
meet, part, regroup later in the day, go out again, and receive different sets of
visitors. One might be tempted to think that such visiting was curtailed by the
darkness of nights without electricity. But Tyrrell, like other eighteenth-
century diarists, routinely stays up late: in August 1808 she spends the day
with a group of people at Hampton Court, not arriving home in Kew until

nine o'clock in the evening. After that they have tea and coffee, and after that one of the guests goes for his violin and is accompanied on the flute: "they played Country dances, and four Couples stood up. I gave them some warm Wine & Water to drink, and they danced till One o'clock, when we separated."[17]

Others show a similar ability to burn the midnight oil—or candle—regardless of the season. Mary Curzon writes to the unmarried Northamptonshire heiress Mary Heber of her stay at Hagley in Worcestershire in November 1776: "We are quite rakes here, for we seldom come home before twelve."[18] Elizabeth Raper, daughter of an East India merchant living in Eltham, just outside London, writes of going into town for the day, and returning home: "Dark by that we got to Eltham ... Arrived safe at Foot's Cray between 7 and 8. Mr. Hotham was determined on going several times, but somehow he staid all night. Read Hogarth's Analogies, supped, sung, and came up to bed before one."[19] The shopkeeper Thomas Turner describes one particularly memorable night out (and in) in February 1757 that he spends with his neighbours and the local vicar:

> About 10.20 we went to supper on 4 boiled chicken, 4 boiled ducks, some minced veal, sausages, cold roast goose, cold chicken pasty, cold ham ... After supper our behaviour was far from that of serious, harmless, mirth for it was downright obstreperious mirth mixed with a great deal of folly and stupidity. Our diversion was dancing (or jumping about) without a violin or any music, singing of foolish healths, and drinking all the time as fast as it could be well poured down ... [about three thirty] I came home ... This morn about 6 o' clock, just as my wife was gladly got to bed and had laid herself down to rest, we was awakened by Mrs. Porter, who pretended she wanted some cream of tartar. But as soon as my wife got out of bed, she vowed she should come down ... Then the next thing in course must be to have me downstairs, which I being apprized of, I fastened my door ... As soon as ever it was open, they poured into my room, and as modesty forbid me to get out of my bed in the presence of women, they drew me out of bed (as the common phrase is) tipsy turvy ... and instead of my clothes, they gave me time to put on my wife's petticoat. In this manner they made me dance with them without shoes and stockings until they had emptied their bottle of wine and also a bottle of my beer.[20]

Hospitality took different forms, and Turner's twenty-four-hour drinking binge was the exception rather than the rule. Wild evenings like this one, or large house parties, were different from a single friend coming to drink tea or a couple staying to play cards for an evening. Not everyone threw themselves into the constant round of visiting with sustained enthusiasm. The diarist John Evelyn had complained about "the tediousness of *Visits,* which they make *here* so long, that it is a very tyranny to sit to little purpose."[21] A century later, they were still tiresome. A letter of July 1785 from the gossipy young Elizabeth Iremonger to her friend Mary Heber identifies rounds of visits as the great evil of domestic sociability.[22] Visits were different from invitations in that they were unsolicited, numerous, and often short. Like many other young women of her age, Elizabeth Watkins, living in Gloucester, recorded her daily activities in a pocket book, a formatted diary that contained columns for account and note keeping. Elizabeth used hers to record what she felt about her visitors, as well as when they came. She notes on 1 March 1771: "Mrs. Clifford call'd in. I am very indifferent"; on 7 April, "Mrs. Lee drank tea here—a stupid kind of evening"; on 6 May, "Miss Elderton call'd in the morn. I do not like her at all."[23]

Social visits might have been tiresome, but they were a compulsory feature of polite town life. Not every day was perceived as suitable for seeing others. The clergyman James Hervey worried about the way in which the Sabbath was becoming the default visiting day. It was fine, he thought, to spend time in the company of others on Sundays if they were religious: "But, alas! where do we find such Company? When do we hear such Conversation? The general Conversation is all Impertinence. Not so much as seasoned with a Spice of Religion."[24]

For those of a more worldly outlook, friendships and alliances could be cemented through the right kinds of visiting, and the trading of visiting cards, small rectangular slips of paper or pasteboard on which the owner's name was written, engraved, or letterpress printed, provided a paper trail of who had been where. Once deposited at a genteel address, cards were kept on semi-display within handmade visiting card holders.[25] *The Ladies' Complete Visiting Guide* (1800) presented the visiting card as the chief measure of sociability, and visiting as a "serious occupation." The author claimed that he had in his manual "hereby reduced to a system the first acknowledged felicity of polished society—*friendly, learned,* and *fashionable intercourse.*"[26]

Virtue and Display

Within the wholesome space of the home, some entertainments were seen as more suitable than others. James Fordyce devotes a large part of his discussion of home leisure time to the insidious evils of card playing—a staple of many an evening in, but in his eyes a dangerous transgression of "the laws of humanity and friendship."[27] The "lust of gaming" should, he argued, be more properly replaced by gentler arts, and in particular needlework.[28] The great virtue of needlework was, he observed, that it enabled one to engage in other improving arts at the same time. Not all needlework was equal—"slighter and freer patterns" were recommended over intricate "fancywork," because they were less likely to strain the eyes, took less time, and would be more useful.[29] Fordyce cited the example of a woman of nobility and virtue:

> who never sat idle in company. . . . Being a perfect mistress of her needle, and having an excellent taste in that, as in many other things, her manner, whether at home, or abroad . . . was to be constantly engaged in working something useful, or beautiful; at the same time that she assisted in supporting the conversation, with an attention and capacity which I have never seen exceeded. For the sake of variety and improvement, when in her own house, some one of the company would often read aloud, while she and her female visitants were thus employed.[30]

The paragon described here is exemplary because she is never idle in her leisure time, and she uses it to combine several of Fordyce's favoured activities: she makes beautiful or useful things, she engages in rational and intelligent conversation—and, to top it all, she is enlarging her mind and those of the women with her by listening to a book read aloud.

Reading aloud was doubly beneficial because it kept one from idleness, and provided an improving and entertaining soundtrack to other domestic activities. The bluestocking letter writer and artist Mary Delany recommends Boswell's *Tour of the Hebrides* as an excellent book to listen to while doing knotting work; Eleanor Butler, one of the "Ladies of Llangollen," living in artistic retirement in a village in North Wales, describes reading to her companion Sarah Ponsonby, who was meanwhile occupied in drawing, making a map, doing cross-stitch, or decorating her journal.[31] Nearly all the reading recorded in Elizabeth Tyrrell's London diary takes the form of one woman reading aloud, while the rest of the group work. And it was not only women who read to stave off idleness, or who combined reading with work. Robert Sharp, a Yorkshire schoolmaster and shopkeeper, declared that "there is not a more uncomfortable thing (at least to me) to see a person lolling about in a Chair, spending his time with nothing, never looking at a Book, for my part sooner than be debarred from reading, I would suffer the odious punishment of the tread Mill."[32] Nicholas Blundell was indefatigable in his home and garden improvements, planting, mending, cleaning—his diary records a life busy with tasks around his estate. He too records the utility of reading as a soundtrack to work: "After dinner I tryed to set some Rayzors and Mr. Aldred red to me the Prognostications of Esqr Bigerstaff."[33] For those further down the social scale, the relationship between reading and work was different. The self-taught publisher James Lackington describes his zeal for reading while he was an apprentice shoemaker. He recalls that he and his fellow apprentices were so eager to read as much as they could that they allowed themselves only three hours' sleep a night, and that "one of us sat up to work until the time appointed for the others to rise, and when all were up, my friend John, and your humble servant, took it by turns to read aloud to the rest, while they were at their work."[34] Hugh Miller, from an artisan family in the small Scottish coastal burgh of Cromarty, describes how his uncle James, a harness maker, managed to read while he worked:

> He often found some one to read beside him during the day; and in the winter evenings the portable bench used to be brought from his shop at the other end of the dwelling, into the family sitting-room, and placed beside the circle round the hearth, where his brother Alexander, my younger uncle, whose occupation left his evenings free, would read aloud from some interesting volume for the general benefit—placing himself always at the opposite side of the bench, so as to share in the light of the worker. Occasionally the family circle would be widened by the accession of two to three intelligent neighbours, who would drop in to listen; and then the book, after a space, would be laid aside, in order that its contents might be discussed in conversation.[35]

The opportunities for reading at work depended on the workplace. In artisan workshops where discipline could be relaxed, where there were opportunities for contact with older employees and masters who were better able to afford reading material, a unit was provided within which readers could group together to buy books and newspapers. Those who worked in groups had the advantages of conversation.[36] Keen readers took their chances where they found them. The servant John Jones describes how he used to hurry in laying the dinner table, so that he might gain a few minutes to explore the contents of the bookshelves in the dining room.[37] An anonymous stonemason, employed as a roundsman (a travelling labourer), taught his horse the route of his journeys, and from then on, read while he travelled.[38]

These accounts show us very different functions of reading in relation to work. For leisured men and women of the gentry and middle classes, to do craft and handiwork while another person read aloud was companionable, and virtuous because it meant that neither was idle in their leisure time. But for the working man or woman, reading aloud at work was a way of improving oneself through learning and alleviating the tedium of manual labour.

These two worlds—reading as soundtrack for recreation and reading while undertaking paid work—could collide within the eighteenth-century home.[39] Servants were often part of the shared reading experience. Gertrude Savile spent several happy days walking in the fields with her maid, Peell, and a book. The maidservant in Thomas Turner's household often listened to her employer's reading, and Hester Piozzi's maid listened while she read the *Spectator* to her daughters.[40] An often cited scene of reading aloud was during the lengthy process of hairdressing and the curling and powdering of wigs. This habit was so prevalent that an article entitled "Hints on Reading" in *The Lady's Magazine* of 1789 claimed that "hair-dressing has been very service-able to reading—Look at the popular books of a circulating library, and you will find the binding cracked by quantities of powder and pomatum between the leaves."[41] The editor went on to recommend, tongue firmly in cheek, that "for the hour of hair-dressing, which is sometimes an hour of torment, I would reserve newspapers and political pamphlets—and so get rid of all my plagues at once."[42]

Being Seen

Fordyce describes his female paragon who sews, converses, and listens as a spectacle: it is by witnessing her conduct that he infers her moral compass. Despite the didactic emphasis on the unaffected freedom of the home, domestic recreation was closely linked to display. It was important to be seen to be doing and saying the right things when visited or visiting.

The history of home decoration reveals that the mid–eighteenth century was when householders began to take serious interest in the spaces in which they received others. Wallpapers, carpets, and sets of china were bought in large quantities by women and men eager to impress their visiting friends.[43] As the middling sort of Britons became a nation of shoppers, so their homes became crowded with fashionable new things to show off to their visitors. Teaware, silver plate, sugar tongs, candle snuffers, pepper casters, japanned trays, and numerous other items were advertised, bought, and shown off on a huge scale.[44] The author of *The Lady's Companion* warned that formal visits were often nothing more than custom-sanctioned nosiness: "many go to see those, for whom they are perfectly indifferent whether they find them alive or dead, well or sick," and claimed that such visits "are but insidious Instructions of a Spy rather than the Good Office of a Neighbour."[45]

Given that part of the game of visiting was to examine how others lived, the same principles of aspirational display applied to the activities of the people within these rooms as to their contents. James Gillray's satirical portrait entitled *Farmer Giles and his wife shewing off their daughter Betty on her return from school* parodies the aspirations of middling-sort domestic culture, the neighbours having been summoned round to hear the daughter's piano rendition of a popular folk tune while her parents beam on, heedless to the fact that no one (including the dog) is listening (fig. 9). A conduct book from the mid–eighteenth century entitled *The Lady's Preceptor* offers readers sound advice on how to prepare to speak during a visit. Conversation during a visit should be approached with the same care and preparation that one would apply to matters of dress or hair. Cautioning his readers not to fall into the trap of "caressing the first Dog that comes to their Relief, . . . without which they would not have known how to have behaved," he advises them on how to sparkle:

> If the Occasion of the Visit does not afford you a Subject for Conversation, take care not to be so unprovided with one, as to be obliged to the Weather or the Hour of the Day for your Discourse. It is not at all amiss to consider, before-hand, what Topicks are suitable to the Company you are going to see, and to make yourself in some measure Mistress of them.[46]

Conversation was part of the performance involved in social exchanges, and even within the relatively informal contexts of domestic visiting, it was

Fig. 9. James Gillray, *Farmer Giles and his wife shewing off their daughter Betty on her return from school*, London, 1809, etching (Library of Congress, LC-USZC2-3808)

important to do it right. In theory, conversation brought out the best in people, since "in company we frequently say a thousand smart and ingenious things which never would have come into our head while alone."[47] Yet it demanded practice, as the compiler of the Ernst family commonplace book observed: "Men of the World can only shew their wit by their Conversation. It is not therefore astonishing they should aim at doing that which makes them shine."[48]

No one could have been more aware of the need to learn how to acquire conversation pieces and verbal wit than poor Dudley Ryder. Ryder's diary spans only a couple of years in his youth, but it offers an extraordinarily candid account of one man's struggle to be sociable.[49] Most of the time what Ryder is really worried about is what to say and how to say it. He watches other men, who seem to talk freely and with charm, but observes of himself: "I find I am mighty apt to look silly and a little uneasy when I am in the company of ladies."[50] Ryder thinks that he can learn to speak well in company by reading books. The books he favours are not didactic works on eloquence or manners, but books that seem to him to embody stylistic traits that he can emulate. So he notes that no book is more fit "to learn one the polite way of writing and conversing than Horace, and one cannot be too familiar with him."[51] He admires Boileau for his informality, and declares that he will read frequently *The Tatler*, "to improve my style and accustom myself to his way of thinking and telling a story and manner of observing upon the world and mankind."[52]

It is worth pausing here to consider the way in which the aesthetic qualities valued in the literature of the period—ease, conversational style, wit—were read as a code for living, however ill-suited they seemed to be to one's own character. Ryder's anxious and self-conscious attitude towards reading may not be typical of all men of the early eighteenth century, but it gives us an insight into the way he translated what he found in books into his own personal social predicaments. He is rather scornful of his cousin who, he says, has spent too much time doing the wrong kind of reading: she "has not the talent of conversation, says very little, reads much and delights mightily in books of gallantry, romances and tragedies but her great defect is her ignorance of mankind."[53] Some books equip you for conversation, and some, apparently, hinder it.

However artificial it may seem today, Ryder's candid narrative of his own struggle to converse with ease, and the role that reading played within this, is important for understanding how people *used* books in the eighteenth century.[54] When James Fordyce came to write his sermon "On Female Virtue with Intellectual Accomplishments," reading and using one's reading were presented as a fundamental part of that accomplishment. He declared that reading could entertain and edify, enable one to enjoy solitude, but also "qualify you to shine in conversation."[55] Later on we will see how this influenced the forms of books that were published, specifically collections of writing deliberately packaged and edited to provide material for social occasions.

In the context of domestic sociability, what you read and what you said were often seen as a show to present to the world, rather than as a fundamental aspect of intellectual or personal identity. The writer and journalist Harriet Martineau looked back scornfully at this practice, within which the female reader was

> expected to sit down in the parlour with her sewing, listen to a book read aloud, and hold herself ready for [female] callers. When the callers came, conversation often turned naturally on the book just laid down, which must therefore be very carefully chosen lest the shocked visitor should carry to the house where she paid her

next call an account of the deplorable laxity shown by the family she had left.[56]

The spectacle of the reading woman and the conversation that her book furnished her with were typically ways in which visitors were to evaluate a person and a home. For Martineau, this window-dressing is explicitly gendered.

Books as indicators of the moral propriety of their female owners can be seen in prints and novels throughout the eighteenth century, which often use the titles of books visible in the home as a sign of moral rectitude—or otherwise.[57] In Richard Sheridan's play *The Rivals*, Lydia Languish, a young woman with an insatiable appetite for romantic fiction, has to cover up in haste the true nature of her reading material when her family are about to enter her room: "Here, my dear Lucy, hide these books.—Quick, quick.—Fling *Peregrine Pickle* under the toilet—throw *Roderick Random* into the closet—put *the Innocent Adultery* into *The Whole Duty of Man*—thrust *Lord Aimworth* under the sopha . . . leave *Fordyce's Sermons* upon the table."[58] Novels are quickly shoved out of sight, and what remains on show is what is respectable—the conduct book *The Whole Duty of Man* and Fordyce's sermons.

Similar principles applied to male reading. One anonymous satire of the period takes as its subject the college room of a young man. The poem is a response to Jonathan Swift's poem "The Lady's Dressing Room," which had famously described a male lover's horror at the seedy contents of his beloved's dressing room, cluttered with cosmetics and bodily sweat and grime. In the response poem, "A Description of a College Room," we are given a peep into the chaotic moral universe of a young man about town:

> Where various books confus'dly lie,
> *Scotch songs,* with deep *philosophy,*
> A *Prior* here, and *Euclid* there,
> A *Rochester* and *book of prayer;*
> Here *Tillotson* with *French romances,*
> And pious *South* with *country dances.*[59]

Again, we read the moral calibre of the man from the books on his table: songs and dances muddled up with Tillotson's sermons and Euclid's classical geometry, and the Earl of Rochester's libertine verse alongside a book of prayer.

Spaces for Reading

Eighteenth-century literature and visual art often use books as a vocabulary of moral rectitude. The choice of books on display within a house—whether being read or in sight on table or shelves—was significant. In larger houses, it had an added significance because of the eighteenth-century shift towards the use of the library as a general living space.[60] Descriptions of domestic libraries of the sixteenth and seventeenth centuries typically reveal places of retreat and solitude, which were primarily aristocratic. Over the course of this period, the contents of the private library evolved—by the end of the seventeenth century, there would have been fewer continental books in learned languages, and more works printed in England, in English.[61] Some of those library owners would have acquired their books for their intellectual content, and others, as status symbols—the two are not mutually exclusive.[62] As we will see later, an expanding print trade and a burgeoning demand for new volumes and titles created, by the mid–eighteenth century, a body of consumers—small estate owners, tradesmen and their families—eager to buy books and to show them off in their homes. In larger houses, or country homes, the library was an important place for public display.[63] Culturally *arriviste* professionals, keen to learn how to manifest their learning in their homes, read guides on how to arrange and index the books in their library.

In 1759 William Palmer, a London lawyer, acquired a manuscript entitled "Memorandum for making a distinct catalog of a library."[64] The document assumes no prior knowledge of how a library should be arranged, or books marked, so it begins from the basics: the room must be fitted up with shelves placed so as to accommodate folios, quartos, octavos, and below "in such manner as to appear the most agreeable to the eye."[65] Care must be taken not to deface the bindings with the shelf mark, and that when people borrow books, they must name and date their borrowing in the catalogue. This is a manuscript aimed at someone who owned books, but needed fairly basic guidance on how to arrange and record his new possessions.

In aristocratic circles, the library gradually became a communal centre of the house, as it was later to become in the homes of middle-class collectors of books. By the end of the eighteenth century, the library had become the main informal living room in many country houses.[66] When Mrs. Lybbe Powys went to Middleton Park in Oxfordshire in August 1778, she found a library connected to the drawing room where "besides a good collection of books, there is every other kind of amusement, as billiard and other tables, and a few good pictures."[67] As this suggests, a library contained more than books—prints, coins, busts, and other antiquarian or natural history items, often the focus of conversation, were also in this space—though as William Parkes cautioned in *Domestic Duties* (1829), it was important not just to assemble these objects but also to find out something about them, or otherwise they would be "mere baubles" and to "display a collection under such circumstances is to emblazon ignorance."[68] The furnishing of the library to accommodate entertainment and group recreation is evident from descriptions and images. By the mid–eighteenth century comfortable library chairs and sofas, along with several writing tables, began to be supplied as standard furnishings.[69] These comfortable items of furniture gave more flexibility to the library as a space, as well as enabling people to read together. Women's reading became associated with sofas and softness rather than with the intellectually rigorous upright reading of men, and young women were castigated for this unbecoming lounging.[70] Sofas brought their own dangers: it is notable that the library sofas of eighteenth-century novels are more often the places for troubled heroines to lie down and recover, rather than to explore the life of the mind.[71]

Over the second half of the eighteenth century, sales in book-related furniture and accessories boomed. There was a thriving trade in replica Chippendale library furniture, and in various other items for library decoration: reading chairs, stands, desks, globes, busts, were all available to the middle-class library owner. Hepplewhite's *Cabinet Maker and Upholsterer's Guide,* offering furniture designs for the middling class, provides designs for desk and bookcases, secretary and bookcases, library cases and library tables, and even "cornices for libraries." Hanging shelves were recommended for "closets or Ladies' rooms."[72] Those without libraries could combine storage items for books and papers, in pieces such as the "Secretary and Book Case" or the "Desk and Bookcase." *New and Elegant Designs [. . .] of Household Furniture in Genteel Taste* (1760), a selection of copperplate designs aimed at a slightly lower sector of the market, boasted a whole section on library and book-related furniture. There were combined writing tables and bookcases, ladies' bookcases, pediment bookcases, "embattled" bookcases, gothic bookcases, library tables, and "open pediment bureau & bookcase" designs (fig. 10).[73] As for the contents of these pieces of furniture, they too were touched by a new culture of book display. Homeowners embellished their books with labels that connected the contents of their library to their social

Fig. 10. "Lady's Bookcase," from
*Household Furniture in Genteel Taste for the
Year 1760*, by a Society of Upholsters,
Cabinet-makers, &c., printed for Robert
Sayer, London, 1760 (© The Geffrye,
Museum of the Home, London)

status—bookplates, like book bindings, could be designed around the armorial
design of the family.

We should, however, be cautious in assuming that because people
owned furniture with which to store books—bookcases, escritoires, library
cases—they necessarily used them for that purpose. Records of domestic
thefts from the eighteenth century show that householders often used locked
bookcases to store anything that was valuable, which meant that they
contained much besides books. The record of one theft from a locked library
bookcase in a London house lists the following as the stolen contents: "one
bank note, value 100 l. and one other bank note, value 30 l. three gold snuffboxes, value 100 l. one repeating gold watch, with a brilliant diamond button,
value 30 l. one silver candlestick, value 20 s. one silver standish, value 20 s.
and 400 l. in money."[74] No books were in the bookcase.

The library was not the only place in which to read or keep books, and most middling-sort householders would not have had a library. A collection of ninety inventories from the houses of middling-sort Londoners, held at the Geffrye Museum in Shoreditch, gives an insight into the location of books in these more modest households.[75] Looking at the lists of furniture, prints, books, china, linen, and plate, room by room, sometimes reveals where books were kept and, presumably, used. There are few mentions of books or bookcases in upstairs rooms or bedrooms—and only one house has a room called a "library." Only one home lists books within a servant's room. By far the majority of these readers' books are housed in their parlours, suggesting habits of reading within a social space. In a 1740 inventory for the house of John Mitford, a merchant in Bow, we discover that in the "common parlor" (as opposed to his "back parlor" and the drawing room) there is an eight-day clock, nine chairs, a tea board, a dumbwaiter, and "a fine parrot in it [sic] Cage & Curtain," and in addition, a "Stand for a Book." The fact that this stand is surrounded by the other accoutrements of midcentury visiting suggests that books were read communally. In the 1800 inventory of the late Nicholas Browning, a baker living in Cripplegate, there are two rooms in which "several old books" are listed alongside "a parcel of waste paper" (it's not clear whether they are part of the waste paper). In his parlour, we find a stuffed parakeet, along with "mahogany secretaire and bookcase with glazed door and pedimenthead," along with ten assorted chairs and, again, various visiting accessories: "a mahogany knife case, an inlaid tea caddy and silver sugar ditto, a spice box, a pair of sugar knippers a pair of snuffers and stand, a cribbage board, a cork skrew, a small mahogany angle beaufet with glaised doors two china bowles, two basons and a wilton carpet."[76] The parlour was the place of entertainment, with its card tables, gaming boards, musical instruments, and books and reading were part of that domestic culture. It was the prime visiting room in a middle-class eighteenth-century house, and often arranged to facilitate groups sitting together.[77]

In grander houses, a drawing room, often used for tea and coffee after dinner, was also a reading space, and the midcentury fashion for upholstered seating, particularly long pairs of settees flanking a chimney piece, would have facilitated group entertainment.[78] As the century goes on, we can see an increasing move towards more informal seating arrangements, which seems to suggest that people might have congregated in both larger and smaller groups, the arrangement of the furniture having been flexible enough to accommodate both.

The furniture of the period tells its own story about changing expectations around sociability. An example is the introduction of casters on both sofas and tables in the mid–eighteenth century, which reveals a demand for furniture that could be moved around to serve different functions. Similarly, tables acquired flaps: no longer a heavy fixed piece in the centre of the room, the table was a more flexible piece of furniture.

Fanny Burney's discussions with her father over the furnishing of her small new cottage in Westhumble in Surrey illustrate some of the issues to consider when thinking about buying a table for a parlour: ". . . and if my dearest father will be so good—and so naughty at once, as to crown our *salle d'Audience* with a gift we shall prize beyond all others, we can think only of a table. Not a dining one, but a sort of table for a little work and a few books, *en gala*—without which, a rooms looks always forlorn."[79] In the event, her father bought two card tables, which were placed on two sides of the room, and Fanny observed of this, "I think no room looks really comfortable, or even quite furnished, without two Tables—one to keep the Wall, & take upon itself the dignity of a little tidyness, the other to stand here—there—& every where, and hold letters & *make the agreeable*."[80]

Tables here are used for holding the things one needed "en gala" or "to make the agreeable." That included books and letters. Burney's dreams of her parlour as a place of informal entertainment are a shift towards the sociable clustering that we see depicted in the influential landscape designer Humphry Repton's contrasting images of a dingy cedar parlour, from the earlier part of the century, to the light, bright, and sociable "modern Living Room" of 1816 (fig. 11). Repton's images are being used to make a point about the new airiness and relaxed sociability of living spaces by the turn of the century. In contrast with the formal circle and the austere and dark formality of the Cedar Parlour, the living room gestures to the outside world through its connection with a conservatory, and is home to four separate sets of people, enjoying its books, seating, and vista in different ways.[81] The tyranny of the fixed circle of social intercourse, typical of the earlier period, was over. Instead, we see a child reading to adults from a huge folio, a silent solitary reader, and women reading from or discussing a book together at a table.[82] Different forms of reading were possible within the same room, with seating arrangements such as these—and the abundance of daylight prevented the need to share artificial light. Repton expects his new room to deliver a lot— nothing less than a transformation of domestic sociability and culture, in which dullness is banished, to be replaced by a cultural utopia in which no aspect of learning seems inaccessible. This opening up of culture came hand in hand with the architectural opening up of spaces.

The idea of sitting around a fireplace is a common feature of many evocations of domestic reading and culture in the eighteenth century.[83] Beyond its emblematic sociability, the fireside also had the obvious practical benefit of being warm, and often, the greatest source of light in a house. Prolonged reading could be a chilly business. The prolific diarist and traveller Anne Lister struggled with her cold and draughty Yorkshire house, and her endeavours to keep reading despite physical adversity are recorded in some detail in her diaries.[84] For her, reading is a source of entertainment and solace in times of emotional distress. She breaks out in eulogy at one point: "O books! books!

INTERIORS

Fig. 11. "Interiors: The Old Cedar Parlour and The Modern Living Room," from *Fragments on the Theory and Practice of Landscape Gardening*, by Humphry Repton, published in 1816 (Private Collection / The Stapleton Collection / Bridgeman Images)

I owe you much. Ye are my spirit's oil without which, its own friction against itself would wear out."[85] Her reading habit was not, however, a salve to her body in quite the same way. In order to keep her particularly vulnerable parts warm while reading, she goes to the breach makers—in July—and orders a pair of leather knee caps.[86] Here is her account of the ceremony she must go through to be able to sit and read and write:

> Plaid wrapped fourfold round my loins, & 2 greatcoats put on over all, besides my leather knee-caps on & a thick dressing gown threwn across my knees over coats & everything. I sit close to the window, all things considered the only seat in the room that suits me. A large high green baize, fold screen on my right to exclude air from the door. The curtains drawn so as only just to admit light enough, to keep out air from the window.[87]

This is a diary entry written on 19 June!

For those who could afford it, the fireside must have been the central focus for gathering and reading in most households, because of the light and the heat that it provided. Hearth tax records from the mid–seventeenth century show that 80 percent of registered houses had one fireplace, 14 percent had two and only 6 percent had three or more.[88] The light generated by the fire would have been more substantial, and perhaps less smoke-filled than the tallow candles and rush lights that were the lighting options for all but the very wealthy. The surviving book catalogue for one country house in Scotland suggests something of the distinctive role of the fireside in book culture. Library records of the time are normally organised by genre and by size of book, rather than location—a catalogue lists contents in divinity, history, law, belles lettres, noting in order of diminishing status, folio, quarto, and octavo and below. But the catalogue for Carmichael House, in South Lanarkshire, organises its content by place. There are historical and religious works in the wainscot presses, legal texts in the chest in the library, books on husbandry in the chests in the dining room. But the works listed in "the press by the fire" are almost all books for entertainment—works of imaginative literature, poems, plays, and romances, many of them dating from the seventeenth century.[89] Those books must have been there because they were the books most likely to have been read as part of an evening's entertainment.

The idea of *reading* around the fire acquired a symbolic significance in idealised versions of home-entertainment. As Richard Twining, son of a

successful banker and tea and coffee merchant, recollects of his family practices: "Well do I remember the evenings at Isleworth, when after supper we
formed a wide circle round the fire, my father often reading some of these
olden rhymes to my mother and ourselves. 'Visions of the past I greet ye
still.' "[90] The fireside circle was the subject of many poems in celebration of
modest domesticity. Nathaniel Cotton's popular poem "The Fireside" used
the titular image as an emblem of companionable marriage, while William
Cowper's poem *The Task*, a paean to virtuous rural domesticity, conjures up
the pleasure and virtue of this fireside scene in its celebrated description of
winter evenings in the countryside. The post was opened, the newspaper was
read, and the family settled down for its pastimes:

> Now stir the fire, and close the shutters fast,
> Let fall the curtains, wheel the sofa round,
> And, while the bubbling and loud-hissing urn
> Throws up a steamy column, and the cups
> That cheer but not inebriate, wait on each,
> So let us welcome peaceful ev'ning in.[91]

The ongoing allure of reading by the cosy fireside is evident in the titles
of the popular literary compilations of the mid–late eighteenth century,
packaged to suggest domestic harmony and sociability: *The Banquet of Wit:
containing a choice collection of Bon-Mots, Jests, Repartees, for the Amusement
of the Fire-side* (1790); *A Companion for the Fire-side; or, Winter Evening's
Amusement. Containing a curious collection of entertaining and instructive essays,
visions, Relations, Stories, Tales, Fables* (1769).

On the upper floors of homes were bedrooms, closets, and dressing
rooms, which also offered venues for more intimate communal reading. The
adolescent Eliza Tyrrell describes her friend reading one of Amelia Opie's
Simple Tales to her in bed, and while she is dressing in the morning, and this
informal scene reflects what must have been widespread practice.[92] The most
undocumented and probably the most frequent forms of communal reading
were in very small groups, between two or three people, in couples, families,
and friends. The learned and cultured "ladies of Llangollen," Eleanor Butler
and Sarah Ponsonby, who lived for forty years in domestic bliss in north
Wales, write about reading together as part of their intimacy. In her diary
entries, Butler presents the relationship between reader and busy listener as a
shared cultural space. She writes on 24 September 1781: "Read Madame de

Sévigné. My Love drawing. From seven till nine in sweet converse with the delight of my heart, over the Fire. Paper'd our Hair."[93] On October 7, she is "Reading Rousseau to my Sally. She drawing her map upon Vellum, made a great mistake in one of the tropics which spoil'd her morning's Work . . . Incessant rain the entire evening. Shut the shutters, made a good fire, lighted the Candles . . . A day of strict retirement, sentiment, and delight."[94]

For the self-educated bookseller James Lackington, marriage represents the chance to share a world of reading together for the first time: "I was in raptures with the bare thoughts of having a woman to read with, and also to read to me."[95] Lackington's sentiments on mutual reading are echoed by the writer and engineer Richard Lovell Edgeworth; although several rungs up on the social ladder, he shows the same enthusiasm for a joint reading experience: "I strenuously endeavoured to improve my own understanding, and to communicate whatever I knew to my wife. Indeed while we read and conversed together, during the long winter evenings, the clearness of her judgement assisted me in every pursuit of literature, in which I was engaged."[96]

Books both passed the time and provided the basis for conversation and discussion.[97] Bookish converse was not the exclusive preserve of married couples, however. Mary Delany talks of the pleasure of spending evenings reading with a female friend, which gives them both the chance to consider the book fully: "we quite chew it and dwell upon its taste."[98] Reading, whatever the subject matter, brought Delany closer to her friends, as is evidenced by the wet day in November 1774 when it "never ceased raining," and she decided to stay indoors and read with her friends: "We are now consoling ourselves, with books [. . .] they entertain us and tell us pretty moral tales; they banish scandal and politicks, but not *one moment's remembrance* of the friends we admire, respect, and love."[99] The point of reading, for Delany, was not personal literary development, but the sharing of experience, as she remarked when explaining her friendship with the Duchess of Portland: "we read and like the *same* books, we talk them over without interruption, we are fond of the *same* works; and the pleasures of these occupations are increased by participation."[100]

Reading and Leisure

Anxiety over how to employ leisure hours permeates the conduct literature of the eighteenth century, an inevitable consequence of the rising affluence that kept increasing numbers of middling-sort women idle in the house rather than out in the workplace.[101] An article from the *Gentleman's Magazine* from 1801 lamented the social changes in the role of women in the home: "Now [...] these farmers' daughters [...] instead of dishing butter, feeding poultry, or curing bacon, the avocations of these young *ladies* at home are, studying dress, attitudes, novels, French, and music, whilst the fine ladies their mothers sit lounging in parlors adorned with the fiddle-faddle fancy-work of their fashionable daughters."[102]

Unbroken leisure became a symbol of a family's status.[103] One of the ironies of eighteenth-century social history was that having time to spare was both the desired reward for hard work and a source of concern. Thomas Gisborne, author of *An Enquiry into the Duties of the Female Sex* (1798), announced piously in his chapter "On the Employment of Time": "Time is a sacred trust consigned to us by the Creator of the universe."[104] All those sacred hours needed to be used, and used well. Educational reading and study played an important role in this—Gisborne says that "the habit of regularly allotting to improving books a portion of each day [...] cannot be too strongly recommended."[105] Within the home, women were often represented as men's leisure companions: one male physician writes in 1740 that ladies were "made to serve us as Play-toys after our more serious Occupations."[106] In her treatise *Letter to a New-Married Lady* (1777), Hester Chapone warned her readers of the potential ennui of marriage, and suggested what could be done to avoid it. She cautions them to beware "of all things" "his growing dull and weary in your company."[107] One way of avoiding this fate is to read with him: "And though you should not naturally be disposed to the same taste in reading or amusement, this may be acquired by habit, and by a hearty desire of conforming to his inclinations and sharing in his pleasures."[108]

Chapone's idea that a wife should bend to her husband's tastes and interests was not shared by everyone. Other women used the practice of reading with their spouse to different ends. Jane Collier's satirical conduct book *An Essay on the Art of Ingeniously Tormenting* (1753) contains a section on how to rile a husband by refusing to listen to him while he reads: "If, for example, he desires you to hear one of Shakespeare's plays, you may give him perpetual interruptions, by sometimes going out of the room, sometimes ringing the bell to give orders for what cannot be wanted till the next day; at other times taking notice (if your children are in the room), that Molly's cap is awry, or that Jackey looks pale."[109] As Collier reminds us, not every marriage was a happy one, and not every home was a bower of bliss. Books and newspapers could screen couples from one another, and create barriers to communication.[110]

Gillray's paired engravings of *Harmony Before Matrimony* and *Matrimonial-Harmonics* literalise the ideas of domestic concord, depicting the soundscape of before and after marriage (figs. 12 and 13). In the first plate the couple sing love duets together and read Ovid, their voices, minds, and bodies in happy union. Pets play peaceably, and the room is an elegant haven of culture. In the second, set in the breakfast room, the emotional chaos of dissension is audible and visible. The wife sings alone: the pages of her open music book are headed "Forte," and her song is "Torture Fiery Rage / Despair I cannot can not bear." On the piano lies music: "Separation: a Finale for Two Voices with Accompaniment," while on the floor is "The Wedding Ring—a Dirge." The husband, carelessly dressed, consults the *Sporting Calendar* and looks dejected. The decibel level is augmented by a screeching baby, its nurse-maid frantically waving his rattle, accompanied by a hissing urn of coffee, a barking dog, and two screeching cockatoos. The *Art of Tormenting* sits open on a chair. It's worth bearing in mind that the happy evocation of homely converse celebrated in so many advice manuals sat alongside a vigorous visual and verbal tradition depicting miserable homes and marriages, often divided in their cultural consumption.[111]

So far this chapter has been concerned with the world of sociable reading inside the walls of the home. To assume that this was the only place in which individuals read together would be a mistake. They also read in taverns, and coffeehouses, circulating libraries, and other gathering places. And even within the domestic arena, there was more to the home than the house. For the more affluent middle class and gentry, at one remove from the house itself was the summer house, a nearby structure that allowed for the possibility of cool but covered outdoor space. Its primary function was as a "pleasure-house," a different location within which to spend leisure time. The design and scale of summer houses varied considerably—simple and rustic, classical, or person-alised, reflecting the whims and eccentricities of their owners. Some were open, but some evidently were sufficiently protected from the elements as to enable their owners to store books within them: the records of at least two cases of book theft in the first half of the eighteenth century show that these locations were vulnerable to burglaries. Thomas Thompson, the owner of what he describes as "a little house in Weybridge," reported a burglary on 14 December of the previous year, when "they cut through the Wall of my

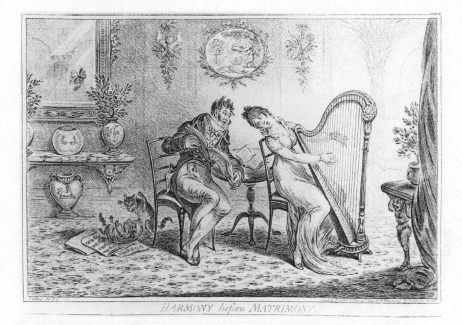

Fig. 12. James Gillray, *Harmony Before Matrimony*, London, October 1792, engraving (Library of Congress, LC-USZ62-100133)

Fig. 13. James Gillray, *Matrimonial-Harmonics*, London, 25 October 1805, engraving (Library of Congress, LC-USZ62-100134)

Summer-house, and threw out one hundred Books more than they took away; I found them upon the Ground in my Neighbour's Orchard; they took away seventy Octavo's, Quarto's and Folio's; twelve Volumes of Rapin's History, in Octavo, &c."[112] Thompson obviously had a fairly substantial collection within his summer house. The tendency to locate a "pleasure-house" at a remove from the main house meant that they could be used for solitary *or* social activities. Reading within them could take both forms.[113]

A lot of reading also happened *en plein air*. Idealised neoclassical images of families reading together in groves and grassy banks that adorn the frontispieces of eighteenth-century books may romanticise the outdoor scene, but they represent a common practice. Heavy taxation on both glass and candles during the eighteenth century must have made many middling-sort homes fairly dingy places, so it is not surprising that readers took their culture outdoors. Mary Rathbone, a Shropshire Quaker woman, records that she "sat in the garden and sewed, while my Bro. Richard read 'Sandford and Merton.' " On other occasions a relative reads the *Spectator* to her in the garden, and on another, Cook's voyages.[114] Mary Delany frequently reads outside, in a grove or grotto, and even on the beach—in "a little sand grotto."[115] As we have seen, Gertrude Savile walks with her maid and reads in the fields. She also goes for a trip to Clapham Common with her mother, and while there reads her "Agnes de Castro," a short piece of prose fiction by Aphra Behn. The next day they go a few miles up Kingston Road, where she begins another novella by Behn, *The Fair Jilt*. They finish this the following day, during their afternoon in Wimbledon; and later on, after supper, they read part of Behn's *Oroonoko*.[116]

Savile's reading trips are a reminder of the importance of being able to carry around eighteenth-century leisure reading—a factor frequently mentioned in advertisements for books and in prefatory material. *The Aviary, or, Magazine of British Melody* described its collection of 1,443 songs as "all within the Compass of a portable Pocket Volume."[117] The compiler of *The Companion: being a Choice Collection of the Most Admired Pieces from the Best Authors* (1790) claimed to contain "such literary provision as may save the trouble and expence of the carriage of many volumes" and was ideal for carrying around, being "of a proper portable size."[118] Just as modern travellers would take a novel, an iPod, or an iPad as a time-killer, so in the eighteenth century on journeys one read while travelling—or waiting to travel. Horse-drawn transport, not to mention potholed roads, would have drawn out the length of even the shortest trip. When John Chubb made his long journey as a teenager from Somerset to London, he was travel-sick most of the way to Bath, but then recovered enough to get profoundly bored on the rest of the journey, later writing to his father: "I never wanted a book so much in my life as in the Coach to day."[119] Mary Delany notes in a letter following a journey: "Sally breakfasted at Causcomb in her way to Stow, and brought a book for our amusement in the coach, entitled "Letters from Lady Catesby to Lady Henrietta [translated by Mrs. Brooke]"; they are odd, interesting, and pretty for a love story—a translation from the French; some pretty sentiments and uncommon characters. It is on the whole amusing, and answered the end for which it was lent us."[120] Like many travelling to Ireland, Delany was at times delayed by bad weather, and records that "'The Rambler' and 'Adventurer' entertain us by turns—we give the preference to the 'Adventurer.'"[121]

The physical and social contexts in which people read assumed many kinds, and as we shall see, this variety came to shape the form of the book itself. Once we relocate the book in the parlour, garden, or carriage, we can start to see how the history of reading in its social context is inseparable from other areas of eighteenth-century life: concerns about public sociability, idleness, loneliness, the virtues of conversation, the cementing of intimate relationships. People looked at each others' houses and watched each other read. As they did so, they made judgements: not just about how well someone else read, but the kinds of books that person was reading. Books read at home could have a very personal significance for their readers and listeners, but they were also part of the way in which one displayed a self for the world.

3. Using Books

Books are a Guide in Youth, and an Entertainment for Age; they
relieve us under Solitude, and keep us from being a Burden to
ourselves, help us to glide over the Rubs of Life, and lay our Cares
and Disappointments asleep; and, in a word, when well managed
afford Direction, Discovery and Support.
—Abbé d'Ancourt, *The Lady's Preceptor,* 1743

Is it possible to recover a history of how and why we read communally? In
the previous chapter we saw how the social history of the book was closely
linked to other practices—to ideas about sociability, the conventions of
visiting, the use of leisure time, the nature of domestic spaces, the value of
conversation. While increasing literacy and access to books undoubtedly
made solitary reading possible for some, there were many reasons why individuals continued to read together.[1] Some of these had to do with control
over what was being read, and how: the perceived social benefits of being
together, of the book as the basis for communal entertainment, performance,
and discussion. But there were also straightforwardly practical reasons—
light and sight. It is in some ways extraordinary that people read as much as
they did in the eighteenth century, given the practical challenges they faced.
Up until the advent of the Argand oil lamp, and cheap supplies of North
American mineral oil in the early nineteenth century, domestic lighting was
primitive, and prohibitively expensive. The darkness was very dark indeed,
as James Boswell's diary reminds us:

> About two o' clock in the morning I inadvertently snuffed out my
> candle, and as my fire was long before that black and cold, I was in a
> great dilemma how to proceed. Downstairs did I softly and silently

step to the kitchen. But, alas, there was as little fire there as upon the icy mountains of Greenland.[2]

Lighting was determined by class, with the poorest households dependent on homemade rushlights, tallow dips, and oil lamps, all of which were smoky and smelly, and needed constant attention.[3] Tallow candles, made of animal fat, needed continual snuffing (trimming the end of the charred wick) to prevent them from guttering and smoking. The best form of lighting, available only to the affluent, was wax candles. These were sold by weight, and substantially taxed. They were rated according to the number of candles that could be bought by the pound: known as 4 s, 6 s, 8 s, 10 s, and 12 s to the pound, with 4 s being longest and thickest. The choice and size of the candle was determined by the expected length of the event—which the host would duly have to consider. Candles were moved around in candle-sticks, and were placed in the socket of sconces, often with mirrors behind to reflect more light. Unless candles were used in great numbers (this only by the extremely wealthy), the darkness would be relieved by pools of light provided by individual candles, rather than suffused with ambient light. In many cases the brightest light would still be that coming from the hearth fire.[4]

Some rooms were harder to light than others. It was calculated that it would take six candles to light a wainscot room, eight for a stucco, and ten for a room hung with paintings.[5] Not all candles were wax, and there were social distinctions between those who used wax candles and those who used tallow dips—the latter were often given to servants and children. But some were not allowed their own lighting at all. James Lackington records of his time as an apprentice: "I had such good eyes, that I often read by the light of the Moon, as my master would never permit me to take a candle into my room, and that prohibition I looked upon as a kind of persecution."[6]

Further down the social scale, there were not even adequate windows. English agricultural cottages had always had too few windows, and it was even worse in Scotland. The soldier and journalist Alexander Somerville recalls that his parents, who were itinerant labourers in the Borders, and great consumers of religious literature, developed their own practical solution: "My father and mother had a window (the house had none) consisting of one small pane of glass, and when they moved from one house to another in different parts of Berwickshire in different years, they carried this window with them, and had it fixed in each hovel into which they went as tenants."[7] Reading alone in the evening in a separate room, or even in the same main room as others, was expensive, not to mention inexpedient (fig. 14). Why strain the eyes with insufficient light and small print when a single person with a well-lit book could do the work of many?

Even with artificial lighting, there were other technical obstacles to easy reading, namely limited ophthalmology. Reading aloud gave those with failing vision access to books and letters, and many read with others' eyes. The author and literary hostess Elizabeth Montagu writes to the Duchess of Portland: "I follow your Grace's advice, I do not work at all, and I read by my sister's eyes."[8] Mary Delany, also concerned about the effect of reading on her eyesight, assures her friend that she will "never read more (and seldom so much) as *two hours together*, but rest between, and chuse good prints for candle light; and that only three days in the week."[9] William Burgess, a fifteen-year-old Huguenot schoolboy from Marylebone, records in his diary

Fig. 14. *A Father Reading to His Family by Candlelight*, engraved by Thomas Cook after Daniel Dodd, frontispiece to a book published by John Marshall and Co., 1783 (Private Collection / The Stapleton Collection / Bridgeman Images)

weekly visits to read French to his ill and aged grandfather.[10] Numerous readers relate eyestrain to the dimness of candlelight.[11]

The position of the candle in relation to the page could be critical. On a dark day in February 1818, Anne Lister records in her diary: "Could not do much, my eyes were so very tired, particularly the right. I have read too much by candlelight lately & neither managed day nor candlelight properly. I have sat with it too much in my face & not thrown properly on the paper."[12] One of the problems with reading by a single candle was that one needed to arrange it so that the light was cast on the page, without glaring too much in the eye, a phenomenon commonly believed to damage the sight. And then there was the fire hazard. In its "Hints on Reading," the *Lady's Magazine* of April 1789 declared that "Some people who complain much of want of time during the day, endeavour to make up reading by reading in bed at night.— The insurances offices against Fire are not much pleased with this mode."[13]

The Lancashire landowner Nicholas Blundell had an ongoing battle with sore eyes. His attempts to tackle the problem are sustained and varied, reaching their acme in the summer of 1710. Over an extended period he buys "Spectacles by way of Preservation" and tries various cures—his recipe book contains twenty-nine different prescriptions for "Sore eyes" or "Rheum in the Eyes" or "Burning in the Eyes."[14] He records that "Dr. Cawood took me in hand to cuar my eyes. He made an Issue in each Eare."[15] This ear-based treatment, perhaps predictably, does not seem to have worked, and a month later we discover that "I began by orders of Dr. Cawood to take drops, eye bright tea, and to put Clary Seeds in my Eyes."[16] It might seem strange to us that Blundell put more energy into recipes, clary seeds, and ear surgery to improve his sight than spectacles, but this was an age when glasses were a very recent invention. One mid-nineteenth-century medical writer could only look back on this spectacle-less age with dismay and pity, declaring that glasses were the key to social and aesthetic pleasure: "[they] enable us to see the faces of our friends in the same apartment or across a table, to enjoy the beautiful in external nature or in art, and to count the stars in the firmament . . . how miserable must have been the condition of the aged and shortsighted before the invention of spectacles."[17]

Spectacles existed from the sixteenth century onwards, but it was not until the late eighteenth century that they began to be used widely. It is noticeable that many of the references to spectacles in the literature of the time treat them not as crucial aids, but as slightly absurd accessories. Comic stories circulated about the poorly endowed judge who is told to use a magnifying glass rather than spectacles to see his member; Spaniards were stereotyped as putting their spectacles on only at dinner time for the sake of fashion; Cowper wrote a joke poem about whether the spectacles belonged to the nose or the eyes.[18] It was only through the widespread use of spectacles in the late eighteenth century and the early nineteenth that conditions such as myopia, astigmatism, and hypermetropia began to be diagnosed and treated.[19] The great eighteenth-century development in spectacles was the addition of sides—up until then, they rested precariously, on the nose. This raises questions about how people read aloud in the era of sideless glasses. Was it really possible to stand and deliver in ways described by domestic oratory manuals while simultaneously holding glasses to the nose and clutching a small print book? For many, the memorization of passages of verse and prose must have been almost essential for truly effective delivery.

Reading, and particularly reading small type, was commonly believed to damage the sight, and a primary response to eye problems was simply to stop reading. As a young child, Laetitia van Lewen (later Pilkington) was banned from reading by her mother, because of her poor eyesight, and when she was caught one day illicitly reading Dryden's *Alexander's Feast* to herself, she feared a whipping. At the failure of cures, Nicholas Blundell is similarly urged to abstain from reading to avoid further complications. The abolitionist and member of Parliament William Wilberforce was noted for his fine elocution and powers of oratory from a young age, when the master of his grammar school in Hull used to set him on a table, and make him read aloud to the other boys. However, Wilberforce's eyesight began to deteriorate early in adult life, and his correspondence often describes the difficulties that this presented. He informs his daughter that he would have written sooner and more fully only that "my eyes were so weak, and that, in such a state, writing by candlelight does not suit me, especially after a full day's work following a bad night."[20] For him, reading aloud was a necessity. In certain circumstances it could be a pleasure: his son recalls (not without nostalgia) that "when being read to in his family circle, which was his delight, he poured forth all his stores, gathering around him book after book to illustrate, question, or confirm the immediate subject of the evening."[21] Wilberforce, however, did not always enjoy the process of being read to as much as this anecdote suggests; he writes of the disadvantage of having to have a volume of Mme de Staël read to him, instead of fully appreciating it by himself.[22] Elsewhere he remarks that he found it difficult to concentrate so well on books when only listening: "I might hope to do something but for the want of eyes . . . I cannot make the same use of passages I notice in books that are read to me as if I had read them with my own eyes, and could know them at a glance."[23]

Readability

As Mary Delany's mention of choosing "good prints for candelight" suggests, the size of print was crucial to healthy reading. The popular octavo format for the more affordable end of the market made for very small type—the equivalent of 10 point Times New Roman. But some popular books were published in editions with type 50 percent bigger than standard. In his *Essay on Vision* (1789), the royal optician George Adams estimated that the distance at which "natural" vision normally operated was such as to enable a person to read a "large fair Print" at a distance of fifteen or sixteen inches.[24] The *Essay* was intended, it claimed, for those whose vision was weak or impaired, and would enable them to arrest further decline, understand what was happening, and choose the right kinds of spectacles. But given that glasses were nothing like as widely used as in post-nineteenth-century Britain, the size of type was more likely to have been the key to enabling access for a broad readership.

An advertisement for Mary Davys's novel, *The Reform'd Coquette* (1736), announces that this edition is "printed on a large Letter, for the Use of antient Ladies."[25] The sixteenth edition of the forbidding *An Answer to all the Excuses and Pretences which Men ordinarily make for their not coming to the Holy Communion* offered a version of the work "printed in a very large Letter, for the Curious, Aged, and such as cannot read a small Print" (fig. 15).[26] The example of Davys's novel in a large print is unusual. Looking over book catalogues and advertisements, one notices that the small-format books most likely to be advertised "in a large print" or "a very large type" are most commonly domestic devotional works—the Bible, the Book of Common Prayer, or *The Whole Duty of Man*. Portability combined with type size were a prized combination for the everyday reader: a bookseller advertising "An Octavo Prayer, of very large Letter, fit for the Pocket" recognised the practical needs of his constituency.[27] When John Cuthbert, a missionary in Sierra Leone, wrote back home with information about his travels, he added at the end of the letter: "I shall esteem it a favor if you will send me a hymn and psalm-book, large print, for the French have got my spectacles, and my eyes are dim."[28]

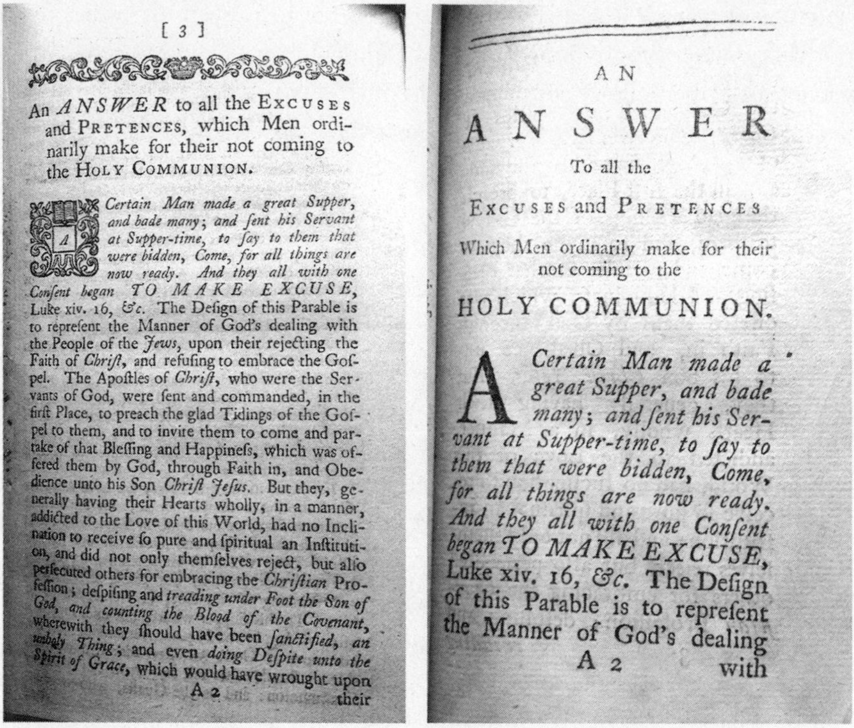

[3]

An *ANSWER* to all the Excuses and Pretences, which Men ordinarily make for their not coming to the Holy Communion.

A *Certain Man made a great Supper, and bade many; and ſent his Servant at Supper-time, to ſay to them that were bidden, Come, for all things are now ready. And they all with one Conſent began* TO MAKE EXCUSE, Luke xiv. 16, *&c.* The Deſign of this Parable is to repreſent the Manner of God's dealing with the People of the *Jews*, upon their rejecting the Faith of *Chriſt*, and refuſing to embrace the Goſpel. The Apoſtles of *Chriſt*, who were the Servants of God, were ſent and commanded, in the firſt Place, to preach the glad Tidings of the Goſpel to them, and to invite them to come and partake of that Bleſſing and Happineſs, which was offered them by God, through Faith in, and Obedience unto his Son *Chriſt Jeſus*. But they, generally having their Hearts wholly, in a manner, addicted to the Love of this World, had no Inclination to receive ſo pure and ſpiritual an Inſtitution, and did not only themſelves reject, but alſo perſecuted others for embracing the *Chriſtian* Profeſſion; deſpiſing and *treading under Foot the Son of God, and counting the Blood of the Covenant*, wherewith they ſhould have been *ſanctified, an unholy Thing*; and even *doing Deſpite unto the Spirit of Grace*, which would have wrought upon

A 2 their

AN

ANSWER

To all the

Excuses and Pretences

Which Men ordinarily make for their not coming to the

HOLY COMMUNION.

A *Certain Man made a great Supper, and bade many; and ſent his Servant at Supper-time, to ſay to them that were bidden, Come, for all things are now ready. And they all with one Conſent began* TO MAKE EXCUSE, Luke xiv. 16, *&c.* The Deſign of this Parable is to repreſent the Manner of God's dealing

A 2 with

Fig. 15. A comparison of the 16th edition (ordinary type) and the 17th edition (large type) of *An Answer to all the Excuses*, both published in London, 1744 (© The British Library Board, DRT Digital Store 1578/6566)

Occasionally, publishers betray something of the relationship between the format of books and the needs of their users.[29] In a 1759 letter to Lady Barbara Montagu, Samuel Richardson explained that "Now and then, when the Words *making, taking* &c come to be *divided* in a narrow Page, for the sake of Young Readers, who are sometimes try'd by Seniors in Reading to them, put in the Letter *e, at the End of the Line,* to give the Full Sound of the Word *make*-ing instead of making."[30] For Richardson, the demands of reading aloud meant greater care needed to be taken in enabling readers to see the way in which one word ran between lines. Compilations occasionally advertised the presentation of the work within, and its suitability for reading aloud. The preface to *Beauties in Prose and Verse* (1783) claimed that "The Paper is good, the Type large and distinct, and calculated for reading publicly, without laboring under the disagreeable necessity of looking so very minutely, and frequently erring from the smallness of the print."[31]

Reading aloud was not only a solution to weak eyesight. It was also looked upon as a great solace in times of illness and for the dying. Frances Edgeworth's memoir of Maria Edgeworth is peppered with accounts of reading to the sick: after Maria's prolonged illness in 1805, the "first pleasure she was able to enjoy, when just strong enough to come down and lie on the sofa in the library, was the hearing Charlotte read out to her the 'Lay of the Last Minstrel.' "[32] Maria writes of having read *Evelina* to her sister Lucy, and takes the opportunity to stress the importance of storing up reserves of lighter reading to alleviate ill health: "It is a great advantage to young people not to swallow down entertaining books too early, for then nothing is left for the solace of illness."[33]

Mary Delany read frequently to her aged and ailing husband, Alexander Pendarves, often in trying circumstances: "When he had the gout, he could never bear (even in the midst of winter) the least fire in his room, and I have read three hours together to him, trembling with cold all the time."[34] Others believed that books offered more than mere distraction, and that selected reading could help to alleviate feelings of melancholy or depression. Dudley Ryder describes a visit from a friend thus afflicted:

> When Mr. Whately came in he was extremely dejected and got into one of his melancholy fits. The poor man could not put on one pleasant look nor speak a word. He told me now he expected never to be happy and cheerful more. I did what I could to divert him out of this humour, but all in vain. I did not know but reading over the *Guardian* wherein his case is exactly described might touch him and please him and therefore read it, but he was unmoved at the description of himself, when I mentioned Milton's poem upon melancholy and endeavoured to change his melancholy into that agreeable one which Milton there describes. But all in vain.[35]

Mr. Whately was evidently unmoved by his friend's advice, but the fact that Ryder thought reading could have a therapeutic effect is not uncommon. Many comic collections of the time claimed to offer "a cure for the spleen." Reading aloud played an important role in the care of the dying. This would often have been spiritual in nature—but not always. The Birmingham bookseller and stationer William Hutton describes the scene at his father's deathbed:

> On the morning of Monday my brother read [an unidentified secular book] to my father for I believe two hours. When he was asked if he chose to have the reading continued, he answered, "Yes." But,

whether he understood what was read, whether the voice soothed
him, or whether it was a mechanical fondness for a book that still
remained, I am not able to determine.[36]

Hannah Reynolds Rathbone, the wife of a Shropshire Quaker minister,
records that on Sunday, 27 December 1807, her husband read his annual
sermon to his immediate family, as it turned out for the last time: the following
year his friend read it to the family in William Rathbone's bedchamber, as he
lay dying in bed.[37]

Yet at the same time, books could be damaging to the health of the
listener, or the reader. The poet John Byrom's diary describes the illness of
his sister Ellen: "Thursday: sister Ellen had had a very good night, was very
well all morning, but at noon all on a sudden changed to worse again. She
fancied it was their reading (for they were reading Clarendon's history) that
disturbed her."[38] The poet and letter writer Anna Seward was to blame her
lung problems on an overenthusiastic reading of Shakespeare: "I think I
injured myself there [as a guest in Nottingham] by complying with the earnest
request of different companies, that I would read scenes from Shakespeare
aloud . . . To read Shakespeare without energy and great exertion, is not
within my chapter of possibilities. One evening I read all the principal scenes
in Macbeth aloud, and have never breathed freely since."[39]

Reading Habits

So what kinds of reading habits did shared reading foster? One recent literary
critic has described the difference between silent reading and oral reading in
terms of performance and introspection: when a reader reads aloud, he or
she is an actor of someone else's words, but when the reader is silent, the
process is more introspective, and encouraging of self-reflection.[40] Reading
aloud need not preclude self-reflection—many commentators testify to their
habits of reading aloud to themselves as a way of better immersing themselves in the words in hand. And when reading is shared, there are two experiences to consider. One person in that exchange vocalises the text, and the
other (or others) becomes a silent auditor. The exchange creates a space in
which both vocal projection and silent reflection happen at the same time—a
duality reflected in many paintings of pairs of readers, which show us the
moving lips and intent delivery of the reciter, alongside an absorbed and

contemplative listener who is often looking away from the reader and book, lost in his or her own imaginative world.[41] In looking at absorbed listeners, we read into them the interiority associated with the experience of reading in general. This feature of the appearance of reading as an emblem of private self-communion is also present in fictional works describing single readers. As the book historian Leah Price has observed, in fictional accounts of reading as a form of separateness, the book's function as a prompt for interiority depends less on its being looked at by the character who holds it, than on that person's being looked at himself.[42]

We can see from diary entries that for some, sociable reading involved a lot of reading of short sections of different kinds of books rather than dedication to a single text over a long period of time. Such habits of skipping and browsing were not unique to this time, nor exclusive to shared reading, as book historians have argued. Writing of "the long history of discontinuous reading," Peter Stallybrass observes that it was the move from scroll to codex (or to book) that enabled for the first time the use of bookmarks, and enabled transitions backwards and forwards within a text. "When cultural critics nostalgically recall an imagined past in which readers unscrolled their books continuously from beginning to end, they are *reversing* the long history of the codex and the printed book as indexical forms."[43] Early modern readers were moving away from continuous reading toward browsing, not the other way around. There is nothing unique about twenty-first-century partial reading, and thinking about these older habits offers a different perspective on present-day anxieties about "distracted reading."[44] Rather like modern-day channel surfing, eighteenth-century readers and listeners moved between different genres to suit their mood or interest. Anne Lister's diary from the early nineteenth century is a perfect example: she and her companions picked up bits here and there to read aloud: a review of an oriental romance, Richard Polwhele's sermons, prayers, a section of the family tree, a new novel by Walter Scott, Samuel Johnson's *Tour of the Western Isles of Scotland*, Caroline Lamb's *Glenarvon*. Not everyone read in this several and simultaneous manner. The clergyman and scholar Thomas Twining found it hard to keep two books on the go at once, and commented to his brother: "As to your reading prose between whiles, it would be very well if you had the leisure I have; but even I . . . always find, when I attempt to read two books together, that one swallows up the other, unless the subordinate, under-plot books be very light and easy reading."[45]

The *Lady's Magazine* also expressed concern about chaotic habits of reading, counselling its faithful that "Reading . . . should be regular—not jumping from history to novels, from novels to divinity, and from divinity to poetry." The editor proffered the story of a great friend called "Eugenio," who adopted a particular timetable for his book consumption: "in the morning he reads the newspaper—at noon studies history—after dinner books of entertainment—in the evening new books and pamphlets, because as he says, they have very frequently a tendency to make him sleep sound."[46]

Anne Lister, however, seems to have relished the chaos of multiple book reading, and consumed many different kinds of books out loud with her companions, her brief notes recording her responses and observations. But how often did someone like her actually read the whole book? In Lister's case it seems impossible that she read all of everything, given the variety of works consulted. Many of her records of reading suggest that she has picked up a work midway through, not necessarily intending to read the whole: "I was on the amoroso till M— made me read aloud the first 126pp., vol.2, of Sir Walter Scott's last novel *The Monastery* . . . Stupid enough."[47] It doesn't sound as though she had read the first volume, or was planning on reading the rest. She notes later that she has read the first hundred pages of the third volume of the German novelist and dramatist Kotzebue's novel *Leontine de Blondheim*, and as before, apparently without having read the earlier volumes. Interestingly, this only partial exposure to a book does not seem to have hampered or diluted her emotional response. The effects of the hundred pages she had read, despite having not read the first two-thirds, were powerful: "I have read it with a sort of melancholy feeling, the very germ of which I thought had died for ever. I cried a great deal over the second & more over the third this morning."[48] Sometimes her acquaintance with a novel was even more piecemeal, and took the form of extracts presented in a critical review: "Just after tea read aloud to my aunt the very favorable review of *Lallah Rookh; an Oriental Romance* by Thomas Moore . . . The extracts from this poetic romance are very beautiful."[49]

Lister's habits of sampling, excerpting, and revisiting are crucial to thinking about how books functioned for their readers. We know that Lister only read parts of things because she recorded page runs and volume numbers in some detail in her diary. The historical evidence of communal reading suggests that many eighteenth-century readers and listeners were not, or were not able to be, "completists." They did not expect that a book could only be enjoyed by cover-to-cover immersion, and the practice of reading together discouraged this. Members of a household or a family were quite likely to catch only part of a work. Sarah More writes to the clergyman Thomas Whalley about the rage for his recent pamphlet called "Animadversions," which she has only heard by accident in her house: "I have been running up and down ever since, catching a page of it as I can, from a lady who is reading it to Patty in her bed, all equally wondering who can be the author."[50]

Should we be surprised by these habits of partial reading? Perhaps not. It could be argued that skim-reading does not prevent us from appreciating a text, and may in fact be a more efficient way to read books, as the French critic Pierre Bayard has argued in *How to Talk About Books You Haven't Read*. Bayard suggests that the partial reading of a book offers a way of "respecting their inherent depth and richness without getting lost in the details."[51] He cites what Paul Valéry wrote about Marcel Proust's work shortly after the novelist's death in late 1922: "Although I have scarcely read a single volume of Marcel Proust's great work, and although the very art of the novelist is an art that I find inconceivable, I am nevertheless well aware, from the little of the *Recherche du Temps Perdu* that I have found time to read, what an exceptionally heavy loss literature has just suffered."[52] Unembarrassed by his partial knowledge, Valéry went on to argue that the fact that *À la Recherche* rewarded such incomplete reading was in itself a sign of its brilliance, its value evident in its remarkable ability to be opened at random to any page.[53]

Valéry's justifications may be slightly casuistical, but they offer us an alternative perspective on the value of different kinds of reading practice—one that is helpful for thinking about the partial reading habits of the eighteenth century. Library borrowing records from the eighteenth century show that books were not always read in sequential and complete order, but in many cases, were perused through "desultory reading."[54] Readers took out odd volumes, and read these independently, without necessarily going on to read the series in its entirety. The records of one particular circulating library show that at least one of the multivolume novels lent out had lost its last volume, but still attracted readers. The desultory readers range from schoolboys to adults, and the fact that many of these people took out one volume of a novel, and then returned a considerable time later to read more, suggests that this practice of not reading the whole of a novel, from start to finish, was not just a matter of a reader losing interest.

So what kinds of books were browsed in this way? Perhaps not surprisingly, Samuel Richardson's long epistolary novels were often withdrawn incompletely, particularly *Sir Charles Grandison*, which was borrowed seventeen of twenty-eight times in this way. After Richardson, Henry Brooke's picaresque sentimental novel *The Fool of Quality* attracted the most desultory reading. Fielding's *Tom Jones*, on the other hand, seems always to have been borrowed complete. Some stylistic features of eighteenth-century novels lent themselves to partial reading: many of the most browsed books listed were originally published in serial form, and the same qualities that made for good serial publication—set pieces, discrete narrative chunks, and recapitulation—also attracted the common browser. The picaresque plotting of a work such as *The Fool of Quality*, or Smollett's *Humphrey Clinker*, moreover, aided casual readings—the multiple strands and loose sense of causality in these fictions made it possible to appreciate the part without the whole. The discrete sections of epistolary fiction and the sentimental vignettes were additional features that gave their passages stand-alone appeal.

What this intriguing analysis of partial reading doesn't take into account is how often books were being read for the second or third time to their listeners, who might not have needed to hear the whole book because they had read or heard it before. Sometimes that made little difference to their ability to remember the book—the Yorkshire schoolmaster Robert Sharp writes of the pleasures of rereading: "is there no pleasure in forgetfulness? yes, surely when one has read an entertaining Book and forgot its contents there is the pleasure of reading it over again without any anticipation aye or recollection either."[55] And in other cases, once was enough: "My Uncle is now reading Amelia to my Aunt & Miss Savery so I have taken this opportunity of writing a few Lines to you according to your desire I assure you I don't deprive my self of any Entertainment on that Account for I think that History a second time any one ought to have more patience than I am Misstress off."[56] But for the main part, just as now, in an age of cheap print and universal access, when many enjoy the retelling of a familiar story, so in an age of relatively expensive and inaccessible books, multiple readings must have been common practice.

These habits of browsing and selective reading were widespread—but not universally approved of. At the same time that hundreds, or thousands, of readers were happily dipping and skipping their way through texts, there was also a concurrent perception that such consumption was intellectually lax.[57] Later critics tended to focus their disapproval on the print forms—the collections of beauties, indexes, abridgements, miscellanies, and books sold in parts—that enabled such easy sampling. In *Idler* 85, Samuel Johnson argued that the plethora of compilations and digests available created a generation of indolent readers "growing wise on easier terms than our progenitors." He declares that compilations "only serve to distract choice without supplying any real want" and that the authors of such productions "give us again what we had before, and grow great by setting before us what our own sloth had hidden from our view."[58] According to Johnson, editors were lazy in repackaging the same texts without offering anything new, and readers were negligent for not taking the trouble to read the original. Yet Johnson himself practiced different kinds of reading: he read substantially and in depth, and also lightly, for pleasure, a habit he described as "mere reading."[59] One of the challenges in recovering a history of this kind of partial, skipping, reading is choosing a way of describing it that does not somehow suggest that it is less valuable. The terms we might tend to use, such as "skimming," "dip 'n skip," or "desultory" reading, suggest that they are less valuable than a "deeper," more sustained, engagement with the whole of a text.[60]

Reading together was a common practice in eighteenth-century households for various reasons: because it enabled one to read and others to work, saved eyesight, saved candles. It provided the basis of domestic education, and allowed parents to control what their children consumed. But needless to say, it ran alongside habits of silent solitary reading, and individual reading records remind us again and again of the continuity between oral and silent. Henry Woollcombe, a young attorney living in Plymouth and writing his diary in the last decade of the eighteenth century, read for moral and cultural self-improvement. Woollcombe, who was to go on to occupy a series of important public offices in Plymouth, remained single all his life, and his diary shows us the life of a man who acquired the time and money to pursue with some seriousness his intellectual interests.[61] Over the course of his increasingly prosperous career, he amassed a collection of histories, belles lettres, romances, and legal texts.[62] He was first and foremost a silent reader, who used his diary to record his opinions on the works he had covered. The diary for 1796 begins with a bold ambition:

> When I reflect on the last year & consider how much I read, & how little I have retained, in fact not much more than the mere title of the Books, I naturally could wish to form some method by which I might look back with greater pleasure on the past than I now do; for

this purpose I have adopted the following plan, & I sincerely hope it may produce the desired effect, that it may tend not only to my gaining benefit from what I read with regard to worldly Knowledge which I am well aware is not to be despised, but that I may so amend my life that I may at last arrive at that blessed mansion which is designed only for the good.[63]

Woollcombe's plan was to record all the books that he read. It did not initially flourish. After a couple of desultory entries, the entries tailed off and the notebook degenerated into the briefest notes, in French, on the activities of the day. The following year he began to realise the scheme in earnest, using his comments to evaluate the books he had read, and often, to compare his responses with critical judgments from the *Spectator* or Samuel Johnson. Woollcombe's preferred mode was silent reading, usually of a complete work. He was not a casual browser, but exhibited instead a purposeful determination to cover certain kinds of material: "I purpose to read one Number of the Rambler every day (Sunday excepted) and when that is finished to begin some other periodical Paper."[64] Although influenced by criticism he had read elsewhere, particularly in Johnson's *Lives*, he liked to strike out in new territory with his own evaluations: "Tickell appears to me to be too Prolix in all his pieces."[65] He was sometimes disappointed by the disparity between his experience of a literary text, and the common critical consensus: "This evening I retired soon after from the Family & read some of Thomson's Summer. I cannot say I am much pleased with it, whether this be owing to my expectations being excited so much by the encomiums I have heard bestowed on it or from what other cause I cannot determine."[66] Henry Woollcombe rarely mentions other people being present, and on the odd occasion when he does, they seem to be an intrusion: "The evenings I was at home this week I read Poetry by different authors whose Lives were written by Dr. Johnson, & after reading it observed what Johnson had said of them, but finding this was not agreable to My mother & Ann this Evening I began Robertson's History of Scotland."[67]

But even though reading alone was his preference, books nonetheless had a social dimension. In letters written before the advent of the diary, his older brother William, in Edinburgh, had advised him of the importance of discussing his reading: "As you are fond of reading, and have upon the whole a good deal of time, unoccupied by your professional duties you have no doubt employed yourself in this way . . . continue to inform me of your course of reading, and of the opinions you form of the different works you peruse. This you may at first find a difficult task, but you know very well that such difficulties are apparent only."[68] William explained to Henry, "You will thus acquire a habit of thinking & judging for yourself, without which a man on entering into life is in danger of having his opinions shaken by all the arts which sophistry can employ, while doubt & uncertainty rush in upon his mind."[69]

Henry Woollcombe's diary preserves this sense of a conversation (with himself) about books, in which he shapes his views and establishes what he thinks in relation to others. Moreover, the diary also records his understanding of reading as an aid to conversation with others. "This Evening I finished Thomson's Seasons not so delighted as I expected to have been but still well pleased that I had read them if it were only for the sake of not being ignorant of the Subject when they were spoken of in Publick."[70] Woollcombe might not have read aloud very often, but his reading, as he saw it, was crucial to his performance in company. He notes with satisfaction having finished Pope's works: "I have derived great entertainment from its perusal [Pope's works], its beauties I hope have not passed me unobserved, and that in conversation I shall appear perfectly acquainted with his Poems as I now consider myself."[71] He also occasionally tries reciting, almost, as if it were, to keep his hand in: "I took up a Book I purchased in Holland but had never yet read entitled 'Chronijk van Amsterdam' I was well pleased to find so readily understood . . . I read at one time aloud & evidently perceived I did not retain the recitation that I hope however to recover."[72]

Henry Woollcombe's reading diary is the work of a man trying very hard—trying to be well informed, to be independent in his thinking, and to apply the lessons of books to his own life. It illustrates the social dimensions of solitary reading, and the importance of looking right across reading experiences to get an understanding of how books were used as part of everyday lives.

Different readers show us other habits. Hannah Mary Reynolds was a Shropshire woman who married a Liverpool Quaker, William Rathbone. Her diary before her marriage is full of references to her personal reading, which was both solitary and communal. She adopts an ambitious "plan of reading" with her brother, and at the start of her diary, periodically records her responses to this. But most of the reading that she records in her diary is with others. She records that "My uncle Joe, Mr. Walker, etc., etc., dined with us; read for amusement Boswell's 'Journal of a Tour to the Hebrides' ";[73] "J. Thresher drank tea with H.B., J.A., and me in the dining-room. Read Mrs. Piozzi. R.L., etc., in the parlour";[74] "Ran into the garden with E.R. W.R read to us in the *Spectator* in the afternoon. Engaged with the microscope."[75] It is notable that this reading is almost always secular, and for entertainment— not what one might expect from the pious wife of a prominent Quaker who held "open house" on Sundays for the young men who worked with him. The reading aloud is done by a variety of people, and although those involved are often elders, they also read this entertaining material. In January 1787 her father-in-law reads *Paradise Lost* to everyone; on a very wet day one September, the children stay in the parlour where their father reads James Thomson's *Seasons*. After her husband's death her family have a whole series of evenings devoted to Blair's *Lectures on Rhetoric and Belles Lettres*. Later on, her son reads Scott's epic poem *Marmion* and Thomson's verse allegory *The Castle of Indolence*. It is difficult to know from the evidence of the diary whether the prominence of these group readings of secular works reflects the relative frequency of their occurrence or their importance to Hannah Mary, or whether these were recorded and her religious reading was not because the spiritual was so everyday and taken for granted.

Despite their apparent authenticity, diaries are not transparent records of lives—and in particular, of reading lives. The complex nature of their evidence is made plain in the case of a teenage boy named Ralph Jackson. Jackson was an adolescent apprentice from Richmond in North Yorkshire, sent by his father to work with William Jefferson, a Newcastle hostman (a kind of merchant middleman, working in this case in the coal trade). Ralph began his journal when he left home in October 1749, and continued it until his death in 1790, by which time he had metamorphosed from a gawky teenager enjoying catching larks and playing "burn ball" (a kind of basketball), hardly able to spell, to a substantial landowner, businessman, and magistrate. The first words he writes in his diary are:

> My father told me when I began to keep this Journal—
> Let not that Day pass by
> whose low descending Sun,
> Views from thy hand
> No noble action done.[76]

From the start, the diary keeping was instigated by his father as a way of encouraging his son to spend his time well. And as it turned out, the diary was also read by his father as a way of checking up on his son.[77] During the first few months of the apprenticeship, Ralph mostly recorded card playing—and only one visit to church. Over his first Christmas break, at home in Richmond, Ralph's father evidently read his son's journal, and commented on the frivolity of his use of time. After Christmas, on the boy's return to Newcastle, there was a noticeable increase in references to churchgoing, and much less about cards. Ralph's father continued to supervise his son's diary keeping. In January 1752, while staying at home, Ralph recorded "my Father put me into a Method of keeping my Acco^{ts} and I wrote in this book in my Fa^{rs} Closet."[78] In town, Jackson lived with his master William Jefferson, a widower or bachelor with no children. The other people in the house were an elderly servant named George and a domestic, Jenny. There is a certain amount of sociable domestic culture in the household—Ralph mentions several times that his master "told some merry stories" before they went to bed. At one point early in his stay, he asked Jefferson for some reading matter, and was provided with "The Compleate Traidman," possibly a copy of Defoe's *Complete English Tradesman*.

Ralph Jackson did not have a ready supply of his own books, but drew on the resources of the household to furnish his needs. When he got back to Newcastle after the Christmas holiday in early 1753, he received a parcel from Richmond that contained a book entitled "Telemachus." His parents had not made a habit of sending him reading material, but their choice of François Fénelon's didactic fiction, *The Adventures of Telemachus, the Son of Ulysses* (1699), which was described in the preface to the 1742 edition as "the most proper book that ever was written to form the minds and hearts of Youth" clearly signalled their desire to shape Ralph's conduct through his reading. In describing the educational travels of Homer's Telemachus, who is guided by the sage Mentor, Fénelon's narrative offered a series of lessons in secular morality, and the nature of government.

The story of what Ralph Jackson did with this book is interesting. Ralph wrote dutifully on many occasions of reading his book, which he usually took over to his friend Billy Tindell's to read in company. But over the course of 1753 Ralph began to seek self-improvement in alternative ways. By the middle of the year he had developed a pattern of reading together—he nearly always took *Telemachus* to Mrs. Tindell's to read, but he also carried

Nelson's Geography, The Gentleman Instructed, and sometimes, his German flute with which to entertain the Tindells. Over the summer of 1753 the diary became fuller and fuller of references to going to church, to hearing Methodist speakers, to reading sermons to his friends Billy Hudspath and John Scafe, and to reading *The Whole Duty of Man* to himself while walking along. Jackson began to use his journal to record not just what he had heard or read, but also the important religious sentiments he was learning. It is as if the diary stopped being a record of the social and professional advancement his father wanted him to achieve, and started to become a more confessional record of his spiritual life. *Telemachus* did not fit in with this new mindset, and in June 1753 Ralph Jackson announced: "I went to Mrs Tindells & read in that bad Book of Telemachus, I went into my Masters Room then I went down stairs & read in the Whole Duty of Man & in the New Testament."[79] Two days later, he packed up *Telemachus,* along with an old shirt, and sent it back to Richmond.

From this point on, Ralph recorded a steady pattern of exclusively religious reading. He got up at five or six in the morning to read *The Whole Duty of Man,* or "the Crucified Jesus," and usually went round to the Scafes' to read sermons and discourses: "I bought some Goose berries & carried them to Thos. Scafes, where I read concerning prayer, Mr Scafe was out of Humour so I endeavoured to pacify him and read prayers."[80] There was no more reading at Mrs. Tindell's, no more geography or magazines or *Robinson Crusoe.* Ralph assumed responsibility for the spiritual development of his teenage friends, and the servants in the house, regularly reading to Billy Hudspath or George, the servant. This was a very different kind of communal activity: "I read the lessons for this day as likewise some Chapters in Genesis for I now intend with Gods assistance to read the old & new Testaments quite through without leaving any part unread."[81]

It didn't last forever. By 1756 the entries were again perfunctory, with little reading. But the diary demonstrates the way in which individual personal development demanded different kinds of friends, different kinds of reading, and different kinds of recording. Ralph Jackson went from taking his new secular books round to a neighbour's, where he might also get a fire, tea, and a snack ("I also went to Mary Davison's but she had not a fire on so I only got a biskett that was there") to reading the Bible in his kitchen, sermons at another neighbour's, and extended solitary reading of religious works by himself early in the morning.

Reading Apart?

Ralph Jackson's story hints at some of the divisive aspects of reading. In his case, growing religious conviction leads him to see his habits of secular communal reading as immoral. Moving towards Methodism, he becomes, for a time, alienated from the family with whom he used to read Fénelon. It reminds us that not all domestic reading was socially cohesive. The autobiographies of labouring-class readers in the late eighteenth century commonly register a strong sense of the contrast between their attempts to acquire culture and the competing bustle of the rest of their household, who were often heedless of the call of the written word.[82] Such memoirs tend to figure shared literary encounters as happening outside the home, not within it. Narratives describe a meeting with another working man who has also set out upon a course of self-improvement, a figure commonly described as "a lover of books," "a reader and thinker," or "a reading man."[83] Here, the name "reader" came to signify not just one who could read, but one who shared an aspiration to rational enquiry and moral improvement. In these autobiographies, the home was a space of cultural loneliness, an element of the physical and intellectual hardship experienced by the self-educating working man.

These literary separations of labouring-class homes remind us that reading was not always a bonding experience within a social setting. Some readers, then as now, used reading as a way of deliberately setting themselves apart from others. Charles and Fanny Burney's account of Samuel Johnson's visit to their house reveals a man using books as a barrier: having studied the contents of Charles Burney's bookshelves with some absorption "almost brushing them [the books] with his eye-lashes from near examination" he found what he was looking for, a volume of the French *Encyclopédie:* "He took it down, and, standing aloof from the company, which he seemed clean and clear to forget, he began [. . .] very composedly, to read to himself; and as intently as if he had been alone in his own study. We were all excessively provoked: for we were languishing, fretting, expiring to hear him talk."[84] Johnson also took reading matter with him to dinner, sitting at the table with his book wrapped up in the tablecloth or in his lap, where again, it formed a bulwark against talking and engaging with others.[85]

Johnson's exclusionary reading on these occasions was silent, but there are also examples of reading aloud as a form of social division.[86]

Sometimes reading ruined what was read. Mary Berry, growing up with her grandmother in Yorkshire, tells of how her grandmother

> made me read the Psalms and chapters to her every morning; but, as neither explanation nor comment was made upon them, nor was their history followed up in any way, I hated the duty and escaped it when I could. The same consequence took place by the same dear parent making me read every Sunday a Saturday paper in the "Spectator," which, till the middle of life, prevented my ever looking at those exquisite essays, or being aware of the beauties of the volumes they were in.[87]

Poor reading could create bathos or bluster, and listeners judged their readers harshly. Anna Seward lamented of her friend Mr. Stokes, a doctor from Chesterfield who comes to visit in September 1798: "He has absolutely no impassioned or metrical intonation, but, instead of it, the oddest cadences, that have no congeniality with the passion or sentiment which the words express. An author's vanity could meet no severer damp than from hearing Dr. S read his or her compositions. He has the art of sinking the manly melodies of Milton's blank verse into the vapidness of Phillip's and of Glover's." Writing of his wife, whom she admires in many other ways, Seward struggles to transcend her dislike of her accent: "A hardness in sounding the consonants, which mark the provinciality of Derbyshire and Lancashire, is so great a disadvantage to the grace of her conversation, as scarcely to be balanced by the uncommon strength of her ideas, the efflorescence of her fancy, and the accuracy of her language."[88]

Even accomplished orators sometimes misjudged the demands of domestic entertainment. One memoir describes John Henderson reciting at home: "I once heard him read part of a tragedy, and but once; it was in his own parlor, and he ranted most outrageously [. . .] It was clear he had not studied that most excellent property of pitching his voice to the size of the room he was in."[89] Elocution guides allude to the social shame of reading poorly in company, warning children of the embarrassment of speaking with monotony, "like an Ignorant Boy, who understands not what he reads."[90]

There also seems to be an element of coercion in some accounts of communal reading—not just amongst recalcitrant children, but also for adults forced to listen against their better wishes. In a letter of September 1794, Mary Berry describes the trials of a wet day indoors with her guests, the

Churchills, who are apparently heedless of others in the room. She tells her correspondent that she cannot answer a letter at full length,

> for the Churchills are here in the room while I write; it has rained heavily ever since breakfast, and they can neither go out in their chaise which they had ordered, nor into the garden; and just as I was going to begin my letter, the newspaper came in, and he has been reading it aloud to us paragraph by paragraph, half of which are bad news of retreats of our army [. . .] Before I could digest half this, he came to a sale of milch cows—I don't mean the King of Prussia, nor that we are again one of his milch cows; but Mr. Churchill, who wants some for Lewisham, and has been reading of them to his wife, till I have not a clear idea left.[91]

The Churchills' disregard for their companions, and their insistence on reading even when not welcome, is not unusual. Reading aloud could be perceived as self-indulgence by those forced to listen to it. Richard Cumberland's account of his stay at Eastbury, the country house of George Bubb Dodington, suggests the element of vanity in his host's recitation. Dodington evidently picked his readings with an eye only to his own particular talents: "His selections, however, were curious, for he treated those ladies with the whole of Fielding's *Jonathan Wild*, in which he certainly consulted his own turn for irony rather than theirs for elegance, but he set it off with much humour after his manner, and they were polite enough to be pleased, or at least to appear as if they were. His readings from Shakespeare were altogether as whimsical, for he chose only passages where buffoonery was the character of the scene."[92]

Those who insisted on reading out their own work in company were easily mocked. The playwright George Colman the younger records an evening with a man called Mr. George Keate, who regaled Colman and his father with a melancholy story about having lost all his hair, including facial hair, due to excessive fright. Already struggling "from the difficulty of suppressing a vulgar and uproarious horse laugh," Colman says that "Having finished his history, he [Keate] began a subject much more doleful, by pulling from his pocket a manuscript play of his own writing, and asking my father (Oh horror!) to let him read it to him."[93] The ennui of the listener is palpable in such accounts. The classical scholar Richard Porson was, according to John Taylor, profoundly insensitive to those around him. Porson's rudeness is manifested in his enforced recitation: "I afterwards used to meet Porson every night at the Turk's Head in the Strand, where he . . . often tired the company with his recital of a burlesque parody of Pope's exquisite poem of 'Eloisa to Abelard.' It was doubted whether this travestie of Pope's beautiful poem was his own writing, but the warmth and frequency of his obstrusive recitations, evidently manifested parental dotage."[94]

Listeners were also not blind—or deaf—to the subtexts of social recitation. The reading of a particular passage could be a way of saying something unsayable, or a particular form of social spite or teasing. Accounts of Lady Anne Miller's parties at Easton Hall in Lincolnshire, in which a Roman vase was filled with handwritten poems, then read out in turn by the assembled gentlemen, tell a couple of times of readers embarrassed by an inappropriate poem, introduced by a mischief-making guest.[95] Frederick Reynolds describes a literary soiree in which Sir Horace Mann accidently reads aloud a smutty poem to the woman sitting next to him, because some wags in the group have swapped "true English single entendres" for the double entendre mottos that were the intended amusement of the gathering. Reynolds reports that Mann tore up the motto and walked out of the room, while the lady who had heard the lines "continued alternately to blush, titter, and fan herself."[96] These occasions may only be a feature of more elevated literary gatherings, but they suggest that the literary parlour games of the era were not always entirely benign.

Preparation for Reading Aloud

As the evidence suggests, many books were read only in excerpt form, with the most striking passages selected for delivery. So how did one go about this? Some readers-aloud clearly applied themselves a good while beforehand. Fordyce's instructions for his young ladies tell them that "there can be few occupations of greater entertainment or utility, than that of imprinting on the mind those passages from any good author, which happen to please and affect more than ordinary; either by repeating them often at the time, till they are got by heart, or by writing them down, or sometimes by doing both."[97] Some reciters preselected passages from texts suitable for their audience. Maria Edgeworth, for instance, whom we met earlier in this chapter, describes her father's discerning reading to his children:

He took delight himself in ingenious fictions, and in good poetry; he knew well how to select what would amuse and interest young people; and he read so well, both prose and poetry, both narrative and drama, as to delight his young audience. . . . From the Arabian Tales to Shakespeare, Milton, Homer and the Greek tragedies, all were associated in the minds of his children with the delight of hearing passages from them first read by their father.[98]

Book marginalia offer some evidence of this kind of preparation. The surviving books of Philip MacDermott, a Dublin physician, show the way in which he had clearly marked up passages for delivery, isolating particular moments. His tiny copy of Byron's *Childe Harold's Pilgrimage* is covered with marks of explanatory footnotes, glosses, and appreciative comments. Alongside this there are annotations that suggest he was looking for passages to share through reading aloud or recitation. At the beginning of the fourth canto he has written at the bottom of the page: "Passages of surpassing beauty Quote—Stanzas 1—2—3 11—12—13—14—15—16—17."[99] As this suggests, passages of verse marked in books would often have been memorised, a practice central to the art of oral delivery. When the five-year-old Laetitia Pilkington is caught in the forbidden act of reading Dryden's *Alexander's Feast*, her parents' immediate response is to ask her to learn it by heart to recite before them, for which she would earn a shilling in reward. A copy of John Gay's *Fables*, owned by a young girl called Frances Stone, reveals her pattern of studying and learning passages of verse: over the course of two years, the work is given dated annotations that she is being taught (with breaks in the holidays) and lines of verse are marked up in sections, probably assigned as an elocution exercise, and for reading aloud to a family group.[100] Thomas Gisborne, instructing young female readers in "The Employment of Time," advised them to learn passages of verse not only to enrich their minds in the present, but also "when old age, disabling the sufferer from the frequent use of books, obliges the mind to turn inward upon itself; the memory, long retentive, even in its decay [. . .] still suggests the lines which have again and again diffused rapture through the bosom of health."[101]

As subsequent chapters of this book reveal, other readers compiled their own selections of passages for the entertainment of friends and family. The long-standing tradition of commonplacing, the transcription of selected passages of prose and verse into a personal collection, continued throughout the eighteenth century, and the commonplace book was used as a storehouse of materials for these social occasions.[102] Readers indexed their reading, enabling them to keep track of what they had read, and record titbits that could be usefully deployed on later occasions. Anne Lister notes in May 1818:

> All the morning till very near 3, copying notes from loose papers into Extracts, vol. B, & writing out an index to my volume of poetry & scraps for which, by the way, I must find out some more tractable name. One thing occurs to me after another. I have now thought of looking over all my extracts & making a universal index of similes, e.g. strong as Hercules, licentious as Tiberius; modest as Daphne, etc., & to make this index extend thro' all my future reading. It would certainly be useful; for when one wants a good simile, it is often astray.[103]

Lister's emphasis on making reading "useful" reverberates throughout the history of this time, and is crucial to understanding how people approached books. As her diary entry suggests, useful does not always mean practically informative but rather, socially enabling.

Propriety

Preparation for reading wasn't just about identifying elevated passages; it was also about choosing the right kind of text. One thing that's hard for us to judge at this distance in time is the boundary between polite and impolite. We might tend to assume that this distinction was gendered, that men drank punch and sang rude songs, and women sat and demurely sewed while they listened to a sentimental novel being read aloud. But it's clear that these assumptions mask a more complicated story. In Thomas Turner's diary entry cited earlier, it is the vicar's *wife* who comes round drunkenly at six in the morning to force him into more drinking and dancing. Recent work on popular culture in the eighteenth century reinforces this, showing the ongoing popularity of cruel and bawdy jokes and stories amongst men and women.[104] The politeness or rudeness of home entertainment at the time is illustrated by the jest books and riddle collections produced in their hundreds throughout the eighteenth century. These compilations demonstrate that double entendres seem to have been a key part of witty amusement; readers and listeners enjoyed riddles and conundrums; and performed dialogues were often based on playing with rude and polite meanings of words and phrases. Diary entries and letters tell a similar story. Elizabeth Tyrrell describes an evening of comic performances and riddles in March 1809: "George went to Tea at Mrs. Fishers to hear a young Lady play and sing—Mrs. Henshaw brought her books of Riddles and Charades &c which amused us the whole Evening—George came home soon after eleven well pleased with his visit."[105] Miss Drake writes to her friend Mary Heber about some books they have exchanged, and shows that while some jokes might be seen as "indelicate" they were still enjoyed: "General Conway's Riddle was certainly on an indelicate subject, but, not withstanding that, I think Mrs. Fanshawe's answer very smart and clever."[106]

Men might, however, be alarmed by the equal propensity of women for rudeness or innuendo. Our man about town, Dudley Ryder, is sometimes thrown by what he hears. He writes in May 1716: "The worst of Mr. Powell's conversation is that he is apt now and then to make use of *double entendres*, which shocked me very much and I wonder Mrs. Marshall seems so well pleased with them and so little shocked at them."[107] On a subsequent occasion he notes that "we passed away the evening in comical conversation enough. It chiefly turned upon bawdy and *double entendres*, than which I perceived nothing is more touching to Mrs. Marshall. I don't know that I ever talked so much to any woman in that way as I did at that time."[108]

Our expectations of what appropriate entertainment might consist of for men and women may well need some revision. Sylas Neville recounts his trip to see an old acquaintance in Richmond in North Yorkshire. Neville lauds his host as a "good & venerable [. . .] worthy old gentleman," who welcomes him into his family and home with "much kindness and civility." By way of illustrating the "vein of humour" that runs through his conversation, Sylas then recounts three of the jest stories his host has told him. One is a story about a husband and wife who fight like cat and dog. When at last the husband dies, the wife goes to close his eyes, and he suddenly opens them shouting out "another peep, you bitch!"[109]

Mary Delany, who disapproved of reading novels, and many other forms of popular literature, clearly enjoyed pretty bawdy fare. On one hand, her correspondence shows us a woman increasingly interested in how to reconcile sociable reading with proper decorum. She thinks Chesterfield's letters are "very hurtful in a moral sense," and writes to her impressionable friend Miss Sparrow, telling her to imprint Hester Chapone's advice manual to young women on her mind.[110] But she was not, as this might imply, closed off from more risqué sources of readerly pleasure. During an evening after dinner in Dublin, she comments that "All the while I have been writing, Don and Kelly have read with an audible voice Hans Carvell and some other pretty things of that kind, and how can one help listening? but I would stop my ears had I anything to say that would be entertaining."[111] "Hans Carvel's Ring" was a hugely popular poem by Matthew Prior, reprinted over and over again in jest books and poetic miscellanies. It's not really "pretty" in any modern sense. It is a story about an impotent husband, female infidelity, and Hans Carvel's pact with the devil. The "ring" given to Hans Carvel by the devil to restore his potency turns out to be Mrs. Carvel's anus, and the poem ends with the wife shouting out the immortal line "You drunken Bear? / You've thrust your Finger G-d knows where."[112] An ending described by Samuel Johnson as "not over-decent," it is hard to square with the image of a rather prim-sounding Mary Delany—but it was part of what she heard and knew, and reminds us of the complex social norms of the era.[113]

If we look at the way jest books and riddle collections from the eighteenth century are packaged, we can see that they contain a mixed fare. A midcentury collection called *Sir John Fielding's Jests* is subtitled *New Fun for the Parlour and Kitchen*. This suggests that it has an appeal both above and below stairs, with and without company. Its content has, supposedly, migrated from the public, and largely male, environment of the alehouse: the reader is told that the jokes and stories within are "Carefully transcribed from Original Manuscript Remarks, and Notes made on Such Occasions, and at the Shakespeare, Bedford Arms, and Rose Taverns . . . where the above Celebrated Genius and his Jovial Companions (*the drollest Wits of the Present Age*) usually met to Kill Care and promote the Practice of Mirth and Good Humour."[114] The compilation is packaged as being more or less decent: "Stale Jests, insipid Poems, and gross Indecencies, we have carefully avoided."[115] So what was "decent"? Within the first fifty pages we encounter comic tales about sex, defecation, prostitution, infidelity, and smelly feet. It is certainly tamer than other collections of the period, but the subject matter is not really decorous.[116]

As a response to the moral heterogeneity of popular print collections, some compilations attempted to delimit their content as entirely suitable for family consumption. Thomas Bowdler's famously censored edition of *The Family Shakspeare* (1818) advertised itself as an edition "in which nothing is added to the original Text: but those words and expressions are omitted which cannot with propriety be read aloud in a Family." However, in reality, selections of texts for reading aloud in a family frequently contained mixed fare that must have been hard to navigate at first glance.

Even when collections were packaged as family-friendly, not all approved. A copy of *The Pleasing Instructor* (1795), a collection of prose and verse that was subtitled "the Entertaining Moralist, consisting of select essays, relations, visions and allegories," is physical testimony to one reader's attempts to censor family reading (fig. 16). On page 359 of one copy of the collection, we find a section of text papered over to obscure the poem beneath. The owner has used soap chandler's labels to cover up a poem by Matthew Prior called "The Ladle." The poem in itself is not very offensive—it retells the story of Ovid's Baucis and Philemon, in which two gods come down to earth, spend an evening with a mortal couple, and offer them three wishes. In this version, the couple accidently wish for a ladle to be stuck up the wife's bottom, and their third wish is its removal. It wasn't suitable for one owner, who used glue and paper to restore propriety for family use.

Not everyone prepared so carefully for reading. Some scanned a page and selected on the spot, seizing quickly the appropriate piece of text. Thomas Holcroft describes an elderly friend who used to "Carry with him a small pocket volume of Milton, or Young's Night Thoughts . . . and as soon as dinner was over, he regularly took out one of his favourite authors, and, opening the book at random, requested the person who sat next him, whether a stranger or one of the usual company, to read aloud a certain passage which

Fig. 16. Canceled pages, obliterating Matthew Prior's "The Ladle," found in *The Pleasing Instructor*, 1795, private collection (Courtesy of Andrew Honey, Oxford)

he thought very beautiful."[117] Maria Edgeworth, describing her father's admiration for the poet and naturalist Erasmus Darwin's scientific verse, recalls: "I have sometimes seen him, when its merits have been questioned, offer to open the Botanic Garden at a venture, and to read aloud from the first page that might occur. His quick eye selected the best lines in the page, and those to which, in reading, he could give contrast and variety."[118]

The *Botanic Garden* is a substantial poem, published in two books, and running to over two and a half thousand lines, with copious notes. But, like the other examples cited here, it was a work that readers took up and read in parts. And again, thinking about habits of consumption offers insights into how books functioned generically. The long narrative or discursive poem, typified by the *Botanic Garden,* is a popular genre in eighteenth-century literature, and one alien to many modern readers. This kind of extended verse form was typically divided into books, interspersing passages of description, philosophic thought and political argument across thousands of lines of rhymed couplets. The most popular example of the long discursive poem was James Thomson's *Seasons,* a four-book nature poem first published in the 1730s. We know that many men, women, and children knew, read, and loved this poem. What we don't know is how they read it, and what they liked about it. It is not obvious to modern eyes why it should have been the most popular poem of the eighteenth century. It is long, diffuse, uneven in quality, and has been puzzled over by modern readers for its lack of coherence—both intellectual and stylistic. Even at the time, there were readers who thought it could benefit from more concision. Samuel Johnson recounts his experimentation with the drastic pruning of Thomson's verse: "Shiels, who compiled *Cibber's Lives of the Poets,* was one day sitting with me. I took down Thomson, and read aloud a large portion of him, and then asked,—Is not this fine? Shiels having expressed the highest admiration. Well, Sir, (said I,) I have omitted every other line."[119]

But perhaps these notions of unity and concision are beside the point. Modern readers and critics try to find coherence in literary forms, but we know that habits of reading, particularly social reading, involved repeated dips and excerpts, and the selection of marked passages. In the case of *The Seasons,* the fact that it was at times inconsistent might not have been a problem for generations of readers looking for discrete passages and moments to read aloud. As we will see later on, these habits of excerpting also shaped the forms of printed books. The miscellanies and magazines of the eighteenth century packaged portions of verse, prose, and music for readers who wanted diversity and accessibility rather than comprehensiveness. Their titles and title pages tell us this, offering a variety of metaphors for this practice of culling excerpts: they present us with "beauties," "flowers," "foundlings" entertainingly arranged, or alternatively a "museum" or "repository" to browse through. The virtue of the compilation was that it preselected comic, sentimental, dramatic, or lyrical moments from whole works, anticipating the ways in which texts were used by their readers.

Reading in this extracted way was undoubtedly common practice—but was it an entirely good thing? Hannah More, writing at the end of the century in *Strictures on the Modern System of Female Education* attacked the "Swarms of *Abridgements, Beauties* and *Compendiums,* which [. . .] may be considered in many instances as an infallible receipt for making a superficial mind."[120] More, like Samuel Johnson, argued that such publications sold learning too cheap: they encouraged young women to know only the names of renowned historical figures, yet nothing of their actions or character. The "few fine passages" of the poets acquired in collections of extracts "inflame young readers with the vanity of reciting" yet "neither fill the mind nor form the taste."[121] It was, More argued, all too easy to trace back the hackneyed quotations of "certain accomplished young ladies" to their shallow sources, the works of the "beauty mongers" who pumped out their volumes of accessible literary fragments. More's attack was connected to her wider critique of the notion of social accomplishment—in her eyes, a cultivation of surface rather than interior merit. Her comments demonstrate contemporary debate over the appropriate nature of improvement—and its implications for our understanding of the history of domestic reading.

꩜

People read aloud for many different reasons in the eighteenth century. They did it because they had to, and because they wanted to. Families gathered together for their evening "duty" of reading psalms and prayers; parents read to their children, and asked their children to read to them; married couples and friends read together for entertainment, improvement, to pass the time. Their reading could be performative, or it could be to create a basis for conversation; it could act as a form of literary criticism, an occasion to try out one's work in front of others. The sick and the dying were read to, but it was also thought that excessive reading could make one unwell. The reading of a single book could be sustained over many days, or only read in short sections, alongside a medley of other books; some readers would merely read in their own persona, while others "did the voices." The assiduous marked up striking passages beforehand, but others simply read what they found—sometimes, to unfortunate effect. Beyond enriching our knowledge of these practices, learning about the contexts of communal reading gives new insights into the form and content of eighteenth-century literature. Books were shaped by expectations about use: the stockpiling of amusing stories or rhymes or jokes, a predilection for the sentimental vignette or the comic dialogue, the collecting of striking and unrelated passages of verse; familiarity with particular speeches from Shakespeare, rather than the whole play; the reading of volumes of novels out of sequential order. As subsequent chapters will explore in more detail, once we start to focus on the social lives of books, we begin to view them in different ways.

4. Access to Reading

Miss Streatfield's maid came to ask Mrs. Thrale whether she
could lend her "*Milk and asparagus lost.*" So she sent her Milton's
Paradise Lost, and this proved to be the object requested.
— Miscellaneous manuscript note in papers of Fanny Burney

Telling the story of readers and their reading lives at home means asking
where they got books from. Historians commonly tell us that the period saw
an explosion in print culture and the birth of "Grub Street." Alexander Pope
and Jonathan Swift described a London clogged with lowbrow sixpenny
pamphlets and innumerable odes, novels, and travel books, the kind of books
that were destined to have a longer life as waste paper than literature, and to
end up, in John Dryden's memorable phrase, "martyrs of pies, and relics of
the bum." Before 1700 up to 1,800 different printed titles were produced annu-
ally. By 1800 that number had grown to 6,000.[1] It is ironic, then, that at the
same time this perceived expansion was under way, it was also extraordinarily
difficult for most of the population to access literature—possibly harder than
it had been a hundred years before.[2] Recent quantitative studies of the
eighteenth-century book trade have emphasised how expensive books were—
and thus should be regarded as luxury objects of that time.[3] In addition,
literacy was limited, and had not changed very much in half a century.[4]

However, thinking about books shared in homes forces us to look beyond
the headline statistics of book prices and literacy figures. Books and reading
material were a significant presence in eighteenth-century domestic life and
were deeply embedded in the culture of home. Even small samples of data
about middling-sort book ownership show a rise in the prevalence of books in
homes in the eighteenth century.[5] But perhaps more importantly, there were

multiple points of access: alongside booksellers and their new books, there were newspapers and periodicals, second-hand stalls and shops, circulating libraries, abridgements, adaptations, books sold in numbers, and old-fashioned sharing, borrowing, and lending. Books, newspapers, pamphlets, and letters could be and were read aloud, in the home, in groups, in public places.

All of this created ways into literature for a broader reading public, and offered alternative models for literary consumption. So, for example, we might assume that at eight shillings and sixpence, well over the value of a week's wages for the average labourer, the first London edition of Jonathan Swift's *Gulliver's Travels* was way beyond the reach of all but a tiny social elite.[6] But popular works such as *Gulliver's Travels* existed in multiple formats: as small versions on rough paper, as chapbooks, as abridgments, as newspaper serializations (fig. 17). Within less than a month it was possible to buy for sixpence a key to the meaning of the book.[7] The pages of the *London Journal* were full of Gulliverian asides, and by 26 November a fictional contributor to the *Weekly Journal* could breezily observe "almost every Body has read the travels of my Brother *Lemuel Gulliver*."[8] There was serial publication in *Parker's Penny Post* by the end of November. Daniel Defoe's *Robinson Crusoe,* which began life as a providential travel narrative in 1719 and has come to be acclaimed as, variously, the first English novel, a true symbol of the British Empire, the embodiment of economic individualism, and the portrayal of a Christian everyman,

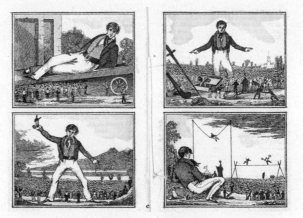

Fig. 17. An illustration from an early-nineteenth-century chapbook, *The adventures of Captain Gulliver in a voyage to Lilliput,* Glasgow, published by J. Lumsden and Son (Glasgow University Library, Sp Coll Bh13-c.28; by permission of University of Glasgow Library, Special Collections)

must have been more likely known in the eighteenth century as the emblematic folkloric adventurer that popped up everywhere in homes, taverns, and coffeehouses. It was possible to buy a brass fireplace ornament of Crusoe and Man Friday; a Staffordshire figure; a rag book for children, a pop-up "juvenile drama," a whole string of chapbooks, and by the mid–nineteenth century, an extensive range of cheap chinaware for children.[9]

The fate of both Swift's *Gulliver's Travels* and Defoe's *Robinson Crusoe* and their rapid dissemination into contemporary culture is a testament to the speedy transmission of some titles, which were quickly translated into formats to suit every taste and pocketbook. But alongside this story of a fast-moving print culture sits a much slower version of literary history. The evidence of reading shows a considerable time lag—people must have happily consumed much older texts, because those were the ones they preferred, or could get hold of. Book inventories from homes all over the country show older publications significantly outnumbering recent ones. Examining middling-sort London inventories, we see that where texts are itemised, by far the majority are at least three decades old. In the 1740 inventory of John Mitford, a merchant in Bow, we find seventy-four books in total. Only five of these were published in the previous decade. Twenty-one dated from the seventeenth century—the majority of these were folios, perhaps because they had been inherited, or bought second hand.[10] The appeal—or the availability—of older texts is also reflected in compilations. Miscellanies of prose and verse advertised the novelty and contemporaneity of their content, but tended to be full of works written some time before.[11] Household book collections reflected the buying or reading interests of generations, and as costly material goods, were unlikely to be discarded. The works available at any one time were in general more likely to have reflected the reading fashion of the past century than the current decade. Collections such as Bell's multivolume *Poetical Works of the English Poets*, or John Cooke's editions of prose writers and dramatists made an evolving canon of earlier English writers accessible to new readers—but these kinds of compilations tended to be heavily weighted towards previous decades of popular authors and texts.[12]

There is also massive variability in the uses of disposable income. Book historians may have determined what the twenty-first-century equivalent of two shillings was—but we cannot from that infer a public appetite for choosing to spend money on particular cultural forms. At two shillings, a copy of Eliza Haywood's *Love in Excess* might have cost the same amount as

a week's lodgings, but may have been seen by some as a more useful investment than a new hat.

So what do we know about book-buying power? Looking across the
social scale, a baronet had an annual income of somewhere in the region of
£1,500; a clergyman £50–70, a gentleman £280, and merchants and traders
somewhere between £200 and £400. Shopkeepers and tradesmen, on the
other hand, brought in £45 per annum, farmers and freeholders £40–90,
labourers and outservants £15. There was no income tax as we know it, but
there were some hefty import charges and wealth duties. The capacity to
spend large amounts of money on new books, let alone on theatre or paintings, must have been pretty narrowly restricted to the upper reaches of
society.[13] Jacob Vanderlint's 1734 calculation of average household budgets
estimated for a family "in the middling Station of Life," came out at four
shillings a week "pocket expences" for the master of the family, two shillings
a week for the wife and children to enjoy "fruit & toys etc.," and four shillings for the entertainment of friends and relations. The whole lot came to
about £315 a year, not including £75 savings to secure the future of the wife
and children, should the husband die.[14] Vanderlint put the minimum annual
income for a "gentleman" at £500.[15] There was no allowance for entertainments within the labouring-class family. Within these income bands some
people will have had more money than others—bachelors, those with smaller
families, and those who happened to enjoy a period of good health would
most likely have had more ready cash than the head of a large sickly household with dependent relations.[16]

Access and Class

Within the book market there was a tiered pricing structure: small numbers
of high-end expensive works were at the top, with increasing numbers of
cheaper works beneath them.[17] It was not until the early nineteenth century,
and the advent of steam-powered printing, that British readers saw anything
like the mass production of affordable literature.[18]

With a likely weekly expenditure of two to four shillings for all kinds of
entertainment, a middling-sort household was not regularly going to buy six-
shilling books. And certainly in the tier beneath, for the labouring man, there
was slim chance of buying any kind of print priced above a penny. The kinds
of editions that we are used to seeing as eighteenth-century literature,

single-author works that contained plays and poems, were affordable by those of "the middling sort" but not regularly, and not in large numbers. The Geffrye Museum sample of London middling-sort inventories shows a wide variation in the quantity and value of books owned by tradesmen in the capital, but there are no records of householders with more than a hundred books. If there is a book mentioned in the inventories, it is always a Bible or New Testament—beyond that, there are some readers who own fewer than ten bound books, and others who have up to ninety.[19] Across the board, the sample suggests a tendency towards devotional works and volumes of travel writing and history, rather than novels, poetry, or plays. There are very few classical works or those in foreign languages. This kind of reading pattern matches the habits that other book historians have identified in middling-sort readers.[20]

Samuel Johnson stated airily in the *Rambler*, "Every size of readers requires a genius of correspondent capacity."[21] He was right in that the eighteenth-century print trade was a heavily differentiated market. Cheap or cheaper print was bought by a wide range of customers across the social spectrum. Almanacs, annual publications containing a variety of information, including astronomical data, tide times, and planting dates, were best sellers in the seventeenth century, second only to the Bible in sales figures.[22] By the mid– to late eighteenth century, the almanac had been supplanted, or complemented, by pocket books, small portable diaries which contained an amazing range of useful information, including poetic extracts, recipes, songs, the fares of hackney cab drivers for various London journeys, or lists of hotels. Chapbooks and "little books" also offered easier access to print. Sold by itinerant hawkers or chapmen (from the old English word "céap," meaning trade or business), these were aimed at adults, often less affluent and less literate customers. Costing only a few pence, and typically decorated with woodcuts, they ranged from ballads, cut-down seventeenth-century romances, Mother Shipton's prophecies, stories of British heroes such as Guy of Warwick, true-life criminal tales, religious material, to scaled-down versions of prose fiction.[23] There were, for example, chapbook versions of *Pilgrim's Progress*, *Robinson Crusoe* and *Moll Flanders*, *Tom Jones* and *Joseph Andrews*, *Gulliver's Travels*, and *Gil Blas*.[24]

These cheap books were not only bought by those at the bottom end of the social scale. There is substantial evidence of gentry reading of ephemeral material, including chapbooks, ballads, almanacs, and pamphlets, suggesting that an apartheid in print culture between popular and elite cannot be sustained.[25] Costing more—but still less than the original text—were the large numbers of abridgements that appeared throughout the eighteenth century. As early as 1705 John Dunton observed that the hack-writing of reduced versions of books was so prevalent that "*Original* and *Abridgement* are almost reckon'd as necessary as Man and Wife."[26] Publishers presented their newly shortened works as a public duty, a way of making literature affordable to a greater portion of the population. Thomas Cox's 1719 abridgement of *Robinson Crusoe* claimed that since Defoe's work had the laudable aim of helping readers to "learn the Art of Patience in Submission to the Divine Will," his version would further that design, and "make it circulate thro' all Hands," not only by making it more portable, but also by lowering its price "to the Circumstances of most People."[27]

The merits of such works were not exclusively economic—they were also significantly shorter and quicker to read. It is interesting to note how many of the authors of early contemporary responses to Richardson's blockbuster *Clarissa* cried out for an abridgement of the seven-volume novel.[28] When *Clarissa* was eventually issued in abridged form, the polyvocal epistolary narrative was replaced by a single retrospective impersonal narrator— the story told in an entirely different way.[29] There will have been a whole section of the reading public who read *Clarissa* and could discuss it, and cry over it, but did not know it in the full form familiar to modern critics. Because they have not traditionally been valued by collectors, and not been preserved in the same way as more prestigious formats, abridgements have not survived in anything like the numbers in which they were published. Yet despite these poor rates, 75 percent of surviving titles of *Robinson Crusoe* (not even a particularly long book to start with) in the eighteenth century are abridgements—forcing us again to ask what was the "real" Robinson Crusoe for Defoe's contemporaries and their children and grandchildren? How are we to know that when a diarist or letter writer mentions reading *Gil Blas* or Captain Cook's voyages, they weren't reading a cheaper, reduced version, perhaps published in parts? Which version did most users know? It is a question that applies to many of the cheaper formats available at this time.

Subsequent chapters of this book describe the ways in which miscellanies, collections of beauties, and domestic editions of Shakespeare repackaged literature for new and less affluent readerships. The compiler of *The Companion: Being a Choice Collection of the Most Admired Pieces from the Best*

Authors (1790) suggested that its assortment of stories and elegant extracts "from such poems as are too long to be ingrossed at full length"[30] would "in some measure supply the place of a library to those who are not in circumstances to lay out much money in purchasing books of amusement and instruction."[31] The three-volume set would provide families with access to "many admired pieces, which cannot be procured without also purchasing perhaps ten times the bulk of such matter as they would not spend time in reading."[32] The patchy documentary evidence of the history of reading, and particularly sociable reading, often obscures the details of sources and formats such as these. We would be mistaken if we assumed that every glancing reference to someone reading a bit of Thomson's *Seasons* or a chapter of *Joseph Andrews* aloud to their friends or family was perforce from an expensive calfskin-bound multivolume quarto.

The rapid development of periodicals and newspapers in the first half of the eighteenth century did much to multiply the number of habitual readers in England. With important exceptions, novels were printed in small runs of 750 or even 500 and seldom reprinted. By contrast, runs of a publication like the *Monthly Review, or Literary Journal,* which contained lengthy book reviews of new books and pamphlets, including extracts, alongside "occasional Articles from Abroad," reached 3,000 in 1768 and 3,500 in 1776.[33] Numerous books would have had a much wider circulation in the extracted form of review essays than they ever did as entire works. Magazines and serialised publications were fairly cheap and therefore affordable by a broad cross section of the community. Accounts of subscribers often reveal a mixed audience: from aristocracy and gentry to artisans, apprentices, shop assistants, and servants. Most issues cost sixpence in the period 1746–80; a year's subscription usually came to six shillings sixpence, roughly the price of a single new two-volume novel.[34] As Chapter 7 illustrates, magazines and periodicals were to become one of the primary outlets for short fiction in the later eighteenth century.

The wealth of contemporary pictures of newspaper reading suggests the public appetite for newsprint; it also illustrates the social nature of people's reading. Because of the way in which newspapers were shared, sales or circulation figures hide the real scale of readership. Diarists and letter writers routinely record the reading aloud of the evening paper to a group, or the circulation of periodicals between friends. There seems to have been extensive traffic between friends and acquaintances involving magazines and periodicals. The Cornish vicar John Penrose writes snootily of two women he meets in Bath: "I cannot say much of the Sociableness of Mrs. Marsh and Mrs. Graham. The chief, almost the only Communication we have with each other, is, that I lend them my *London Chronicle*, and they lend me their *Daily Gazetteer*."[35] Such practices were for Penrose, as for other readers, a good way of accessing a wider range of newsprint than they would wish to buy for themselves. Nancy Woodforde, living in rural isolation with her uncle in Suffolk, is always pleased to receive her neighbour Mr. Du Quesne's *Gentleman's Magazine*, or his cast-off London papers.

These more ephemeral print sources commonly left their mark in the verse or anecdotes copied into manuscript commonplace books, presumably because they sprang from a form less likely to be stored for future reference. The source of the borrowing is rarely acknowledged, but some readers kept notes. When the rector of Hodnet in Shropshire, Reginald Heber, transcribed a squib entitled "Ultimatum" in his commonplace book, he also noted, "This spirited & pointed little party jeu d'esprit was copied out of an Irish newspaper."[36] Eliza Chapman, compiling her manuscript book of favourite verse also jotted down the newspapers she had taken her cuttings from: the *Morning Herald*, the *Morning Post*, the *Mirror*.[37] The Madan family sometimes copied and sometimes cut and pasted bits of news, jokes, and sections of "Poet's Corner" into their family scrapbook, as did Harriet Pigott in Oswestry, sandwiching the contents together along with home-grown verse and drama, children's thank-you letters, and watercolour sketches. These compilations reinforce the importance of newspapers and periodicals as vehicles for a range of reading matter. But while recognizing the extent to which newspapers and magazines inspired the collection of fragments of favoured text, we should also remember that those pieces were probably collected in part precisely because they were ephemeral. Readers might not have felt the urge to copy out other admired forms of literature when they had them safely stored on bookshelves (we might consider, too, the extent to which borrowed texts were also likely to be commonplaced, because of limited access). Magazines and periodicals rarely feature in book inventories; while it is common to find multivolume editions of the *Spectator*, the piecemeal consumption of assorted ephemeral publications leaves little mark in formal lists of reading matter.

In addition to newspaper and magazine serialization, books were also available sold in parts.[38] All sorts of things were available in this format—you could get anything from medical dictionaries to Rapin's *History of England, Paradise Lost*, Barrow's sermons, books of algorithms, treatises on conveyancing, painting, or penmanship. The trade in books in parts really began to take off from the 1730s onwards, with different formats of books to suit different incomes—parts enabled readers to assemble anything from a folio on fine paper to a duodecimo. George Crabbe wrote in *The Library* (1781): "Abstracts, Abridgements, please the fickle times" and "Bibles, with cuts and comments, thus go down / E'en light Voltaire is number'd through the town."[39] And because it was usual in the eighteenth century for books to be sold in sheets and bound by the purchaser, the only real difference between buying, say, Chambers's *Cyclopaedia* (fourth edition, 1741) in one go and buying it in parts, three sheets at a time, was that by buying in sections, the consumer got two folios for sixpence a week, rather than paying a prohibitive four guineas all at once. The part buyer might have been more likely to read the early sheets of their work before the buyer of the whole, because regular subscribers often had access to parts before the whole work was on sale.[40] The *Grub Street Journal* professed outrage at "that strange Madness of publishing Books by piece-meal . . . I bought, the other day, three pennyworth of the Gospel, made easy and familiar to porters, carmen and chimney-sweepers."[41] The author is incensed at the overt commodification of books, and in this case, Holy Scripture, which could be sold off in small quantities, as one might buy a few ounces of flour or sugar. It is a slightly disingenuous argument; the print trade had always been a business in which products were created and priced for particular markets. The difference with part books was that they opened up access to a group of consumers who might have been frozen out of the market by the high prices of whole books. But if we look at the types of titles available in parts—from the collection of antiquarian tracts in the Harleian miscellany to an appendix to the Greek Thesaurus—it is evident that selling in numbers was a sales technique with a social reach far beyond the "porters, carmen and chimney sweeps" imagined in the *Grub Street Journal*.[42]

New Readers

Evidence of historical literacy is complex. While literacy was still very partial by 1800, it had increased over the course of the seventeenth and eighteenth centuries, growing from 1 percent of women and 10 percent of men able to read in 1500 to 40 percent of women and 60 percent of men by 1800.[43] One of the recurrent consequences of the rise in literacy, both generally and amongst women in particular, was a much-voiced concern about what was being read, and how. Literacy as a route to self-improvement and self-advancement was one thing—but literacy as a conduit for distracting knowledge and fantasy was quite another. Much of this anxiety was focussed on fiction reading, as we shall see. But it was not all about novels. One contributor to the satirical *Grub Street Journal* of September 1734 lamented that

> so many persons in the lowest stations of life, are more intent upon cultivating their minds, than upon feeding and cloathing their bodies . . . I used to think, that nineteen in twenty of the species were designed by nature for trade, and manufactures; and that to take them off to read books, was the way to do them harm, to make them, not wiser or better, but impertinent, troublesome, and factious.[44]

He was writing in 1734, and clearly even by this point there was some concern about the social consequences of the popular transmission of knowledge and information amongst the middling classes. Half a century later on, this concern was directed at lower social levels of the reading population. New forms of popular publication bristled with prefaces eager to reassure the socially conservative that they were serving up only the most improving intellectual diet. Sarah Trimmer, a devout evangelical Anglican and wife of a prosperous brick and tile maker from Brentford, produced a series of educational resources designed to provide stimulating moral instruction for the young. The *Family Magazine*, a periodical she founded in 1788 and edited until 1789, offered suitable material for middling-sort families eager to read. In the prospectus for the magazine, she confronted the issue of the public appetite for reading: "it is an undeniable fact, that those families in the middling and higher classes of life, who in their hours of recreation seek amusement *at home* in the perusal of *well chosen books*, are by far the happiest. The deplorable effects of *ignorance* among the common people of this country have been long felt, and it is time to try what cultivation will do."[45]

The change over the century is marked. The *Grub Street Journal* contributor of 1734 had focussed his dismay upon the middling classes, those in trade and manufacturing, who were liable to become impertinent and factious through reading. Sarah Trimmer, a woman of trade writing fifty years later, takes it for granted that reading the right kind of "well chosen" books at home is wholesome exercise for the middling sort, and that this could and should be rolled out to their social inferiors. But she acknowledges anxieties about the effects: "The only argument against the instruction of the Poor . . . is, That an improvement in knowledge will set them too nearly on a level with their employers . . . surely the danger of all this may be prevented, by furnishing the Poor with books peculiarly appropriated to their use, and calculated to make them *contented* with their condition, and emulous to *fulfil the duties of it*."[46]

Servants

Sarah Trimmer clearly thought that servants and those lower down the social scale should be encouraged to read—albeit, the right kinds of material. The Geffrye inventories show that only one or two mention a book or two as part of the property in a servant's room—and none of them mention bookcases in servants' quarters.[47] Yet some employers went out of their way to encourage their servants to learn to read. As in Trimmer's case, this was often for religious reasons.[48] There is some evidence that by the late eighteenth and early nineteenth centuries a select number of large houses had their own servants' libraries—various National Trust country-house libraries betray the remnants of such collections, although there is more substantial documentation from the mid– to late nineteenth century. A collection of chapbooks in a very early nineteenth-century canvas binding in the Bodleian library is inscribed "Moreville House Servants Library," presumably referring to Morville Hall in Warwickshire. Its contents suggests that it might have been a book reflecting the employer's idea of good reading rather than the employees' preferences, since it consists of a series of cautionary tales about drinking and gambling.[49] Individual servants were probably sometimes given suitable reading material by their employers; booksellers' records show that John Parker, a Warwickshire clergyman bought four copies of Eliza's Haywood's *A Present for a Servant-Maid*, presumably to give to his employees or parishioners.[50]

There are also signs, especially later in the century, that servants bought reading material through booksellers, in much the same way as their employers. The surviving records of the Clays' bookselling business in the Midlands shows servants buying printed material, either in book form or as serialization, for intellectual curiosity and self-improvement. Titles such as *Every Man his Own Lawyer* and *The Complete Letter-Writer* offered the opportunity to acquire new skills, which were becoming more and more essential in eighteenth-century society. Religious works were popular, and so, increasingly, was literature for entertainment. While records suggest a minimal interest in long narrative fiction, we can see that servants of all kinds, like the middling-sort tradesmen, farmers, and artisans, were increasingly interested in magazines and other inexpensive forms of literature. In the Clays' records are numbers of sales of plays and music, along with belles lettres. An unnamed group of servants at Brockhall, a large Northamptonshire manor house owned by the Thornton family, ordered a total of five plays from the Clays, and it seems likely that servants in this and other great houses bought plays to read aloud or perform amongst themselves.[51]

Not every servant accessed reading matter in such a benign way.[52] The Old Bailey's records of book thefts list numerous instances of books stolen by servants from their employers, along with other valuable material goods. The books were commonly sold to second-hand dealers, but some accounts suggest that they were taken for reading. In a case of 1761, Mary Gaywood, the wife of a London gardener, living in the Neat Houses on Millbank, accused her maid of twenty years of stealing books and kitchen items.

> Last Tuesday night she went away, and not coming on the Wednesday, we missed a cream pot; I went to Westminster, where she lodg'd, in John's-street, thinking she was not well; going up stairs, I saw her reading in a book; I looked to see, and found it to be the Pilgrim's-progress, my own book. I turned round, and saw my cream-pot; then I went to the window, there lay a Prayer-book, a Testament, and another book, entitled The Groves of Diana, all my property, some with my maiden, and some with my married name on them.[53]

In a later case, William Francis, the servant of General Robert Melville was found with two of his master's books on him, after a break-in at the house. Giving his defence in court, he explained that he had been teaching himself to read: "When I was there in the last summer, I was dusting the books and putting them away, and I got these two books and was reading them, I was teaching myself to read, and in a very great mistake I put them into my box: here is a person here that I lent one of them to, I told him at the same time that the book was General Melville's."[54]

The fact that learning to read by borrowing employers' books was seen as an acceptable defence by 1781 probably reflects quite a widespread practice of servants being permitted to use their employer's library or bookcase, and numerous biographies of eighteenth-century labouring-class writers tell of literary aspirations awoken by this kind of contact (fig. 18).[55] Surveys of the contents of working-class homes in the early nineteenth century show that very few contained no books at all—there might be a few chapbooks, the odd volume of travel and exploration, and a couple of old newspapers and journals.[56] But on the whole the tiny book collections of such settings were dominated by religious works—the Bible, and perhaps a prayer book, the odd religious commentary, and maybe *Pilgrim's Progress.* Owning such religious books was not the same as reading them—John Clare noted wryly that "the Bible, is laid by on its peaceful shelf, and by 9 cottages out of 10, never disturbed or turn'd to further than the minute's reference for reciting the text on a Sunday."[57] Bibles probably served as much use in their common role as a place for transcribing births and deaths in a family than in actually being

FEMALE LUCUBRATION. ETUDE NOCTURNE.

Fig. 18. Philip Dawe, *Female Lucubration,* London, 1772, mezzotint on laid paper (Geffrye Museum, 93/2009; © The Geffrye, Museum of the Home, London)

read. In the context of such restricted domestic resources, labouring-class readers wishing to familiarise themselves with secular literature undoubtedly drew on material found in their employers' homes.

The idea of the gentry library as a source of elevation was also perpetuated in the middling-sort magazine fiction of the mid– to late eighteenth century. Stories in the *Lady's Magazine* repeatedly offer images of lower-class girls who visit country houses and are allowed to participate in an elite-class lifestyle whose most appealing feature is ready access to books: sometimes they are able through their literacy to prove their right to join the library-owning classes by marrying the son of the house.[58] Such accounts envision the homes of the higher orders as beacons of erudition and culture, vistas of learning for those who came into contact with them.

But for those who owned the libraries, it was also noted that possessing books was not the same as reading them. Defoe's *Compleat English Gentleman* describes the library of a country squire as comprising a Bible, a volume of family records, three mass books, four or five prayer books, some old newspapers, a few ballads, an old bass viol, two fiddles, and a music book. The squire asks a friend: "What should I do with books? I never read any. There's a heap of old journals and news letters, a bushell or two, I believ; those we have every week for the parson and I to talk over a little, while the doctor smokes his pipe." The friend replies: "O but, Sir, no gentleman is without a library. 'Tis more in fashion now than ever it was."[59] Defoe's piece exaggerates the phenomenon of the philistine book owner, but it and similar comments are also a useful caution in interpreting the evidence of library catalogues and book inventories, upon which so much of the history of reading is based. A catalogue on its own will never really enable us to understand the correlation between the listing of a book as a possession and its significance for its owner.[60] Neither will it tell us what was actually read, as opposed to kept for its value: were the books retained by a family the well-read ones or the valuable and high-status elements of a collection?

Geographical Access

In England, the organization of the book trade depended on a transportation network radiating out from London. By the early nineteenth century, 90 percent of all British titles were published in London. Although there were an increasing number of provincial booksellers, they were more likely to operate as distributors of books, or perhaps newspaper printers, than as publishers of new titles.[61] When Pope, Swift, and Gay located Grub Street, the epicentre of popular publishing, in the heart of the city of London, they were reflecting a reality of the book trade and the wider economy. London was both the site of hundreds of trades and industries and a huge consumer market that dominated the British economy. That market population exploded from roughly 100,000 in 1650, a number that stayed relatively stable till 1750, to 900,000 by 1800 and nearly 2 million by 1830, bringing a far more diverse ethnic and social makeup.[62]

At the same time as this was happening, the country was being reshaped by what has been called "the English urban renaissance," the growth of affluent provincial clusters of cultural aspiration, leisure, and luxury trades.[63] Although most books continued to be printed in London, literary activity evolved as part of an increasingly sophisticated urban culture throughout the rest of the country. The urban renaissance manifested itself in the growth of leisure activities: public concerts, provincial theatres, assembly rooms, beautifully landscaped walks for promenading, bowling greens—and a significant increase in booksellers, libraries, and newspapers, enabling provincial readers to engage in ever more wide-ranging cultural debates and enthusiasms. In his 1780 life of Milton, Samuel Johnson compared the mid-seventeenth-century epic poet's age with that of the present, noting, "To read was not then a general amusement; neither traders, nor often gentlemen, thought themselves disgraced by ignorance. The women had not then aspired to literature, nor was every house supplied with a closet of knowledge."[64]

By the mid–eighteenth century, forms of access to print were evolving fast. One recent estimate suggests that "in 1700 there may have been about 200 booksellers operating in 50 different towns . . . By the mid-1740s the list of subscription agents for *The Harleian Miscellany* reveals the existence of 381 traders in 174 urban centres."[65] The growth in the trade is reflected in the evidence from individual towns and cities. So, for example, even by the 1730s, Birmingham had seven booksellers, and within a decade, its first local newspapers. There were various local libraries, from the private subscription library founded in 1779, with a vast range of scientific and theological works, to the nine or more commercial circulating libraries established by 1800.[66] The city's Lucas's Circulating Library boasted holdings of 2,535 books, from romance and novels to travel, history, and science. Norwich between 1700 and 1759 boasted thirty booksellers—not all of them operating at the same time. In smaller towns, such as Great Yarmouth, there were eight booksellers working in the same period.[67]

Depots of Learning

One of the most talked-about literary aspects of this new polite urban and provincial literary culture was the circulating library (fig. 19). The circulating library, which also often sold medicine or insurance, provided readers with a range of books that could be borrowed on fixed terms for a certain amount of time (they were called circulating not because the libraries moved around, but because the books did, to different readers). These organizations provided users with a relatively affordable supply of literature. Their membership was determined in part by subscription charges, which varied from one organization to another.[68] Within an individual library, there was a range of price structures—readers could choose between the sizes of books

Fig. 19. Isaac Cruikshank, *The Circulating Library,* pen and ink and w/c and wash on wove paper (Yale Center for British Art, Paul Mellon Collection, USA / Bridgeman Images)

they borrowed, or their age, and secure a reduced subscription fee (old or small being cheaper). Subscription libraries were particularly useful for those travelling, who were away from home and could not carry all the books they were likely to read over a given period. Libraries in resort towns were linked to other forms of entertainments.[69] When the Reverend John Swete visited Sidmouth in March 1795 he wrote excitedly: "every elegancy, every luxury, every amusement is here to be met with—iced creams, Milliners shops, cards, billiards, plays, circulating libraries and as I saw a smart Gentleman take a novel from his Pocket in the public shed—I presume such to be the fashion of the place!"[70] Once Weymouth, on the Dorset coast, became fashionable in the 1780s, a bookseller named James Love, who also rose to celebrity status as "the fattest man in England" marketed his bookshop as a house of public entertainment, named "The Pantheon of Taste." The venue, open from six o'clock in the morning to ten in the evening, housed, in addition to its books, a billiard room, musical circulating library, and public exhibition room, and Love claimed to receive 130 newspapers two hours earlier than the Post Office.[71] As this suggests, some circulating libraries were promoted and depicted as social spaces. They were not the hushed environments that we now associate with libraries, but, at their best, elegant spaces full of people to converse with.[72]

Estimates of how many circulating libraries existed in the eighteenth century vary wildly from two hundred to a thousand. We know that they really began to flourish in the 1740s. They differed greatly in their holdings—an early study of the percentage of fiction in circulating libraries showed that some institutions contained up to 90 percent fiction, while at others it was only 5 percent.[73] And there were other variables. Libraries in affluent spa towns, such as Cheltenham or Bath, visited by well-to-do tourists, charged higher prices for a greater range of books. From the labels from British circulating libraries collected in the Papantonio Collection, we can see that libraries sold a range of other goods alongside book rental, including stamps, paper hangings, theatre tickets, and insurance.[74] Some libraries fitted the contemporary stereotype of the library as a magnet for novel readers, and boasted a big list in narrative fiction. The Waters' library at Kettering in Northamptonshire had only 188 books, yet most of these were narrative fiction, much like Rogers' circulating library in Stafford, with a collection of 350 books, all novels.[75] On the other hand, there were libraries that hardly mentioned novels in their advertising, and aimed instead for an extensive coverage of many instructive and nonfiction works.[76] One study of the contents of London circulating libraries shows that novels made up only 20 percent of what was available.[77] The Clays' bookselling enterprise and their library in the Midlands demonstrate "the relative insignificance of novels in provincial print culture: almanacs, school texts, Bibles, common prayer books, divinity, sermons, history and belles lettres were much more popular."[78] The circulating library in Margate boasted no fewer than six hundred sermons available for borrowing. Other studies have shown the extensive availability of plays for reading at home, and of sheet music for domestic performance.

Because they effectively created a wider reading experience for users who did not traditionally have their own extensive selections of books, circulating libraries became a touchstone for conservative outrage about social mobility, the independent activities of women outside the home, and the respective merits of different kinds of literature.[79] The Reverend Edward Mangin, writing in 1808, rehearsed popular objections to circulating libraries and their readers in a blustering *Essay on Light Reading as it may be supposed to influence Moral Conduct and Literary Taste* (1808). From the start, Mangin had only particular kinds of books in his sights: "*novels, romances, and poems of a particular class.*"[80] He disapproved of everything about circulating libraries, from the way their contents were treated, to the kinds of people who used them, to the effects they had on their readers. He describes the careless use of books "turned over, thrown down, taken up again, cut open, read, and returned to the shop with the usual and flattering marks of having seen service; viz. a leaf or two turned out, scratches of pins, scorings of thumb-nails, and divers marginal illustrations."[81] He declared that he didn't mind novels being a form of "*occasional* relaxation to the very *high* and the very *low,*"[82] from the peeress to the housemaid, but the readers he was most concerned about were "The sons and daughters of the gentleman and the tradesman, who are, as it were, the very life-blood of the realm."[83] These vulnerable kinds of people, especially the daughters, were encouraged in false expectations about the nature of the world and their place within it, which could only ruin them in later life.

Mangin's comments illustrate the extent to which engagement with literature was bound up with questions about who ought to be reading, and what they ought to read. His essay assumes that those who borrowed from the library were relatively unused to the world of books, and thus ill defended against what they found within. It is a view echoed by Thomas Gisborne, who declared that the contents of circulating libraries were "frequently contaminated by the contagion of folly and vice" and would "travel in routine from house to house, [and] obtrude themselves on those who would not have sought for them."[84] But the reality was that women constituted only a small proportion of readers, and that numerous users, particularly the more affluent, both borrowed from libraries and possessed books of their own.[85] A circulating library was a different—rather than the only—way of getting hold of books. Anne Lister's diaries show her using the circulating library in Halifax as a day out, a place to see people, to get hold of books she doesn't own but would like to read. The shopkeeper Thomas Turner bought books, borrowed books from friends, and used Edmund Baker's circulating library at Tunbridge Wells. Access to reading material in the eighteenth century was a mixed economy, with points of entry to suit almost all. The anonymous author of a pamphlet offering guidance on how to set up a circulating library distinguished between the various users of a potential library, or "depot of learning." He says that the rich can subscribe for a year, for a guinea, the middling sort for three months, for four shillings—and "those whose means are not so good, but have leisure time, may indulge in the luxury of reading for a month, at the trifling expence of eighteenth pence or two shillings."[86]

Contemporary advertisements for circulating libraries in resort towns and large cities emphasised their role as sites for discussion and the exchange of ideas as well as just access to rentable texts (fig. 20). The author of the *Tunbridge Wells Guide* considered the town's circulating library, like its coffee-house, to be a place where "social virtues reign triumphant over prejudice and prepossession." As public spaces, both demonstrated "the easy freedom, and chearful gaiety" made possible by such venues, particularly in the case of the library in which, unlike some coffeehouses, women were allowed.[87] In the anonymous satire *Bath: A Poem* (1748), a trip to Leake's, a bookseller's and circulating library within the spa town, is described as a social pastime and spectator sport: "Now, with a motly Throng, resorts the *Fop*, / To kill an Hour, to Leake's fine spacious shop."[88] Not all circulating libraries operated as social centres—some offered merely a collection of books, which could be ordered by reference number from a catalogue.[89]

Circulating libraries were not the only source of borrowable books for the eighteenth-century reader. The landscape of reading was being trans-formed by multiple innovations in access to texts. Subscription libraries and

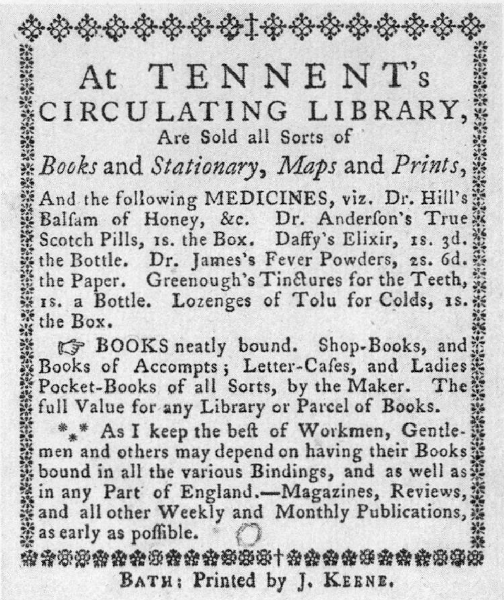

At TENNENT's
CIRCULATING LIBRARY,
Are Sold all Sorts of
Books and *Stationary*, *Maps* and *Prints*,
And the following MEDICINES, viz. Dr. Hill's
Balfam of Honey, &c.   Dr. Anderfon's True
Scotch Pills, 1s. the Box.   Daffy's Elixir, 1s. 3d.
the Bottle.   Dr. James's Fever Powders, 2s. 6d.
the Paper.   Greenough's Tinctures for the Teeth,
1s. a Bottle.   Lozenges of Tolu for Colds, 1s.
the Box.
    ☞ BOOKS neatly bound.   Shop-Books, and
Books of Accompts; Letter-Cafes, and Ladies
Pocket-Books of all Sorts, by the Maker.   The
full Value for any Library or Parcel of Books.
    ₊ As I keep the beft of Workmen, Gentle-
men and others may depend on having their Books
bound in all the various Bindings, and as well as
in any Part of England.—Magazines, Reviews,
and all other Weekly and Monthly Publications,
as early as poffible.
BATH: Printed by J. KEENE.

Fig. 20. Advertisement for Tennent's
Circulating Library, Bath, c. 1780
(The British Library, RB.31.b.95[63])

book clubs flourished, and again they illustrate the socialization of reading practices, as Stephen Colclough has shown in his illuminating study of the reading and borrowing habits of a Sheffield apprentice, Joseph Hunter.[90] Book clubs and subscription libraries were not-for-profit organizations made up of a collection of people who clubbed together to buy books, which were sometimes sold on—rather than money-making enterprises run by a book-seller or tradesman.[91] For the price of the subscription, the whole household was able to get hold of a common library. As in the case of circulating libraries, prices varied. They usually had a substantial entry fee, and a smaller annual cost. The Liverpool Library, founded in the early 1760s, charged an entry fee of one pound eleven shillings, with an annual subscription of five shillings, although these charges, like those of many other libraries, rose significantly in subsequent decades. Lancaster Amicable Society in 1785 asked for a similar entry fee, but a twelve-shilling annual subscription.[92] Although the surviving records of book clubs are patchy, it is clear that such organizations often included opportunities for their members to discuss and debate the books bought. The eleven founding members of the Boston Literary Society in Lincolnshire agreed from the start that they would have structured discussions about their reading, as well as about their own responses to it.[93] Book clubs of all sorts were generally founded on the premise of reading as a sociable activity.[94] Members often met in inns or public houses or coffeehouses, and the clubs were clearly perceived to offer more than merely access to texts, because even readers with substantial book collections joined them.[95] In *The Country Book-Club* (1788), Charles Shillito mocks the excessive conviviality of some of these groups (fig. 21). Imitating Pope's *Dunciad*, he scoffs at the assembled company of surgeon-barber, squire, self-taught scholar, and vicar, who gossip about the scandals of the village and surround themselves with cheap print, before, soaked in punch, they descend into literary anarchy:

> Riot, boundless riot is the word.
> Replenish'd goblets jealous jars create;
> Soon follow open war, and foul debate.
> Each champion aids, as with revenge he glows,
> His powerful logic with more powerful blows.
> Now books are made their *missile* force to try;
> Swift as artill'ry balls, huge volumes fly.
> [. . .]
> At length the potent juice obscures each brain,
> And Chaos holds his universal reign.[96]

Even when there is little evidence of the actual meeting of groups, readers sometimes left records of the books they were consuming. Frances Hamilton, of Bishops Lydeard in Somerset, a doctor's wife, and then widow, joined the Taunton reading society, founded in 1766. Her diaries and account books of the 1780s and 1790s record the books that came in and went out amongst the group, along with some of her thoughts on what she was reading. Her policing of borrowing illustrates the fast turnaround in reading amongst her set—on 26 February 1791 she records "rec'd Feb 3rd delivered Feb 26 fine—this book ought not to have been kept more than three days. Address for the National Assembly." The next item is "Christian Vigilance by Joshua Toulmin MA. Rec'd Feb 19th delivered Feb 26th to be kept 3 days only."[97] These were short works, but other book groups record a similarly tight borrowing period, of a week on average. It suggests that group reading of books might have been more time intensive than other kinds of reading, which could stretch over weeks, as readers browsed amongst a range of works. Hamilton doesn't record any group discussions of her borrowings,

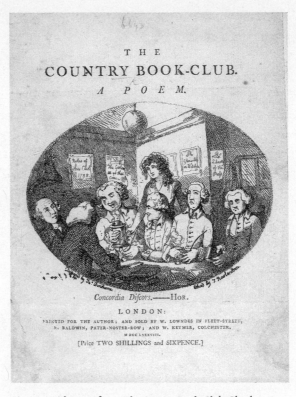

THE

COUNTRY BOOK-CLUB.

A P O E M.

*Concordia Difcors.——*Hor.

LONDON:

PRINTED FOR THE AUTHOR; AND SOLD BY W. LOWNDES IN FLEET-STREET,
R. BALDWIN, PATER-NOSTER-ROW; AND W. KEYMER, COLCHESTER.
M DCC LXXXVIII.

[Price TWO SHILLINGS and SIXPENCE.]

Fig. 21. Title page from *The Country Book-Club,* Charles
Shillito, London, 1788 (© The British Library Board,
11641.g.12)

but her notes illustrate the social function of the reading: in October 1788
she records receiving the *Poetic Works of the Revd William Smith,* which is
accompanied by a version of Longinus on the sublime. She is greatly struck
by it: "a credit to the Author, & reflects a lustre on Longinus himself. To the
unlearned also it may be of use, and give pleasure. It will enable him to read
with more satisfaction, when he can read with more judgement, & distinguish the perfection & fault of a writer." She goes on: "He will be the better
able to bear his part in conversation and appear with credit, when his observations are just & natural. Such compositions while they form the understanding to a true taste kindle an inclination to Literature."[98] Hamilton clearly
thought that a grasp of the principles of literary criticism would enable an
aspiring entrant into the world of culture to acquit himself well in conversation. Other entries suggest a more direct use of books in company, and she
records a collection of jokes and impromptus.[99]

It is hard to generalise about book clubs or subscription libraries because their remits were so varied.[100] Innerpeffray Library was situated in a very remote rural location in Perthshire, and intended to benefit the education of the local population, especially students. The collection was serious and scholarly, with an emphasis on all branches of knowledge, especially practical knowledge, and the organization of civil society. Although isolated, its concerns were not parochial, with numerous books in French, Italian, Latin, and Greek, and a substantial holding in world histories and atlases. The eighteenth-century collection contains very little fiction, drama, or poetry, and the heaviest borrowings were for historical and religious books. There was a reading room attached to the library, and a school—the social function here was very much educational, for adults as well as children. This was not unusual. A study of subscription libraries in Georgian Leeds demonstrates the importance, and often unrecognised role, of libraries in providing useful knowledge to support the professional training of those involved in trade and commerce.[101]

One of the interesting quirks of the borrowing records at Innerpeffray is that some users borrowed books jointly—presumably because they were planning to read together.[102] The Roseland Book Club, on the other hand, situated in south Devon, held an annual dinner at the Queen's Head in the small town of Tregony, when, according to Richard Polwhele, "the town is more than usually illuminated by the splendour of carriages without," and "the feast of reason, and the flow of soul" within.[103] It became known as the Powder Literary Society, because its members, except for their steward, the Reverend Trist, were all women. The membership was limited to thirteen, and the society's aim was the reading of books of history, travels, biography, politics, and belles lettres.[104]

Robert Burns's accounts of his attempts to stock the Monkland Friendly Society, a small parish subscription library that he managed in Lanarkshire, reveal some of the difficulties in book-borrowing ventures. The library was initiated by the patron and antiquary Robert Riddell. Riddell started by getting a number of his tenants and farming neighbours to form a little society. They agreed to join for three years, and to pay five shillings at entry, and at the meetings, held every fourth Sunday, they paid another sixpence. With these funds they could buy books, decided by a majority, and then took it in turns to have first pick of the month's reading. Burns's job was to deal with the Edinburgh bookseller Peter Hill, who sold them the contents of the collection. Burns's letters to Hill on the subject began full of optimism about the project and its potential, and as he was writing its history, he observed that providing material for the lower classes in this way is "Giving them a source of innocent and laudable amusement; and besides, raises them to a more dignified degree in the scale of rationality."[105] The problem was that the members did not want to read the same kinds of books that Burns favoured. Burns wanted to order secular works, but the readers were much keener on religious books: "The Adventurer–Joseph Andrews–Don Quixote–The Idler–Arabian nights entertainment–Dr. Price's dissertations on Providence, prayer, Death & Miracles–Roderick Random–&–the 5th Volume of the Observer—for these books take your fair price, as our Society are no judges of that matter, & will insist on having the following damned trash, which you must also send us, as cheap as possible.[106]

Burns goes on to list the "damned trash," a series of works of practical divinity. His increasingly irascible letters to Hill expose a clear gap between his idea of reading material and what the subscribers want. The users of the Monkland Friendly Society planned to use their reading to advance themselves spiritually rather than culturally, betraying the tension in contemporary ideas of what "self-improvement" might mean.

Book clubs appealed not just because they provided people with easy access to books without having to buy them, but also because in an era of rising enthusiasm for all sorts of clubs and other structured forms of sociability, they located reading, and the discussion of books, alongside a range of communal pursuits. The allure of such associations for even the young is evident in the diary of George Sandy, an apprentice writer to the signet, or apprentice solicitor, living in Edinburgh.[107] At the time of the diary, 1788–89, Sandy was fifteen, and in it he describes his decision to start a "Boys club" with two other friends, Hugh Watson and James Milligan, which was to be modelled on the convivial clubs of his elders. Its main interest was visiting places of interest in the Edinburgh suburbs at the weekends, accompanied with a dram of whisky or "Crambambuli." The group also, ambitiously, aimed to form a little collection of books, a gallery and a museum. There was no entry fee to join the book club, but the members had to deposit a book, a coin, or a painting. Sandy appointed himself "Secretary and Scribe," wrote the minutes, and evidently enjoyed stamping documents with his special seal—his early enthusiasm for officialese must have been well exercised in his subsequent career as secretary to the Bank of Scotland. The books were kept in Sandy's home, so it made sense for him to be the librarian. Within the collection, he had thirty-four books, Hugh Watson five, and James Milligan seven. The boys soon argued about the rules for the library, and at one point Sandy banned Milligan from using it. The entries in the diary show the way the collection was used to move books between one member and another:

> 1788 March 17th "This day the History of the Devil on Two sticks & the Gentle Shepherd added to the Library. Jas. Milligan got the loan of Pennant's Tour Vol. 1st."[108]
>
> Tuesday 18th "Geo. Sandy having got the loan of Johnson's Tour from Andrew Duncan J.M. proposed making reprisals by keeping it for the book which the said A. Duncan lost of his some years before. We will accordingly try what can be done."[109]
>
> Saturday 29 "At night H.W. & G.S. went to the auction where the former bought a Collection of voyages & travels, at 14 pence. N.B. it was a very good bargain & thereby hangs a tale."[110]

The records of the book club or library suggest the boys' enjoyment of the mechanisms of official club life—they send one another various formal documents about items lent and borrowed, and pompously invoke the founding documents of the library in 1787 when disagreements occur over borrowing of books.[111] For Sandy and his friends, the apparatus of the club and the wider world of sociable culture that it represented was as important as the resource it provided.

Readers drew on multiple sources to fuel their reading habits, including buying books or borrowing them from friends and family, joining book clubs and circulating libraries, and reading serialised portions of books in magazines or newspapers. John Penrose's letters, sent while he was staying in Bath for some months in the 1760s, offer a glimpse into the range of potential transactions involved in the supply of reading material. A figure at times bewildered by his unfamiliar surroundings, Penrose was a retired clergyman visiting the resort from parochial Cornwall, hoping to cure his gout at the spa. In between the teas, carriage rides, and visits in Bath, he encountered Methodism, play recitals, and pleasure gardens, none of which particularly stirred him, although he did puzzle over aspects of the everyday ("The Price of Butter here is very uncertain").[112] His correspondence of 1766 and 1767, which he imagines being read out aloud to his whole family, details his two trips, and was a way of keeping in contact with his home and keeping up a semblance of what was usual to him in an unfamiliar environment. When Penrose first gets to Bath, he is delighted at the offers of books he has received, which mean he won't have to pay out for the circulating library.

> He [Dr. Grant, a clergyman] has offered me the use of any Book in his Study, so has Col. Sewell the Use of any Book in his, and the Ladies upstairs have lent me *Johnson's Shakespeare,* so I have not yet subscribed (and I don't know that I shall subscribe) to the Bookseller's Library. Mr. Vivian too, who is a Subscriber, has offered me any Book in the Catalogue, during the Fortnight he is to reside here.[113]

The fact that he is promised access to library books through a subscriber suggests some of the difficulty in measuring the reach of circulated texts—his Mr. Vivian was almost certainly not allowed to borrow on behalf of another. Subsequent letters show the way Penrose's reading, and his efforts to obtain books, ground him in an absent place, enabling him to maintain relations with his family and to create new and elaborate ways of forging intimacy. He copies out for his family things that he has recently read and enjoyed. Delighted at the novelty of being at the hub of fashion, he promises to send home *The New Bath Guide,* a satirical account of the town and its people. It is a piece, he thinks, hardly worth the paper it is written on, "But it is the Fashion to read it: and, who would be out of the Fashion?"[114] Penrose discovers that there are numerous complications arising from the costs of books being sent to the wrong place, and, already worried about his living costs, he fears they are too expensive to post on:

> I have sent a Letter by this Post to Mr. Feroulhet, desiring him to send the *London Chronicle* to Penryn as usual. You will be so good as to put the Papers away safely, after Mary and Charles have done with them. I apprehend, when Mr. Enys went to London, he stopt his *London Chronicle* from coming: if he did not, I desire you will speak to one of Enys Servants for Number 1466 which the Carelessness of Borrowers hath lost for me here.[115]

The saga of various missing *London Chronicles* continues to preoccupy Penrose, and draws in an ever wider web of acquaintances as he tries to sort out where a given issue has gone and should go: "My *London Chronicle* for the Wednesday & Thursday, the 15th and 16th of April, did not come to me. If it was sent by Mr. Feroulhet to Penryn thro' inadvertence (as possibly it might), then all is well: if not, desire Mrs. Hawkins to let me have hers, not sent hither, but preserved at home in order hereafter to bind with the rest: if Mrs. Hawkins', be not to be had, let me know, that I may write to London for another."[116] Some of the books Penrose wants cannot be sourced in Bath, even through the extensive network of book lenders, and so he writes home asking for help: "In the Gallery Book-case, you will find Abernethy's *Sermons* four vols and another vol. of *Tracts & Sermons* by the same author. I desire you to let me know the first Text in each of the vols."[117] Preparing to leave, Penrose realises he needs to coordinate the return of all his borrowings: "As the Time of departure is drawing nigh, I have sent home to the Owners all the literary Productions, which I had borrowed for my Amusement. They are Hume's *History of England, vol. the 1st.*—Wood's *Account of Bath, vol. the 2nd.*—*The New Bath Guide*, a poem,—Colman's *Terence*—Rotherham's *Essay on Faith*—and the *1st Book* of Massillon's *French Sermons*."[118]

John Penrose's accounts of his travails illustrate the way in which borrowing connected him with newfound acquaintances and enabled him to share his experiences with those back at home. But book buying as well as borrowing was also an extremely sociable activity. George Sandy's account of his friends' trip to the book auction, their bargain, and "the tale" around it points to a common feature of diaries and accounts of book acquisition: the entertainment value of acquiring books, whether new or, as in many cases, second hand. Existing auction catalogues with prices show that sales were helped along with convivial entertainments—good wine and a handsome supper as part of the fun when buying books was an entertainment. An advertisement for an auction of books held at the Queen's Head Tavern in Paternoster Row, London, in September 1740 promised "Dinner to be on the table at exactly One o' Clock, with a Glass of good Wine."[119]

In the rapid commodification of the book market, bookselling success relied on gimmicks and fashionable innovations. Sales were promoted as events and entertainments in themselves: from illuminated winter evening sales and ice fairs on the Thames to the summer spa resort sales flourishing by the 1750s.[120] There was a thriving trade in second-hand books.[121] Trade-ins and second-hand purchases will have been the norm for many consumers, and turnover of previously owned goods would have been faster than in our own time, because of the common occurrence of early death.[122] Those keen on books evidently kept an eye out for their neighbours' possessions. In South Yorkshire John Wilson catalogued local families' book collections in his commonplace book, presumably with a view to acquisition. Meanwhile, Nicholas Blundell goes to the sale of his late neighbour Molyneaux's books, which takes place at his home, the Grange: "I dined at the Grange. Was present at ye valewing of Bookes. I bought some."[123] Book buying often happened in domestic spaces. In Blundell's case, people come to his house to sell him books, or he finds them at other houses, rather than going to booksellers' shops.[124] Robert Sharp, a schoolmaster in a Yorkshire village, also describes a travelling bookseller, along with some of his eccentric sales pitch: "I was at Robt Marshall's when he was there, he offered Awd Beck a Cooking Book for 1s. which he affirmed contained all things necessary to be known by any Cook whatsoever; the large Books he said were good for nothing but muddling their heads, and then they would be either under or over doing the Joints."[125]

Diaries and letters also show us the buying habits of people who don't talk about the books that they read, like the tantalizingly unforthcoming Norfolk parson James Woodforde. Woodforde lists numerous occasions on which he buys books: "To Mr. Bacon at Norwich for 2 Volumes of Peerage 8/0. To Ditto for Book on Wills 3/0. To Ditto for Norwich Mem. Book 1/8. To Ditto for Court Calendar 2/0. Total 14/18."; "For Musick Books at Bacons, pd. 1.0."; "Mr. Barker of Dereham, Bookseller, called on me about 2 o'clock, paid him a Bill of 0.8.6. I asked him to stay and dine with us which he did."[126] Yet unlike his niece, with whom he very often reads, he does not say anything about what he does with the books, or what he thinks about them. Was it that he didn't think that that was the kind of account keeping his diary was for? Or that he found the transactions particularly interesting?

Sociable Exchanges

As these examples suggest, much of the exchanging of books, and of opinions about them, took place by post. Opinions were aired and shared, often in a three- or four-way epistolary communication. Elizabeth Iremonger writes to her friend Mary Heber: "I agree with Mrs. Wrightson in her partiality to Southey's Poems, with which I formed an acquaintance when I was at Bristol . . . Does Mrs. Wrightson also like his *Joan d' Arc* & his *Letters in Spanish Literature?* I have seen Extracts from Cleri's book in the Reviews, which— together with the Conversations I hear about it—are sufficient for my curiosity as it is an old & disagreeable Subject."[127] Eliza Pierce, a young Devon woman living with her ailing aunt and uncle, wrote regularly to Thomas Taylor, the man who would become her husband. Seeking refuge from the longueurs of what she feared might be a lifelong commitment to caring for her relatives, Pierce found respite in discussing books in her letters to Taylor. She compares notes on her reading of Milton's *L'Allegro* and *Il Penseroso*, enjoys the copy of *Tacitus* Taylor has sent her, and sneaking out of her uncle and aunt's reading of Fielding's *Amelia*, says that Fielding should have stopped writing when he was on a roll, with *Tom Jones*. She later describes the epistolary exchanges she has as conversation, commenting in January 1766: "There is certainly something very agreeable, to chat in this Manner with the pen (excuse the expression) about Books & other peoples affairs, but at the same time one ought not to be unmindfull of ones own."[128]

Mary Delany was a great borrower, lender, and sharer in literary matters. Her letters are littered with references to her exchange of reading materials by post with those with whom she could not be physically close, like her sister, her niece, her grand-niece, and her best friends. "Since we cannot be together, the next greatest pleasure is to be occupied in the same study, and I read 'Sir Charles' [Grandison] with double pleasure as I think he may be also entertaining you at the same time."[129] Exchanging reading material had the same function as reading aloud: the forging of closeness through enjoyment of the same literary works. Again, Delany triangulated sets of acquaintances through the swapping of books: "My best acknowledgments are due for your obliging favour in furnishing Mr. Oakover with his copy of my book. I here return you another book, with my sincere thanks . . . I have received *Women's Worth*, etc., as fair as when it went out of my hands, so that Mrs. Dewes and Lady Anne Coventry will always be welcome to the perusal of any curiosities in my collection."[130]

Much work remains to be done on the role of family libraries in disseminating books amongst the wider community.[131] A case study of the papers of Elizabeth Rose, the lady laird of Kilvarock, near Nairn in the Scottish Highlands, offers a glimpse of the way in which such informal domestic circulation came to shape reading experience. Rose's letters, diaries, and lending catalogue show how her family library informed the education of the children of the family, and the degree to which shared reading by the fireside helped establish a bond between her and her stepdaughters.[132] The use of the books was not confined to these female relations—a tenant farmer, a local solicitor, and clergymen also drew on the Kilvarock resources. Elizabeth

Rose's letters to the friends and acquaintances to whom she lent her books show her discussing those books, again testifying to the element of intellectual exchange involved in book swapping or lending.[133] Rose was not confined to her own library, but also used the local circulating library, along with the collections in neighbouring country houses. Domestic book borrowing was a mixed economy. Like many other readers, she found that the constraints of borrowing determined usage—so she sometimes had to rush to copy down extracts in order to return them, and read multivolume books in the wrong order.

The extensive trade in printed, often individualised bookplates is a material testament to this world of domestic book sharing.[134] Plates were a way of both personalizing a book and enabling it to circulate more widely amongst friends and family. They imply a seriousness about the act of owning books, and of seeing them as part of an individual collection. Because books were largely bought in sheets, and bound according to the tastes and income of their owners, to pick up a book, any book, enabled users to read in it an indication of the status of its owner, or the perceived value of the work. Of course, it was not only women who swapped books. Walter Gale, a schoolmaster from Mayfield, exchanges books amongst friends, in his case, within a more local ambit.[135] His diary illustrates book swapping as part and parcel of more general sociability: "We went together at noon to Elliott's, where he [Mr. Hassell, a conjuror, or astrologer] treated me with a quatern of gin, and I gave him a dinner at Coggin's Mill . . . At nine he returned to Heathfield, carrying with him my Little's *Introduction to Astrology*. He gave me directions to write to Mr. White of Rotherfield, to demand Raleigh's History of the World, which he had in his hands."[136]

Nancy Woodforde records a whole series of book loans, and the ways in which these texts are then read aloud at home with her uncle. Often noting how frustrated she was by a lack of company, her diary reminds us of the potential tedium of parish life in the country. She laments on 30 November 1792: "No Person has call'd on us since the 13th and nothing has happen'd worth mentioning since the 16th. I have spent the latter end of this month in walking, reading the History of England and making Shirts for Uncle."[137] In the context of her limited access to a wider world, she records every injection of literary stimulation. Their acquaintance Mr. Du Quesne is an especially good provider of reading matter, supplying her with the *Gentleman's Magazine*, Buffon's *Natural History*, and various London papers. She then reads these aloud with her uncle. The local squire, John Custance, and his wife are another reliable source. One rainy afternoon in March 1792 she goes to the recently built Weston house, where Mrs. Custance was in a period of confinement after childbirth (one of many—she had eleven children in as many years, three of whom died in infancy). Nancy describes her evening. She had taken along her *Carlton House Magazine* for Mrs. Custance:

> As I thought it may entertain her for a short time, as any little thing is amusing to a Person in confinement. I din'd with Mr. Custance and we had a deal of Conversation about Books and other things so that I spent my time very agreeably. I went up to Mrs. C. Room after dinner and sat and chatted with her near an Hour . . . It was a very wet evening there, Mrs. Custance sent me home in her Coach, Betty came with me in it also—I got home to tea. Brought home the second Vol: of Baron Trenck and Mrs. Custance lent me the first Vol: of Hogarth illustrated by John Ireland.[138]

In this case, Nancy spends some time downstairs with the man of the house, discussing literature of presumably some substance, which results in a loan of the second volume of the life of the Austrian soldier Baron Trenck. She then pops upstairs to deliver his wife a loaned copy of a magazine, covers some celebrity gossip (she says they discussed the Duke of York's gambling), and returns home with a loan from Mrs. Custance of John Ireland's study of William Hogarth. The books lent then live a secondary social life, read by Nancy to her clergyman uncle, or by him to her.

∂χϵ

In our age in which text of all kinds is so freely available, it is hard to imagine the excitement felt by previous readers at the possibility of gaining access to a new book. A foray into the world of book sharing, buying, selling, and borrowing reveals the intricate texture of cultural interactions. Through these examples we can glimpse the world of shared print, shared stories, and shared enthusiasms. Although early editions of most books were accessible only to a restricted section of the reading population, they became available to many more through various forms of printed dissemination. Texts circulated in multiple forms, to suit different markets. As this and later chapters illustrate, many of the ways in which readers consumed texts were in forms that have left little trace, such as newspapers, borrowed books, serializations, and abridgements. Formal and informal institutions of libraries and book clubs framed reading within broader notions of sociability, or education, and often created spaces within which the life of the mind could be enjoyed in company. The acts of lending and borrowing evident in the diaries and correspondence of the era created networks of exchange through which individuals gained access to an increased range and quantity of books. Reading forged opportunities for contact with other people, as well as for developing one's own cultural intelligence or sense of entertainment.

5. Verse at Home

My dear Polly
I have just finished reading your valuable collection [of verse] and I
think you have shewn great taste in the choice of them.
—Harriet Binny

Verse had many uses in the eighteenth century. Family members shared pious lines on themes of providence and affliction, neighbours exchanged comic verses on local elections, lovers wrote one another sentimental verses on the death of favourite pets, and young women sent back and forth their musings on friendship. Readers and listeners also hooted with laughter over riddles, enigmas, drinking songs, and conundrums, puzzling and jovial rhymes to cheer a winter's evening and, in theory, purge melancholy. People embroidered poetic maxims into samplers, admired lines from Samuel Butler's *Hudibras* on transfer-printed jugs, and enjoyed ballads and broadsides pinned to the wall. The story of the popular transmission of verse reveals the close connection between printed selections—in newspapers and magazines, or poetic miscellanies—and the uptake of poems by individual readers. It exposes the powerful impact of popular print forms in shaping the literary canon and literary taste for many middling-sort readers. And it also demonstrates that a lot of readers and editors were fairly blasé about who wrote what. In the eighteenth century (the so-called age of the invention of authorial copyright, dating from the Statute of Anne in 1710), a substantial quantity of verse was not assigned to an individual author—nor were distinctions made between homemade verse and that by well-known poets.[1] Poetry seen through the lens of its social uses shows much more emphasis on theme, personal connection, and social entertainment than on the original author.

Readers and editors repurposed poems as it suited them. Long poems were chopped up into shorter, thematic pieces; substantial philosophical discussions were shortened into quotable aphorisms, illustrating a lively culture of creative disregard for authorial intention.

What then, is particular about verse? Does it do the same kinds of things as other forms of writing? It would be possible to discuss reading books at home by thinking about the functions of literature, such as instruction, piety, laughter, or sentimentality, and downplaying the generic differences between drama, prose, and verse. But there were certain characteristics of eighteenth-century verse that ensured its take-up was different. Most obviously, it is the genre most closely related to an oral tradition—to make metre and rhyme work, we need to hear, or imagine, how a poem sounds. The transition from print to vocal performance is assumed, even if it doesn't actually happen. Moreover, the couplet form and the liftable, aphoristic quotability of much eighteenth-century verse made it highly transferrable into a whole range of media, from commonplace books and printed miscellanies to cups and rings and samplers. The relative brevity of entire poems ensured it was possible to copy them out, collect them, compose them, read them out, or send them with a frequency not possible for the longer genres such as plays, novels, or essays. As we shall see later on, those genres were also transformed into formats suitable for reading in parts—but poetry had an unmatchable portability. The domestic afterlives of verse—the fact that it would be cut up and turned into quotable snippets by readers and editors—surely came to affect its composition. Did the aphoristic tendencies in eighteenth-century verse stem from the knowledge that these were the parts most likely to be quoted by readers? Was text constructed—like the "search optimization" built into websites and online publication in this century—to encourage extraction and citation? And how far did poets write in anticipation of amateur reciters? The poet Anna Seward argued that writers should not hem themselves in by using only easy sounds that could be mastered by the clumsiest reader. To do so, she argued, would limit the verse. Instead, she said, the poet should accept "unavoidable circumstances."[2]

Commonplacing and Compilation

One of the most important contexts for thinking about how eighteenth-century readers used poetry together and in their homes is the Renaissance tradition of commonplacing—the copying out and indexing of short texts or sections of text in manuscript books. The practice had its roots in classical education and rhetoric, which had emphasised the importance of taxonomizing different species of argument. Over time, commonplacing came to be interpreted more loosely as the copying out of pieces of favourite reading, and a commonplace book evolved into an eclectic and inventive hotchpotch of materials. Part anthology, part encyclopedia, part recipe book, it can be seen as a form of life writing.[3] There is plenty of evidence of the continuing practice of educated gentlemen and women collecting up classical learning in indexed volumes throughout the eighteenth century, enough to suggest that there was not a single and decisive shift from one sort of compilation to another. But it is also true that there are research libraries, family archives, and local record offices stuffed full of handwritten volumes from across the eighteenth century that might loosely be called commonplace books—or more commonly, just notebooks of "volumes of verse" in which readers amassed their favourite pieces. These collections were not necessarily informed by a close reading of Renaissance humanist texts, nor were they intended to build an encyclopedic body of educational material with which to understand the world. Instead, they were a way of collecting and personalizing the snippets that readers enjoyed—enabling them to be redeployed in new contexts. Such collections illustrate the way in which contemporaries initiated creative relationships with their reading matter, culling notable pieces to create the literary equivalent of a modern playlist. From early on, commonplacers had been advised to concentrate their selection upon textual forms that used language elegantly, and economically, to articulate ideas without taking up a lot of space.[4] Epigrams were highly suitable. As the commonplace book acquired an increasingly social function, bon mots, sententiae, and aphorisms, often taken from much longer poems, began to pepper the notebooks of eighteenth-century readers.

Commonplace books are but one aspect of the practices of manuscript compilation and transmission that dominated early modern literature. Although the eighteenth century saw a significant expansion of print culture, older habits of composing and sharing through handwritten texts continued.[5] Manuscript exchange had an important social function in bonding groups of like-minded individuals into a community.[6] The circulation of texts, and the habits of imitation, addition, and parody that often stemmed from it, remained fundamental to reading habits in the eighteenth century.[7] Ordinary readers continued to write and copy literature into personal notebooks throughout the eighteenth century.

One of the difficulties in finding these collections in archives is that they are rarely classified in a straightforward way. A "Commonplace" book may turn out to be household accounts, while an "account book" contains diary entries alongside verse transcription and sketches. Some readers started off with one, and ended up with another. The Sheffield tailor George Hoyland began using a notebook for details of his business accounts, and an inventory of furniture, and then employed it to record all kinds of verse and bits of news that took his fancy, much of it taken from contemporary newsprint.[8] Other collections bundled together everything people liked the look of, and the commonplace book grew into a family encyclopedia.

The commonplace book of the Wilson family of Broomhead Hall, in the Ewden Valley, just outside Sheffield, was compiled in the 1730s and 1740s and is a cornucopia of jottings. There are several hands at work in the volume, suggesting a family culture of reading and transcribing useful information. The main compiler was probably John Wilson, the heir to the estate, who attended the local grammar school and then lived in relative retirement in the house, which was fairly isolated from its surrounding neighbours, in a large area of moorland. Wilson's nineteenth-century biographer explains that he had plenty of time to devote himself to amateur academic and literary pursuits because of the stable condition of his estate, which enabled him to "maintain hospitality, and to take a respectable rank among the neighbouring gentry."[9] Wilson, who acquired a local reputation as an antiquary, compiled a substantial manuscript collection during his lifetime, amassing from diverse sources bundles of material relating to the local area, and historical documents concerning neighbouring families. These ranged from depositions concerning the divorce of Anne of Cleves to a verse account called "The Liberties and Customs of the Lead Mines."[10] His family commonplace book is a blend of practical advice, nuggets of knowledge, entertainments, and transcriptions from literary works. The compilation begins with "To find the Longitude at Sea" and moves on to "how to lay out an acre of Ground," followed by legal details on "Term of a Bond" and then some dance music transcribed using an idiosyncratic mode of notation (fig. 22).[11] There are pages of notable facts: "Of Ignorance in Learning," "Of Great Memory," "Unusual Strength," "Of the Famous Wall of China," and lists of "Useful Arts," which include how to polish shot, mend china, make a varnish for a violin, or find out the height of a rock or a steeple.[12] Further on are a series of word games and puzzles with numbers:

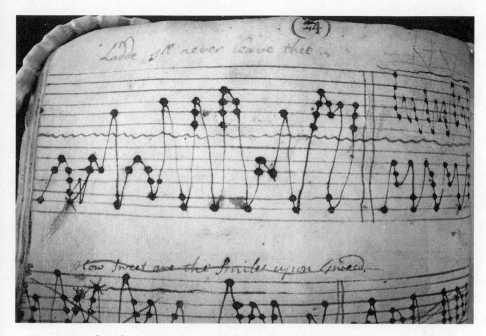

Fig. 22. Page from the Commonplace Book of the Wilson family of Broomhead Hall (Sheffield City Council, Libraries Archives and Information: Sheffield Archives MD 145)

> B not yy nor nice
> Uc how A fool U B
> My love is true
> Which I O U
> C, U, B as true to me[13]

At the back of the volume are inscribed the dates of birth of family members, information that other households commonly entered in a Bible. The book as a whole represents many different areas of the family's interests, enthusiasms, and needs, and its contents are overwhelmingly dictated by utility and application. The "Select Scraps of Poetry" that we find inside the volume are also shaped by these concerns. The verse is a mixture of seventeenth- and eighteenth-century pieces, some of them quite recent. There are extracts from Pope's *Essay on Man*, Milton's *Paradise Lost*, Denham's *Cooper's Hill*, and shorter poems by the Earl of Roscommon, Ambrose Philips, and Jonathan Swift. Very little of the poetry is attributed, and much of it represents a short, retitled section of a longer work. Alongside the works of established writers, there are also anonymous joke poems and riddles—there is one poem written in the margins, entitled "A Love Letter," in which every line ends with a word ending in "ation," another marginal note with the Swiftian aphorism "to live in suspence is the life of a spider." There is little logic to the collection of verse—they seem to be poems that had taken the compiler's fancy, in the same way that he was also struck by "Choice Secrets in Physick" or news "Of Mahomet & his pretended Journey to Heaven." John Wilson's later biographer complained that he should have been a bit more methodical in his compiling. Describing him as a man averse "to arrangement and composition," he accused Wilson of wasting his time in "laborious transcription from books which at all times were easily accessible, that might have been much better employed in digesting into some regular and connected form what he had collected."[14] Today, the Wilson volume gives us a real sense of the way commonplacing could embed literature in domestic culture, selecting imaginative works for their use and application in the home.

Sometimes commonplace books seem to have emerged from a specific social group. An anonymous notebook in the Bodleian library, dating from the 1760s, is entitled "Lusus Seniles; or, Trifles to Kill Time in Confinement and Old Age" (fig. 23).[15] Its compiler, an unidentified man, probably lived in Leicestershire and, judging from the figures identified in the volume, was part of a local professional or lesser gentry social circle. In this collection, it is his group of local friends, rather than his family, who provide the context for the collection.[16] The book contains only verse, transcribed on a number of different occasions, and it has a contents page at the front, and a poem at the end dedicating the whole collection to "Flora," later identified as a "Miss Bridges." One of the first poems in "Lusus Seniles," called "The Amicables," is an encomium to a friendship group:

> The Clock strikes five; fragrant the Coffee steams,
> And butter'd Bread (like Paper) lies in Rheams.
> True as the Needle to the Northern Pole,
> Or Balls inclining to the Centre roll;
> Or as the Dial to the brilliant Sun,
> To meet each other Amicables run.
> The Ev'ning Hours weekly thus they spend
> And in Rotation Friend thus visits Friend.
> But lo! in Feasting, Chatting and in Play
> Too soon the hasty Minutes steal away.[17]

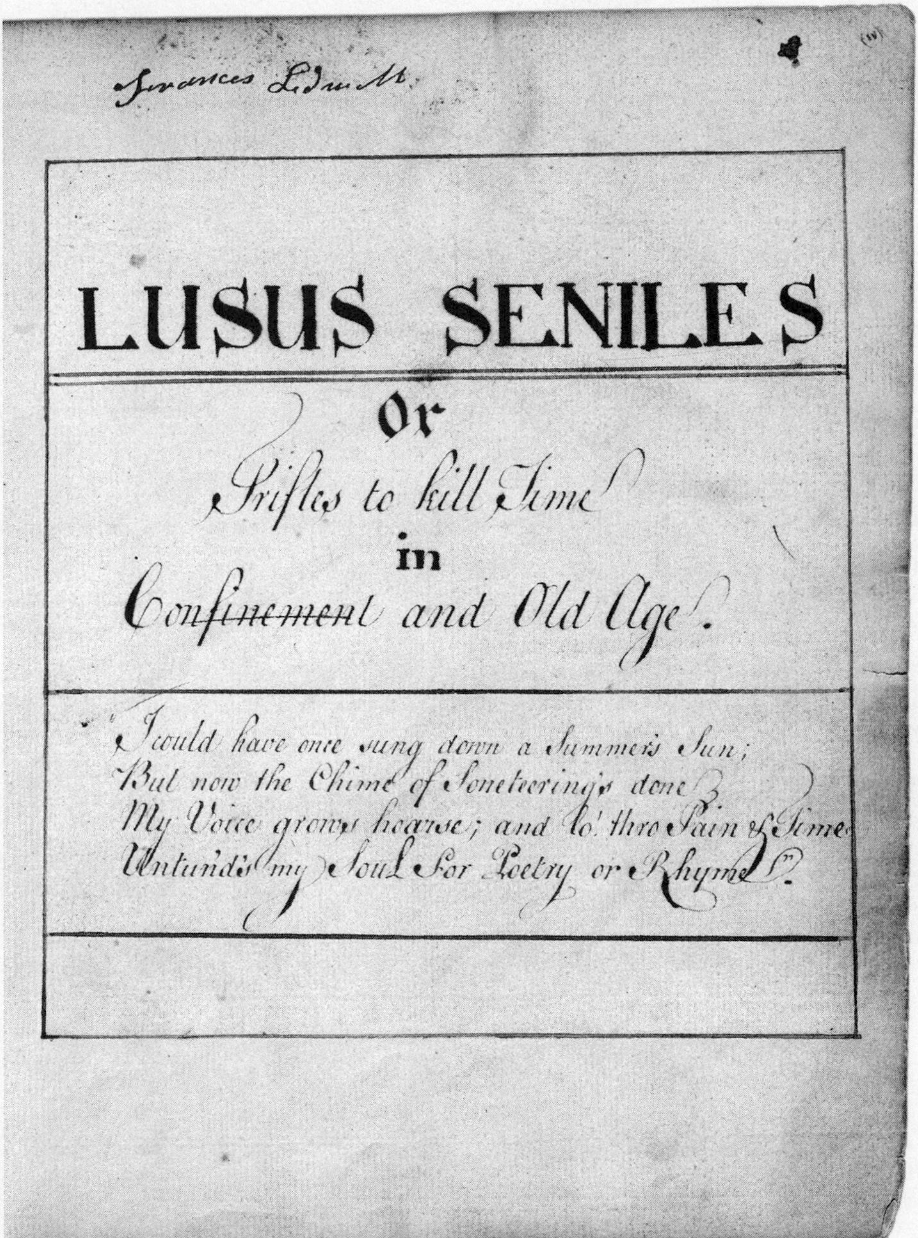

Frances Edn M.

(iv)

LUSUS SENILES

Or

Trifles to kill Time

in

Confinement and Old Age.

"I could have once sung down a Summer's Sun;
But now the Chime of Sonetering's done;
My Voice grows hoarse; and lo! thro Pain & Time
Untund's my Soul For Poetry or Rhyme."

Fig. 23. Title page from "Lusus Seniles; or, Trifles to Kill Time in Confinement and Old Age"
(The Bodleian Libraries, The University of Oxford, MS. Eng. Poet. d. 47, fol. Iv)

We get an unusually vivid glimpse of the type of regular domestic event that the volume both records and embodies. There is mixed company, a group of doctors, military men, and their wives. The food and drink—coffee and bread, nothing excessive—provides the backdrop to this celebration of regular, provincial sociability. The rest of the piece offers a series of brief pen portraits of the members of the group, who are named as "little Squib," "the gallant Major," and "Justinian's son." At the end of the volume, there is a key to the identity of these ciphers, where we learn that Justinian's son is "Dr Smith a Civilian," "the Major" is one Major Hargreaves, and "Squib" is a Dr. West. Other poems assembled in the compilation are concerned with events specific to the members of the Amicables. There are pieces entitled "A Gentleman desires Miss Seaward to characterise the Frequenters of the Litchfield Assembly, held in the Vicar's Hall" and "On an Apple Thrown, which bruis'd the Hon.ble Miss Br-n's Hand (Extempore)."[18] The allusions to common jokes and experiences, and the playful use of code and the key, suggest that the volume was to be shared and circulated.

What is particularly interesting about "Lusus Seniles" is the fact that amongst these familiar, social exchanges are also poems by established authors—and no distinction is made between the personally composed verse and that which had elsewhere appeared in print. The verses that had come from a print source can mostly be found in contemporary poetic miscellanies, magazines, and songbooks, suggesting transcribing was a way of preserving both the transitory nature of social exchange and the casual reading of popular print.

There are many other collections that stem from friendships. Begun in 1768, the notebook of Mary Allanson, member of a Yorkshire gentry family near Ripon, contains verse she had written and collected between the ages of eighteen and twenty-four. It is a compilation Allanson made before her marriage, and is largely made up of poems addressed to female friends, alongside some toasts. There are verses "On the Death of Miss Swan" from 1768; "To Miss Dawson on her birthday Novbr 4th 1769"; and "To Miss Beaumont" from 1771.[19] Again, the notebook illustrates a shared world of compliment with exchanges of verses and the perpetuation of social events in written form. Mary Marshall's hand-sewn collection of romantic and loyal songs and verses, now in the Bodleian Library, dates from the Napoleonic wars, and is partly in manuscript and partly made up of cut-out printed pieces from a range of other sources (fig. 24). She must have shown it to her friend

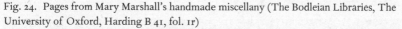

Fig. 24. Pages from Mary Marshall's handmade miscellany (The Bodleian Libraries, The University of Oxford, Harding B 41, fol. 1r)

Harriet Binny, who wrote in the volume, "My dear Polly I have just finished reading your valuable collection and I think you have shewn great taste in the choice of them."[20] Sharing, as this homemade example reminds us, was also about displaying one's literary values to the wider world.

Eighteenth-century commonplace books embody a way of thinking about literary texts that was highly individualised.[21] Copying out favourite verses, pieces of news, or nuggets of knowledge was a form of autobiography—a genre developing rapidly at this time. The practice enabled individuals to shape a narrative of their interests, their responses to the world, and their aspiration through their reading. Yet the commonplace book encapsulated the literary lives of groups as well as individuals. The family scrapbook belonging to Mary Madan contains deeply personal poems such as a father's elegy on the death of his ten-and-a-half-year-old son, William, "who began to Droop August 26th, 1769," pasted in alongside pretty much any morsel of writing that other friends and family members thought useful, ranging from vegetable bills to odes on contemporary figures.[22] Other collections offer a record of the performance of household literary compositions. The commonplace book of Paul Ourry Treby, of Plympton St Mary, just outside Plymouth, illustrates the role of amateur poetry writing in the social life of provincial gentry in the late eighteenth century. Treby's surviving notebooks are decorated with hand-drawn pictures in watercolour of contemporary figures, and like the commonplace book of the Wilson family in Yorkshire, combine items of academic interest and, increasingly, his leisure pursuits—lists of what he has shot or his designs for dog kennels (fig. 25).

In the Treby volume Paul Treby transcribes his rather lumpen verses to the daughters of the neighbouring Trelawney family, one of whom he was later to marry:

> Fair nymphs of Trelawny Laetitia and Mary
> Whose words and whose actions are never to vary
> With health and respect first permit me to greet ye
> . . .
> On Thursday tis fixed should the weather prove fair
> For the party to Plyms rocky banks to repair
> . . .

Fig. 25. Sketches from the diary of Paul Ourry Treby, 1798 (Plymouth City Council [Arts & Heritage Service], Plymouth and West Devon Record Office, 2607/4)

> Duly furnishd with paper pens pencils and meat
> They prepare to draw landscapes with verses & eat
> To pass a long sociable day at our ease
> Be pleased with each other and mutually please.[23]

Writing and sharing verses and paintings are part of the day's activity at a picnic by the river Plym. As elsewhere, these amateur lines, rooted in individual experiences, are combined with transcriptions from established authors—"Pope's Universal Prayer," Herbert's *Court of Death*, *The Castaway* by Cowper. Further on in the volume, Treby records in some detail an evening writing versified toasts to various women. He describes the setting: "Scene. A Winters evening, a good Fire, good humour, mirth, and good wine, each friend called on in his turn to toast the girl he loves best." Then follows a quotation from Horace's Ode 37 and his own poem:

> How much in drinking is our pleasure lost
> If the pure liquor flows without a toast
> Here's one who o'er my captured soul bears sway
> The modest gentle unaffected Grey.[24]

After this, Treby lists the pieces contributed by the friends gathered for the evening, which were obviously read aloud by each participant: "A Song Upon the Miss Harrisons and Miss Ourry by Doctor Geach"; "By Mr. Marshall on Seeing Miss Ourry wet and dirty"; "A Sonnet by Dr. Cropmare on Miss Ourry's sending for roses to Ford the Gardener at Exeter." There is a playful naughtiness to some of the contributions: "To Miss Ourry soon after desiring Dr. Geach to kiss her horse":

> What kiss your horse a strange request
> A stranger thing may come to pass
> At Goodamore when I'm your guest
> You next may bid me kiss your Ass.[25]

Here, as in many such cases, the verse notebook is a thing of youth, capturing an era of passionate attachments, literary aspiration, and playful friendships. John Chubb of Bridgwater's commonplace books begin in this vein—the first entry in the first notebook was written when he was ten, asking his friend Joseph Burrows to come to his birthday. It ends with the rather solemn couplet "That Friendship which in Youth began / Shall grow and strengthen in the Man."[26] Later poems commemorate other attachments—a poem "To Miss xxxxxxxx" paraphrasing the story of Pyramus and Thisbe; or "To Miss Boys of Sherborne." There is a slightly pompous letter to a Mr. James Partridge of Exeter, including translated passages from *Il Pastor Fido,* and a series of translations and imitations of Voltaire, Anacreon, and Horace. "The Lottery: A Cantata" comes complete with arias and recitative, and Chubb also includes a smattering of short dilemmas and epigrams. These texts are social texts, but they are all of quite different kinds. Towards the end, dated 1773, is a satire on the election of a mayor at Bridgwater. It runs:

> 'Twas a question if Symes, or if Cox, should be Mayor,
> If a Fool, or a Rogue, should be plac'd in the Chair.
> Split the diff'rence says _____ and 'tis easily done,
> Let Gard'ner be Mayor—and you'll have both in one.[27]

This poem had a wider circulation than most of Chubb's verse because it was pinned up in the centre of the town. One of its furious subjects, Gardiner, the mayor elect, wrote to Chubb:

> Sir
>
> I am creditably Informed by my friend Mr. Cox That you are the auther of That there eppigrim That was hung up against the Cross the other night if you are so you are a impudent raskel and Durty Scoundrel besides you Have called my son in law Mr. Charles Anderton the mayor capon Which is a lye as my dafter [daughter] says he is no more a capon then yourself . . . if I have a mind to writ and argie i can make Nothing of you so you had better not provoke me again.[28]

This rough, unlettered response is a very different kind of voice and exchange to most of those commemorated in Chubb's correspondence, and it reminds us of the range of literacy and articulacy that amateur writers lived amongst. John Chubb's poems include classical imitations and local political satire, poems to his children, and a hymn for the freemasons. He wrote for and with all these different groups and audiences—and at the same time, he also knew and corresponded with Samuel Taylor Coleridge, who lived nearby at Nether Stowey. If we are to understand the social lives of writing, we need to recognise such potential diversity, and the possibilities of transmission up and down the social scale.

John Chubb's second notebook contains much of the same material as he had transcribed in his first one.[29] In the later version, the poems from the first volume are recopied and glossed to identify particular figures and historical references. "Miss xxxxxxxx" becomes "Miss Fanny Warren." This revision suggests that his notebooks may have circulated amongst friends in his later life, who did not know the occasion of the many impromptu pieces of his youth. A third notebook is composed largely of prose pieces, mainly extracts culled from his reading, and it is prefaced, unusually for such a compilation, with an explanation of its purpose:

> The Collector of ye following Extracts, not being blessed wth the most retentive memory, and often in vain wishing to recall to his mind, ye several sensations, exalted by the rich and exalted ideas, ye generous sentiment, ye useful information, ye sprightly wit, & elegant diction, so frequently occurring in many of ye authors he chanced to peruse, was induced to transcribe into the following pages some of those passages wch most struck his fancy, as possessing many of those excellencies.[30]

John Chubb is an interesting figure because of the breadth of material he left—commonplace books in verse and prose, pictures, and correspondence—unusual in a man of business with no university education or literary career. Moreover, the materials span his lifetime, and show the ways in which compilation and note taking evolved. Chubb's books began as a way of preserving his childish and adolescent effusions, and became a record of his family, his interventions in local political life, and his reading.

The Printed Commonplace

The collection of verse fragments was not only a manuscript phenomenon. One of the publishing successes of the early eighteenth century was the printed poetic commonplace book, a collection of short quotations from English verse and drama alphabetically arranged by theme.[31] One of the most widely circulated in this field was Edward Bysshe's *Art of English Poetry*, which first appeared in 1702.[32] It was a dictionary of rhyming words, and of quotations arranged by theme. The collection enabled readers to flick with ease from poetic illustrations of "Dissension" to "Dolphin" to "Doubt." *The Art of English Poetry* was the sort of book that many owned, and used—but few would admit to. Ostensibly designed to aid budding writers in their own compositions, it served a more general purpose as a handbook of poetic effect, a series of quotations that could be lifted and used to enliven other forms of writing. If you wanted to produce a passionate exclamation on the nature of existence, you could flip to the section on "Life" and choose, amongst others, between John Dryden's "When I consider Life, 'tis all a Cheat; / Yet, fooled with Hope, Men favour the Deceit," Shakespeare's "Life's but a walking Shadow; A Poor Player," or Thomas Shadwell's "Life is but Air / That yields a Passage to the whistling Sword."[33] We know that *The Art of English Poetry* was part of the collections of Alexander Pope, Samuel Richardson, Henry Fielding, Isaac Watts, Samuel Johnson, Oliver Goldsmith, Hugh Walpole, and William Blake.[34] Like Wikipedia in the twenty-first century, it was a fruitful source for many readers and writers who claimed to disapprove of its scholarly shortcuts. It is now established that Samuel Richardson must have used it for many of the literary quotations in his masterpiece *Clarissa* (he replicated some of the same errors in transcription or attribution that Bysshe had made), yet it is nowhere acknowledged in the novel, which for centuries of critics and readers gave the impression of Richardson's wide familiarity with the English literary canon.

The Art of English Poetry was a work expressly designed not for the privacy of a study but for casual consumption. In the dedication, Bysshe states:

> The *Melange* of so many different Subjects, and such a Variety of Thoughts upon them ... may not satisfie you so well as a Composition perfect in its kind on one intire Subject; but possibly it may divert and amuse you better, for here is no thread of Story, nor connexion of one Part with another, to keep the Mind intent, and constrain you to any length of Reading; This is a Book that may be taken up and laid down at Pleasure, and would rather choose to lye about in a With-drawing-Room, or a Grove, than be set up in a Closet.[35]

In content and format, this was, Bysshe suggested, a work for "dip-n-skip," desultory reading. The fragmentary nature of the collection was perfect for picking up and putting down, with none of the lengthy distraction of a sustained story or argument. Form and use are linked; as far as Bysshe is concerned, casual, domestic use (the drawing room rather than the closet)

demands short, browsable forms of writing. We can discern in this phenomenon something of the circular relationship between print and manuscript,
editors and readers. Edward Bysshe had the canny idea of taking the
commonplace book, traditionally an indexed manuscript collection of quotations, and issuing it in a print version. In this new format, the editor had done
the hard work of collecting the "most noble thoughts" of the English poets,
so that his readers could draw on them at ease, without having to have read
the originals. And then what happened to the quotations in *The Art of English
Poetry* was that they were reabsorbed into the literary lives of their readers,
redeployed in novels, letters, and commonplace books.

Such a pattern of borrowing, reusing, and reworking—often
unacknowledged—was a fundamental part of domestic literary culture.
Traditional literary critical questions such as the exact source of an allusion
or the intention behind a textual borrowing have no meaning in this context
of informal, unacknowledged, and possibly unrecognised intertextuality.
Ordinary readers were much less fastidious about the source of their knowledge—including literary knowledge—than we might assume. They took what
they liked, remodelled it to suit their purpose, and, in doing so, gave textual
forms a new, and unpredictable, trajectory through eighteenth-century society.
It is hard to tell where exactly readers got their quotations from. The 1772 diary
or memorandum book of John Andrews of Modbury in South Devon contains
brief notes on repairs and estate management and social visits, and a lot
of information about the weather (fig. 26). These are accompanied by cryptic
short quotations from verse and song. In January 1772 he notes some lines
from James Thomson's *Seasons:* "With tomorrow's Sun our annual Toil /
Begins again the never ceasing round."[36] On 25 February he quotes the song
"O had I been by Fate decreed / Some humble Cottage Swain," from Isaac
Bickerstaff's "Love in a Village." On 15 March, "A Dawn of Hope my Soul
Revives / And banishes Despair," from a libretto by Thomas Arne. On 12
April it is lines from Pope's "Essay on Man," "A Wild where Weeds & Flow'rs
promiscuous shoot, / A Garden tempting with forbidden fruit."

For Andrews, these verbal snippets seem to have offered a way of
glossing his life, using quotations to reflect his emotional responses to the
events of his day—exactly how, we cannot tell. Were the extracts he used the
result of wide reading in the authors quoted, or of browsing in a compilation
of extracted beauties of English verse and song? It is impossible to know
where Andrews got his material from. But given that these quotations were

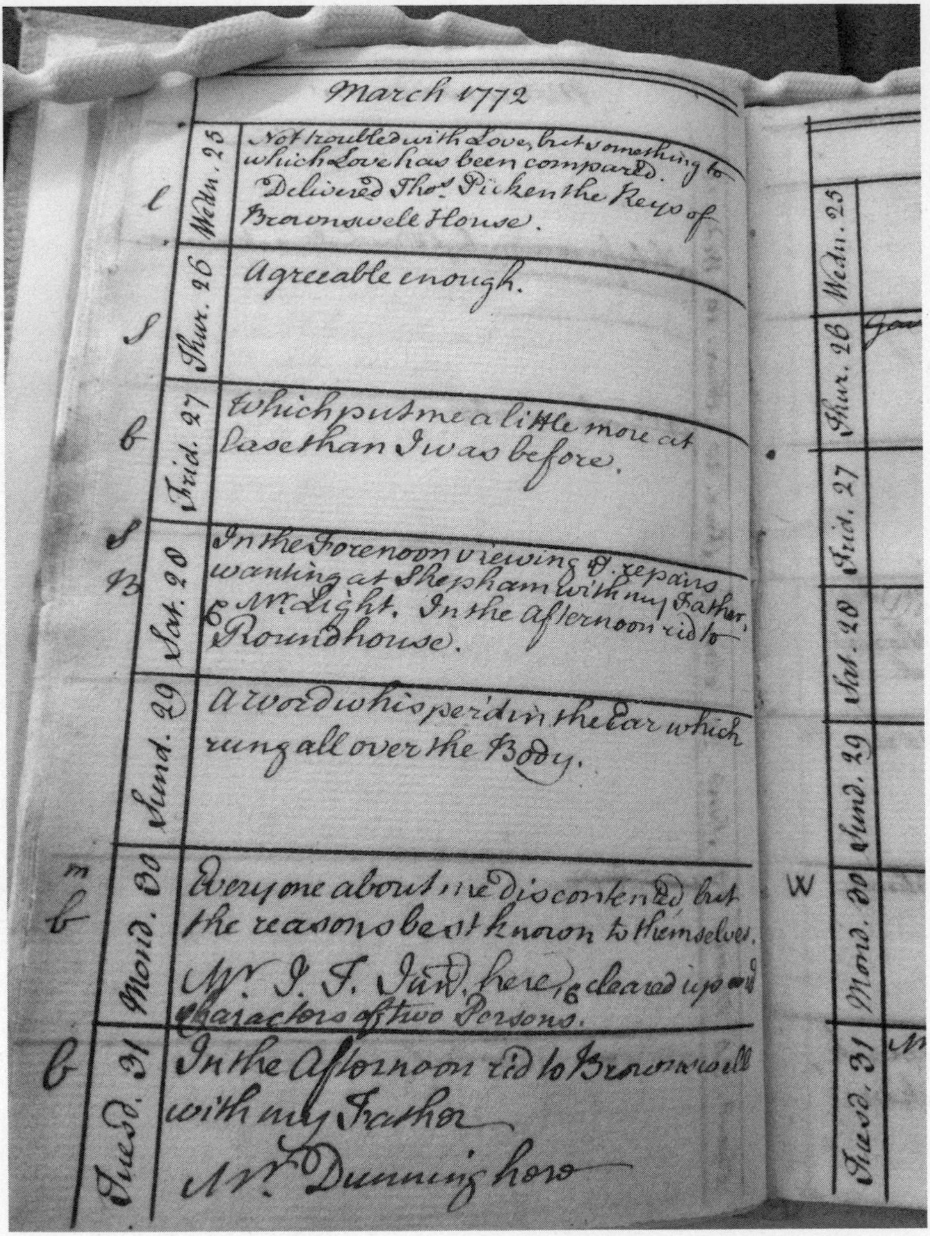
March 1772

l	Wedn. 25	Not troubled with Love, but something to which Love has been compared. Delivered Thos. Picken the Keys of Brownswell House.
S	Thur. 26	Agreeable enough.
b	Frid. 27	which put me a little more at ease than I was before.
S 13	Sat. 28	In the Forenoon viewing Ø. repairs wanting at Shepham with my Father & Mr. Light. In the afternoon rid to Roundhouse.
	Sund. 29	A word whisper'd in the Ear which rung all over the Body.
b m	Mond. 30	Every one about me discontented but the reasons best known to themselves. Mr. J. F. Jun. here, & cleared up ye Charactors of two Persons.
b	Tues. 31	In the Afternoon rid to Brownswell with my Father. Mr. Dunning here

Fig. 26. Diary and memorandum book of John Andrews of Modbury, 1772 (Plymouth City Council [Arts & Heritage Service], Plymouth and West Devon Record Office, 535/11)

excerpts frequently found in printed compilations, it seems likely that this is an example of the printed commonplace book feeding back into manuscript note-taking.

Many more substantial manuscript collections of verse in the eighteenth century offer similar examples of the repurposing of printed verse to suit personal interests and needs. As we have seen, compilers happily mixed their own verses with unattributed poetry by established authors. Andrews's habits of culling verse not from authorised editions but from recent publication in magazines and newspapers or from poetic miscellanies was not unusual. Some compilers didn't even bother to copy everything out, and instead pasted in sections of printed text to a notebook, alongside the material they had transcribed or composed by hand.[37] Mary Madan's verse scrapbook dates from the last decade of the eighteenth century, but its pages are covered with verses copied by members of her family, or cut from magazines, the majority of which long predate the compilation (fig. 27).[38] As a

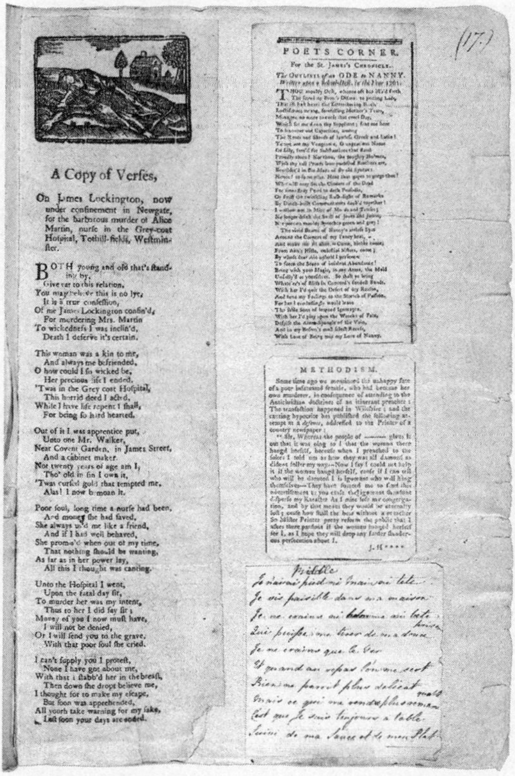

Fig. 27. A page from Mary Madan's verse scrapbook (The Bodleian Libraries, The University of Oxford, MS. Eng. Poet. c.51, fol. 25r)

whole, the volume is a multigenerational magpie's hoard of literary brows-
ings, amateur extempore verse on family members pasted in alongside jests,
bills, pieces of news, occasional verse, and epigrams.

Other collections betray a more intriguing relationship between print and
manuscript. Eliza Chapman's collection is a slim volume of handwritten verse
dating from 1788–89 (fig. 28).[39] It must have been composed when Chapman
was a young woman living in Essex. Many of the poems within
the compilation are from a lover or suitor titling himself "Scriblerus." As in
other handwritten verse collections, the book contains numerous poems
addressed to the compiler: "A Sonnett to Eliza Recovering from Sickness (Nov
1788)"; a poem "To Eliza. From her Favourite Robin Found in his Cage. March

Fig. 28. Title page from Eliza Chapman's poetry
notebook "Poetry, Selected and Original, 1788 & 1789"
(The Bodleian Libraries, The University of Oxford, MS.
Montagu e. 14, Title Page)

1789."[40] Chapman also transcribes her own gift poems, such as "Lines from Eliza to her God-daughter with a present of a Chintz coverlid on her Birth-day. May 27th 1789."[41] A good part of the volume is based in the affectionate exchange of homemade verse between the compiler and her female friends, and her male admirer. But as elsewhere, these personal pieces are intermingled with poetry from print sources: the volume is titled "Poetry, Selected and Original."

Chapman, unlike many other commonplacers, is fairly assiduous in recording her sources. We learn that she took the poem "Retirement 'Written in America by a Native Bard' " from the *Morning Herald*, of 1789.[42] "A Winter Piece" was found in Vicesimus Knox's miscellany *Elegant Extracts*, while "A Sonnet, To Sleep" was gleaned from the *Morning Post*.[43] Not all the borrowings from print sources are acknowledged, however. A piece entitled "To Eliza, Written at Midnight," and signed by "Scriblerus," is dated 1 July 1790. It takes the form of an extended meditation on the purity of the speaker's love for Eliza, and his desire to die and to know that

> When the kind grave shall all my follies hide,
> My fruitless love, my passion & my pride,
> Then sometimes surely shall a gentle woe,
> O'ershade thy mind; the chrystal drops shall flow
> In kind regret for him, whose heart was known
> With its last pulse, to beat for her alone.[44]

They are affecting lines, if a little sentimental for modern tastes. What is remarkable, however, is that although these last lines were probably written by Scriblerus for Eliza Chapman, most of the rest of the poem was not. It was, instead, an adapted version of the bluestocking Elizabeth Carter's religious poem "Thoughts on Midnight," also known as "Night Piece," first published in 1739. All Scriblerus did was to make some changes to the points in the poem where God was addressed directly. So where Elizabeth Carter had piously proclaimed that "To thee! all—conscious presence! I devote / This peaceful interval of sober thought," Scriblerus romantically declared to Eliza Chapman "To thee, my hearts' best tut'ress I devote / This peaceful interval of sober thought."[45] The addresses to divine grace are now pleas to Eliza, and Carter's imagined embrace of death as a prelude to the glorious afterlife is now replaced by Scriblerus's wish for death as a confirmation of Eliza's love.

It is hard to know what to make of this poetic transformation. There is something tasteless in the passing off of an older religious poem as a personal effusion of the moment. But this is an ingenious performance nonetheless. With a few tweaks, we have a passionate and eloquent poem addressed to the beloved Eliza Chapman. Was she intended to recognise the borrowing? The poem is not a parody, and there is no suggestion of an intended imitative relationship with the source text—most of the lines are the same in both versions. We here face some of the unknowns of amateur reading and writing. Did it matter? Did Eliza Chapman know the poem and enjoy the transformation? Or would she have been outraged to discover that her love poem was a thinly disguised recycling of someone else's religious verse?

These examples show us a vigorous culture of personalization and recycling. The ownership of poetry was complex—editors reshaped text to speak in different forms, and readers altered the verse they copied out to suit a particular agenda. There was a readiness to recycle material without acknowledging who had actually written it in the first place. Sometimes it wasn't clear, even to an author, what belonged to whom. Richard Lovell Edgeworth's sense of the distinction between quoting himself and quoting another was blunted by the fact that he could not remember what he had written himself. The novelist Maria Edgeworth described how she and her siblings used to trick her father with his own compositions: "In general he so completely forgot what he had written, that we have often read passages to him, without his recognizing them; and have cheated him into praising these, when he believed them to have been written by another."[46] And we might pause here to consider that our concepts of literary borrowing—that is, plagiarism, appropriation, allusion—are predicated on the assumption that every reader is fully aware of the origin of every text. But, of course, they are not. Readers do not always know where a quotation or fragment has come from, and they also forget what they have read, and what they have written. In an essay on reading, Michel de Montaigne discussed the way in which consuming a book often detached ideas from texts:

> I leaf through books, I do not study them. What I retain of them is something I no longer recognise as anyone else's. It is only the material from which my judgment has profited, and the thoughts and ideas with which it has become embued; the author, the place, the words, and other circumstances, I immediately forget.[47]

The confusions of ownership that seem so striking in the examples of textual borrowing discussed above may sometimes have been unconscious, part of the tidal ebb and flow of words and information that makes up everyday reading habits.

Elocution and Aspiration, Virtue and Values

As we have seen earlier in this book, reading together was linked to social aspiration and moral improvement. Printed verse collections specifically designed for domestic use were intended to teach users how to read aloud well. *Sheridan and Henderson's Practical Reader* guided readers in how to use inflection and tone when reading the beauties of English verse. The editor acknowledged that he couldn't offer instructions for everything, since "so much depends on such a nicety of expression, look and manner . . . Graces like these, which give, perhaps, the greatest beauty, and we may say a kind of bewitching ornament to a poem, cannot be methodized into rule."[48] But having said this, he endeavoured to provide some rules and, using italics, took users step by step through selected passages.

How to Read

COTTON's FIRE SIDE

DEAR Chloe, while the busy crowd,

The two first words in a tender, affectionate manner.

> The vain, the wealthy and the proud,
> In folly's maze advance;
> Tho' singularity and pride
> Be call'd our choice, we'll step aside,
> Nor join the giddy dance.

Lay a stress on the word our

> From the gay world we'll oft retire
> To our own family and fire,
> Where love our hours employs.

Read this line in the manner we recommended the first two words of the poem.

> No noisy neighbour enters here,
> No intermeddling stranger near,
> To spoil our heartfelt joys.

> If solid happiness we prize,
> Within our breast this jewel lies;

If you place your hand gently on the breast, in pronouncing the words, it
will have the proper effect—Jewel *ought particularly to be marked.*[49]

The tips for reading aloud offer a form of rewriting of the original poem—
in this case, overriding the meter. When the editor-instructor asks readers to
put the stress on the word "our," he effectively ignores the form, in order to
lay stress on what he perceives to be the most important element of the poem,
the affectionate companionship between the speaker and Chloe, which is
later to be reinforced by physical gesture. Elsewhere in this volume, readers
are taken through the delivery of fables by John Gay, which are to be read
with a "neat flippancy" of expression, giving due attention to the places that
need an injection of "*strength* and *energy.*"[50]

The performance of light-hearted material seems to require particular
elucidation: there is obviously a worry that users will be so focussed on
perfect elocution that they will forget that the poem in front of them is
supposed to be funny. The author is harsh in his advice here: "This
mouthing-out what ought to go *flippantly* and *trip* from the tongue, at once
destroys the poet's intention, and is peculiarly disgusting."[51] Would-be
speakers should be mindful to avoid all that is "*laboured* or *heavy*" and to
learn to distinguish between which pieces treat of sorrow and grief, necessi-
tating a "*slow, tardy* mode of utterance,"[52] and those that demand warmth and
animation. A wide range of modes is included within the volume: dramatic,
sentimental, and pastoral pieces, fables, and comic dialogue. There are also
hymns, songs, and ballads, which are given their own set of instructions for
spoken delivery, suggesting that musical forms were not always sung, but
often read in performance. The fact that so many verse miscellanies of the
eighteenth century include songs without any notation or indication of tune
may suggest a public who could fall back on a commonly known musical
repertoire, but it may also reflect the practice of reading music as verse. Isaac
Watts's enormously popular hymns were packaged by Cotton Mather as texts
suitable for reading, as well as singing within the home, making them part of
the literature of daily devotion.[53]

As these instructions suggest, poetic miscellanies offered guidance not
just in rendition, but also in the development of literary taste, appealing to
middling-sort readers keen to acquire the polite social skills previously

associated only with an elite. John Walker's *Exercises for Improvement in Elocution, Being Select Extracts from the Best Authors* (1777) was ostensibly aimed at students in elocution, looking for suitable works with which to hone their skills.[54] Walker, a former actor and then schoolmaster, had risen to fame for his elocution lectures and writings, in which he advocated the mechanical school of inflection, in distinction to Thomas Sheridan's "natural" school.[55] The advertisement to his *Exercises* suggested that the compilation might also provide general guidance in cultural *savoir faire:* "Mr. Addison's letters on taste, with some of the finest passages from Akenside's Pleasures of Imagination, and Pope's Essay on Criticism, not only furnish excellent lessons for reading, but form, in some degree, a system of polite knowledge."[56]

As "a system of polite knowledge," Walker's miscellany was aimed at those who wanted to learn how to *talk about* the texts they read or heard. Elocution collections played an important role in introducing new readers to ways of understanding the texts that they were reading aloud. The advertisement of the duodecimo *Exercises in Elocution* refers to its "small size and price"; for some readers such a collection must have provided not just a handy selection of elocution pieces, but also an accessible anthology of great literary works—possibly even their only point of contact with literature. The texts within were arranged with the advertised literary critical passages at the front, as a guide to key concepts. Some readers must have been a bit foxed by the advice on offer. The introductory passages from Addison's *Spectator* presented the two traditional (and conflicting) notions that taste was innate, and conversely, that it could be acquired: "It is very difficult to lay down Rules for the acquirement of such a Taste as that I am here speaking of. The Faculty must in some degree be born with us . . . But notwithstanding this . . . there are several Methods for Cultivating and improving it."[57]

The *Exercises* were designed to provide some of these "methods" for cultivating those who feared they might not have been born with taste. Walker's interventions also emphasised the spiritual aspects of human development. Walker was a converted Catholic schoolmaster, and he used his editorial role to refashion canonical poetic texts to promote cultural, personal, and spiritual education. Introducing extracts from Mark Akenside's long poem, *The Pleasures of Imagination,* he explained that he had added some material to his source text, supplementing Akenside's words with passages from Edward Young's *Night Thoughts* in order to paint a fuller picture of human existence. He said of Akenside: "His picture of man is grand and beautiful, but unfinished. The immortality of the soul, which is the natural consequence of the appetites and powers she is invested with, is scarcely once hinted throughout the poem." To rectify this omission, Walker explained that in his edition

> this deficiency is amply supplied by the masterly pencil of Dr. Young; who, like a good philosopher, has invincibly proved the immortality of man, from the grandeur of his conceptions, and the meanness and misery of his state; for this reason, a few passages are selected from the Night Thoughts, which, with those from Akenside, seem to form a complete view of the powers, situation, and end of man.[58]

In what seems to us now like a bold move, Walker effectively cut and pasted his texts together, turning them, in a stroke, into a poem conveying the kind of religious message he wished had been there to begin with. Akenside's *Pleasures* were given a focus on the spiritual afterlife that they did not originally possess, and were repackaged to fit a wider agenda within the miscellany, illustrating the same habits of excerpting and repackaging that we have seen in manuscript collections of verse.

Collections like *Exercises in Elocution* assembled gobbets of texts, specifically for sociable delivery and to be read aloud, texts that needed to be manageably short. Yet major poems of the eighteenth century, such as Thomson's *Seasons* and Akenside's *Pleasures of Imagination* ran to thousands of lines, and so they needed to be chopped up into smaller sections to fit the browsing, collecting habits of their readers. Poems had entirely different posthumous identities as short excerpts. Alexander Pope's *Windsor Forest,* a substantial political poem on the Peace of Utrecht, was commonly excerpted as extracts on the theme of rural sports (which generally had a wider and longer appeal than political panegyric).[59] The poem was repurposed in other forms: four lines on a pointer dog and his master appear on a creamware tile decorated with a shooting print and entitled "The Pointer," and the same extract was commonly cited in all sorts of discussions of pointer dogs in contemporary newspapers and reference books.[60]

Miscellanies tended to emphasise thematic rather than authorial classification of their contents, and the appearance of excerpts highlights theme rather than author. This is the approach taken in John Drummond's *Collection of Poems for Reading and Repetition* (1762).[61] Drummond thought that variety was the key to good delivery: "as novelty gains attention, and attention disposes to diligence; so variety will prevent a monotony, and brevity, tediousness and impatience."[62] The compilation, which contains no advice on how to read the passages, is organised alphabetically, by theme, from "Advice," "Affliction," and "Age," through to "Wit," "Woman," and "Words."[63] Each heading could include several passages, or "sentences," that were drawn from a number of different authors, without any indication of their original syntax or separate provenance. So, under "Providence" we are given six lines each from Bevil Higgons's *The Generous Conqueror* (1702), James Thomson's *Edward and Eleanora* (1739), and Samuel Johnson's *Irene* (1749). Readers coming across these works in this form would have had no idea that they were separate works, and no sense of the different authorial voices or literary contexts across the pieces selected here. There was also no distinction made between poetical lines drawn from plays in verse or poems—the literary canon was mined for sententiae, or memorable moments, whose significance was decontextualized. This lack of background gave readers only the text on the page with which to infer the appropriate voice or tone for their reading— which was presumably thought enough. It is clear that for many editors and readers, the experience of reading a passage completely isolated from its literary origins was probably a common one.

James Thomson's *Seasons* was one of the most popular poems of the eighteenth century. In addition to numerous editions across the century and beyond, it was commonly excerpted in miscellanies, where it was featured as short poetic extracts retitled "A Prayer to the Deity" or "A Description of the Sun Rising."[64] It also reemerged in the poetry snippets published in pocket books and almanacks.[65] The frequent republication of these particular sections of verse would have dominated readers' sense of Thomson's 5,500-line address to the natural world, possibly at the expense of their grasp of the whole. *The Seasons* included inset sentimental narrative pieces, such as the story of Musidora, or that of Palemon and Lavinia, and these little stand-alone stories feature prominently in later reworkings of the poem, providing the subject for many of the illustrations of *The Seasons*, and for the porcelain, earthenware, and tapestry renditions of the poem that proliferated towards the end of the eighteenth century.[66] Deft-fingered young women embroidered the story of Lavinia while they sat and entertained in their parlours (fig. 29). In structuring his philosophical and religious ruminations around moving fictional stories of suffering country folk, did Thomson anticipate

Fig. 29. Framed needlework embroidery of "Palemon and Lavinia" by an unknown maker, 1815–25, probably made in Pennsylvania (The Phillips Museum of Art, 4869; Courtesy of Franklin & Marshall College and the Permanent Collections of the Phillips Museum of Art, Lancaster, Pennsylvania; all rights reserved)

their later extraction and recitation? We cannot know this, although part of the success of the poem must have been that it offered moments of pathos that could be isolated from the often dense political, economic, and scientific discourse.

One of the notable features of the material afterlife of the poem was that it appealed across very different tastes and markets. In commemoration of the death of John, Second Duke of Argyll (1678–1743), the duke's wife presented a close friend with an inscribed gold snuffbox (fig. 30). Inside the lid are engraved some lines from James Thomson's tribute to Argyll's military heroism, which had appeared within "Autumn." A personal and individually

Fig. 30. Inscription of lines from James Thomson's "Autumn" on the inside of the lid of a gold snuffbox in the form of a shell, made in London, 1741–42 (Ashmolean Museum, WA1946.139; © Ashmolean Museum, University of Oxford)

designed piece of high monetary value, this unique box frames the autumn of Argyll's life within Thomson's lines on the man's valour. It speaks of a set of very personal connections between poem, object, and recipient.

But Thomson's poem was also reiterated in many less elite forms, and featured widely in the earthenware and printed ceramics aimed at middling-sort consumers.[67] With the advent of transfer printing, creamware jugs and pieces in Derby biscuit porcelain were decorated with prints of the episode of Palemon and Lavinia.[68] Staffordshire figures showed the couple in pastoral idyll. Such objects extended the experience of reading, suggesting both a moment and a whole book, the person with whom one read it, or the time of reading it. Householders could relive their enjoyment of a celebrated literary episode by propping it on their shelves, discussing it with their friends, establishing affinity through shared enjoyment of their response.

The choice of the Lavinia episode is interesting in view of its commod-ification. The vignette comes towards the beginning of "Autumn," and follows on from a description of industry and the process of social improvement that it brings:

> Hence every form of cultivated life
> In order set, protected, and inspir'd,
> Into perfection wrought. Uniting all,
> Society grew numerous, high, polite,
> And happy. (115–19)

A few lines later, we meet luxury, who "pour'd out her glittering stores." Luxury and luxury goods were a product of industry, but, as numerous accounts of the period tell us, they were also potential signifiers of the superficiality and effeminacy of eighteenth-century society.[69] It is in the context of this vexed question of the benefits—and fears—of commercial prosperity that the story of Lavinia sits, and the transition to her narrative marks a shift from urban sophistication to rural virtue. Lavinia is a beautiful young labourer, devoted to her poor widowed mother, and Palemon is the wealthy landowner. Seeing a dusty Lavinia in the fields, Palemon recognises her innate nobility and falls in love with her, rescuing her and her mother from the penury of rural hardship. It is a story about inner value rather than exterior appearance. Like the sentimental fictional episodes from Sterne and Richardson discussed below, which were also transformed into discrete consumable forms, it was an antimaterialistic moment vigorously marketed as a saleable commodity.

Verse and Virtue

As we have seen, texts for reading aloud at home were commonly a medium for cultural and theological instruction. There is a close parallel between the attempts to shape female taste and intellectual pursuits in miscellanies and the directions given in contemporary advice literature.[70] Conduct writers attempted to prescribe not only what should be read in leisure time, but also how it should be read. Thomas Gisborne, whom we met in Chapter 2, declared that while young women should avoid novels, they would greatly benefit from the regular reading and memorizing of "select and ample portions of poetic compositions, not for the purpose of ostentatiously quoting them in mixed company, but for the sake of private improvement."[71] It would strengthen the judgment, exalt piety, promote virtuous emotions, and provide a consolation in times of sickness or old age.[72] As Chapter 1 above suggests, contemporary thinking about the elocution movement was slightly contradictory: although it was important that women acquire speaking skills and read regularly, it was critical that the primary function of memorizing and reciting be not ostentatious display, but intellectual and moral self-improvement.

Propriety in speaking and thinking was frequently reinforced through other areas of female activity, including handwriting and embroidery. Thomas Dyche's extraordinarily successful *A Guide to the English Tongue* (102 editions between 1707 and 1800), "shewing a Natural and Easy Method to pronounce and express both Common Words, and Proper Names; in which particular Care is had to shew the Accent for preventing Vicious Pronunciation," included a series of verse quotations that could be used for practice exercises in pronunciation, and in handwriting.[73] Some of these maxims were also sewn into embroidery work by young women, further embedding the tenets of right living within household activity.[74] Mary Wakeling's sampler, embroidered in 1742, when she was ten, contains as its text the lines "Gay dainty flowers go swiftly to decay, poor wretched life's short portion flies away, / We eat, we drink, we sleep, but lo, anon, old age steals on us, never thought upon" (fig. 31). Eleanor Speed, who completed her sampler in May 1784, embroidered at the top "Content is all we aim at with our Store / And having that with little need no more" (fig. 32). She could have taken these lines from any number of compilations, such as *Sentences and Maxims Divine Moral and Historical . . . for the Improvement of Youth in Good Sense, and Correct English* (1712, 1730, 1752) or *The English Spelling Instructor* (1760). For many eighteenth-century readers, especially young girls like these, such a route of textual transmission through educational texts and then into needlework would have been one of the ways in which verse became familiar and used.

The fusion of verse and virtue is prominent in manuscript verse collections. When Eliza Warner, a Warwickshire woman, gathered together the poems she had written or copied, she explained that "This manuscript is for my Neice Susanna Clarke, as she desir'd to have it in remembrance of me. The following pages were collected into their present form, from detach'd papers, for my mother, to whom they are address'd."[75]

The collection, like the Madan and Wilson collections, reaches across generations; Eliza Warner copied out for her mother the poems she had written in her youth, and then recopied them in later life for her niece. The first poem in the collection dedicates the book

Fig. 31. Sampler by Mary Wakeling, 1742, wool embroidered with silk (Victoria and Albert Museum, 394-1878; © Victoria and Albert Museum, London)

> To the instructor of my early youth,
> Who form'd my mind to piety and truth,
> By whose maternal care, I first was taught,
> To speak, to think, and practice as I ought.[76]

The verse contents of the collection are, unsurprisingly, largely concerned with virtuous living—"A paraphrase on the 19th Psalm," "On reading Mrs Cath: Talbots Works," "The Story of Boaz and Ruth." They are transcribed alongside "thoughts and meditations," such as the following rather prim reprimand to those tempted to linger in bed: "what false luxury it is, to lye stretch'd upon the bed of sloth, instead of enjoying those various sweets

Fig. 32.   Sampler sewn by Eleanor Speed, 1783–84, linen, embroidered with silk (Victoria and Albert Museum, T.56-1948; © Victoria and Albert Museum, London)

which nature pours forth to the early risers. Who can refuse to join the universal chorus of Nature."[77] The final poem in the collection gives us an insight into the ways in which Warner viewed the value of literature:

"On Printing"

> From this great source, knowledge & pleasure flow
> Yet hence, are often Drawn, the tears of woe.
> Th' unconscious Characters speak to the heart
> But joy or grief unknowingly impart.
> With pleas'd attention we trace back old time
> And ages past reveal in various rhyme,
> Or else perchance in sober prose review
> The ancient Worthies, the selected few,
> Born for examples rare, to rouse y[e] Mind
> To great exploits, & *humanize* Mankind.

Alas! That such a spring, shou'd ever be
Poison'd with vice, and infidelity!
Be made the dirty channel to transmit
To future times, contaminating wit.
May I with care select the better part,
Books that the passions smooth, & mend the heart.
Or if a while I choose the comic page,
And light amusements for an hour engage,
Such be the authors, who with chasten'd pen,
The follys only, lash, but spare the men.[78]

It is rare to find such a clear exposition of a compiler's everyday reading philosophy. Eliza Warner's selection of poetry was a form of self-collection designed to be passed around to other women in her family as a badge of virtue and a recommendation for their reading.[79]

Purging Melancholy

Eliza Warner was judgmental in her condemnation of the pernicious influence of the "wrong" kinds of reading, and of texts that transmitted "contaminating wit" to their consumers. Her verse collection represents a strain of sentimental, religious verse that can be found in many manuscripts, magazines, and printed compilations of the period. But there are other stories to be told about the ways verse was read and used. One of the most notable aspects of the printed collections of verse is the prevalence of comic, impromptu witty poems, the kind of verse that can raise a laugh rather than sustain serious contemplation. Modern critics and modern anthologies tend to cite Jonathan Swift's clever autobiographical poems as examples of his varied poetic oeuvre. But extensive analysis of the reprinting of Swift's verse in collections and songbooks shows that the most popular poems for eighteenth-century readers were the slight, funny pieces we tend to overlook.[80] In thinking about the social uses of verse, the compilations of comic material are central to understanding what was read and why.

Collections from *The Merry Medley for Gay Gallants* (1755) to *Fisher's Cheerful Companion to Promote Laughter* (1800) drew together miscellaneous extracts in different comic genres, and typically included jests (short prose anecdotes involving some piquant reversal, incongruity, or smart reply), riddles, comic verse, word games, and music. *The Laughers Delight* claimed to offer "an Hour's Laugh at any Time, and design'd on Purpose to make the Heart Merry, and to prevent and expell Spleen and Melancholly, and drive the Evenings away with Mirth and Jollity. Usefull to all especially to those who take Physic."[81] Poetry, alongside other jocular material, had the capacity to drive away unhappiness and promote good humour, and one of the neglected, but important uses of verse in this period is alongside jestbook culture.[82]

The literature of mirth was generally predicated on the belief that unhappiness, in the form of melancholy, could only really be cured by a forceful injection of its opposite—hilarity or joviality. Throughout the sixteenth, seventeenth, and eighteenth centuries a sizeable literature was dedicated to the curative properties of sociable mirth, or as the great seventeenth-century theorist of melancholy, Robert Burton, puts it: "Nothing better than mirth and merry company in this malady [melancholy]. *It begins with sorrow* (saith *Montanus*) *it must be expelled with hilarity.*"[83] This literature of laughter moved across class and gender boundaries. Situated between oral and printed culture, it constantly evoked the social exchanges that it mimicked, and in turn, as jokes and jests and comic poems were copied into commonplace books and letters, it moved back into oral circulation.

Melancholy, defined by the eighteenth-century physician Richard Blackmore as "continual Thoughtfulness upon the same Set of Objects always returning to the Mind, accompanied with the Passions of Sadness, Dejection, and Fear," was regarded in medieval physiology as stemming from a large amount of cold and dry black bile in the body.[84] Only if the amount became disproportionately large in comparison to the other humors did it become a disease.[85] According to the humoral doctrine, antidotal cures helped redress the balance of the four bodily liquids.[86] In the case of too much black bile, a change in lifestyle was needed.[87] Blackmore recommended treatment through horrible-sounding vomitory medicines, laxatives, and other purges. But he also suggested "riding on Horseback, new Company, Change of Place, and Variety of Objects."[88] Exercise and joyfulness were key, and could be attained through walks in the open air, travel, hunting parties, ball games, music, and jokes. Laughter was healing laughter, thought to make the heart swell and produce fresh blood.[89] It was thought especially good to relax after a meal: "The reading of joyful histories and pleasant conversation" lifted the spirits after dinner, according to a popular Dutch health booklet.[90] The recommendation of curative laughter became commonplace over the sixteenth and seventeenth centuries, and was an integral part of Robert Burton's systematic analysis of the causes and cures of melancholy in *The Anatomy of Melancholy*, whose concluding advice is "be not solitary, be not idle." Burton advocates various kinds of exercises of mind and body for the dispelling of melancholy, which range from hunting and fishing to writing acrostics and dancing. Jokes, jests, and merriment were a key part of this recreational picture. To those who considered such light-hearted entertainment demeaning, he continued: "now and then (saith Plutarch) the most vertuous, honest, and gravest men will use feasts, jests, and toys, as we do sauce our meats."[91] Burton sums up his advice on this matter:

> what shall I say then, but to every melancholy man
> . . .
> Feast often, and use friends not still so sad,
> Whose jests and merriments may make thee glad.
> Use honest and chaste sports, scenical shews, playes, games.[92]

Burton was writing in the mid–seventeenth century, but the notion that mirth and joviality could have a curative function is still prevalent in later thinking. The eighteenth-century physician Timothy Rogers recognised a spectrum of melancholy, and for the less severe forms suggests that "[Melancholy] which is not deeply rooted, . . . can be drowned in wine, or chased away with sociable divertisements."[93] Whether readers—or editors—actually believed that the contents of their books could cure melancholy, or depression is hard to tell. But there is clear evidence of the circulation of jovial verse and riddle collections amongst eighteenth-century readers, and an understanding of the pleasures it could bring. Compilations were frequently prefaced with frontispieces depicting groups of men in taverns, sipping punch, pipes out, and chairs pushed back in jovial enjoyment of the comic world offered by the book in question.[94] Similar images would reappear on the jugs, punch bowls, and mugs celebrating jovial, usually male, sociability (figs. 33 and 34).[95]

Polite and Impolite

If one is tempted to see the world of riddles and jokes as one largely rooted in popular culture, then there is plenty of evidence, across England and Europe, of the enjoyment and collection of jokes amongst the elite.[96] At an average price of one shilling bound, jestbooks were far from the cheapest publications on the market—chapbooks typically sold for a half penny to a penny. The price, the format, and the terms on which such collections were

FRONTISPIECE.

The Cabinet of Momus

Our Jibes, and Jests, and Merriment,
Shall set the Table in a Roar.

Fig. 33. Frontispiece from Timothy Broadgrin, *The Cabinet of Momus, and Caledonian Humorist; being a collection of the most entertaining English and Scotch stories, selected from the best authors, in prose and verse, etc.* (London: W. Cavell, 1786) (© The British Library Board, 12316.d.20)

Fig. 34. Punch bowl decorated with a drinking scene, Wedgwood, Staffordshire, about 1775, lead-glazed earthenware, transfer-printed in black and enameled (Victoria and Albert Museum, C.391-1923; © Victoria and Albert Museum, London)

described ("bon mots," "smart repartees") suggest that they were predominantly aimed at a middling- and upper-class readership.[97] As discussed previously, collections of comic poems, squibs, and enigmas were marketed at a range of social groups—from *The Jovial Songster; or, Sailor's Delight* (1784) to *Fun for the Parlour; or, All Merry Above Stairs* (1771), its frontispiece a group of well-dressed women sitting demurely around a table listening to a companion's reading from the book (fig. 35).

Fun for the Parlour is not outlandishly rude, but neither is it prim: there are jests about drunkenness, sexual reputation, shrewish wives, and unhappy marriages:

On an old Scold

Scylla is toothless, yet when she was young,
She had both Teeth enough, and too much Tongue;
What shall we then of toothless *Scylla* say?
But that her Tongue has worn her Teeth away.[98]

Fig. 35. Frontispiece to *Fun for the Parlour; or, All Merry Above Stairs,* 1771 (© The British Library Board, 1607/5125)

It reads as an extraordinarily refined collection in comparison with compilations aimed at all-male drinking groups. *Hilaria, or the Festive Board* appeared
in 1798, "published for the author," who is sometimes identified as Captain
Charles Morris. The collection typifies (in quite an extreme way) eighteenth-
century miscellanies associated with drinking, jestbooks, and comic
songs. Its epigraphs, from Milton and Horace, allude to anacreontics,
classically inspired drinking songs and verses, and the editor strives to
preserve this veneer of respectability in the preface, which introduces the
collection of bawdy and satirical material by citing Milton, Samuel Johnson,
Solomon, and Robert Burns. The festive board turns out to be a bawdy
smorgasbord. There is something to amuse—or offend—all: anti-Irish
songs, political satires, poems about circumcision, pubic wigs, countless
comic verses on unfortunate sexual encounters, and Madam Mara, the
unfortunate soprano:

> Of Handel's fam'd Commemoration,
> And what was let loose there, I sing,
> When the Flats and the Sharps of our nation
> Assembled along with their King.
> Madam Mara (now mark what will follow)
> Her ravishing sounds was imparting;
> Momus play'd off a trick on Apollo,
> And set the sweet lady a f-t-g.[99]

Many of the poems have tunes attached to them, although it is not clear
whether they were actually sung. The collection was designed for communal
reading, presumably for groups of men, at a punch party, possibly at a crude
version of a catch and glee club, at home, or in the tavern. This and other
collections (such as the *Laugh and Be Fat* miscellanies) remind us that the
social culture of libertinism so often associated with the Restoration was
thriving right through the politer eighteenth century. Jestbook culture coex-
isted alongside elegant conversation.

The jokes and riddles of the eighteenth century frequently test the
boundaries of modern sensibilities. Jestbook collections offer many anecdotes based on stock types and situations—the cuckolded husband, the
Welshman, the blind woman, the scold, the congenital idiot. Yet we know
that these jokes were enjoyed, copied down, and repeated with enthusiasm by
numerous contemporaries, for example by Sylas Neville and his friends. This

question of inclusion and exclusion is central to eighteenth-century comic culture. Established satirical types affirmed a norm, a group of readers who were able to laugh, united, at the traits and misfortunes of those outside their group. Was jestbook culture misogynistic?[100] It was, but women also participated in the misogyny. *Fun for the Parlour*, expressly designed for a polite and female audience, is full of jokes about men who resent their shrewish wives, who celebrate their widowerhood, or who are generally unhappy in marriage. While there are jests about drunkenness, there are far fewer jokes about bad husbands. In this case, women laugh with, and at, men who are unhappy with other women, and the dynamics of exclusion are harder to pin down. But the prevalence of jokes at the expense of an outsider exposes the complex link between laughter and social pleasure. Much jestbook mirth, promoted as driving away sorrow, is predicated on laughing at others' misfortunes. Jesting affirmed social bonds amongst those enjoying the joke, but also promoted antagonisms and xenophobia by excluding victims of the jest.[101] As a recent study has shown, jestbooks were only one manifestation of a strain of ridicule and cruelty in eighteenth-century literature that is very hard to square with the notions of benevolence and sensibility that were so influential at the time.[102] We now know that the canon of jokes about disability, sexual violence, deformity, and poverty that runs throughout the comic literature of the era was read and enjoyed by men and women, and at prices ranging from one to three shillings, they were affordable only to those with considerable disposable income. Pleasure and social cohesion could be generated by jests and jokes—but those jokes were often predicated on forms of exclusion that contemporaries believed could induce melancholy. It is not surprising that in his handbook of melancholy, Robert Burton had a twofold attitude towards jokes: they are both conducive to happiness and also, in the form of "scoffes and calumnies," dangerous to the individuals who are mocked.[103]

Shared Laughter

We can begin to grasp the part comic verse, jokes, and riddles played in social networks by looking at the evidence of individual readers. Warwickshire Record office holds a letter series from the 1730s representing repeated exchanges between four well-educated young women in their late teens: Catherine Collingwood, Mary Pendarves, Anne Vernon, and Margaret Cavendish. Mary Pendarves would become the bluestocking Mary Delany, and Margaret Cavendish the Duchess of Portland, one of the greatest anti-quaries and collectors of the century. Catherine Collingwood would become Lady Throckmorton of Throckmorton Hall, and Anne Vernon, later Granville, another aristocratic hostess. At this stage in their lives, they were preoccupied with town gossip and social exchanges. Reading through the letters, it is soon clear that their epistles follow a formula: the addressee is praised, and then berated for not writing sooner. Reports on mutual acquaintances are given. The final section of the letter discusses reading, and usually offers an exchange of some sort of riddle, lighthearted rhyming jokes that affirm the friendship group. The games they circulate are similar to the word-based wit—the epigrams, acrostics, emblems, and anagrams on friends' names—prescribed by Burton as a preventative, or cure for melancholy.[104] They are a form of verbal recreation, a social currency, and are recognised as an important source of pleasure. Anne Vernon writes to Catherine Collingwood on 27 August 1734: "I'm grown fatter then when I had the pleasure of seeing you last, hope you increase in it also, my receipt is laughing, for we have with us a good humoured merry man that Miss Harcourt has persecuted with tricks, if you know of any do send me word, or any pretty ridles or rebus's."[105]

Other letters give an insight into the wider circulation of the jokes. Margaret Portland writes to Catherine Collingwood on 16 September 1733: "I have likewise sent you a Dictionary of hard words which by the time I see you I shall expect that you will be able to Converse with a Certain Gentleman who I hear is going to be married to Miss Spencer Don't put it in Fortunes Box for I must have it again adieu my dear Collyflower."[106] Portland writes a year later, on 16 September 1734: "the Ode I sent you I thought extremely silly but when I see you I will show you the Verses I told you of which are very pretty & you may Copy 'em if you please, they are not by the Club but by the Poetical Footman. I found out your Riddle & have Dazzled a good many People with it, I have sent you one in return that you may send to the Wit."[107] Portland's letters are often partly in code. The schemings between the mutual friends are coded as flowers, and everyone is named: there is a nettle, a rose, and a "sweet William." A letter of 20 October 1734 ends:

> I have had a Letter from the Wit who is very angry you don't write
> to her she sent me a Rebus which I desire you will send me the expla-
> nation of very soon.

If measure of Lace thats Less than a nail
& Where travellers hope to meet with good ale
The Shepherds retreat when the sun is at height
is the name of a Lady we love at first sight.[108]

The letter collection reveals an avidity in the receipt of these puzzles, and suggests that they will pass into further circulation, so the jokes entertain twice, once in the initial reading and then again when deployed amongst subsequent circles of friends or guests.

Other groups of women enjoyed similar exchanges of puzzles and rhyming word games. Elizabeth Tyrrell, the Kew housewife, was married to a City official and spent her time shuttling between visits and trips with her children; she records evenings spent with riddle collections: "George went to Tea at Mrs. Fishers to hear a young Lady play and sing—Mrs. Henshaw brought her books of Riddles and Charades &c which amused us the whole Evening—George came home soon after eleven well pleased with his visit."[109] Higher up the social spectrum, the manuscript notebooks of Elizabeth, Countess of Harcourt, record a game enjoyed by house guests at her home in Nuneham Courtney, Oxfordshire:

In the year 1799 it was a fashionable Jeu D'Esprit for persons to give each other words that were to be introduc'd into little Poems, some of these were shown to the society at Nuneham, they agreed to attempt amusing themselves in the same manner, & before they separated in the Morning, the following words were given.[110]

Lady Harcourt then goes on to list the terms that have been suggested by various members of the group. Her friend Sir Brook Boothby offers the rather pedestrian words "Marvellous" and "when"; Mrs. Hancock proposes "Robin" and "Modest," and (clearly the most aspirational of all) Lady Harcourt throws in "Tremor" and "Abstruse." At the end of the day, the friends gathered to show what they had concocted from the suggestions.

The attraction of such apparently slight pleasures might be seen in the context of the relative idleness and isolation of women of this time. Numerous contemporary publications articulate concerns about the effects of female idleness and boredom, related to the increasing leisure time of middling-sort and gentry women.[111] In Essay 80 of his *Idler*, Samuel Johnson writes of fashionable women who long for town life: "They who have already enjoyed the crowds and noise of the great city, know that their desire to return to it is little more than the restlessness of a vacant mind, that they are not so much led by hope as driven by disgust, and wish rather to leave the country than to see the town."[112]

Conduct writers of the late eighteenth century prescribed reading (the right sort of reading) as an antidote to the frustrations of female ennui. Thomas Gisborne observed that for the daughter of a country gentleman, "Visitors are not always to be found in the drawing-room; the card-table cannot always be filled up; the county town affords a ball but once a month." In the face of such frustrated sociability, young women should draw on the resources of domestic amusements: "Family conversation, needle-work, a book, even a book that is not a novel, in a word, any occupation is found preferable to the tediousness of a constant want of employment."[113] We get an inkling of the boredom of rural retreat in the letters of the Portland circle. Anne Vernon writes from Oxfordshire to Catherine Collingwood on May 24, 1734: "I hope London is more agreable than Cockthrop, for tis here as cold as xmas, and as wet, so I have nothing to doe but work and read my Eyes out."[114] In a later letter, again sent from a country house, she complains: "Do not be so Cruel as to Imagine I don't feel very sensibly the leaving my agreable Friends in London, but I brag of the pleasures of my Solitude more to show my Philosophy than any great Joy they give me, for nothing alone can be very delightful; you Contribute to my entertainment many Ways." Yet she also makes claims for the benefits of rural seclusion: "I had rather you injoy'd some rural retreat, and much rather it were in our neighbourhood, for all country pleasures give me so much pleasure that I pity all my Freinds who do not tast them or have no Opportunitys to learn, for I am persuayded it is like other inclinations, improved by seeing the reasonableness of it."[115]

Vernon's attitude towards country living veers between bored disdain and philosophical encomium. The jokes and games she shares with her friends simulate a circle of wits—on paper—as a way of livening up her rural existence. Clearly, the problem of idleness within the retirement of an isolated country house was only really a problem for those fairly high up the social scale—but the overall trend towards women's lack of engagement in the world of work, and the need to turn their time to account, is one way of explaining the proliferation of polite amusements in printed form. As we can see from the printed pocket books that became increasingly popular from the mid–eighteenth century onwards, puzzles, riddles, and enigmas were considered to be an important part of the polite equipage of a woman. One of the regular features of the *Lady's Magazine* was "Enigmatical Lists," which with anagrams and anecdotes provided appropriate ways for polite young woman to spend their time.

❧

The practices described in this chapter suggest some of the ways in which poetry moved between people as it was borrowed, transformed, laughed, and cried at. Many of the most enduring verse forms are premised on the idea of a poem as part of an exchange from one speaker to another—the verse epistle, the Horatian ode, the comic dialogue are inherently social forms. But as the examples illustrate, almost anything could be shared. The tradition of commonplacing gives us an insight into the ways in which readers personalised what they read and juxtaposed a world of amateur homemade culture with that culled from other, often ephemeral, print sources. In the notebooks of ordinary readers we can discern the creativity inherent in practices of collecting, and what was often a flagrant disregard for issues of authorial property. And in the miscellanies and elocution compilations we see the circular relationship between print and manuscript, as print mimicked handwritten forms, and was then taken up by individual readers to go back into manuscript circulation. Both printed and manuscript collections of verse also illustrate the appeal of lighter forms of literature—the hundreds of riddles and epigrams with which an increasingly leisured class amused itself. Readerly self-improvement came hand in hand with an appetite for the comic, the witty, and the bawdy.

6. Drama and Recital

for we have had all this winter our proper times for everything in
our chamber what is good and in the evening while Nanny and I
did work [Betty] red playes and what else deverted us which made
the long nights pass a way the more pleasently to us all
—Mary Clarke to Edward Clarke, April 1700

In the eighteenth century readers consumed plays as avidly as we now read novels. Texts designed for the theatre swiftly migrated into domestic environments, where they had alternative lives—read silently, adapted into narrative form, recited, or turned into amateur performance. Both the vogue for elocution and the rise of private theatricals at the end of the century shaped perceptions of amateur drama and recitation. There were clear distinctions between reading, reciting, and performing, and these were linked to fundamental issues of propriety.

To Act or Not to Act

The Bertrams' amateur performance of *Lovers Vows* in Jane Austen's *Mansfield Park* is probably the most famous fictional example of the performance of drama at home in this period:

> To the Theater he went, and reached it just in time to witness the
> first meeting of his father and his friend. Sir Thomas had been a
> good deal surprized to find candles burning in his room; and on
> casting his eye round it, to see other symptoms of recent habitation
> and a general air of confusion in the furniture. The removal of the
> bookcase from before the billiard-room door struck him especially,

but he had scarcely more than time to feel astonished at all this, before there were sounds from the billiard-room to astonish him still farther. Some one was talking there in a very loud accent; he did not know the voice—*more* than talking—almost hallooing. He stept to the door, rejoicing at that moment in having the means of immediate communication, and opening it, found himself on the stage of a theater, and opposed to a ranting young man, who appeared likely to knock him down backwards.[1]

The passage above describes Sir Thomas Bertram's surprised disapproval on returning home to find rehearsals in full flow. It is a puzzling moment in Austen's novel for many modern readers, an instance of historical disconnect. Generations of readers have wondered over exactly what was so wrong with staging a play at home. They have interpreted the incident as an indicator of Sir Thomas's tyrannical tendencies, or as Austen's way of signalling the theme of dissimulation.[2] Yet placing this scene within the context of eighteenth-century domestic culture, we can see that it also neatly frames its era's moral distinctions between recitation and performance. In an attempt to override the virtuous Edmund Bertram's scruples about the *Lovers' Vows* performance, Tom Bertram had earlier reminded the would-be actors that his father had always encouraged domestic recitation: "and for any thing of the acting, spouting, reciting kind, I think he has always a decided taste. I am sure he encouraged it in us as boys. How many a time have we mourned over the dead body of Julius Caesar, and *to be'd* and not *to be'd*, in this very room, for his amusement! And I am sure, *my name was Norval*, every evening of my life through one Christmas holidays."[3] Tom reminisces affectionately about the way in which their family had read aloud bits of famous plays, mentioning here lines from *Hamlet*, and from John Home's hugely popular blank verse tragedy, *Douglas*. But in his linking of "acting, spouting, reciting" Tom conflates disingenuously the planned private theatricals, of which his father would not have approved, with the social recitation that was widely acceptable.[4]

It is not a confusion that his father, or many others, would have made. As we shall see later on, the late eighteenth century saw a vogue for amateur dramatic performance, largely associated with a social elite, which generated significant moral debate. But for many middling-sort eighteenth-century readers, it was seen as perfectly fine, even morally improving, to *read* plays, or parts of plays, aloud at home. The quotations Tom alludes to were probably taken from one of the most popular recital miscellanies of the late eighteenth century, William Enfield's *The Speaker* (1774).[5] Enfield was a Unitarian minister and tutor in *belles lettres* at Warrington dissenting academy, and his book was designed to enable his pupils to attain a "just and graceful Elocution." Like many other compilations of the time, *The Speaker* yoked together moral and social improvement.[6] It contained over 140 passages of varying length, and included narrative, didactic, and argumentative pieces, orations and harangues, dialogues, and descriptive and pathetic extracts.[7] The selections were excerpted from literary journals, and from works of individual writers, and the collection had a huge circulation—it was reprinted, plagiarised, and pirated up until the middle of the nineteenth century. Enfield prefaced the book with a substantial essay on elocution, in which he argued that oratorical skill was not to be used by readers merely for social show, but for speaking in public life.[8] Yet as Tom's reminiscence suggests, the collection was also much used for domestic entertainment, in this case, during the Christmas holidays, a period long associated with "gambols."

Enfield does not refer to named elocutionists as models, but other similar compilations traded hard on celebrity association. *Sheridan and Henderson's Practical Method of Reading and Reciting English Poetry,* which we came across earlier, was published in 1796, two decades after the heyday of the elocution movement. It described itself as "a Necessary Introduction to *Dr. Enfield's Speaker,*" and offered practical step-by-step advice on how to develop good oral reading skills. In the preface, the editor lamented the "dry method of theoretical forms" and explained that his new approach was to draw on the evidence of his own experience of celebrity rendition, where "some great master of elocution has afforded considerable pleasure in the delivery."[9] In this case, the great masters were the actor John Henderson, sometimes known as "the Bath Roscius," and the actor-writer and elocutionist Thomas Sheridan, both of whom had reputations as tutors as well as stage actors. The editor claimed special access to these figures, boasting that many of the extracts "I have heard read or recited either in public or in the hour of social enjoyment."[10] We are told that he had witnessed Mr. Henderson read David Mallet's poem "William and Margaret" "in private."[11] Some of the commentary takes the form of a reconstruction of performances by Sheridan and Henderson. Here is Hamlet to the Ghost, as delivered by Sheridan—the interpolated passages are the instruction offered by the editor:

Angels and ministers of grace defend us!

With a low, solemn, awful *voice, as if repeating a short prayer. Then pausing ere you proceed, you raise your voice a little, not forgetting the great solemnity of* tone *and* manner:

> Be thou a spirit of health or goblin damn'd,
> Bring with thee airs from heav'n or blasts from hell,
> Be thy intent wicked, or charitable,
> Thou com'st in such a *questionable* shape,
> That I will speak to thee.

In all these lines observe the same solemnity as before-mentioned, and the word questionable *to be spoken with a peculiarly marked* strong emphasis, *a kind of* burst of expression, *as if feeling a degree of confidence on the supposition that the ghost may be* questioned *without impropriety*

> I'll call thee Hamlet,
> King, father, royal Dane:

Here Mr. Sheridan used to stop for a considerable time, as if waiting for an answer, and then, with a kind of burst of exclamation proceeded—

> Oh! Answer me;
> Let me not *burst* in ignorance;

"burst"—*he used to particularly mark.*[12]

This combination of interpretation and memorial reconstruction offers an intriguing example of the historical performance of Shakespeare. It also demonstrates the close relationship between theatrical performance and the home consumption of drama. On one hand, as we saw already, domestic recitation was strictly differentiated from the morally dubious practices of dressing up and acting out plays at home, and readers were encouraged not to mimic the "cant" of the public stage. Yet on the other, guidance on how to read well was marketed by its association with contemporary plays and actors. The *Sheridan and Henderson* reader was subtitled a "practical method of reading and reciting English Poetry," and most of its contents were not, in fact, taken from plays. Shakespeare's plays were extracted to form stand-alone speeches such as "Othello's Apology to the Senate," "The Seven Ages of Life," and "Hamlet's Address to the Ghost of his Father." In the detailed instructions accompanying each piece the editor addressed his readers' practical hurdles. How was one supposed to pronounce "jocund"? (As if it was spelt "joccund.")[13] Did one pronounce "sans" in the seven ages speech from *As You Like It* the French way or English? (Answer: the English way.)[14]

The reading of plays in the home was full of challenges that were distinct from stage practice. How were you supposed to differentiate between characters when a play was read by one person? In *Chironomia*, Gilbert Austin explained what you should not do: "In the reading of plays in this style [in mere private and family society], the names of the characters are sometimes read in a sort of dry under voice before the passages they are supposed to speak: but this awkward expedient should not be used except to prevent ambiguity [. . .] A person of taste and judgement will feel when he may divest his reading of this incumbrance, and will know when he ought to submit to it."[15] There was also the question of how far to go in impersonating a character—not too far, according to John Rice, author of *An Introduction to the Art of Reading with Energy and Propriety* (1765): "A Reader is not required to wear a Hump with King Richard, nor a great Belly with Sir John Falstaff: Nay, he is not required even to saw the Air with his Hands, to make Faces, to laugh, to cry, nor indeed take any one Step in order to make the Hearer think him a Person of the Drama."[16]

Shakespeare and the Home

The story of the Stratford playwright in print in the home illustrates the way in which celebrity, domesticity, and morality were entwined in the consumption of drama—often in unexpected ways. Over the course of the eighteenth century, Shakespeare became ever more firmly ensconced as the national bard. In the 1660s and 1670s it was still quite normal to discuss the comparative merits of Shakespeare versus Jonson or Beaumont and Fletcher, but a hundred years later he was in a league of his own. The Shakespeare Jubilee, the monument in Westminster Abbey, and the Ladies Shakespeare Club evidence his institutionalization within the national consciousness.[17] Readers could embellish their homes with earthenware figurines of the Bard and his characters, including Ophelia, Cleopatra, and Falstaff.[18] Shakespeare was often depicted leaning on a pedestal with his works beside him. The Derby factory produced three versions of this piece in the late 1750s to mid-1760s, often sold as a pair with one of John Milton (the pairing was a common one, and can also be found in Liverpool porcelain) (fig. 36).[19] They were available both in earthenware and Derby porcelain. The figure, which is based on Shakespeare's monument in Poet's Corner, replaces the Latin of the original with some lines from *The Tempest*.[20] Shakespeare points to a scroll inscribed with a slightly mangled version of Prospero's lines from Act IV:

> The Cloud capt Tow'rs, The Gorgeous Palaces,
> The Solemn Temples, The Great Globe itself,
> Yea all which it Inherit, Shall Dissolve;
> And like the baseless Fabrick of a Vision,
> Leave not a wrack behind.

The words of the aging Milanese ruler are here, as so often, taken as an auto-biographical statement of Shakespeare's views on the imagination, and in this way, the object embodies the historical man, the text of the play, and the bard's memorialization as the great voice of English imaginative writing.

Fig. 36. Porcelain figures of John Milton and William Shakespeare, made in England, c. 1765 (Victoria and Albert Museum, S.76-1988 and 91-1870; © Victoria and Albert Museum, London)

Along with these public and material forms of bardolatry, the era saw the proliferation of a publishing industry around Shakespeare's plays. On the one hand there was a spate of scholarly editions of the plays, in which editors such as Edmund Malone, Lewis Theobald, and Alexander Pope vied with one another in the fastidiousness of their glosses and emendations, and in their attempts to conflate folios and quartos to achieve the holy grail of an original manuscript text. Yet at the same time we also see the rise of more accessible "acting" editions of Shakespeare's plays, which repackaged the contents of Shakespeare's archaic folios for a readership accustomed to reading plays in more accessible modern editions. The reshaping of Shakespeare for modern nonspecialist readers began in the early eighteenth century. In 1709 Jacob Tonson published a series of octavo and duodecimo editions of Shakespeare's plays, edited by the dramatist Nicholas Rowe. These editions were aimed at a small section of the reading public—they were expensive, and at 30 shillings a set were a serious investment. They were no longer in folio format, but in smaller, more portable octavo, with minimal annotation, and were edited so that they more closely resembled modern plays.[21] Amongst other changes, Rowe added and corrected stage directions (especially entrances and exits) to assist readers in imagining the actions of the characters, and perhaps most significantly, he divided nearly half the plays into acts and scenes. One of the most heavily advertised features of the edition was the inclusion of forty new engravings of scenes from Shakespeare. These illustrations depicted costumes, scenes, and staging techniques from the early eighteenth century. Interestingly, not all the plays featured in the illustrations were part of current or recent repertoire. Although Tonson could rely on the fact that theatregoers would recognise and buy *Othello*, *The Merry Wives of Windsor*, or *Julius Caesar* because they would have seen these plays, there was a challenge in selling others, such as *All's Well that Ends Well* or *The Comedy of Errors*, which hadn't been performed for a century. One way of creating a readership for these nonperformed plays was to edit and illustrate them as if they *had* been seen within living memory, imagining scenes in action to suggest that these unknown plays were as worthy of production as the more celebrated dramas.[22] So the early purchasers of the Tonson-Rowe edition could sit at home and imagine the glories of a production of, for example, *The Winter's Tale*, which had in fact not actually been seen on stage for many decades. This domestic edition of Shakespeare's plays created the impression of a theatrical reality that did not actually exist.

Although the Tonson editions were smaller, they were still costly and exclusive. The Bard would not become truly popularised in print until his works became much cheaper.[23] The most significant innovation in the domestication of Shakespeare in the eighteenth century came some sixty years later, in 1773–74, with *Bell's Edition of Shakespeare's Plays as they are now Performed at the Theatres Royal in London, Regulated by the Prompt Books of each House*. As its title suggests, this edition compiled by John Bell was derived from contemporary theatrical performance, the plays edited in accordance with the prompter's text. It was hugely popular, selling 800 sets in the first week, and was the most influential edition of its kind.[24] The reach of Bell's edition went far beyond existing versions of Shakespeare, its estimated sales of 4,500 for the first three editions dwarfing those of Samuel Johnson's or Lewis Theobald's scholarly editions.[25]

Bell's edition, like Tonson's, was not encumbered by much apparatus. It was a small format, came with illustrations, and was composed with a view to "correctness, neatness, ornament, utility, and cheapness of price."[26] Critics often refer to Bell's edition as the first "acting edition" of Shakespeare's plays.[27] But in fact, like the printed playtexts of the seventeenth century, which often had commonplace markers in the margins, these were editions designed for reading at home, aloud or silently—not acting. The plays were prefaced with a long essay on the art of elocution by Francis Gentleman, a one-time actor and now editor who had previously published an elocutionary treatise entitled *The Orator: or, English Assistant* (1771). In his essay for Bell's edition, Gentleman cautioned readers tempted to confuse home and stage:

> When I recommend *action*, I would not be supposed to intend that a speaker should be in continual motion; or that, puppet-like, he is to lift first one hand and then another, merely to lay them down again.—No,—I would have motions few, easy, graceful; and, for my own part, I know not how a declaimer can possibly feel and stand stock-still: but, admit the possibility of this, I will venture to say there is but little probability that his audience will think him in earnest: I know that some delicate persons are afraid of becoming too *theatrical;* but there is a very wide difference between the action of an *orator* and an *actor*.[28]

Bell's edition of Shakespeare's plays was meant to aid those intending to recite at home. It was not an edition for fully developed dramatic performance. Gentleman's essay, like other elocution guides of the time, took readers through individual words and phrases, drawing on theories of the passions, as pioneered by Charles Le Brun. He plucked out sections from the Psalms, Thomas Otway, and Milton, in addition to Shakespeare's plays, to show readers how to deliver the text. The notes to individual plays assumed that the texts were for reading, rather than acting, even if reading wasn't always the best medium. Of *Richard III* Gentleman writes, "Upon the whole it must always read well, but act better,"[29] and of *Twelfth Night*, "Action must render it more pleasing than perusal."[30]

Yet again, there was a mixed message about the relationship between the home and the stage. The reader was definitely not supposed to imitate the practices of contemporary actors, but at the same time, the collection was dedicated to the great Shakespearean actor David Garrick and was accompanied by an engraving of him, while the lists of *dramatis personae* identify specific actors with parts. Gentleman's notes offered a combination of comments on theatrical performance, literary criticism, and practical advice to the would-be reciter.[31] In the first act of *Macbeth*, we are informed that "The characters of *Ross* and *Angus* have been judiciously blended, at *Covent-Garden Theatre*, into those of *Macduff* and *Lenox*, to make them more worthy the attention of good performers and the audience."[32] Then, introducing Macbeth and Banquo for the first time, Gentleman addresses the amateur reader, giving instruction on how to perform the parts "*Macbeth* requires a bold, graceful, soldier-like figure . . . Banquo, being confined to level speaking, demands little more than a good external appearance."[33] And then commenting on Angus's speech on Cawdor's rebellious conduct, he proffers his own critical valuation, noting a "strange lapse" in Shakespeare's characterization of Angus.[34] These interventions seem to be based on an expectation that private readers wanted to understand the plays they read from multiple viewpoints. They wanted to know how to speak individual parts, how to evaluate the play in literary terms, and how to see the ways in which the text they were reading differed from what they might have seen on stage. The theoretical distinctions that modern critics make between "reading" and "acting" editions of the time are too simple to accommodate the multiple ways in which eighteenth-century readers encountering drama thought of themselves. Such readers were at the same time literary critics, audience members, and reciters of Shakespeare's plays.

Bell and Gentleman thought that in order to make the Bard suitable for domestic reading, he would need to be censored. Gentleman wondered, in his preface, "Why then should not the noble monuments he has left us of unri-valled ability, be restored to due proportion and natural lustre, by sweeping off those cobwebs, and that dust of depraved opinion, which SHAKESPEARE was unfortunately forced to throw on them?[35] He explained that he followed contemporary stage practice in omitting from his text passages that were indelicate or redundant. Noting that there might still be some merit in certain lines too lewd for polite rendition, he explains that "some passages, of great merit for the closet, are never spoken; such, though omitted in the text, we have carefully preserved in the notes."[36] Most of the time these notes draw attention to lyrical passages cut in performance but worthy of note to the reader. Glossing Romeo's lines on the poisoned Juliet's lips, he observes: "This speech is well curtailed for stage utterance; but these two lines, which come in after *lips,* well deserve notice; *Which ev'n in pure and vestal modesty, / Still blush, as thinking their own kisses sin.*"[37] Elsewhere Gentleman suggests cuts not usually made in performance but required in the home. In Act I, Scene i, of *Othello,* Gentleman includes Iago's "Sir, you're robbed" speech, and puts in italics the lines "Ev'n now, ev'n very now, an old black ram / Is tupping your white ewe." He tells his readers "The lines distinguished by italics, for sake of decency, should be omitted, though usually spoken."[38]

Gentleman's comments suggest that for the readers of Bell's edition of Shakespeare, private recitation was guided by what was deemed acceptable in public performance. His editorial choices also tell us something about how he imagined the books being used at home. The idea that some passages were kept because they were "of great merit for the closet" suggests that the assumed setting was social reading in a mixed public room, such as the parlour, but that the owner or reader of the edition could also find a quiet moment in the closet to enjoy the censored material.

Bowdlerizing Shakespeare

Bell's edition of Shakespeare had a wider reach and influence than any other contemporary edition of the dramatist. In offering an accessible, sanitised version of the plays, authorised by contemporary performance practice, it paved the way for the most famous trimming of Shakespeare of the era—Thomas Bowdler's *Family Shakspeare,* which appeared in various versions in 1807 and 1818. Bowdler, the man whose editorial stance was memorialized in a whole new verb, *to bowdlerize,* made his aims clear in the subtitle to his work: "in Which Nothing is Added to the Original Text but those Words and Expressions are Omitted Which Cannot with Propriety be Read Aloud in a Family."[39]

Thomas Bowdler had originally trained as a doctor, but had ceased practising and was a member of the bluestocking Elizabeth Montagu's circle. He involved himself in a series of philanthropic projects and was actively engaged in the "Proclamation Society," a group formed in 1787 to enforce a royal proclamation against impiety and vice. Despite the title of the work for which he has become famous, Bowdler was not himself a family man; after a brief and unhappy marriage to a widow at the age of fifty-two, he did not have any children, and lived as a bachelor. Nor was he, in fact, the original author of the family Shakespeare. His sister Henrietta Maria Bowdler had originated the project at Bath in 1807, with the publication of the first edition of *The Family Shakespeare* (the title was spelt differently in his sister's edition). His sister's edition had contained only twenty plays, avoiding such perilous works as *Hamlet*, and throughout had excised sexually explicit passages and religious references that might offend the Anglican reader. Thomas Bowdler had assumed the authorship of this edition by 1809, probably in order to protect the reputations of his sister and the family. His own edition, not published until 1818, included more plays, and restored some of the cuts his sister had made merely because she thought them trivial or uninteresting. One modern critic of the edition claims that Thomas Bowdler made his excisions "rather as an unusually scrupulous television producer might now." His sister, who took out in addition anything she thought was absurd or uninteresting, "treated Shakespeare rather as a normal television producer would."[40] Yet despite this salutary modern parallel, Thomas Bowdler has become infamous for his moralistic intervention in Shakespeare's reception history.

Bowdler's *Family Shakspeare* squarely located morality within the home. "Family" in this title was used to invoke a domestic propriety. The 1807 edition stated that "the present publication . . . is intended to be read in private societies, and to be placed in the hands of young persons of both sexes."[41] And interestingly, Bowdler was to identify the origins of his edition in his own experiences of reading at home: "My first idea of the FAMILY SHAKSPEARE arose from the recollection of my father's custom of reading in this manner to his family. Shakspeare (with whom no person was better acquainted) was a frequent subject of the evening's entertainment. In the perfection of reading few men were equal to my father; and such was his

good taste, his delicacy, and his prompt discretion, that his family listened
with delight to Lear, Hamlet, and Othello, without knowing that these match-
less tragedies contained words and expressions improper to be pronounced."[42]

Bowdler's edition, like Bell's, is premised on an image of patriarchal
delivery, of a man's reading aloud a text that has been made suitable for
mixed company. He fondly imagines potential users of the *Family Shakspeare:*

> It certainly is my wish, and it has been my study to exclude from this
> publication whatever is unfit to be read aloud by a gentleman to a
> company of ladies. I can hardly imagine a more pleasing occupation
> for a winter's evening in the country, than for a father to read one of
> Shakspeare's plays to his family circle. My object is to enable him to
> do so without incurring the danger of falling unawares among
> words and expressions which are of such a nature as to raise a blush
> on the cheek of modesty, or render it necessary for the reader to
> pause and examine the sequel, before he proceeds further in the
> entertainment of the evening.[43]

In a culture of reading aloud, such hazards were an issue. Like the nine
o'clock watershed, or filters for Internet browsing, Bowdler's edition offered
a way of securing one's loved ones from harmful material in an unpoliced
cultural marketplace. A copy of *The Family Shakspeare* could be left in the
parlour, or handed around the tea table with impunity, because potential
dangers had been removed. This was an edition that spoke to the concerns of
a readership without extensive literary knowledge—the reciter did not need
to have a deep familiarity with all of Shakespeare's plays to know what was
appropriate, because Bowdler had preselected for him. We know that readers
in the eighteenth century "improved" texts while reading them aloud to their
families. Frances Burney praises readers who censor the texts before them.
She writes of one family friend: "It is not possible for a man to make a better
husband than Mr. Rishton does . . . He is reading Spencer's 'Fairy Queen' to
us, in which he is extremely delicate, omitting whatever, to the poet's
disgrace, has crept in that is improper to a woman's ear."[44] She later notes
approvingly her husband's censoring of *Gil Blas* for their young son: "excellent Father judiciously omits or changes all such passages as might tarnish the
lovely purity of his innocence by any dangerous impressions."[45]

In presenting his version of Shakespeare, Bowdler enabled any reader
to approach the Bard with the confidence of one who knew its moral pitfalls,

and how to avoid them. His censoring of Shakespeare took the form of plot and language. He replaced the exclamations to "God" to Heaven; Ophelia's death was referred to as an accidental drowning (to avoid the suggestion of suicide); and he made substantial excisions in *Romeo and Juliet* and *Timon of Athens*. Some characters were removed entirely—Doll Tearsheet does not appear at all. At other times Bowdler struggled with the decision to cut, and in the case of *Othello*, which he acknowledges is "little suited to family reading," he suggests that the (presumably male) reader might enjoy its pleasures alone:[46]

> I have endeavoured to erase the objectionable expressions which so frequently occur in the original text, whenever it could be done consistently with the character and situation of the speaker; but if, after all that I have omitted, it shall still be thought that this inimitable tragedy is not sufficiently correct for family reading, I would advise the transferring of it from the parlour to the cabinet, where the perusal will not only delight the poetic taste, but convey useful and important instruction both to the heart and the understanding of the reader.[47]

Here we see a very material distinction between different kinds of reading at home—the book in the parlour and the book in the cabinet. Some readers, it seems, could have their poetic taste gratified even by a play perceived as objectionable, so long as it was in the closed cabinet, not lying around in a public room.

Bowdler's *Family Shakspeare* did not achieve significant popularity until its reputation had been oxygenated by a prominent exchange of views about its merits in *Blackwood's Magazine* and the *Edinburgh Review*, some fifteen years after Henrietta Bowdler's first publication and five years after her brother's. In February 1821 a critical review in *Blackwood's* described the *Family Shakspeare* as no more than a "piece of prudery in pasteboard."[48] This view was stoutly countered in October of the same year by the paper's rival, the *Edinburgh Review*, whose editor Francis Jeffrey declared that, after Bowdler, other editions had become obsolete. Going much further than Bowdler had done, he argued: "As what cannot be pronounced in decent company cannot well afford much pleasure in the closet, we think it is better, every way, that what cannot be spoken, and ought not to have been written, should now cease to be printed."[49] This idea that nothing should be read unless suitable for decent company echoes sentiments found in contemporary conduct literature for women. The author of *An Enquiry into the Duties of the Female Sex* (1798) had earlier suggested that young women be guided in their reading matter by its suitability for reading in company: "Let whatever she peruses in her most private hours be such as she needs not to be ashamed of reading aloud to those, whose good opinion she is most anxious to observe."[50]

Lord Jeffrey's defence of Bowdler's method was used as a frontispiece in subsequent editions of Bowdler's text for the next sixty years, and the exposure guaranteed almost constant reprinting of the text for the rest of the century. From this point onwards, the market for excised editions grew and grew. By 1850 there were seven expurgated editions of Shakespeare on the market, and by 1900 that number had increased to fifty.[51] Many families in the nineteenth century would have encountered the works of Shakespeare, and other authors, only in this form. Modern critics have tended to see this phenomenon as an instance of Victorian prudery. Yet the history of editing Shakespeare for the home in the eighteenth century shows the way in which the radical censoring of the plays was initially born out of eighteenth-century politeness, the elocution movement, and the contemporary norms of theatrical performance. Moreover, the wide availability of Shakespeare's plays for family reading had a legacy the Bowdlers could not have predicted. The decadent poet Algernon Swinburne is perhaps *The Family Shakspeare's* most unlikely defender: "More nauseous and more foolish cant was never chattered than that which would deride the memory or deprecate the merits of Bowdler, no man ever did better service to Shakespeare than the man who made it possible to put him into the hands of intelligent and imaginative children."[52]

Plays in Parts

Swinburne was not alone in seeing the benefits of reading selected passages of Shakespeare to children. Diarists in the eighteenth century regularly testify to the practice of parents reading aloud scenes from Shakespeare to their offspring, choosing passages that would be striking, comprehensible, and wholesome. The Shakespeare editions produced by Bell and Bowdler dealt with the matter of finding the wholesome, at least in the case of Shakespeare. The demand for collections that curated drama for home use, portioning it out into forms suitable for recitation or browsing, is evident in the many other eighteenth-century compilations containing stand-alone excerpts that could be read to groups of listeners young and old. Some of these drew on the celebrity associations of the theatre, and were often titled "spouting collections," ostensibly aimed at the spouting clubs that flourished after the elocution movement. Selections of prologues and epilogues, often the most easily extractable elements of a play, proliferated throughout the eighteenth century. These ranged from *A Second and Last Collection of the most Celebrated Prologues and Epilogues Spoken at the Theatres of Drury-Lane and Lincolns-Inn* (1727)[53] to *The Court of Thespis.*[54] *The British Spouter: or Stage Assistant* (1773)[55] contained prologues and epilogues recently spoken at the different theatres, and identified original speakers. In its introduction, its editor stated that "the Prologue to a Play, whether a Tragedy or a Comedy, ought to contain the whole Quintessence of the Plot, and at the same time be adapted to the reigning Taste of the Age."[56] Part of the appeal of the prologue or epilogue was the fact that it encapsulated, in some sense, a whole play, yet at the same time was a set piece that referred to contemporary fashions and scandals, giving its readers a taster of what they might imagine to be the *beau monde.* Other works combined song and recitation: cheap songbooks from the early nineteenth century gathered material from the pantomimes and musical entertainments at the transpontine theatres, and offered the words to songs "as sung by" alongside comic passages designed to be read in dialect. *The Jovial Songster, Liston's Drolleries, The Actor's Regalio,* and tens of other similar titles enabled a variety of forms of spoken and sung entertainment, packaged for the domestic market.

The abundance of drama in extract form tallies with the evidence of contemporary readers. It is not easy to know which editions or forms of plays were consumed by particular readers, but it is clear from letters and diary entries that when people read drama at home together, they often did so without completing a whole play. They were quite likely to read only a short passage—a selected speech, or a witty dialogue. Diary entries illustrate the way in which a play could be picked up and put down—Eliza Tyrrell spends an hour of reading *Much Ado*, in company, while a group of women are occupied with their needlework.[57] Elsewhere we can piece together anecdotal snippets about reading habits to understand how families read drama at home. The prodigious acting talents of the child actor William Betty were put down to his early exposure in the family circle: "His father, his mother, and his sisters, were all fond of plays and players, and the female part of the family were accustomed to recite scenes from their favourite pieces. Mrs. Betty was an accomplished speaker, and exercised her son from an early period of his existence, in recitation from the best dramatic authors."[58]

One of the consequences of the practice of excerpting was that it blurred the distinction between the genres of drama and verse. By the time lines from *She Stoops to Conquer*, *Zenobia*, or *Tancred and Sigismunda* had been reassembled for casual browsing, they read much like a poem. Many collections actually presented their dramatic extracts as verse: *Thesaurus Dramaticus*, published in 1724, claimed to contain "all the celebrated passages, soliloquys, similes, descriptions, and other poetical beauties" found in English plays ancient and modern (fig. 37).[59] It is made up of snippets taken from sixteenth- and seventeenth-century tragedies that are arranged under thematic headings, beginning with "Absence." Like Edmund Bysshe's collection of extracts of English verse, the compilation mingled verse and drama to create a series of extracts exemplifying verbal and imaginative skill, rather than coherent poetic or dramatic forms.

But was this trade in extraction a good thing for drama? In "On the Tragedies of Shakespeare" Charles Lamb exclaimed:

> How far the very custom of hearing any thing *spouted*, withers and blows upon a fine passage, may be seen in those speeches from Henry the Fifth, &c. which are currently in the mouths of school- boys from their being to be found in *Enfield Speakers*, and such kind of books. I confess myself utterly unable to appreciate that cele- brated soliloquy in Hamlet, beginning "To be or not to be," or to tell whether it be good, bad, or indifferent, it has been so handled and pawed about by declamatory boys and men.[60]

In their *Tales from Shakespeare* (1807), a series of illustrated stories designed for children, Charles and his sister Mary Lamb hoped to offer an example of how Shakespeare might be read afresh, without the engrained familiarity of overquoted set pieces. It is a sign of the burgeoning orality of reading that recitation culture had become so widespread that it threatened to render its central texts meaningless.

The transmission of literary works, often in cheaper forms of print, enabled them to change genres and be used in different ways. Shakespeare's plays were novelized for children by the Lambs' *Tales from Shakespeare*. By the 1820s and 1830s there was a thriving market in the adaptation of

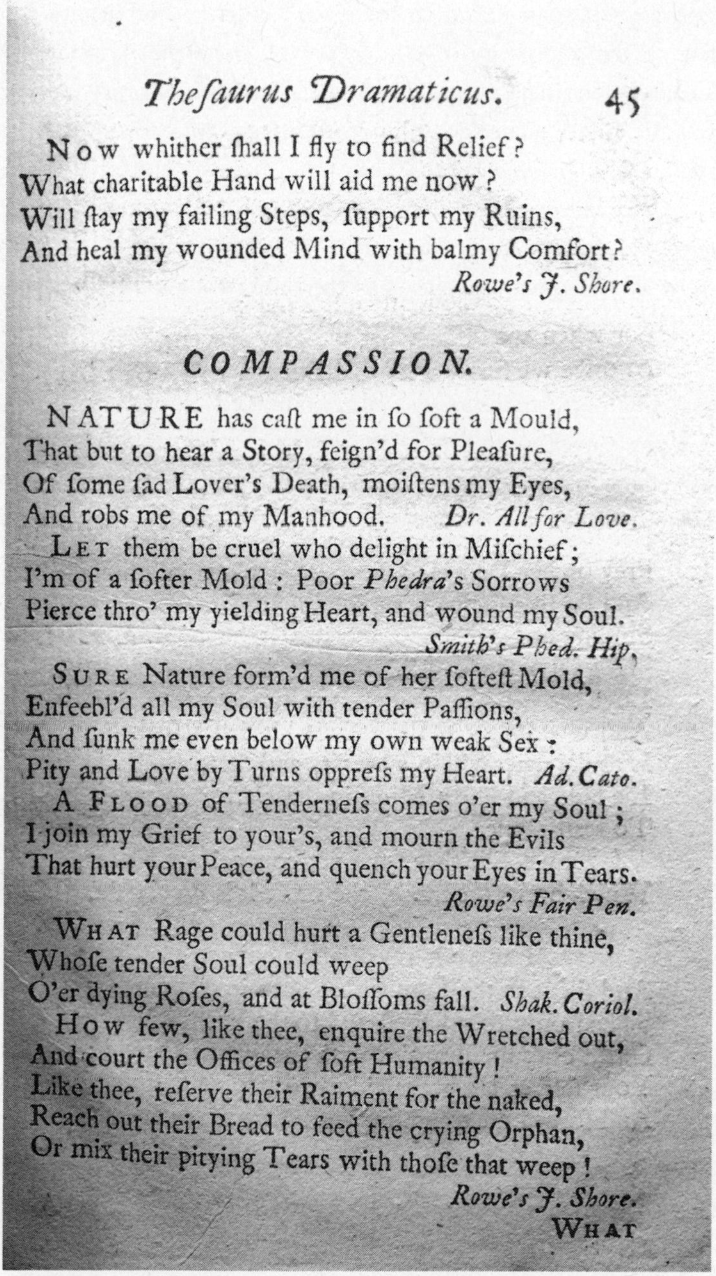

Thefaurus Dramaticus.   45

Now whither fhall I fly to find Relief?
What charitable Hand will aid me now?
Will ftay my failing Steps, fupport my Ruins,
And heal my wounded Mind with balmy Comfort?

Rowe's J. Shore.

COMPASSION.

NATURE has caft me in fo foft a Mould,
That but to hear a Story, feign'd for Pleafure,
Of fome fad Lover's Death, moiftens my Eyes,
And robs me of my Manhood.   *Dr. All for Love.*
Let them be cruel who delight in Mifchief;
I'm of a fofter Mold: Poor *Phedra's* Sorrows
Pierce thro' my yielding Heart, and wound my Soul.

Smith's Phed. Hip.

Sure Nature form'd me of her fofteft Mold,
Enfeebl'd all my Soul with tender Paffions,
And funk me even below my own weak Sex:
Pity and Love by Turns opprefs my Heart. *Ad. Cato.*
A Flood of Tendernefs comes o'er my Soul;
I join my Grief to your's, and mourn the Evils
That hurt your Peace, and quench your Eyes in Tears.

Rowe's Fair Pen.

What Rage could hurt a Gentlenefs like thine,
Whofe tender Soul could weep
O'er dying Rofes, and at Bloffoms fall. *Shak. Coriol.*
How few, like thee, enquire the Wretched out,
And court the Offices of foft Humanity!
Like thee, referve their Raiment for the naked,
Reach out their Bread to feed the crying Orphan,
Or mix their pitying Tears with thofe that weep!

Rowe's J. Shore.

WHAT

Fig. 37. Page from *Thesaurus Dramaticus: Containing all the Celebrated Passages, Soliloquies, Similes, Descriptions, and other Poetical Beauties*, 2 vols. (London, 1724) (© The British Library Board, 643.b.10-12)

contemporary plays in narrative form for adults, as publishers sought to capitalise on the popularity of contemporary stage plays, issuing them as short, cheap prose tracts. John Duncombe's miniature library of tiny books of "Dramatic Tales" turned contemporary stage plays into stories for reading at home: "The plan of the present volume may be conceived as entirely novel—the prevailing taste for the Drama and its continued rise in public estimation, induced the commencement of a series of Original Tales founded upon most of the approved pieces as they are produced upon the English stage."[61] These editions shrank five-act plays into tiny, affordable pamphlets, issued weekly or fortnightly depending on the season, suggesting a decreased market in summer months.[62] The tales combined narrative with dialogue, capturing some of the imagery of the original while making the language accessible: the edition of *Coriolanus* retains Menenius's extended analogy of the citizenry as a belly.

This kind of adaptation enabled the redactor to improve the endings, or the plots. In Bell's edition of *Romeo and Juliet*, Juliet wakes in the tomb before Romeo dies, enabling a brief pathetic exchange. And in the Duncombe edition of *Love's Labour Lost*, the inconclusive year's trial parting of the lovers that ends the original play is replaced with the following happy ending:

> It is almost needless to say that at the termination of the allotted period, Ferdinand, the King of Navarre, and the three lords, presented themselves before their expectant mistresses, who receiving them with the utmost ardour on the termination of their allotted tasks [*sic*]. In a few days afterwards the nuptial rites were performed, and it is recorded that a scene of greater festivity was never witnessed within the walls of the French capital.[63]

Duncombe also published theatrical abridgements, advertising an "Acting Edition of the British Theatre Comprising the Best Pieces As performed at all the London Theatres."[64] For a couple of pennies, readers could acquire heavily abridged forms of stage plays, shrunk into one act. Some were canonical plays, but most were shows recently performed in the major and minor London theatres. They commonly contained songs and pianoforte duets for home performance.[65] For sixpence the curious could purchase John Fairburn's "An Accurate Description of the Grand Allegorical Pantomimic Spectacle of Cinderella, As Performed at the Theatre-Royal, Drury Lane" (1804).[66] Alongside a description of the production, including some of the lines and songs, they also got a fulsome "Critique on the Performance and Performers, by a Lover of the Drama,"[67] together with a separate narrative sketching the story of Cinderella. The whole package was accompanied by four engravings of the performance. Such hybrid compilations offered a substitute for going to the pantomime: the scenes and costumes were described and illustrated, the story was summarised, and the whole show was evaluated to provide a proxy for the real thing.

The traffic was not, of course, all in one direction. At the same time that plays were turned into novels, or collections of poetic sententiae, we also find prose turning into drama—of a sort. Mrs. C. Short's 1792 collection entitled *Dramas for the Use of Young Ladies* offers a guide to polite behaviour in the form of a series of dialogues between young women.[68] The preface explains that "These little Dramas were written for a Society of Young Ladies, in whose welfare and improvement I am warmly interested; and as they have proved beneficial to this small circle, in promoting the habit of speaking with grace and propriety, I conceived they might be useful to others in similar situations."[69] Within we find a set of scenarios, set in the home, that enact different social or moral dilemmas. There is the case of Eliza in "The Fortunate Disappointment," who is unable to marry the man she wishes and fears that "the whirlwind of passions is ready to ingulph, the shoals of inexperience to endanger."[70] In "Domestic Woe" we meet Louisa Denizen, whose lover has just been killed in a duel; she shows others how to bear adversity with fortitude. They are dialogues rather than plays, but the fact that they take the form of conversations reveals a different angle to the generic transformations of drama.

Performed dialogue in the home could be a vehicle for informal education. The conversations staged in Short's collection created an opportunity for young women to practice their speaking skills, and at the same time model correct behaviour. Noting the neglect of women in matters of oratory, Samuel B. Morse commented: "Single pieces are not so proper for them to speak; but well-chosen Dialogues, as the means of teaching the fair sex a graceful, easy, and elegant mode of conversation, will prove of the most extensive benefit."[71] The advantage of dialogues rather than "single pieces," with only one speaker, was presumably that they imitated conversation rather than stage acting or public oratory.[72] As we shall see, the question of amateur female theatrical performance was vexed. But dialogues were a different matter, and were increasingly used as a medium for domestic instruction, as we shall also see in Chapter 8.

Looking at the range of printed spin-out materials coming from the stage, from novel adaptations to librettos, one becomes aware of the range of after-lives a single work could have in the home. It had long been possible to buy the playtext, the songs, the prologues, the epilogues, and illustrations of contemporary plays, and we know that eighteenth-century readers enjoyed a single work in multiple ways. Gertrude Savile, the Nottinghamshire spinster we met at the start of this book, describes going to see John Gay's *Beggar's Opera* on 29 January 1729, observing afterwards that "it was impossible to expect anything so odd and out of the way."[73] She obviously wasn't put off by the novelty of Gay's ballad opera. Two weeks later, having bought the printed edition, she describes reading it out to friends: "I read the Beggar's Opera to them in intervalls, before and after supper. Bed 12. Miserable."[74] Ten days later she returns to the *Beggar's Opera* but this time she was using the music, relating that she has tuned her harpsichord and played some of the songs.[75] A month later she goes back to see the play again, and is astounded by its popularity—it was so busy people couldn't get in: "Glad to get from the dore, where was such crowding and shriking, we were happy to be on the right side for runing away."[76]

Savile's multimedia enjoyment of the *Beggar's Opera* was not unique. Sylas Neville writes in his diary of going to see a performance in the 1760s, and taking the libretto with him to read between the acts while he watched. (Neville was a habitual reader during plays, and complained about one trip to Drury Lane: "I stood at the side so jambed up that I could not read the newspaper I carried; but I saw the Play very well.")[77] He also read sections of plays before he went to see them.[78] One evening he skipped dinner, put Benjamin Hoadly's popular comedy *The Suspicious Husband* in his pocket, and read Ranger's part, played by Garrick, in the coffeehouse before going to see it at Drury Lane. Another evening he read Mary Ann Yates's part of Medea in Richard Glover's tragedy of the same name, before going to see it at Covent Garden.[79] Richard Bagshawe, the compiler of a commonplace book in the mid–eighteenth century, copied out airs from the burlesque opera with the parts assigned to each singer, which were interspersed in the volume with toasts, erotic poetry, and other airs, clearly designed for domestic entertainment.[80]

By the end of the century the market in theatrical byproducts was extensive, with a substantial trade in china, actors' portraits, prints of performances, and Staffordshire figurines. By the early nineteenth century children could act out their own operas and burlettas with miniature toy theatres, which came supplied with cardboard characters and abbreviated scripts (fig. 38). There

Fig. 38. *Hodgson's New Characters in "The Tempest,"* miniature
theatre plates, 1823 (The Bodleian Libraries, The University of
Oxford, John Johnson Collection: Miniature Theatre 1 [6+])

were coloured harlequinades offering reduced versions of various works: the
whole of Lesage's *The Devil Upon Two Sticks,* a hugely popular comic novel,
was available in the form of a folded pamphlet of four panels, which sold for
sixpence plain and a shilling coloured, and enabled readers to "discover" the
story by lifting flaps to reveal different elements of the plot (fig. 39).[81]

At the root of these phenomena was the coalescence of theatrical celebrity and the increasing commercialization of culture. David Garrick, the
actor most frequently depicted in portraiture in the pre-photographic age,
was the perfect subject for this fusion of fame and material embodiment. As
a distinguished actor, successful manager, and gifted playwright, Garrick
used visual images throughout his career to promote his public persona and
cultural preeminence. Through engravings, popular illustrated editions such

Fig. 39. Illustration from *Dr Last; or, the Devil Upon Two Sticks* (London: H. Roberts, 1771) (The Bodleian Libraries, The University of Oxford, Vet. A5 e.892 [1])

as *Bell's British Theatre,* and memorabilia, depictions of Garrick in his most famous roles reached a broad audience (fig. 40). Performers staged evenings of entertainment that consisted of imitations of Garrick in his most celebrated roles. By posing for theatrical portraits, which were publicly exhibited and reproduced as prints or porcelain figures well into the nineteenth century, Garrick was kept in the public eye long after his death.[82] In the eighteenth and early nineteenth centuries, as now, there was a consumer market for plays, characters, and actors as brands—and a host of publishers and manufacturers ready to satisfy the demand for products associated with the theatre.

Homemade Drama

The examples discussed so far have focussed on the reading of plays within the home, and this would have been the way in which the majority of middling-sort families in eighteenth-century Britain encountered theatrical

Fig. 40. *Mr Garrick in Four of his Principal Tragic
Characters*, by an unknown artist, c. 1750–70, engraving
(English School / Private Collection / Bridgeman Images)

culture. But for a smaller group of mainly gentry and aristocratic theatre-lovers, a late-century vogue for ambitious private theatricals provided an outlet for thespian ambitions and a powerful fusion of sociability and creative display. According to one account of amateur theatre, there are records of 120 places in which private theatricals were held.[83] The *St James Chronicle* declared in 1776 that "scarce a Man of Rank but either has or pretends to have his petit Theatre, in the Decoration of which the utmost Taste and Expense are lavished."[84] This was doubtless an overstatement, but the theatrical mania of eighteenth- and nineteenth-century Britain clearly influenced the practice—and just as importantly, the perception—of drama in the home.[85] One of the fullest sources of evidence for these pop-up performances is a scrapbook of tickets, playbills, newspaper clippings, and programmes assembled by Charles Burney and Sarah Sophia Banks, now in the British Library. This archive of theatrical titbits illustrates just how closely many amateur performances aimed to imitate public theatre. They copied the format of an evening at the theatre, so that the main piece was accompanied by ballets, interludes, afterpieces, prologues, and epilogues. Plays came accompanied by the printed paraphernalia of theatregoing— locally handpress-printed playbills and programmes, and very grand houses even sold merchandise. At Richmond House it was possible to buy engravings of portraits that had originally been painted for the scenery.[86]

Newspaper coverage suggests there was considerable public interest in these performances. Snippets of news gave reviews of particular performances, commenting on the acting, sets, and costumes—the *World* had a whole subsection of its review dedicated to "Ladies' Dresses." The descriptions framed the performance much like modern coverage of celebrity events. The event and its glamorous assemblage were celebrated effusively, the play itself only one element of the interest of the evening. Reviews of the Blenheim Palace theatricals of 1789 give a taste of the heady fusion of fashion and exclusivity in this genre of reporting. On 3 December the *World* enthused: "Of the Magnificence, the ease, the amiable excellences of the Duke and Dutchess, the World cannot say enough till the World has nothing else to say."[87] The *Diary* declared that the play was "one of the most splendid, both in the style of execution, and in the numbers and rank of the spectators, of any that has yet been exhibited. The Duke and Duchess of Beaufort and family, Earl and Countess of Abingdon and family, with a long list of beauty and fashion, graced the performances with their presence."[88] As happens today, many of the consumers of this "news" were not themselves present or invited to the event, but could marvel from a distance thanks to the breathlessly enthusiastic accounts. So while the aristocratic spectacles at Blenheim or Brandenburg House belonged to the stratosphere of the social elite, the abundance of contemporary printed descriptions gave such events a cultural reach that extended beyond those attending.

Even though much of what we know about the phenomenon of domestic theatricals centres on the great houses of the aristocracy, there are also less well-documented instances of lesser gentry and middling-sort groups gathering together to produce their own plays. While most of the drama enjoyed in the home in the eighteenth century stemmed from printed sources, some families evidently wrote and performed their own plays. Amongst the papers of the Hebers, a gentry family from Yorkshire, is a manuscript play entitled "Britain Triumphant or the Spaniards foild. A Tragedy. occasion'd by the Success of the British Arms in the West Indies."[89] This patriotic heroic tragedy retold Walter Ralegh's quest for El Dorado in Guiana, drawing parallels with the British endeavours in the Caribbean during the War of Jenkins' Ear. The play was intended to make a comment on contemporary current affairs. The dialogue is punctuated with passionate declamations and heroic sentiments, and the text is marked up with pencil lines to indicate emphasis in delivery. Elsewhere, the margins are marked with annotations giving stage directions, telling the amateur actors when to swoon, exit, or embrace. Other similar surviving documents give a clearer indication of the individuals playing each part, and often survive in multiple copies, so that the actors could learn their lines separately. An anonymous vellum-bound manuscript play in the Bodleian Library named "Eumenes" has listed on its title page the names of the actors, Christopher Wyatt, Mary Sanderson, Ann Jennings, Kitty Wyatt, and one Thomas Jones, identified as the playwright. The play bears the single performance date of 30 August 1750. It is a heroic tragedy based on Plutarch's account of the Greek commander Eumenes. Like the Heber play, the setting offers the opportunity for patriotic sentiment, spelt out in the prologue:

> Of all the human Virtues, none can raise
> A nobler Subject for the Muses praise:
> None, to a British Pitt more gratefull be,
> Than publick Spiritt—love of Liberty.
> By this—Old Rome to height of Greatness rose,
> And free it self—to potent States gave Laws.
> And this—while Albion's freeborn Sons retain,
> They may contemn the Rage of haughty France, or Spain.
> Such is our Theme to Night—from hence proceed
> Our Author's hopes of being well receiv'd.[90]

The manuscripts for "Eumenes" give only vague indications of scenery and location: "Antigonus Camp"; "part of the camp with an eminence"; "A Pavilion." But the faraway locations of both this play and others we know of suggests that a key attraction in home performance was the element of exoticism—at its most basic, an opportunity to raid the fancy-dress box. In the case of the Harris family in Salisbury, Wiltshire, costuming was certainly a major preoccupation. James Harris, an MP, was a lover of theatre and music, and encouraged his daughters, Gertrude and Louisa, in their home recitals and performances, which were staged in the chapel room of their house in the cathedral close. The mother of the family, Elizabeth Harris, sent bulletins about her daughters' productions to her son, James, who was on the Continent. Her correspondence is preoccupied with silks, brocades, and headdresses. She wrote of her daughters' 1768 production of James Thomson's *Tancred and Sigismunda:* "it is a most complete thing[,] & their dresses both for the tragedy & entertainment are remarkably pritty, I may say fine."[91] Two years later, in the lead-up to another show, she writes: "Our time is wholy occupied in preparations for the play & Pastorall. Miss Wyndham acts Creusa, & will be as fine as silver trimmings & diamonds can make her[,] the last of which she will have a large quantity. Gertrude acts the Priestess. Her dress is taken from the antique[:] it is white sattin, quite simple & elegant, only fasten'd by a row of large pearls round the wast[;] on her head she wears a white kind of veil & round it a row of Alexandrian laurel."[92]

One of the distinctive features of the Harrises' plays was that the performances were often all female, the men's parts played by the daughters and their friends. In one letter, Elizabeth Harris describes Louisa in the male role of Illysus in William Whitehead's *Creusa: Queen of Athens* (1750): "a pritty inocent looking boy & did her part incomparable."[93] But Louisa's donning of male clothing, even in a private performance, was controversial.[94] Louisa wrote to her brother shortly after the production of *Elvira,* enclosing some "vile verses" that had been published about the play in a local newspaper, the *Bath Journal.* She comments dismissively that "You may easily imagin these verses were sent from some vinegar merchant in Salisbury who [could] not gett admitted to the performance," but the poem's content evidently caused some offence in the family, as her older sister records that her father destroyed his copy before she could see it. The object of criticism was the cross-dressing of the Harris sisters:

"On the Ladies of the Close of S[alisbur]y now acting Elvira"

> In Good Queen Elizabeth's reign
> IN a decent an[d] virtuous age
> That they ne'er might give modesty pain
> No female appear'd on the stage[.]
> But lo! what a change time affords[:]
> The ladies 'mong many strange things
> Call for helmets, for breeches and swords[,]
> And act senators, heros and kings.
> Sign[ed] Leo[95]

According to this disgruntled poet, the introduction of women playing male parts was in sad contrast with the virtuous practices of yore—in which the roles were played by boys. There were obviously different views about the dramatic morality of the past. Whereas editors such as Francis Gentleman and Thomas Bowdler censored Shakespeare's drama to eliminate the indecencies of his age, others, like the author of the *Bath Journal* poem, wistfully looked on the early modern stage as a time of virtue, because there were no women performing on it. Elizabeth Harris's correspondence shows her concern for the reputational issues associated with her daughters' performances, and her letters to her son frequently reassure him as to the propriety of what they are doing, reassuring him that the audience was "All ladies except elderly gentlemen, such as the Bishop of Salisbury, & Doctor Hele,"[96] or, that "Louisa was a pritty innocent looking boy."[97] She tells him of the ways they have controlled any potential impropriety: "I had a card sent me by some gentlemen to desire to be admitted behind the scenes—a modest request—as the whole performers consisted of young ladies. Your father & I were both in the theatre & he with the most audible voice forbid all gentlemen what ever from being admitted on the stage."[98]

Many of the surviving records of domestic performance from the time suggest concern over cross-dressing. Mary Clarke, mother of four daughters and wife of the Somerset MP Edward Clarke, wrote to her husband of a family visit in 1699:

> I must confess I beleve I should have bin prevailed on to have humoured the girls so far as to have gone to Sutton, they being so very pressin, if I had not found by them that they was to act a play, and they had bin so indiscreet to undertake to act mens parts, which I think was an undertaking sutable to theyr age and bigness, but not so proper for me to like, and I beleve impossoble for me to hinder if we should go unless I spoyled the play, and theareby make myself apear sower and morose, and I think it is time enough for them to think of wearing the britches yet, much more to put them on or any other dress that might become such a part in a strange place in this censoriouse age.[99]

Mrs. Clarke's concerns about the appropriateness of her daughters dressing as men, or "wearing the britches," were understandable. Women had only been permitted to act since the Restoration of Charles II in 1660, and in the decades after this innovation, associations between licentiousness and female performance had flourished, not least because so many of the Restoration actresses were mistresses of the king and his entourage. Playwrights teased their audiences with the idea that they were "selling" access to the women who performed.[100] Although the playwrights and managers advocating the introduction of women claimed that a female presence would reform and refine the stage, the most obvious consequence of the introduction of actresses was the sexualisation of contemporary drama, as dramatists and theatre managers went out of their way to exploit the novel and titillating presence of the female body on stage. One of the ways in which female bodies were displayed visually was through the creation of breeches parts—in which women dressed as men. Cross-dressing and comedies of gender confusion had flourished on the Renaissance stage, where they were used to take advantage of the staging conditions in which women's parts were played by young boys. In the late seventeenth century the same plot devices were employed to showcase women's legs. In the tight breeches of male dress, actresses revealed far more of their bodies than was possible in conventional female attire (fig. 41). Numerous

Fig. 41. Engraved portrait showing Mr. Smith and Mrs. Mary Ann Yates as Lord and Lady Townley, Act 1, Scene 1, of *The Provoked Husband; or, a Journey to London*, by Sir John Vanbrugh, 1776 (Harry Beard Collection, Victoria and Albert Museum, S. 2469-2013; © The Victoria and Albert Museum, London)

prologues and epilogues alluded to the spectacle of female bodies: in 1672 John Corye wrote that " 'Tis worth your money that such legs appear; / These are not to be seen so cheap elsewhere."[101] Breeches parts remained a source of consternation—or risqué delight—throughout the eighteenth century, as both the Clarke letters and the response to the Harris daughters' performance suggests.

Morality and Private Theatricals

Private theatricals aroused a furore of virtuous disapproval in contemporary onlookers. Recitation was pleasurable and improving—but the kinds of lavish theatrical spectacles that became fashionable in the later decades of the eighteenth century were widely perceived as corrupting. Critical attacks highlighted the dangers of confusing stage and domestic practice. Vicesimus Knox, the educationalist and compiler of the popular recitation anthology *Elegant Extracts,* was severe in his condemnation. In an essay criticizing the current fashion for performing plays at home, he began by noting the positive social attractions: "Nothing can enliven a rural residence more effectually than the prevailing practice of representing plays in a neighbourly way by friends and relations. Music, poetry, painting, fine dresses, personal beauty, and polished eloquence, combine to please all who are admitted to partake of the entertainment."[102] But warming to his theme, Knox warned of hidden dangers: the ruinous cost of such productions, and worse still, the erotic temptations that followed the acting out of romantic scenes (to which stage actors were apparently immune by virtue of their professionalism). "Paint and gaudy dress" encouraged vanity and folly, while amateur actresses immersed in the sentimental displays of the emotion were, he thought, likely to neglect their families:[103] "Let us see no more your black velvet train, your disheveled hair, and your white handkerchief. Be no longer desirous of personating the afflicted parent on the stage, but go home and be the good mother in your nursery and at your family fire-side."[104]

Knox's arguments defined the home as a place of responsible parenting and household duty rather than as a venue for show and entertainment.[105] He suggested that those who truly loved drama should either see it in a public theatre, or "If, indeed, they are lovers of dramatic poetry, and possess taste and sense enough to be delighted with fine composition, independently of dress, stage-trick, and scenery, why will they not acquiesce in reading the best plays in their closet, or in the family circle?"[106] His advice makes explicit the responsible reader's choice—between the superficial temptations of dramatic performance and the improving benefits of recital in the family circle or closet.

Other critics also focussed on the unseemliness of certain kinds of dramatic performance in the home, worrying that would-be actors were likely to confuse their roles in life and art, to the degree that "the open embraces of the Actor are exchanged without difficulty for the private of the Seducer."[107] Richard Cumberland, who, unlike Knox, declared himself a friend to amateur theatre, urged would-be players not to try to perform unsuitable roles from the public stage: "How can a lady stand forward in a part, contrived to produce ridicule or disgust, or which is founded upon broad humour and vulgar buffoonery?"[108] His real fear was not, however, for the social elite, but for their imitators, young women "of humble rank and small pretensions" whose "vain ambition of being noticed by their superiors betrays them into an attempt at displaying their unprotected persons on a stage, however dignified and respectable."[109]

Flaunting It at Porkington

Such public censure undoubtedly came to shape performers' presentation of what they were doing—as we have seen, the correspondence of the Harris family, in Salisbury, shows the way in which some families tried to navigate moral consternation around their amateur performances. Others took a markedly different approach. Harriet Pigott, an unmarried woman in her thirties living with relations in rural Shropshire, was involved in a series of thespian endeavours with local landowners and gentry living nearby between 1807 and 1810. Pigott, who was later to travel and to publish accounts of her voyages in Europe and experiences of contemporary society, at this time kept two volumes of letters, playbills, and literary cuttings relating to the plays performed at "Porkington," or Brogyntyn Hall, near Oswestry, on the Welsh borders. The "Salop theatricals," as she called them, offer an example of a well-documented but little-known cluster of theatrical activity. The Salop group clearly set themselves apart from their more conventional neighbours and their moral concerns, and their activities were far from the norm in middling-sort households. Yet the documents surrounding this group give us a sense of the way in which amateur drama was often

Fig. 42. Watercolour sketch of a scene from the "Salop theatricals" (The Bodleian Libraries, The University of Oxford, MS. Pigott d. 22, fol 153r)

embedded in other, more familiar exchanges of jokes, poem and letter writing, and local sociability (fig. 42).

The plays were performed at Brogyntyn, home of Pigott's friends the Ormsby-Gores, and at Pradoe or Prudhoe Hall, home of the Kenyon family, during the Christmas and New Year period.[110] Neither of the houses used as a venue seems to have had a purpose-built theatre, but the players erected a stage for regular theatrical activities—the playbill for one of the perform-ances at Pradoe reveals that the coach house was used as a performance space. Harriet's correspondence suggests that she was the literary ringleader of the little group of local friends who acted. Her letters document the social exchanges around the plays: correspondents often sign off their letters using the name of the character they are playing or have recently played, such as "Walter Scot," "Princess," "Buckingham," or "Leontes." They discuss their parts in their letters, debating the suitability of individual roles. Thomas Leeke, son and heir of Ralph Leeke, a local landowner who had made a fortune through the East India company, wrote to Harriet in late 1809 concerning his future role in Thomas Francklin's tragedy *Matilda,* which was performed in January 1810: "I am unacquainted, and consequently will accept Seward conditionally, vizt [*sic*] provided he is not a pathetick proseing Stick, which is quite out of my way."[111] Another would-be actor friend writes advertising his services for entertainments to held during the Christmas period:

> I am Madam a tall Boney Man large Stout & finely made. My Complexion is a dark brown My Eyebrows finely arched & strongly Marked. My nose triangular partaking of the Roman Grecian & aquiline Curve My eyes sparkling black will turn *every way* and express *any Passion* that you, Sweet Lady in your great goodness shall offer. I can express the humble suppliant or the distracted lover, the Buffoon in low Comedy, or the Elegant Man of Fashion As an inmate of yr large & splendid Mansion you will find me perfectly unexceptionable, gentle & unassuming ready to promote cheerfulness & good humour not like many of *our* Countrymen addicted to the Bottle & quarrelsome in my cups though quite ready to take a jolly Glass when Conviviality requires & any of yr Guests demand it.[112]

His playful description of his qualifications for a part (which include a sketch of himself in character) included not only his acting skills, but also his contribution to the life of the house during the rehearsal and performance period, when he would presumably have stayed there (fig. 43).

The Salop theatricals, like other similar ventures, involved a dinner and dancing afterwards. The playbills collected by Pigott show that the main play was followed by an interval for tea, then a comic afterpiece, then supper, and then dancing. A handwritten playbill advertises the "Tragedy of the Earl of Warwick," followed by an interlude, an entertainment "newly translated" from Molière, the comic opera of *The Cave of Trophonius,* and the whole lot "To conclude with the favourite Comedy of the Knife & Fork, And a Dance."[113] In with her playscripts and letters Pigott bound invitations, valentines, charades, jokes, notices of dances, and illustrations, all involving the same group of young local gentry involved in the theatricals. The correspondence documents ongoing flirtations between Pigott and the assorted men who play parts in the plays. Charles Wingfield's letters were particularly saucy—a letter of 8 December asks her what she meant by "a part of lady D marked 'O,'" suggesting, through some enclosed sketches, that she should

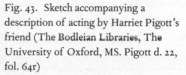

Fig. 43. Sketch accompanying a
description of acting by Harriet Pigott's
friend (The Bodleian Libraries, The
University of Oxford, MS. Pigott d. 22,
fol. 64r)

have clarified whether she meant breasts or buttocks. He also penned an
imitation of Marlowe's "Come Live with me and be my love," which he
finished by drawing attention to Pigott's forthcoming breeches part:

> Dear Pig! It is beauty both us bewitches
> Since I must the truth on't reveal
> For when I write bad verses, and you wear the Breeches,
> We shew, what we ought to conceal.[114]

In adopting the breeches part, Harriet Pigott and her friends were
invoking the risqué associations of cross dressing that had developed through
the late seventeenth and eighteenth centuries. They addressed dress in one of
their manuscript prologues, written for "The Beauty and the Beast. An
Oriental Entertainment Taken from real life Written Composed & represented with unbounded applause at The Hon[ble] Thomas Kenyon's Prado."[115]
Pigott, in the role of the Princess Cossima (at this point dressed in breeches)
declares:

But Men won't act—why then Women may
To fill a gap in this our Tragic Play
Therefore without more prefatory speeches
(throws off the Pelisse)
I doff the Petticoat, and try the Breeches.
If any of you Husbands apprehend
Your Wives should take example from yr friend
It wou'd grieve us much to think that any strife
Should from our Play ascend to real life
And breed dissension betwixt Man & Wife[116]

This prologue playfully diffuses any suggestion of gendered role reversal, but other pieces within the collection offer a more spirited challenge to moral disapproval. In his essay on private plays, Richard Cumberland had focussed part of his criticism on the inappropriateness of performing prologues and epilogues in refined private settings. For him, these add-ons were extremely unbecoming: "I should blush to see any lady of fashion in that silly and unseemly situation: They are the last remaining corruptions of the antient drama; reliques of servility, and only are retained in our London theatres as vehicles of humiliation at the introduction of a new play, and traps for false wit, extravagant conceits and female flippancy."[117]

The prologues and epilogues seem to have been relished by Pigott and her little group, who exploited their potential to engage directly with the audience, offering an insouciant affront to conventional mores.[118] In a prologue for the "Tragedy of Theodosius," performed on 2 December 1807, the author, who is possibly William Gell, writes:

Though 'tis most generally understood,
That these theatricals "can do no good:"
Yet this is not a question of alarm,
Unless it's fairly prov'd, that they do harm.—[. . .]
O charming subject for a coterie!
Delightful relish to a cup of tea!
Where with each drop let sneaking scandal flutter,
With innuendos wrapt—in bread and butter—And
though they strive to know by ev'ry means,
They can't guess what we do—behind the scenes.[119]

Gell, Pigott, and their friends were treading a fine line between mocking the groundless fears of detractors and titillating their audience with the suggestion that, as suspected, their local "coterie" was up to no good behind the scenes. Pigott's family were already controversial. Her uncle, Charles Pigott, was a radical and a satirist, and the author of scurrilous exposés of high society in *The Jockey Club* and *The Female Jockey Club*. His older brother, Robert, was also a radical and a fervent advocate of vegetarianism and of the sexologist James Graham's "Celestial Bed," a glass-covered contraption in which couples were encouraged to procreate surrounded by piped oriental music, live turtle doves, and working automata. Harriet Pigott's correspondence with friends and neighbours betrays an awareness that not everyone would approve or wish to attend, and the collection is a reminder of the contested nature of performance, in which even within a fairly confined provincial circle there were a multitude of views on what was, and was not, acceptable.

Plays and theatrical culture took many forms in the eighteenth century. On one hand, drama presented a threat to domestic virtue—from the moral hysteria over the damaging effects of Shakespeare's bawdy to the idea of mothers neglecting their children in favour of their thespian ambitions. Yet on the other hand, there was a market for recitation collections, and Shakespeare editions intended to provide material for wholesome rendition in the family circle or in the closet. The domestication of Shakespeare's plays cleansed them from the low humour of their age, and presented the Bard's lines as wholesome fare for all to enjoy. Yet at exactly the same time that some families were furnishing their parlours with these materials, others, like those in the Porkington theatricals, were enjoying the teasing role play and performance licensed by the vogue for private theatricals. The home was a space in which the morality of culture was both policed and wilfully transgressed.

7. Fictional Worlds

Made an end of "The Adventures of Abdella." I can find
no morrall or design in it. 'Tis a collection of silly but very
entertaining Lyes, of Fairies, Enchantments etc. Such books I read
as people take Drams, to support for an hour sinking Spirits, and
alass! the more is taken, the more is nesassary.
—Gertrude Savile, diary entry for 22 October 1728

The rise of the novel is the big story of eighteenth-century literature. At the beginning of the century, readers had little more than short continental prose fictions, or romances; by the end they had great tomes from *Clarissa* to *Evelina*, from *Tristram Shandy* to *The Mysteries of Udolpho*, thousands of pages of invented lives and stories that were consumed in books, anthologies, part books, abridgements, and magazine instalments. Although historians have recently emphasised that novels represented only a fraction of the trade in printed books, some going so far as to challenge the very notion of a "rise of the novel," the development of a tradition of extended prose fiction had a transformative impact on the landscape of literary culture at this time.[1] The rise of narrative fiction has been seen by critics as the reason for, amongst other things, a crisis in poetic identity, the rise of the solitary reader, and the development of a complex sense of self. The development of the novel also generated what now seems like bizarre mass hysteria over the uses of this new form—reading novels was thought by many to be seductive, dangerous, and enervating for those who consumed too much, too fast. If we are to understand fully how and why eighteenth-century readers enjoyed reading together, we need a sense of the cultural and moral debates surrounding this new genre. But we also need to recognise that at this time fiction took many forms—and not all of them were long novels. Myriad collections of extracts and beauties, abridgements, short magazine fiction, and compilations of jests and comic stories created reading experiences that were shaped by use and company.

The Rise of the Novel

For most of the eighteenth century, novels were not called novels—they were more likely to be called "histories," "tales," "lives," or "adventures." It was only by the end of the period that the term "novel" was widely used to describe what we now recognise as novels—that is, fictional narratives in extended prose, often set in the present day (or recognizably recent past), with a focus on individual experience, and often, a claim for the authenticity of the worlds they described. In earlier decades, and particularly towards the beginning of the century, many novels went under the guise of nonfiction— they pretended to be "true life" accounts of the persons they described. Readers of the "first" English novel, *The Life and Strange Surprizing Adventures of Robinson Crusoe, of York, Mariner . . . Written by Himself* (1719) were led to believe (and many did) that what they held in their hands was a genuine travel narrative.[2] Over the course of the century we see a creeping acceptance of fictional stories, though many novels retained the conceit that the story within was based on found papers or firsthand sources. But a suspicion around *how* novels were read, and by whom, remained.

The novel might be seen as the antithesis of sociable reading. Ian Watt's formative account in *The Rise of the Novel* (1957) linked the novel's focus on individual experience with the development of individualism in economics, and in society more generally.[3] Another landmark study stated that the novel is "an essentially . . . isolationistic form."[4] It has been argued that eighteenth-century novels substituted fictional relationships and fictional intimacy for the real thing, imitating the dialogue and sociable exchange that had previously characterised shared reading experiences, by conjuring up loquacious, engaging narrators who addressed their readers directly in conversation, as if they were friends.[5] At the same time, the novels themselves told stories that emphasised individuality, giving the impression of access to solitary experience. Both these things are true. Many narrators did simulate conversations with their readers, and one of the distinctive characteristics of the eighteenth-century novel as opposed to, for example, continental romance, was its focus on individual subjectivity. But neither factor negates the evidence in diaries, letters, and records of libraries and book clubs, that there were friends, families, and lovers who read novels together, out loud, giving voice to the conversational addresses of the narrators they encountered. One of the arguments of this chapter is that it was partly because of the contemporary perception that novel reading was a dangerously solitary exercise, especially amongst young women, that communal reading was encouraged in families and domestic environments. Reading together could be a way of mediating the solipsistic elements of novel consumption.

By the late eighteenth century there was a well-developed opposition to novels and novel reading that was as much about who read, and how, as it was about the books themselves.[6] Vocal commentators pointed to a nation of women addicted to the seductions of fiction. That ever-vigilant cultural critic and educationalist of the previous chapter, Vicesimus Knox, lamented the way in which sentimental fictions

> Not only tend to give the mind a degree of weakness, which renders it unable to resist the slightest impulse of libidinous passion, but also indirectly insinuate, that the attempt is unnatural . . . Every corner of the kingdom is abundantly supplied with them. In vain is youth secluded from the corruptions of the living world. Books are commonly allowed them with little restriction, as innocent amusements: yet these often pollute the heart in the recesses of the closet, inflame the passions at a distance from temptation, and teach all the malignity of vice in solitude.[7]

Knox here conflates several dominant narratives about the novel: its erotic temptations, the danger of readerly overidentification, the fashion for solitary reading, and the widespread availability of prose fiction. The last thirty years of literary criticism have seen an explosion of scholarly interest in the eighteenth-century novel. A preoccupation with narrative fiction—its issues of gender, identity, materiality, and power—has propelled many women authors and women readers to the centre of the canon after centuries of neglect.[8] And as part of this second "rise of the novel," modern critics have tended to repeat the same kinds of claims about novel reading as those made above by Knox (without the moral disapproval). Novels were read alone, by young women who identified closely with the heroines they read about, and who had easy access to fiction through circulating libraries, book clubs, and cheap editions. But was this really true?

Other kinds of evidence suggest a more complex picture. Jan Fergus's study of provincial reading and the sales and circulation of books in the Midlands shows that, in fact, men were the primary purchasers and borrowers of novels. Within the communities around Daventry and Rugby a whole range of sources, from schoolboys' subscriptions to the *Lady's Magazine,* to records from booksellers, shows substantial evidence of men's interest in fiction even by and about women.[9] Other recent national studies of book clubs and libraries have confirmed this pattern.[10] And conversely, the anecdotal evidence found in women's diaries and letters suggests that novel reading was generally only one part—and usually a minor part—of the mixed fare of the middle-class reading public. Diarists of all sorts record novel reading alongside the reading of histories, poetry, plays, natural science, sermons, and periodicals. Records of circulating libraries in the eighteenth century—organizations suspected by many contemporaries as being the breeding grounds of unhealthy novel reading—show that novels were not the most prevalent or the most borrowed genres in subscription libraries, generally coming second to books of voyages and topography.[11]

And we are wrong to lump all novels together. Even amongst the disapproving, not all novels were equally bad. Writing of his breakfast-time reading aloud with his daughters, the vicar William Jones observed in his diary: "Novels, even of the best sort, I would read very sparingly—as I would have recourse to drams. *Rosanne* was introduced to our breakfast & tea-readings by my Dosy, who has great influence over me;—& I was much pleased. *Gertrude* I rejected, a year or two ago; but we are now reading & admiring the character of dear *Gatty Aubrey.*"[12] There were obviously lines that could and should be drawn. The founding rules of a literary society in Leicestershire read: "No Novel, or Play shall be admitted into the Library but such as have stood the test of time, and are of established reputation."[13] The magazines and reviews of the 1760s and 1770s supplied their readers with countless lists of acceptable and unacceptable novels. The *Lady's Magazine* pronounced on the exceptional few that could be recommended—these included *Evelina, The Man of Feeling, Millennium Hall, Julia Mandeville, The Female Quixote,* and the novels of Richardson.[14] And by distinguishing between "good" novels and the mass of fiction that merely encouraged vice and folly, magazines and libraries and book clubs could in effect both defend the novels they rated and demonstrate their ambivalence about the form.

The furore around narrative fiction was probably a gross distortion of the realities of reading by women and men of the time, but it nonetheless came to shape the way novels were presented in relation to domestic spaces. Opponents of novel reading focussed on the excessive consumption of fiction by young people, especially women, whose solitary, compulsive reading of fiction in their closets was apt to encourage lascivious thoughts and false expectations. Novels were addictive, serving only to increase the appetite, and critics drew on a vocabulary of gorging, devouring, and digestion. Thomas Gisborne, the conduct writer we have already encountered, described with some alarm the steady corruption of a girl's virtue: "The appetite becomes too keen to be denied; and in proportion as it is more urgent, grows less nice and select in its fare. What would formerly have given offence, now gives none. The palate is vitiated or made dull. The produce of the book-club, and the contents of the circulating library, are devoured with indiscriminate and insatiable avidity."[15] The Edinburgh novelist and editor Henry Mackenzie, writing in the *Lounger,* further developed the dietary metaphor: "when the sweetened poison is removed, plain and wholesome food will always be relished. The growing mind will crave nourishment."[16]

Some readers clearly internalised this notion of addiction. Gertrude Savile, the Nottinghamshire diarist we met previously, writing in 1728, well before the novel was fully established in print or criticism, writes disparagingly: "Made an end of 'The Adventures of Abdella.' I can find no morrall or design in it. 'Tis a collection of silly but very entertaining Lyes, of Fairies, Enchantments etc. Such books I read as people take Drams, to support for an hour sinking Spirits, and alass! the more is taken, the more is nesassary."[17] Savile often read romances and novels alone, after supper, and her diaries make a connection between melancholy isolation and the reading of this type of prose fiction: "All day alone. Had nothing to do but indulg the depth of mellancholy which I think I am at present more hopelessly overhwhelm'd in than ever. Din'd and Sup'd alone. Lay on the bed as much as I coud. Read 2 books of the life of Baron Debross, an old storry."[18]

Visual representations of women's reading reflect this emphasis on the solitary female reader.[19] Although books had long been depicted in Western painting as emblems of moral virtue or self-improvement, during the eighteenth century they began to reflect the perceived sexualisation of novel reading.[20] In images such as Auguste Bernard D'Agesci's *Lady Reading the Letters of Heloise and Abelard* (1758–59), the book in hand is associated with sexual license and solipsistic dreaming. Within D'Agesci's painting we see a solitary reader overwhelmed with passion, lips open, hands languorous, and on her table, next to a billet-doux, a book entitled *The Art of Love*. The lighting and the proximity of the book, the dress, and the bosom invite us to see a link between all three—it is this novel that has transported its reader into a state of distracted arousal. Many paintings and prints of solitary readers depict a degree of absorption in which the painted reader becomes a synecdoche, a shorthand, for the interiority depicted within the fiction itself and the intimacy of the reading experience (fig. 44).[21]

It was precisely because of the perceived linkage between novel reading and vulnerable young minds and virtues that the conduct literature and the novels of the eighteenth century endorsed the collective reading of fiction within the family circle. Many thought that the problem with novels was that because of their availability in cheap formats, through circulating libraries, what women read could no longer be controlled by those around them. In her

Fig. 44. *Reflections on Clarissa Harlow*, by Gabriel Scorodumoff after Sir Joshua Reynolds, London 1785, stipple and etching (British Museum, 1838,0714.4. © The Trustees of the British Museum)

manuscript account of changing mores in Scottish society over the course of the eighteenth century, Elizabeth Mure declared that in the early eighteenth century "The booksellers houses were not stuffed as they are, *now* with Novels & Magazines the womens knowledge was gained only by conversation with the Men, not by reading themselves, as they had few books to read that they could understand."[22]

In the context of such broad changes in reading, writing, and bookselling, shared domestic reading was presented as a kind of cultural prevention. It protected women against the dangers hidden within novels, while simultaneously reinforcing the values and the discipline of wholesome family life. To consider a novel within the context of the family circle was a very different thing to envisaging it in the hands of the idle and unguided young. By way of recommending a collection of romances, the *Critical Review* of December 1764 suggested a suitable setting: "The reading of them may prove a very innocent and diverting amusement, during the holidays; the father on one side of the fire, the mother on t'other, and the children just come from boarding-school round them, may read it by turns—*Probatum est.*"[23] In reading together, the reciter could take guidance from those around: ideally a young woman would read in the domestic circle, and she would discuss what she read with her parents or preceptor, so that any misapprehensions into which she slipped could be corrected.[24] She could use the notion of family reading as a benchmark for what to read on her own—if a book wasn't fit to be read in company, it wasn't fit to be read at all.[25] Communal reading offered the chance to gloss what had been read, and many descriptions of family reading frequently imply that the readings were interrupted for commentary, either by the reader or by his or her audience. The radical and feminist Mary Wollstonecraft argued that a pointed delivery could shape reception: "If a judicious person, with some turn for humour, would read several [romantic novels] to a young girl, and point out both by tones, and apt comparisons with pathetic incidents and heroic characters in history, how foolishly and ridiculously they caricatured human nature, just opinions might be substituted instead of romantic sentiments."[26]

The Morality of Reading Aloud

One of the reasons why young women, in particular, were seen to be so susceptible to the "giddy and fantastical notions of love and gallantry" imbibed from novels was that they were perceived to read differently from

men. The female reading experience was not ballasted by intellectual engagement, but was apt to lapse into affective identification with the characters
described.[27] Unable to apply rational judgment to distance themselves from
the worlds evoked in the pages before them, women, it was claimed, responded
instead with their hearts and imaginations.[28] Sometimes this was a benefit.
James Fordyce happily affirmed these distinctions in relation to devotional
books. Speaking of Scripture, he advised young women to focus on "facts the
most astonishing to the imagination, and Sentiments the most touching to the
heart." In the case of Bible reading, this engagement with the emotions was a
positive attribute, granting women a more intense piety and a stronger sense
of belief.[29] But in the context of the novel, the same gendered predilection
for affective engagement was a danger zone and the cause of much moral
hand-wringing. Moreover, class exacerbated these issues. Young women from
middling-sort backgrounds or lower were rendered doubly vulnerable to lack
of critical distance by both their sex and lack of education.

Reading together replaced the subjective identification of silent absorption with the socialised framework of the group. Eighteenth-century novels
are peppered with positive instances of communal reading. Sometimes this
practice is shown to enable those involved to establish the correct interpretation of a text. In Fanny Burney's *Evelina*, the heroine describes the way in
which she reads with her suitor, Lord Orville: "When we read, he marks the
passages most worthy to be noticed, draws out my sentiments, and favours
me with his own."[30] Similarly, shared reading is modelled in Richardson's
sequel to *Pamela*, *Pamela in Her Exalted Condition*, in which Lady Davers
describes the way in which she and her rather frivolous friends have been
educated by their communal reading of Pamela's story: "We have been
exceedingly diverted with your Papers. You have given us, by their Means,
many a delightful Hour, that otherwise would have hung heavy upon us; and
we are all charm'd with you . . . Lady Betty says, it is the best Story she has
heard, and the most instructive."[31] Lady Davers and her friends are the kind
to read novels badly. In both cases, the experience of reading together enables
those present to step back from the text in hand and to establish a critical
distance through sociable discussion. Other novels emphasised the way in
which reading together lets characters communicate with one another, or
acquire critical judgment. In *The Mysteries of Udolpho*, Emily recalls the way
in which her suitor Valancourt had read to her: "she had often sat and worked,
while he conversed, or read; and she now well remembered with what

discriminating judgment, with what tempered energy, he used to repeat some of the sublimest passages of their favourite authors; how often he would pause to admire with her their excellence, and with what tender delight he would listen to her remarks, and correct her taste."[32] In Charlotte Smith's early novels, reading is shown to be a way of establishing social bonds and strengthening friendship—in *Emmeline; or, the Orphan of the Castle* (1788) the heroine takes much comfort from reading with a sympathetic friend.[33]

These fictional examples are not evidence of actual practice, but they do illustrate the notion of reading aloud as a corrective to the solipsism of reading silently. The championing of the sociable novel is manifest in the publication of Samuel Richardson's *Pamela*. *Pamela* is a work that embodied controversy about the value of prose fiction. As a story of a servant girl who resisted the approaches of her master, only to be rewarded by marriage to him (once he had reformed), Pamela polarised contemporary opinion. Was it a morally uplifting fable about the triumph of virtue over vice? Or a voyeuristic encomium to a young jilt? Richardson was concerned that his readers might enjoy his book for the wrong reasons. *Pamela* was a work designed "to inculcate Religion and Morality," not a titillating romance. And part of Richardson's strategy in securing the "right" kind of reading of his novel was to present it as a book that was and should be read in company.[34] In his letters he emphasised the way the novel had evolved as a communal exercise. Explaining how he brought *Pamela* to completion, he recalled that it was his wife and a young woman staying in the house who effectively enabled him to finish: "when I had read them some part of the story, which I had begun without their knowing it, [they] used to come in to my little closet every night, with—'Have you any more of Pamela, Mr. R.? We are come to hear a little more of Pamela.' "[35]

When Richardson revised *Pamela* for its second edition, he did so by surrounding it with documents that illustrated its use in the family circle. Aaron Hill, along with many of Richardson's friends, had written to the author in praise of his novel. In the second edition, Richardson cited Hill's letters in response to the barrage of criticism of the novel's inflaming and "low" scenes. In the first excerpt used, Hill declared that "I have done nothing but read it to others, and hear others again read it, to me, ever since it came into my Hands; and I find I am likely to do nothing else."[36] Hill's comments identify *Pamela* as the kind of book to be shared, not read furtively alone in closets or languorously on sofas. His emphasis is on the novel within the family: " 'Tis sure, that no Family is without Sisters, or Brothers, or Daughters, or Sons, who can *read;* or wants Fathers, or Mothers, or Friends, who can *think;* so equally certain it is, that the Train to a Parcel of Powder does not run on with more natural Tendency, till it set the whole Heap in a Blaze, than that *Pamela,* inchanting from Family to Family, will overspread all the Hearts of the Kingdom."[37]

Hill took the metaphors of contagion used by contemporary critics of the novel, and reused them to suggest that Pamela's virtue was infectious. He effectively repositioned the novel in the parlour, where it was relished as the topic of polite discussion amongst wholesome families. Hill finishes the letter with an anecdote about one particular collective reading of the novel, involving a young child. The little boy stole into an assembled family group while Hill was reading an affecting passage in which Pamela momentarily contemplated drowning herself after having tried to escape from the house of her pursuer. Hill says that the child had sat in front of him with his head hung low.

> He had sat for some time in this Posture, with a Stillness, that made us conclude him asleep: when, on a sudden, we heard a Succession of heart-heaving Sobs; which while he strove to conceal from our Notice, his little Sides swell'd, as if they wou'd burst, with the throbbling restraint of his Sorrow . . . All the Ladies in Company were ready to devour him with Kisses: and he has, since, become doubly a Favourite—and is perhaps the youngest of *Pamela's Converts.*[38]

Hill's anecdote reversed the expectations around novel reading. Novels were thought to be bad for unformed minds, yet here we have a story of a child who is a "convert" to Pamela, who is visibly moved not by her sexuality but by her moral sentiments. The group reading provided him with controlled access to the book, and his response was applauded by the other adults, who affirmed his "right" reading of the novel. The little boy's physical response to the text becomes a testament to the novel's ability to refine the feelings of everyone who hears it.

There were paradoxes at the heart of novel reading. On one hand, young people were warned against the tendency of novels to "pollute the heart in the recesses of the closet, inflame the passions at a distance from temptation," as Vicesimus Knox put it. Readers became too involved in fictional worlds, and were thus unable to distinguish between life and fantasy. On the other hand, a child's ability to manifest an emotional response in a social setting was lauded as evidence of precocious sensibility. While Aaron Hill's anecdote, part of the paratextual puffing of *Pamela*, is hardly representative of all readings of the novel, its use illustrates the way in which the *concept* of reading together could be used to shape the idealised presentation of a novel.

Sentiment and Show

A lot of the debate about whether novels were a good or bad thing focussed around sentimental fiction.[39] The emotional reactions prompted by the genre's tales of distressed beggars, orphans, servant girls, or travellers were at one level deplored as self-indulgence: "I have actually seen mothers, in miserable garrets, *crying for the imaginary distress of an heroine*, while their children were *crying for bread:* and the mistress of a family losing hours over a novel in the parlour, while her maids, in emulation of the example, were similarly employed in the kitchen."[40] Yet in accounts of social readings of sentimental fiction, crying in public at a novel was, as in Hill's anecdote above, commonly seen as evidence of genuinely humanitarian sympathy.[41] Novels were celebrated for their ability to provoke tears within a reading circle. The clergyman Thomas Twining wrote to Charles Burney of the reception of Fanny Burney's *Cecilia:* "I know two amiable sisters at Colchester, sensible and accomplished women, who were found blubbering at such a rate one morning! The tale had drawn them on till near the hour of an engagement to dinner, which they were actually obliged to put off, because there was not time to recover their red eyes and swelled noses."[42] An anecdote about a reading of *Clarissa* illustrates the virtues of the novel in a similar way:

> A lady was reading to two or three others the seventh volume of Clarissa, whilst her maid curled her hair, and the poor girl let fall such a shower of tears upon her lady's head, that she was forced to send her out of the room to compose herself, asking her what she cried for; she said, to see such goodness and innocence in distress; and a lady followed her out of that room and gave her a crown for that answer.[43]

This hairdressing story offers a bizarre sense of the way in which physical emotional response was valued—in this case, literally, through the payment of the crown. The crying maid's accidental participation in the theatre of feeling becomes a testament to the power of Clarissa's story. In both this anecdote and Hill's story of the little boy, the tears are inadvertent.[44] Critics of the sentimental novel lamented the way in which readers deliberately and indulgently immersed themselves in a vale of woe—yet these stories about positive sentimental reactions are about an accidental response.

Sometimes readers seem to have felt that the act of reading aloud actually increased their sentimental response to a literary work. Harriet Martineau recounts the way in which the novelist Amelia Opie used to try out the effects of her writings on a little audience before the manuscripts went to press. Martineau records the transformative impact of reading aloud: "I remember my mother and sister coming home with swollen eyes and tender spirits after spending an evening with Mrs. Opie, to hear 'Temper,' which she read in a most overpowering way. When they saw it in print, they could hardly believe it was the same story."[45] Eighteenth-century compilations of prose designed for recitation are full of sentimental vignettes from novels, and we might pause to consider how far the sociable practices of reading aloud determined the composition of the original work, making it ripe for the kind of extraction that was so prevalent at this time. Collections of sentimental scenes had the dual advantage of giving readers and listeners the chance to enjoy acute pathos, while also claiming to be morally improving: the editor of *Beauties of English Prose* claimed that from his selection of passages "the unfeeling Heart (if such there be) may learn an excellent lesson from the pathetic story of Le Fever; the Tyrant may be taught humanity."[46] Henry Mackenzie's *Man of Feeling* was heavily excerpted in compilations, and seems to have become a litmus test of emotional response. Writing in adulthood to Walter Scott, Lady Louisa Stuart remembers the agonies of trying to respond in the right way: "I remember so well its [*The Man of Feeling*'s] first publication, my mother and sister crying over it, dwelling upon it with rapture! And when I read it, as I was a girl of fourteen not yet versed in sentiment, I had a secret dread I should not cry enough to gain the credit of proper sensibility."[47]

Within titles such as *Beauties in Prose and Verse* (1783), *Waylett's Beauties of Literature* (1791), or *Beautiful Extracts of Prosaic Writers* (1795) individual sentimental episodes acquired an afterlife of their own. The tale of Maria in Sterne's *Sentimental Journey* or Sterne's account of the death of Le Fever in *Tristram Shandy* were reprinted again and again, becoming stand-alone classics in a repertoire of sentimental recitation. Maria was available in multiple material forms—as a Staffordshire figurine, jasperware medallion, bas-relief bracelet, vase, pin dish, belt clasp, tea set, and numerous prints, paintings, and book illustrations (fig. 45).[48] The episode in which Sterne's narrator, Yorick, comes across a lovelorn maiden was used as the frontispiece to Enfield's recitation collection *The Speaker,* and Mrs. Poplin of James Cobb's *English Readings* declared that she loved it the best of all her texts for performance. Hester Thrale remembered her daughters' comic parodies of the way in which they had been taught to read the passage in school: "They used to repeat some Stuff in an odd Tone of Voice, & laugh obstreperously at their own Ideas—upon Enquiry we found out that 'twas the pathetic Passages in *Sterne's Maria* that so diverted & tickled their Spleen."[49]

So how exactly was one supposed to read an extract of sentimental fiction aloud? We can get some idea from *The Reader, or Reciter,* a collection that included quite specific instructions. The editor included a whole section on Sterne's fiction, which when "feelingly read" afforded great delight to the

Fig. 45. Pale blue jasper show buckle with white relief of Poor Maria, 1785–90 (Wedgwood Museum, 5576; photo © Wedgwood Museum/ WWRD)

reader of "taste and discrimination."[50] Introducing the story of the death of Le Fever, he guided the reader through the piece. She or he was instructed to adopt a "manly pathetic tone" and to be guided by Sterne's typography: *"The words in Italics still more pathetic than what we advised before."*[51]

One of the obstacles facing reciters was the punctuation of speech.[52] The history of the punctuation of fiction in the eighteenth century reveals very little consistency over the ways in which direct speech, reported speech, and shifts from one character to another should be indicated. The modern habit of using inverted commas for direct speech was not standardised, and a wide variety of markings appeared to suggest who was speaking, often employed at the same time. Italics or dashes could be used not only to indicate a change of speaker, but also to add emphasis. A passage from Charles Johnstone's *Chrysal* shows a bewildering array of dashes, inverted commas, and italics, each of those typographic elements used in an attempt to clarify who speaks when (fig. 46).

A further difficulty in reading, according to the guide offered in *The Reader*, appeared in the tonal shifts between one narrator and another. In the case of Sterne's *Tristram Shandy*, to capture the character of the ingenuous Uncle Toby, "there must be a blunt unrestrained honesty, blended throughout the whole, to shew at once the person you are delineating."[53] The corporal, on the other hand, should speak with "coarseness of expression."[54] The reader must be careful to distinguish between the two speakers, "without which the proper effect will be entirely destroyed."[55] Then there were the peculiarities of Sterne's syntax—the fragmented sentences in which "Care must be taken to express the many half and unfinished periods in the writing of Sterne with that force of which they are susceptible."[56] Attention was drawn to Sterne's liberal use of dashes—for which he had already acquired a reputation amongst conservative punctuators, one of whom remarked: "I know no other author, whose works have been so terribly be-dashed, or who has been generally considered more unintelligible."[57] Malcolm Parkes, author of *Pause and Effect: A History of Punctuation in the West*, argues that the frequent dashes and exclamation marks in Sterne's writing are so placed to enable readers to exploit fully the sentimental or dramatic potential of the narrative in reading aloud, and this is clearly how they are being interpreted here.[58]

Within *The Reader's* treatment of Sterne's passage, the imagined reader was also cautioned against hamming it up: *"nothing affected, or apparently studied, will do; but let it all be simple, candid, and ingenuous . . . Mingle a good*

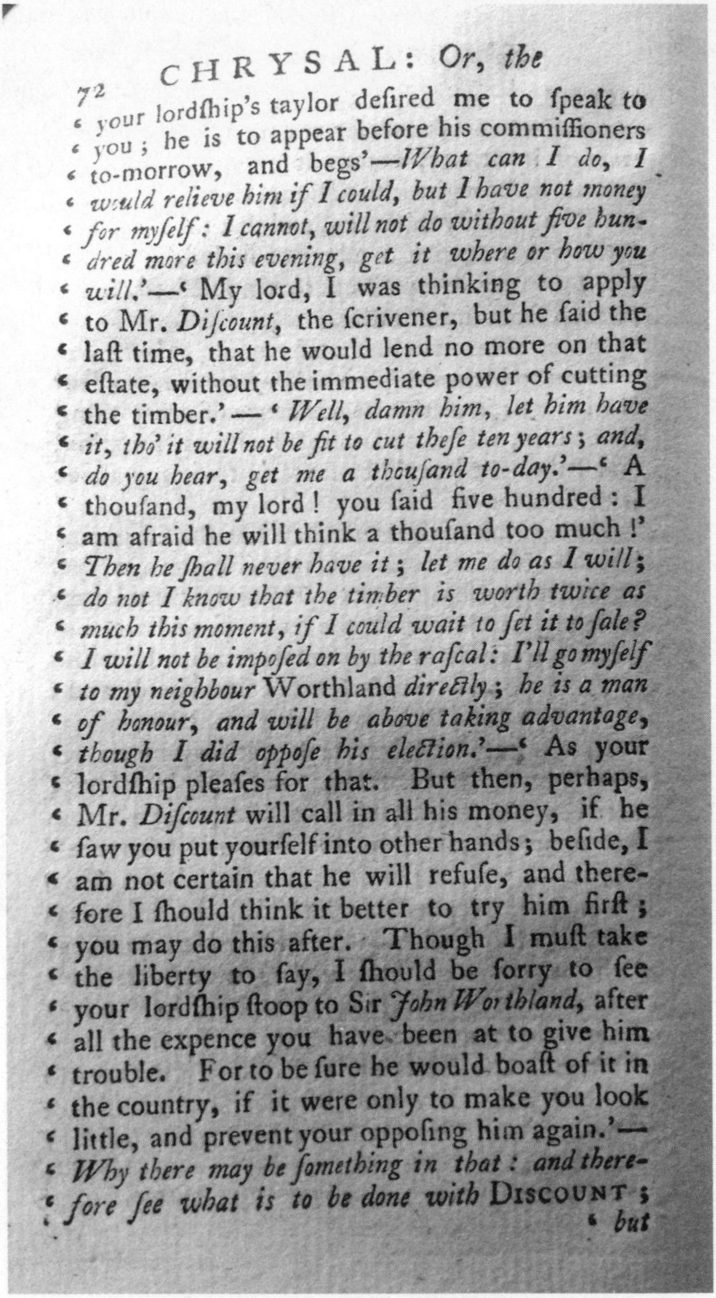

CHRYSAL: *Or, the*

72
' your lordfhip's taylor defired me to fpeak to
' you; he is to appear before his commiffioners
' to-morrow, and begs'—*What can I do, I*
' *would relieve him if I could, but I have not money*
' *for myfelf: I cannot, will not do without five hun-*
' *dred more this evening, get it where or how you*
' *will.*'—' My lord, I was thinking to apply
' to Mr. *Difcount*, the fcrivener, but he faid the
' laft time, that he would lend no more on that
' eftate, without the immediate power of cutting
' the timber.'—'*Well, damn him, let him have*
' *it, tho' it will not be fit to cut thefe ten years; and,*
' *do you hear, get me a thoufand to-day.*'—' A
' thoufand, my lord! you faid five hundred: I
' am afraid he will think a thoufand too much!'
' *Then he fhall never have it; let me do as I will;*
' *do not I know that the timber is worth twice as*
' *much this moment, if I could wait to fet it to fale?*
' *I will not be impofed on by the rafcal: I'll go myfelf*
' *to my neighbour* Worthland *directly; he is a man*
' *of honour, and will be above taking advantage,*
' *though I did oppofe his election.*'—' As your
' lordfhip pleafes for that. But then, perhaps,
' Mr. *Difcount* will call in all his money, if he
' faw you put yourfelf into other hands; befide, I
' am not certain that he will refufe, and there-
' fore I fhould think it better to try him firft;
' you may do this after. Though I muft take
' the liberty to fay, I fhould be forry to fee
' your lordfhip ftoop to Sir *John Worthland,* after
' all the expence you have been at to give him
' trouble. For to be fure he would boaft of it in
' the country, if it were only to make you look
' little, and prevent your oppofing him again.'—
' *Why there may be fomething in that: and there-*
' *fore fee what is to be done with* DISCOUNT;
' *but*

Fig. 46. Lines from *Chrysal: Or, the Adventures of a Guinea* by Charles Johnstone, 2nd edition, 2 vols. (London, 1761), 1:72 (© The British Library Board, 12611.e.5)

deal of simplicity in your pathos."[59] Facial expressions were important at key moments, as the reader is urged to *"contract your brow into grief."*[60] Learning to read aloud forced readers to work with diverse elements of the text: using the author's often unorthodox punctuation and syntax to pattern the meaning of the prose, differentiating between different kinds of delivery for different speakers, and colouring third-person narration with the "manly pathos" demanded of the sentimental subject. One of the unsettling features of Sterne's narratives, noted by many modern critics and readers, is the way in which a work such as *Sentimental Journey* is at once bawdy and sentimental. In recording Yorick's responses to the people he meets in his unfinished journey round Europe, Sterne mocked the erotic tensions underlying sentimental encounters, but at the same time, created moments of genuine emotional pathos. This combination of irony and sentimental engagement is hard for us to negotiate now, and it also affected the performance of Sterne's fiction for would-be reciters of his own time. When the editor of *The Reader* came to introduce the celebrated story of Maria in the *Sentimental Journey* he addressed head-on the fact that the narrator, the rather unsentimental postillion, seemed to undergo a dramatic change of character in narrating the pathetic tale. He explained to his readers: *"You must not throw into the delivery of the postilion any thing of the coarse vulgarity that would be so necessary in assuming the same character in another situation. Your expression must be feelingly simple and artless in order to coincide with the meaning and intention of the writer."*[61]

Character and Personation: Being Someone Else

In the context of reading aloud, an inconsistent characterization was not so much a problem for realism as a challenge for performance. The reader needed to be careful not to assume that the same person's voice should be performed consistently throughout the text. The postilion was sometimes coarse and bluff, and sometimes meltingly pathetic—and the reciter had to work out which was which. This must have entailed some preparation, at the very least, in the form of a silent read-through beforehand. Feeling should be embodied through a contracted brow or a downcast look—yet at the same time, it should all be artless and natural. Not everyone who read fiction aloud followed these kinds of rules—but we can see the challenges implicit in giving feeling to fictional prose. Again and again *The Reader, or Reciter* encourages its users to distinguish between different speaking voices or narrative positions within the novel by adopting different tones and manners for those characters. This seems to have been an approach shared by other guides to recitation, which reflect a concern for the balance between narration and personation:

> In the Recital of mere Narratives, of Descriptions, and of argumentative or persuasive Discourses, the Reader stands in the Place, and speaks in the Person of the Writer; but in the Rehearsal of Conversation-Pieces, he must diversify not only his Mode of reciting, in Conformity to the Subject, but also in Conformity to the Character. Thus the same Narrative and Description, if spoken by different Personages, must be differently recited.[62]

Other instructors differentiated between the degrees of emotional involvement felt by a narrator. In *Principles of Elocution*, John Wilson stressed the reader's responsibility to reflect the "natural personation" of the happy or suffering subject: "Descriptions, in the *first* person, must be read differently from those in the *third:* for when joyous or sorrowful scenes are described by the happy or suffering subject, the reader is incapable of doing them justice, unless he counterfeit the feelings, and exemplify the tones of natural personation; but when the same scenes are described by a spectator, the emotions must be less vivid, the tones less varied, and the emphasis less forcible."[63]

Novels were not easy to read well aloud. As these accounts show, the elocutionary movement put pressure on readers to work out how involved the narrator or speaker was in their story—were they emotionally engaged in the action? Was a description coloured by their sentiment? It is often the case in eighteenth-century novels that free indirect speech, or reported speech, is marked out with the same inverted commas as if it were direct speech—suggesting that it was to be delivered differently from straight narration.[64]

These questions of personation show again some of the tensions within popular literary culture—and how they may have been addressed through communal reading. For the vulnerable lone reader, it was bad to lose sight of the difference between fictional romance and real life, and to overidentify with a novel's characters.[65] Reading out loud offered a chance to engage with a fictional identity through performance—while recognizing that it was only a performance, and only one part of a larger narrative structure in which there were many voices. So in some ways it could counter the problems of overidentification. It was all very well to feel the pain of the corporal's account of the death of Le Fever, but one needed to be ready to switch back into the quixotic narrative style of Tristram's narration. Various elocution writers made the point that reading a novel should be more like reading a play than a breathless monovocal racing through of the plot. Gilbert Austin, author of *Chironomia* (1806), observed that "In reading these works aloud to the public circle, custom, arising from the eager desire of unravelling the story, has determined that the mere narrative should be read with unusual rapidity." But, he emphasised, this practice should not be emulated, because "the interesting scenes demand impressive reading, and many of the scenes, which are constructed like those in a regular drama, require to be read in a similar manner."[66]

It's hard to know how contemporary readers felt about these issues of identification and distance presented by the novels they read, or to know what correlation there was between the reading advice offered by recitation manuals and the experience of actual practice. Numerous critics have noted the degree of dialogue in, for example, Frances Burney's novels—there are many conversations between distinctly individuated character voices that could be performed effectively as a comic dialogue. A well-read novel may well have sounded more like a read play than a novel. Jane Austen's niece Caroline records her reading aloud *Evelina:* "once I knew her take up a volume of Evelina and read a few pages of Mr. Smith and the Brangtons and I thought it was like a play."[67] Caroline was not alone. What struck many contemporary readers of the novel most was the ways in which it represented speech.[68]

In addition to *Evelina*'s frequent quotations of dialogue, the epistolary form of the novel replicated one of the most familiar scenes of oral reading, that of the reading aloud of correspondence within a domestic group. We can get quite a strong sense of this from a series of letters from Susannah Burney to her sister Fanny detailing how the recently published *Evelina* is being read in her household. Susannah acts as a spy on her sister's behalf, listening behind the door while her father reads to her mother, and noting down everything said about the book in her presence. Her father is praised for his ability to give life to the dialogue within the novel: "Dr. Burney does read the conversations, and mark the characters so well, 'tis quite delightful."[69] As Susannah feeds back readers' responses to Fanny, it is striking that rather than simply identifying with the heroine, Evelina, those reading and listening have a critical distance on the novel, taking greatest delight in its comic dialogue and finely delineated moments of pathos. The novel is described in "scenes," as if it were a play, with some of the most popular being the conversations in which Madame Duval is comically goaded by Captain Mirvan, which are relived in the accounts given by various readers described by Susannah. Susannah also tells of the point at which her father reads out Evelina's meeting with her father: "'I declare,' said he . . . 'I never remember crying so at a Tragedy—*had I not taken pains to check myself—I should have blubber'd*—I never read any thing higher wrought than it is—I do protest I wish it could be brought on the stage . . . I think I would advise its being part of a Drama.' "[70]

Charles Burney's sense that the novel is comparable with a play is echoed in Susannah's reportage, which suggests that the novel is perceived to fall into separate scenes, which are punctuated by considerable discussion. Her father apparently interrupts his reading all the time to comment on individual characters: "My father stopt to laugh after every speach of the Captain's—'that's excellent'—'*isn't* that good?'—'there's wit in spite of all his grossness in every word he says.' "[71] And the reading group as a whole uses the epistolary format to punctuate the reading experience with discussion: "we have read it in a most delightful manner—not hurried it over—but stopt to laugh and talk it over between almost every letter."[72] This fragmentation of the narrative doesn't preclude emotional response; Susannah's readers are just as likely to cry, or laugh until they cry, even when the story is broken up into separate sections, with discussion in between. In many ways, *Evelina* is read and appreciated as if it were a dramatic work, reminding us of the way in which the sociable reading of literature blurred generic distinctions. But it is also broken up into different sections rather than read at a long stretch. Poems got turned into moral sententiae, and plays became verse snippets or dialogues to be read aloud. Similarly, novels sometimes had afterlives as performed conversations. One of the consequences of thinking about books as social objects is that we realise that the demands of use frequently overruled the strictures of genre.

The Novel and the Self

Reading aloud enabled alternative forms of engagement with fictional works in which the relationship between reader and character could be seen as a matter of performance rather than immersion. For those anxious about the seductions of the novel, this may have mitigated the perceived dangers of reading. But we should not lose sight of the fact that there were also numerous readers who wouldn't in any circumstance have dreamt of confusing fictional characters with their own selves. John Murgatroyd, an Anglican clergyman living in the West Riding in Yorkshire, kept a commonplace book in which he recorded his reading of novels from the 1750s. Those remarks show him mining the novels he read not as a reflection of his own experiences and identity, but rather using them as a storehouse of pertinent sententiae and pronouncements.[73] So he reads, like many of his contemporaries, the picaresque novel *Gil Blas*, and he commonplaces useful observations, taking pleasure, for example, in recording a maxim from Cicero amongst its pages. When he reads *Tom Jones*, another novel about a young man's formative experiences travelling around the country, in different social groups, the notes he makes are mostly to do with love, passion, and loose women—as if he were trying to learn from those phenomena, rather than identify with the man experiencing them. Murgatroyd treats novels like he treats the other nonfictional texts he reads, using them as a source of insight and information about the world, not as a point of reference for his individual self. John or Jack Chubb, the merchant from Bridgwater, reads novels in a similar way— his prose commonplace book is full of useful extracts from factual works, anecdotes and maxims, and alongside them are passages from Godwin's *Caleb Williams* that he has titled "On Duelling," and "On Poverty," followed by extracts from Scott's *Waverley*.[74]

Other, more worldly and educated readers read fiction for entertainment and escapism, well aware that what they were consuming together had little application to real life. Although Gertrude Savile's diaries are full of references to her miserably reading romances alone on her bed, there is never any sense that she identifies with the characters or scenarios depicted. For Savile, fiction is lowbrow escapism: "I lye in Lady Cole's room, the best in the house; Peell with me. Spent this time very idly alass! I drive on the sad hours with 'Astraea.' Romances, foolish as they are, are better than worse."[75] Worse, for Savile, is indolence. When she does quote pieces of literature that seem to her to express her mood or sense of isolation, they are not from novels, but from poetry or *Spectator* essays. Mary Delany read with her friends, and exchanged books and ideas about books with them all her life. Her letters are full of references to reading novels together with her companions, and she does so with a kind of gleeful acknowledgement that what they are reading is not to be taken seriously, and in no way to be confused with real life.

We rise at eight, meet altogether at breakfast at ten, after that sit to work, Phill holds forth, Zaide—'tis a pretty romance. How I love Belasive, Alphonzo's [*sic*] mistress, and pity him, though his folly wrought his destruction.[76]

We have begun Clelia, she is a much better French lady than an English one; our hours of work and reading are from breakfast to dinner, and from five to seven our walking hours.[77]

We have been diverted lately in reading the renowned history of Reynard the Fox. The fair of Killala has added largely to our library—Parismus and Parismenos, the Seven Champions, Valentine and Orson, and various other delectable histories too numerous to be here inserted. Philosophy, romance, and history amuse us by turns.[78]

We have just finished part of a novel entitled L'Honnete Homme, or the Man of Honour; it is a fine character, but we have left the hero of the story in *so forlorn a condition* that we repent having read it, as we don't hear when the rest will be published. We are now reading Guadentio di Lucca, an entertaining, well-invented story, that pretends to be true.[79]

All these books seem to be enjoyed by Delany and her companions as diversions, entertaining ways of passing the time—not fictions confused with life.

Anna Margretta Larpent, an avid reader who left seventeen volumes of manuscript diaries covering the period 1773–1830 and marked up under the headings "Reading," "Writing," and "Society," provides a detailed picture of an active reader engaging with all sorts of different books.[80] She shows a marked preference for works by and about women, and French and English novels constitute the largest category of the books she read. Despite the fact that she shared the conventional view that novels should be approached with caution—"too seducing, too frivolous, too dangerous"[81]—she recommended select works such as *Evelina* and the *Spiritual Quixote*, and read a whole succession of novels, often by women, that dealt with the affairs of the heart. Her diaries suggest that her response to imaginative literature was strongly emotional, but that this was sharply differentiated from the kind of passionate desire found in romance. For Larpent, emotional engagement with fiction was based on virtuous sentimental response, which encouraged sympathy, not self-abandonment. She writes of Jane Austen's *Persuasion:* "They are people one can see daily—feelings one has felt or heard of daily—incidents simple & only complicated by the common effects of common causes & yet the mind is carried on by the Nature & truth which animate the story & we feel as we should in hearing that of a friend."[82] Yet her absorption was never so complete as to suspend her critical and moral faculties. Novels, when used properly, could be a source of moral profit and edification. In this respect, she resembles the moralist Hannah More, who wrote, "to those who exercise a habit of self-application a book of profane history may be made an instrument of improvement" and vice versa "without such an habit the Bible itself may, in this view, be read with little profit."[83] Like many other readers of her time, Larpent's family circle discussed novels, along with nonfictional works, which provided the assembled group the opportunity to evaluate and criticise the works read.[84] These very different approaches suggest caution in making generalizations about how historical readers responded to the books they encountered. Yet what they do indicate is that across the vast spectrum of opinion amongst those reading and moralizing about novels, there was a consensus that *how* one read was as important as *what* one read.

Novel Fashions: Sharing the Moment

Reading together was undoubtedly shaped by contemporary debates about novel reading. But while communal reading of fiction could be seen as a moral prophylactic, it could also be a way of sharing the same cultural experience, as Mary Delany and so many other engaged readers did with their friends. And if we are to consider the social lives of books, we might also think about the ways in which novels were shared in other material forms. One of the distinctive features of the rise of long fiction was the overt fashionability of the novel, and the sense that arose of certain novels being what "everyone" was reading. It has often been said that what really marked Richardson's *Pamela* out from its fictional predecessors was the public respectability of its consumption, the "Pamela Vogue."[85] Like a new style of gown, the novel was a fashionable object, widely imitated (and derided) amongst a wider and wider section of the reading population. Readers wanted to be seen with their new book. Anna Laetitia Barbauld claims that when Richardson's novel first appeared, amongst the ladies circulating at the Ranelagh pleasure gardens, "it was usual for ladies to hold up the volumes of *Pamela* to one another, to shew they had got the book that every one was talking of."[86] But they didn't have to hold up the book to show that they too were one of Richardson's new admirers. Thanks to a burgeoning trade in themed merchandise, they could flutter a *Pamela* fan, play a hand or two with *Pamela* cards, pour their friends tea in *Pamela* themed cups, display Joseph Highmore's *Pamela* prints on their walls, see the waxwork of their heroine in Shoe Lane, or dine at Vauxhall in the newly decorated *Pamela* pavilions.[87]

These commodities enabled readers to display their participation in the most fashionable new fiction—and to talk about it. The social life of the book spun out into the myriad related objects and forms that it had inspired, from prints to plates and teapots. The fact that so many of these items were an intrinsic part of the culture of visiting and public entertainment embedded popular fictions within sociable exchange and enabled consumers to take the world of the book into encounters far beyond the physical novel itself.[88] Pocket books, small portable diaries, sometimes included—along with notable dates, riddles, verse snippets, and information on fashion—depictions of scenes from recent novels. The *Norfolk Ladies Memorandum Book* for 1787 was advertised as "embellished with a beautiful descriptive plate, representing an interesting scene from Cecilia." The scene depicted is titled "The Transport of Sensibility," accompanied by the lines from the episode involving Mrs. Hill, the struggling carpenter's wife: "When we are gone, who is to help our poor Children!—I will, cried the generous Cecilia" (fig. 47).[89]

The choice of this particular episode, frequently selected for illustration in editions of the novel, demonstrates the way in which sentimental moments were privileged in such extracts.[90] A much cherished sentimental vignette in eighteenth-century fiction was the encounter between Sterne's travelling parson, Yorick, and a begging monk, Lorenzo, in *A Sentimental Journey*, in which the two men exchange snuffboxes. In this episode, Yorick refuses to give alms to Father Lorenzo, and then realises his error when he sees the monk in conversation with an attractive woman. As a peace offering, Yorick gives Lorenzo his tortoiseshell snuffbox in exchange for the monk's much less valuable horn box. The gift giving as a moment of emotional engagement spoke to many contemporary readers. Not only was the passage reprinted in *Beauties of Sterne* and other compilations, but snuffboxes bearing the words "Pater Lorenzo" on the outside, and "Yorick" on the inside were apparently available, enabling users to reenact in part the exchange between the two men as they shared a pinch of snuff.[91]

Novels thus became talking pieces through sociable souvenirs—snuffboxes, tea sets, public entertainments, and fans. In some cases those branded

THE TRANSPORT OF SENSIBILITY.

"When we are both gone, who is to help
our poor Children?
I will! cried the generous Cecilia.
From Page 148. Vol. I.

Fig. 47. "The Transport of Sensibility," an
illustration from *Cecilia* by Frances Burney,
1:148 (Henry W. and Albert A. Berg
Collection of English and American
Literature, The New York Public Library,
Astor, Lenox and Tilden Foundations)

objects reflected the significance of the object within the fiction they celebrated. Consumers who bought the Lorenzo snuffbox were well aware of the
snuff taking in Sterne's *Sentimental Journey*, while those who had purchased
the *Pamela* fan might have recalled their heroine dressing up with her fan to
act the part of a "Gentlewoman," or later, in the sequel, biting her fan in frus-
tration when meeting Lady Davers.[92] Those who cherished their Staffordshire
figurine of Maria and her faithful little dog could relish the way in which its
maker had replicated each detail of Sterne's description of her outfit, from
her twisted hair to her green-ribboned dress (fig. 48).

Some of these objects record more obscure literary enthusiasms. A
creamware jug in Liverpool Museum is transfer printed with a romantic
couple in a rural landscape, a groom at a distance holding their horses.[93] The
lines beneath it are taken from Elizabeth Helme's now largely unknown 1787
novel *Louisa; or, the Cottage on the Moor*. Does the jug reflect the work's widespread appeal in this decade? The two-volume novel, it turns out, was

Fig. 48. "Poor Maria" Staffordshire figure (Courtesy of
Andrew Dando Antiques)

published in Geneva, Leipzig, and Paris within two years, and saw eight
editions within eight years. This artifact is probably testament to a literary
moment now lost to us.

Literary keepsakes created a new, material afterlife for the celebrated
scenes they depicted, and as discussed earlier, extended the book beyond the
act of reading, and out into domestic spaces and social encounters. We can
never know what sorts of conversation these objects enabled. Perhaps, like
the merchandising surrounding a Disney franchise, they merely allowed an
expression of solidarity amongst purchasers, a sense of being in the same
cultural and consumer moment. But it seems ironic that at the same time that
novels aroused considerable critical anxiety about private reading, we also see
an overt consumption and display of novel pleasures. Some books were not to
be spoken of, while others were emblazoned all over homes and lifestyles.

Episodes and Moments

The creation and consumption of souvenir literary objects in the eighteenth century are an extension of the culture of excerpting found in prose compilations, which also offered novels "in epitome." These material and textual afterlives generally represented only a part of the whole—a selection of the most memorable or the most useful. Richardson's *Pamela* is a novel that articulates the complexities of individual decision making through a series of letter exchanges—but as a fan, it became a set of emblematic scenes illustrating Pamela's exemplarity and the rewards of virtue. A poem advertising the new product made it very clear that the fan was designed to enforce a single reading of the novel. Martha Gamble, a well-known fan maker, puffed the new accessory with these lines:

> Virtue's Reward you in this Fan may view,
> *To Honour's Tie,* Pamela *strictly true:*
> But when by conjugal Affection mov'd,
> A Pattern to her Sex, and Age, she prov'd.
> In ev'ry amiable Scene of Life,
> Beneficent, fond Parent, loving Wife.[94]

Within the print tradition of beauties, editors gave their readers not continuously plotted fiction with a coherent narrative, but little sections of relevant or enjoyable text that could be read alone or aloud within a relatively short time span. So how does this model of discontinuous reading relate to the structure of the eighteenth-century novel? Many of the dominant accounts of eighteenth-century fiction have emphasised the way in which the early novel privileged interiority for the first time.[95] Such a model would seem to lend itself towards a solitary reader and continuous reading. There were other trends associated with fast, silent reading. Critics of the novel—especially in its gothic and sensational versions—lamented the ways in which readers raced from page to page, hardly stopping to read the words in their desire to unravel the plot: "curiosity is kept upon the stretch from page to page, and from volume to volume, and the secret, which the reader thinks himself every instant on the point of penetrating, flies like a phantom before him" (fig. 49).[96]

While many of the Gothic novels of the later eighteenth century easily bear out this observation in breathlessly plot-driven narrative that constantly defers full revelation, there are plenty of other examples of the way in which fictions of the time are structured episodically, making them easily extractable

Fig. 49. James Gillray, *Tales of Wonder!* London, 1802, hand-coloured etching (Library of Congress, LC-USZ62-139066)

either by individual readers or editors. Whether we think about the multiple inset narratives packed into the amatory fictions of the early eighteenth century or the discrete adventures of *Robinson Crusoe,* many kinds of fictional forms worked well as sequences of stand-alone episodes. The unconnected experiences of the objects featured in the narratives or novels of circulation of the later eighteenth century were also broken down into smaller parts—either through reading in instalments or publishing in instalments. The novel of sentiment achieves emotional effect by fragmentary structure, often denying resolution in the short episodes it presents.[97] Sarah Fielding's *David Simple,* like Mackenzie's *Man of Feeling* and so many other sentimental fictions, has a plot constructed largely from the stories that the protagonist hears about other people's lives—stories that stand alone as exemplars of human suffering, and have little sequential relationship with one another.[98] Such fictions were extensively culled by editors and anthologists as a series of moments. Elsewhere, novelists drew on the picaresque tradition in continental fiction—Smollett's much republished *Roderick Random* and *Peregrine Pickle* drew on the idea of the knight errant and his unconnected adventures as evolved through *Don Quixote* and *Gil Blas* (which Smollett had translated) to tell stories of modern-day travellers narrating a series of causally unlinked experiences in their voyages round the country.

Not everyone got the hang of reading from episode to discrete episode, however. One of the gems of the Clays' reading records studied by Jan Fergus involves the efforts of a boy called Arthur Miller, who was allowed to take out the first volume of *Peregrine Pickle* for a further week (having returned the second volume) because "the first he cant make out therefore must have it next week."[99] Miller's case aside, disconnected fictional structures were on the whole eminently suitable for reading in short bursts, with plots and characters that did not require an extensive knowledge of the immediately preceding chapters or even volumes.

And there is plenty of evidence to suggest that eighteenth-century readers read fiction occasionally and partially. They did so with all kinds of books, from sermons to voyages and long poems—but such habits are more of a challenge to our understanding of novel reading. As we have seen, Anne Lister's diary reveals a woman who habitually noted in her daily entries records of runs of pages of a range of genres, very rarely reading more than a short section of one volume. In her case, and probably that of many other readers, partial immersion in a novel doesn't impede emotional response, and we might pause to think here about the equation of solitary immersion and emotional response. Other diarists enable us to map out the pattern of reading within a home. The young Elizabeth Tyrrell's account of her family's reading in her diary of 1818 gives us a flavor how this might have worked. On 25 June she describes her visit to a family in Mortlake: "we played in the garding and after dinner the Miss Andrews and Miss Eliza Bullock went to pay a visit at Barnes and the two Miss Pykes Miss James and I worked and then read part of Shakespeare's play of (Much Do about nothing)." Elizabeth's social life is a constantly changing cycle of interconnected groups, as on this day. She goes with one friend to visit other acquaintances; more join them; the groups separate, re-form, and read part of a play together. They only read a portion of the play, and they never reassemble to read more. She records a more continuous engagement with Fanny Burney's novel *Cecilia*. We first hear that her mother reads part of the novel to her and her sisters on 29 June, while they work, continuing the following day. Two days later, the mother goes out for a walk while one of the sisters reads. Ten days later some young female friends, the Pykes, come round, and one of them reads *Cecilia* while the rest of the girls, and Elizabeth's mother, work. At the end of July *Cecilia* is still being read, and this continues until mid-August, when the mother reads the final part, after which Elizabeth pronounces, "I like it beter than either Everlina or Camilla two which Mamma read to us or that we have read to ourselves."[100] The novel had been read in parts over a span of six weeks in total.

Elizabeth Tyrrell's diary entries show some interesting things. Some books, in this case Shakespeare's *Much Ado,* were only read as short extracts; others, like *Cecilia,* were read over a long period of time, as were, presumably, *Camilla* and *Evelina,* the additional Burney novels that the family had read together. It is not surprising that it took a while—*Cecilia* was a long novel, consisting of five volumes in duodecimo. But because of the constantly changing pattern of sociability within the Tyrrells' household, the readers and listeners involved in its complete delivery varied considerably. What does this tell us? We can see that when novels weren't published in serial instalments, they were probably consumed in serialised form, and not everyone would have been familiar with the previous instalment. There must have been a lot of catch-up necessitated, and one can trace some of this recapitulation of plot and segmentation of story in the style of novels themselves.

Anna Larpent's diary entries also record the partial reading of multiple books on a single day. On 1 July 1780 she hears her sister Clara read Rollin's *Histoire Ancienne,* then reads to a group of friends the sentimental novel *Marianne,* while the friends work on sewing and embroidery. After dinner she works, while another guest reads Hugh Kelly's comedy *School for Wives,* and then after supper, in mixed company, she reads some more passages from *Marianne.*[101] None of these groups of readers recorded in the diary can have heard or read more than a small portion of the whole novel.

The evidence of book borrowing in the period also suggests habits of partial reading. Jan Fergus's study of readers in the Midlands reveals the prevalence of browsing within multivolume novels, even within incomplete sets.[102] She has shown that this desultory or incomplete reading takes up some 17 percent of all the borrowing from the Clays' circulating library—with a higher proportion of these kinds of readers being women and schoolboys.[103] Some readers began in the middle of a work. Mrs. Hervey of Warwick takes out only volumes 2 and 3 of Richardson's four-volume *Pamela* from her circulating library; a Miss Sawbridge seems to have made a regular habit of incompletion, taking only the third and fourth volumes of *Amelia,* and in one year, 1779, taking out only two unspecified volumes of the anonymous *Sir William*

Harrington (four volumes) and five of six volumes of *The Arabian Nights*.[104] Informal borrowing, especially of multivolume sets, shows a similar phenomenon. Readers seem to have seldom lent or borrowed multiple volumes—so they inevitably experienced gaps between one volume and the next, a disruption of the chronological ordering, or were unable to read the whole set at all.

The diary of the young Edinburgh apprentice lawyer George Sandy records the backwards and forwards of books between him and his friends, in their small book club. They only ever exchange part of a multivolume set: "Jas. Milligan got the loan of Pennant's Tour Vol. 1st.";[105] "Got the loan of the First volume of Strutt from James Milligan."[106] Later, Sands lends the first two volumes of Henry Brooke's sentimental picaresque novel *The Fool of Quality*.[107] Letter exchanges also document people reading volumes in isolation or at some distance from other parts of the same book. John Penrose, visiting Bath in 1767, writes to his wife telling her about the books he has bought: "I have bought Fanny the 3rd vol. of *Clarissa*, a dirty dab price 1 s. Dolly says, the other vol. she wants, is the 7th. If so, I cannot get it. I could have any odd vol. except that and the 1st."[108] Presumably Fanny had access to volumes 1–2 and 4–6 and had read at least some of them without her missing volumes.

Short Forms

The argument just made for the discontinuous or interrupted nature of eighteenth-century reading experiences assumes that fiction predominantly took the form of full multivolume novels. But we also know that this wasn't the way in which a majority of middling-sort readers had access to fiction. It was much more likely that they read it in magazine extracts than in expensive multivolume novels. The volume of magazine publication of fiction greatly dwarfs the range or quantity of fiction published in book format, and there was a lot of fiction out there that did not fit with the "rise of the novel" narrative—fiction rarely mentioned in publishers' lists, and rarely appearing in reviews, which had a wide currency in eighteenth-century England.[109] The growing prevalence of this literature has been attributed to the growth of a new reading audience, which was "naïve, sentimental, and eager for the airs of gentility."[110] A publication like the *Lady's Magazine*, perhaps the most continuously successful magazine, running over sixty-two years, gives some indication of the aspirational nature of its readership, one not entirely *au fait* with literary culture. Essays entitled "Hints on Reading" gave instruction on what kinds of books to read and when to read them. So, reading to pass the time while having one's hair done could be appropriate, but reading in bed was a fire hazard and conducive to bad dreams. Elsewhere it was emphasised that readers should not make the mistake of reading the ending of a novel first, and so spoiling the ingenuity of the plot.[111]

Short-form fiction ruled in the middlebrow market of the magazine, and the distinctive feature of much of the magazine publication was in drastic abridgements or so-called epitomes—forms not that different from the lengthy summaries or extended quotations in early book reviews. Magazine editors favoured the "detached episode" produced by writers like Johnson, Goldsmith, Brooke, Mackenzie, and later, Charlotte Smith and John Moore. Publications such as *Harrison's Novelist's Magazine* (1780–88) drew together fictional genres we rarely consider—translations, Chinese or oriental tales, moral tales, works by women writers—and suggested that they were worth keeping or preserving.[112] The *Lady's Magazine* was fronted with a piece of prose fiction, in the form of an independent tale or romance or as part of a continuation of a story, broken up into conveniently and tantalizingly presented gobbets. Readers were enticed with titles like "The Intimation: A Tale," "The Casket," "Love Without Wings," "The Fatal Effects of Despair: A Tale."

The abbreviated forms of fiction that evolved over the course of the century in magazines were not the only template for short stories. The miscellanies and books that proliferated also offered short comic prose pieces for the delectation of their readers. They are not what we usually think of as eighteenth-century fiction, but the vein of jovial narrative that runs through popular print culture in this era, often accompanied by the verse riddles discussed in Chapter 5, is an important part of understanding how people read imaginative stories. It offers a counter to the idea that the sentimental and the sensational were the only kinds of narrative available, and also a different way of thinking about readerly identification with fictional characters. Many jestbook or story compilations were expressly aimed at sociable delivery. The title page of *Fisher's Cheerful Companion* (1800) declared its purpose "to promote Laughter; being a Humorous Collection of Interesting Stories for a Winter's Evening Fireside; or Amusement for Summer, in a Shady Retreat."[113] Inside we find a series of short comic tales: "The Three Dexterous Thieves," "The Hunch-back'd Minstrels," "The Humorous Miller." These are narratives whose pleasure lies in the comic reversal and the quip—offering kinds of reading experiences very different from the intense emotional engagement of the gothic or sentimental. Another collection, which advertised its wares on the title page as including "diverting stories" and "droll dialogues," bore a preface in which the art of storytelling was explained.[114] The editor started by saying that there were five different kinds of storytellers: "the Short, the Long, the Marvellous, the Insipid, and the Delightful."[115] Having described the traits of each one, he closed by emphasizing the most important point of all—to keep it short:

> If any Person, of what Rank soever, shall presume to exceed Six
> Minutes in a Story, to hum or haw, use Hyphens between his Words,
> or Digressions, or offers to engage the Company to hear another
> Story when he has done, or speaks one Word more than is necessary,
> or is a Stammerer in his Speech; that said it shall and may be lawful
> for any one of the said Company, or the whole Company together to
> pull out his, or her, or their Watches, to make use of broad Hints, or
> Innuendos, for him the said Story Teller to break off, although
> abruptly: Otherwise he is to have a Glove, or Handkerchief crammed
> into his Mouth.[116]

The *Merry Medley*'s irreverent portrait of group listening reminds us of the ways in which time and space were shared in communal reading. To perform for others often meant negotiating the interests and the egos of those present in the social circle, and tailoring one's offering to suit their attention span (fig. 50).

The *Merry Medley* is like many other jestbook and comic story collections, an assortment of tales about individuals not known to the reader, which were designed for use in company. Stories relating to particular figures become detached from their original author and circulated as part of a wider collection of witticisms. But in circulation, they continued to evoke the witty world that generated them. Most of the stories in jestbooks are based in towns, usually in London. Many were advertised by association with the haunts of town wits, and with their urbanity. There is much topical metropolitan humor in accounts of celebrated "frolicks" and "humbugs"; jokes about the London stage and high politics, and about famous courtiers or men of fashion.[117] Both manuscript and printed jests were a genre of recycling and updating—the scores of jestbooks published across the eighteenth century reused much of the same material, in slightly different formats and orders. Yet many of the jokes also retained a certain biographical specificity. Although lots of tales

Fig. 50. James Gillray, *"The feast of reason, & the flow of soul,"—i.e.—the wits of the age, setting the table in a roar,* London, 1797, hand-coloured etching (© Courtesy of the Warden and Scholars of New College, Oxford / Bridgeman Images)

centred around stock types—the shrewish wife, the Irishman, the cuckold—other comic narratives were based on real-life celebrity jokesters, Sir John Fielding, Baron Munchausen, the Earl of Rochester, Charles II, or Beau Nash. *Joe Miller's Jests,* perhaps the most frequently reprinted collection of the era, purported to contain the witty jests of Joe Miller, the early-eighteenth-century actor. *Sir John Fielding's Jests* are said to be "carefully transcribed from original manuscript remarks, and notes made on such occasions . . . where the above celebrated Genius and his Jovial Companions (the drollest Wits of the Present Age) usually met to Kill Care and promote the Practice of Mirth and Good Humour." The idea was that readers could use a collection such as this to re-create a sort of celebrity jokester's alehouse evening entertainment within their own homes. The reality was that the content of this particular collection was material recycled from innumerable other jest-books, and was highly unlikely to have come from manuscript jottings of the *bon mots* of John Fielding. But it is premised on the idea that it is pleasurable to have joviality by proxy, a kind of borrowed fun.

This is also the case in some of the longer narrative collections. One publication, *Baron Munchausen's Narrative of his Marvellous Travels and Campaigns in Russia*, is described as "recommended to Country Gentlemen; and, if they please, to be repeated *as their own* [emphasis added], after a hunt, at horse races, in watering-places, and other such polite assemblies; round the bottle and fire-side."[118] The fictional collection of stories within, assembled by the German writer Rudolph Erich Raspe, was inspired by the historical figure of Hieronymus Karl Friedrich von Münchhausen, a German nobleman who had gained a reputation as an imaginative after-dinner storyteller, creating witty and highly exaggerated accounts of his adventures in Russia. Over the ensuing thirty years, his storytelling abilities gained such renown that he frequently received visits from travelling nobles wanting to hear his stories. Raspe took the reputation of the real von Münchhausen and created a fictional character upon whom a whole assemblage of implausible anecdotes could be hung.[119] So what began as a real-life collection of tall tales was fictionalised as a vehicle for assorted travel anecdotes, which could in turn be appropriated by their readers for rendition "to be repeated as their own." Here we get a completely different conception of the relationship between reader and fictional character, or narrator, one in which far from there being an anxiety about overidentification with the imagined world, readers were *encouraged* to appropriate fictional anecdotes as their own. W. Carew Hazlitt observed astutely in 1890: "We are not apt to ask ourselves the question, who delivered the joke, or ushered it into print? There are cases, of course, where the author of a sally or rejoinder, himself repeats it to a third party, possibly in its original shape, possibly with embellishments; but there must be, nay, there are numberless instances in which a funny thing is given to a person, not because he said it, but because he might or would have done so."[120]

The journey from oral culture to print has come full circle. Jokes that began in oral tradition were published in printed form, and those tales were then reappropriated back into a shared cultural exchange of storytelling. Jestbooks and collections of comic stories offer a sense of the multiple perspectives on fiction available. We are accustomed to thinking of the eighteenth-century novel of manners as dramatizing conversation, and some critics have argued that the fictional conversations in novels provided a model for young women wanting to learn to speak in company.[121] Jestbooks and comic stories offered material for improving conversation in another way, supplying their readers with ready-made wit with which to delight their companions.[122] Rather than seeing eighteenth-century jestbooks merely as a continuation of a traditional genre of popular entertainment, we could see them as part of the broader culture of eighteenth-century self-improvement, like the elocutionary manuals that taught aspiring middle-class readers to read with assurance before their friends. Jestbooks offered handholding for those keen to become the jovial and entertaining sociable man or woman at the centre of the group.[123] *Fun for the Parlour* was said to be "calculated to render Conversation agreeable, and to pass long Evenings with Wit and Merriment."[124] The intangible art of "good conversation" was a cornerstone of eighteenth-century polite sociability, and collections such as this one were part of this project.

⧲⧳

It is hard to understand the role of fiction in the eighteenth-century home without engaging with contemporary debates (however unrepresentative of the reality) about the nature of reading and readers. Concerns about novels, and their dangers, undoubtedly shaped the ways in which fiction reading was perceived, and led to an emphasis on the value of communal activity and discussion. Again and again wholesome domestic shared reading is set against the dangerous isolationism of the solitary female reader. But there were other issues at stake, such as how to perform character within prose fiction, and how to combine dialogue with narration. Both the books that attempted to offer advice on reading fiction aloud and the anecdotal evidence of novel reading suggest that good fiction reading resembled dramatic dialogue. And the novel was not the whole story. One of the most illuminating aspects of exploring the life of fiction in the home is the relative importance of the fictional forms that are rarely considered by modern readers and critics. Magazine instalments, abridgements, and jestbooks offered very different ways of considering the relationship between imagined and lived experience.

8. Piety and Knowledge

You employ your evenings in reading the History of England
to my mother & sisters & you are not perhaps aware of the
many advantages you may derive from this.
—William Woollcombe to Henry Woollcombe, 17 November 1793

We might expect imaginative literature to be the stuff of entertainment and sociable exchange—as they still are for many readers in the twenty-first century. But what about history, science, or religion? How were those books shared? Library catalogues and diaries show that the borrowing, selling, and reading of sermons, histories, and travel writing dwarfed that of literary works. Records of books sold in parts show that by far the largest genre available in this form was history, followed by geography, topography, and travel, then biblical commentary, church history, and treatises on morality. Imaginative works come some way down the list.[1] The expanding print market created newly accessible formats across many areas of intellectual enquiry, and the display of generalist knowledge about historical figures, botany, or astronomy was a prominent part of polite accomplishment for both men and women.

There were multiple reasons why eighteenth-century readers consumed nonfiction works together at home—for piety, self-improvement, entertainment. And there were some who just didn't want to immerse themselves in imagined worlds, favouring a more utilitarian approach to their reading. In the late 1770s, William Jones, a clergyman, went to Jamaica to work as a tutor to the sons of an estate owner named William Harrison. There he had access to his employer's books: "A well-chosen Collection of valuable Books on most subjects Mr. Harrison's Library affords, which I enjoy an unrestrain'd use of."² Jones clearly read widely in the library he had found—but Harrison did not. Jones recalls:

> Perused, last Sunday evening, with Mr. H., much of Dr. Young's *Night-Thoughts*. I with difficulty refrained from tears, while I smiled at the simplicity, which was that of a child, with which Mr. H. (in tears) observed, "Were I to indulge in reading much of such books, I should be extremely fond of them, but it wou'd absolutely incapacitate me for attending to my Business; I shou'd not attend the next Court of Admiralty; shou'd not care, whether I were worth a dollar in the world, &, consequently, shou'd neglect my children & Family."³

For someone like William Harrison, books were not for entertainment or distraction—they were useful and educational.

Religion at Home

As we have seen in the first chapter, the elocution movement was closely related to the changing world of the pulpit. Religious environments not only affected what people read together; they also shaped how they read. In the fifteenth and sixteenth centuries reading out a prewritten sermon was frowned upon, seen as a sign of laziness and mechanical delivery, which could not convey the passion of genuine religious oratory or a sense of real spiritual authenticity. But by the late seventeenth century it was increasingly acceptable for preachers to read out prewritten sermons.⁴ It's not difficult to imagine many of them welcoming the change. The author of some of the most popular printed sermons of the eighteenth century, John Tillotson, started off by preaching from memory, but said that the effort of trying to remember so much "heated his head so much, a day or two before & after he preached, that he was forced to leave it off."⁵ In theory, the sermon as written was the brainchild of the preacher himself, but it could also be the work of another. The possibility of not spending Saturday night writing another original treatment of the Scripture must have been appealing to many clergymen, and the huge market in printed sermons during the eighteenth century was a gift for the overworked, uninspired, or lazy.

One ingenious priest turned publisher, John Trusler, printed sermons in a special handwritten script, a lithographic typeface that imitated copperplate handwriting, so that keen-eyed members of the congregation peering down from the galleries would think the text the work of the preacher rather than an off-the-peg version (fig. 51).[6] Trusler assured potential users that they would not be caught out in their shortcut: "only 400 copies of any one sermon, are, at any time vended; that they do not pass through the hands of the booksellers, of course, the Clergy may rest satisfied that they never can be too general."[7] By the early nineteenth century it was possible to buy Charles Simeon's skeleton sermons, a collection of 2,536 pro forma sermons on every book of the Old and New Testament. These *Horae Homileticae* contained the basic outline of content, which could be filled in according to the preacher's wishes, giving the reassurance of guidance with room for individual detail.

The shift from the idea of the sermon as impromptu oratory to one based on the reading out of written discourse undoubtedly changed the nature of late seventeenth- and eighteenth-century sermons. Without the need to commit the whole thing to memory, the author of the sermon could produce a much more

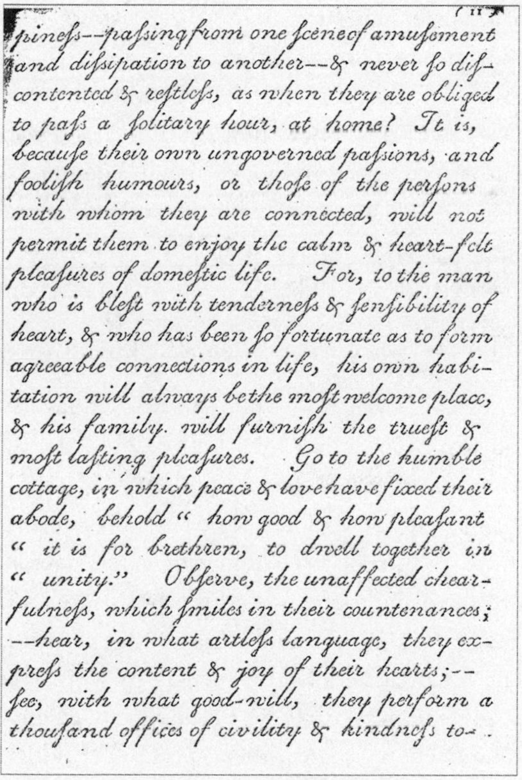

piness--passing from one scene of amusement and dissipation to another--& never so discontented & restless, as when they are obliged to pass a solitary hour, at home? It is, because their own ungoverned passions, and foolish humours, or those of the persons with whom they are connected, will not permit them to enjoy the calm & heart-felt pleasures of domestic life. For, to the man who is blest with tenderness & sensibility of heart, & who has been so fortunate as to form agreeable connections in life, his own habitation will always be the most welcome place, & his family will furnish the truest & most lasting pleasures. Go to the humble cottage, in which peace & love have fixed their abode, behold " how good & how pleasant " it is for brethren, to dwell together in " unity." Observe, the unaffected chearfulness, which smiles in their countenances; --hear, in what artless language, they express the content & joy of their hearts;-- see, with what good-will, they perform a thousand offices of civility & kindness to-.

Fig. 51. Page of printed copperplate script from *On Domestic Happiness* by John Trusler (London, 1785) (© The British Library Board, 4477.d.120)

structured piece of debate, more like a moral essay than a fire and brimstone harangue.[8] But if prewritten sermons were less taxing on the memory, they were also apt to degenerate into monotony in the hands—or mouth—of a bad reader. Trusler, who was renowned for his accessible and powerful sermons, lamented: "Though a discourse be penn'd with the greatest judgement— though it be elegantly written and even addressed to the passions, still if it be delivered as is too commonly the case, with a tone between singing and saying and with all the art of nasal eloquence [. . .] what can he [the preacher] expect but that his congregation should smile at his oratory or doze over his doctrines?"[9]

Early elocution manuals from the 1760s and 1770s were intended to rectify the problem, and to give clear guidance on how to read well and inspire the devout flock, as we have seen. Trusler's *The Sublime Reader* gave specific instructions on the delivery of every aspect of the prayer book. In an advertisement for the volume, he diplomatically suggested that even the most well meaning of ministers might sometimes get distracted when conducting their services: "Disturbances of any kind, irreverent or irregular conduct in the people, absence of parishioners, their coming in after the Service is begun, and, many other causes, will tend, at times, to take off his attention from the Office he is engaged in, and make him, in a degree, forget himself."[10] Trusler was taking no chances with his potentially distracted pupils; he provided them with marked-up versions of every aspect of the church service, in which italics were used to indicate epithets, capitals for substantives, commas and dashes for shorter and longer pauses.

In spite of the dangers of poor delivery or poor content, for many churchgoers the sermon was the high point of the Sunday service, and worth shopping around for. Much more than a gloss on a passage of Scripture, sermons were a moral compass, a source of entertainment, a method of fundraising, and a form of politics.[11] They were part of the broader political and cultural life of their readers, perused alongside verse, pamphlets, or newspapers dealing with the same topics.[12] And their pleasures and benefits could also be enjoyed at home. By the mid–eighteenth century printed sermons were so prevalent that preachers felt that the clergy were in competition with print, and that parishioners preferred reading a selection of published sermons to coming to church to hear them speak.[13] Sermonists warned of the dangers of this: "it is a very dangerous mistake in many among us, to think that the reading the Scriptures or a good Sermon at *Home* is sufficient, whilst they neglect the Publick Ministry of God's Word in the *Church*."[14]

For those too old, ill, or infirm to go to church, reading a sermon together at home was often the best substitute for formal religious practice. Henry Prescott, a church administrator living in Chester in the early eighteenth century, reveals that when indisposed on a Sunday he read the Psalms and the lesson for the day at home.[15] Anne Lister, living with an infirm aunt, sometimes observed religious practices in a domestic setting: "My uncle went to morning church but my aunt staid at home with me. Heard her read the psalms & chapters & then came upstairs & lay down most of the day."[16] On other occasions, like so many of her contemporaries, Lister goes to church in the morning and then spends the evening reading a sermon aloud to members of her family.

Across the evidence of many different kinds of diaries and readers, we see that Sundays were generally reserved for religious reading. Henry Woollcombe, the young lawyer from Plymouth, was not alone when he commented in his diary: "I have long accustomed myself to read Books Moral or Divine on the Sabbath."[17] In her diary of Norfolk parish life, Nancy Woodforde reads a sermon every Sunday to her uncle (he rarely if ever mentions this in his diary).[18] One Gloucestershire diarist, Elizabeth Prowse, writes in 1759: "Sunday evenings, Sacred Musick at Mincing Lane, & our rooms both well filled, the one with our particular Friends, the other with the best Performers joyned our Own Band."[19] In Amelia Steuart's household in Perthshire, her brother spent Sunday evenings sustaining his family with rather less jolly religious entertainment: "in the evening my Brother read a discourse on Death & the advantages of having it always in our view." The following week, "at night my Brother read to us from Parsons directory, chiefly upon the punishment of the wicked in Hell. Gave a most dreadful description of their tortures."[20]

The sermon preached at church had a role in the home even if it wasn't read out there in printed form. On their return from church on Sundays parents were expected to rehearse with the whole family in the text and content of the sermon.[21] Instructional and catechistical manuals for Anglicans and Dissenters stressed the role of the family in religious education, and usually contained morning and evening prayers for each day of the week, with graces for before and after meals, prayers for times of special stress, and scriptural passages for rote learning.[22] The family unit—with its penumbra of servants, apprentices, and unmarried relatives—played an important role in the instruction and practice of Christian faith.

Even if people could not read themselves, they had long bought printed texts and books in the expectation that they would be read aloud to when the opportunity arose.[23] It was the duty of Christian heads of households to read aloud to their families, and as formal education expanded, so the possibility that children might do this for their parents became ever more likely. Given the scale of production, the family Bible was becoming a more common possession by the end of the seventeenth century, and, as Richard Baxter observed, "some few that cannot read get others to read to them, and get a good measure of saying knowledge."[24] The same was true of the catechisms containing the basic articles of faith that clergymen like Baxter read to their unlearned parishioners, who would learn them by rote.[25] Diaries and spiritual journals show frequent echoes of the phrases from the Prayer Book, suggesting that many people were committing the Orders for Morning and Evening Prayer and the collects and probably the Psalms to memory.[26]

Some diarists left records only of their religious reading practice, listing no reading at all for recreational purposes. The recusant Catholic Nicholas Blundell faithfully documented the saplings he planted, the pies he had been given, and the neighbours he received, but of his life with books, he simply commented, "I read a Spirituall Booke most of the after Noone in my Closet"[27] or "I read in a Spirituall Booke by my Wife whiles she was writing Letters most of the after noone."[28] His habit of recording devotional reading clearly reflects one of the most significant roles that group reading played within the home; but the fact that it is recorded in the absence of any other reading may also speak of the nature of the eighteenth-century diary as a form of spiritual testimonial. In Blundell's case, it has a special significance because of the proscriptions against Catholics. We can tell from Blundell's account book and capacious diary that he went to book sales, bought his neighbours' books at auctions, ordered from booksellers in Liverpool, and borrowed from friends and acquaintances living nearby. But he only consistently records his reading of religious books. The son and grandson of Royalist recusants, his faith was not one he could practice in an open setting. While there is little overt comment on politics or religion in the diary, the consequences of his Catholicism are evident in his reading life. He writes at least twice that he has "red much in Quid me persequeris."[29] *Quid me persequeris* ("Why are you persecuting me?") was a small book, written by his grandfather, dealing with the penal laws in force against Roman Catholics. This grandfather, William Blundell, had had a few copies printed to distribute amongst friends, and the circulation and preservation of this work, like that of other Catholic or Jacobite texts at this time, became in itself an emblem of faith.

As the political climate intensified in the early years of the eighteenth century, Nicholas Blundell responded by moving some of his books from public to private spaces in his house, putting "schoolbooks and spirituall books" in his personal closet. Fifteen years later, his books and pictures, presumably Catholic or Jacobite, were seized and burned at the custom house on his return from a trip to Flanders. Reading with others, for him, was part of creating a social identity for a minority religion. When he writes "My Wife and I went to Richard Harrisons and sat some time there. We read in the Dining Roome in a Spirituall Booke"[30] or "My Wife & I read to my Aunt Frances Blundell in a Spirituall Book in the Parlor," we get a glimpse into the powerful cohesive role of reading together within the recusant community.[31]

In a 1725 sermon decrying a decline in private morality, Edward Chandler invoked the established notion that "a man's house was a little Oratory, where the master himself prayed with all his family, and read a portion of Scripture to them."[32] Practical devotional books offered guidance for those responsible for maintaining their own "domestic oratory." *The Whole Duty of Man,* written by Richard Allestree, and first published in 1658, was in twenty-five editions by 1690 and well over fifty by the mid–eighteenth century, and was the dominant religious work of the period. It was so widespread that it was probably known to everyone in the country, and along with a Bible, a catechism, and a Book of Common Prayer, it would have been the book most commonly found in a household's reading. Many of the eighteenth-century editions were subtitled "Necessary for all Families." The *Whole Duty* took each reader through a cycle of self-examination and meditations, and extended editions were accompanied by prayers, concordances, and biblical extracts for home use. It contained advice on domestic prayer:

> A second sort of Publick Prayer is that in a Family, where all that are Members of it join in their common Supplications; and this ought also to be very carefully attended to, first, by the Master of the Family, who is to look that there be such Prayers ... If either himself, or any of his Family can read, he may use some Prayers out of some good Book; . . . if they cannot read, it will then be necessary they should be taught without Book some Form of Prayer which they may use in the Family.[33]

Other titles supplemented the *Whole Duty,* works designed for family and personal use and especially concerned with fostering regular devotional habits, including daily family prayers and private prayer.[34] Children were often asked to read part of the family evening duty, as a form of education and instruction, sometimes during meals. In working-class families where children had learnt to read, while their parents could not, it was they who made books speak. James Lackington famously described the changing cultural habits amongst "the poor country people" who previously "spent their winter evenings in relating stories of witches, ghosts, hobgoblins, &c. now shorten the nights by hearing their sons and daughters read tales, romances, &c."[35] In this account, the reading performed by the young is primarily fiction—and as Richard D. Altick points out, the scenario is highly implausible, given the high cost of the novels and romances Lackington describes.[36] But the potential literacy of the children of the poor was also crucial to religious education in the late eighteenth century.

Martha More, sibling of Hannah More, worked with her sister setting up schools for local children in Somerset. In her *Mendip Annals,* she describes the large groups of illiterate adults attending the reading aloud of sermons and prayers in the evenings: "it is a vast consolation to know, that every hard-working parent in this parish . . . can find a child who can bring the additional refreshment of reading to him a few verses of Scripture."[37] These Somerset children were taught reading, the Bible, and the catechism—though, interestingly, they were not taught how to write, a practice that continued into the late nineteenth century.[38] For some children it was literally a punishment. The Newcastle engraver Thomas Bewick tells how as a boy he was punished for getting into a fight and subsequently, "I was obliged to attend my master to church twice a day, every Sunday, and, at night, to read the Bible, or some other good book, to old Mrs. Beilby and her daughter, or others of the family."[39]

Thomas Turner, the mid-eighteenth-century schoolteacher turned shopkeeper from East Hoathly, writes often of reading religious matter at home: "In the evening finished reading Wake's Catechism, which I think a very good book and proper for all families, there being good instructions in it and also something which is prodigious moving."[40] Turner was typical of his class. Practical devotional works had a reach right through the middling and lower social groups. Detailed studies of book ownership in rural Wales show that such books drew a substantial number of subscribers from a reading level below that of the parish gentry. The book collection at Townend, the home of many generations of the Brownes, a yeoman farmer family in the Troutbeck Valley in the Lake District, shows a large collection of sermons and practical divinity. The inventory collection assembled by the Geffrye tells a similar story. Some householders had nearly a hundred books, and some only two or three, but the collections are heavily weighted towards devotional material. Alongside the Bible, the New Testament, and the Book of Common Prayer, the most popular items are Nelson's *Festivals and Fasts*, Foxe's *Book of Martyrs* and *The Whole Duty of Man*. In addition to this literature of daily piety, we also see readers addressing more substantial theological works. The dense arguments of printed sermons might sometimes have been easier to follow at home than in the crowded and noisy arena of the communal church, as John Trusler noted: "Long sermons in which abstruse points of divinity and morality are systematically discussed are beyond the capacity of two thirds of congregations—short and plain ones or large portions of scripture paraphrased are better harkened to."[41]

The diaries of Thomas Turner amply illustrate the variety of types of religious reading and the influence of ingrained habits of Christian self-improvement on a reading life. Married from a young age, Turner was a regular Anglican churchgoer with bourgeois, thrifty habits (he had, for instance, the habit of dining on the leftovers of previous meals for days on end). He was also a prodigious reader. In the period covered by the diaries, he read, and commented upon, most of the major works from the mid–eighteenth century, including Swift's *Tale of a Tub*, Pope's *Dunciad* and translation of Homer ("the language being vastly good and the turn of thought and expression beautiful"),[42] Richardson's *Clarissa* ("a very well-written thing"),[43] Gay's *Fables* ("a very good lesson of morality"),[44] and Thomson's *The Seasons* ("describe[s] nature very justly").[45] He also read sixteenth- and seventeenth-century works ("think Hamlet's character extremely fine and on the whole think it a good play"),[46] John Locke's *Essay on Human Understanding* ("a very abstruse book"),[47] and Milton's *Paradise Lost* ("it exceeds anything I ever read for sublimity of language and beauty of similes").[48] But for Turner, as for many of his time, these secular works were almost invariably viewed through a religious lens. He had no time for mere entertainment: "In the evening read part of a book entitled *The Prudent Jester*, which I think is a poor silly empty piece of ribaldry."[49] He read *Paradise Lost* as a testament to divine creation, and the notes he makes on what he has read frequently turn on their moral exemplarity: "My wife read the 20th and 21st numbers of *The Guardian* to me, which I think extremely good, the first of which shows how indispensable a duty forgiveness is and the last how much mankind must be delighted with the prospect of the happiness of a future state."[50]

Turner treated most of his reading, of whatever kind, as an advice manual whose wisdom was to be internalised as a matter of pressing importance. His comments are occasionally evaluative, but more usually a way of commonplacing the useful insights gleaned from what he has read. During the course of his diaries he consumes a bewilderingly wide range of books in his quest for knowledge, such as Bishop Burnet's *History of the Reformation*, Joseph Tournefort's *Voyage into the Levant*, Hervey's *Theron and Aspasio*, Richard Mead's *A Mechanical Account of Poisons*, *The Complete Letter Writer*, and Henry Bracken's *Farriery Improv'd*. He seems to be particularly struck by the advice on offer from periodicals and magazines, treating periodicals as a kind of social or cultural bible, and recording in his diary their examples of debauchery, virtue, or piety that speak to him. Sometimes he wondered if he just liked them because they reflected his own opinions: "In the evening read part of the London Magazine for July, in which I find a great many excellent pieces, more than I ever remember to have seen in any one magazine. Perhaps I may be partial in my opinion, and only think them excellent as they agree with my own sentiments, for we are apt to be partial in our judgment of men and books as they agree and are similar to our own thoughts."[51]

Before we assume Turner's approach to be the naive self-identification of a self-educated man, it's worth bearing in mind that other, better educated men felt the same way, and expressed their desire to act and talk like the figures in the periodicals they read. James Boswell declares in his *London Journal*: 'I felt strong dispositions to be a Mr. Addison . . . Mr. Addison's character in sentiment, mixed with a little of the gaiety of Sir Richard Steele and the manners of Mr. Digges, were the ideas which I aimed to realize."[52] The trainee lawyer Dudley Ryder also tried to emulate the periodical writers in his behaviour: "Came into my closet. Read some of the *Tatlers* . . . Intend to read them often to improve my style and accustom myself to his way of thinking and telling a story and manner of observing upon the world and mankind."[53] Sylas Neville reads the *London Magazine* in March 1771 and is powerfully struck by a letter "on the effects of an improper mode of beginning life," noting that it "deserves to be seriously perused by every young man in danger of entering into vicious female connexions, & the dreadful guilt of seduction is truly painted in the poetical & moral ballad of Henry & Eliza in the same Magazine."[54]

What is notable about Turner's diaries is that the works he reads communally are in general religious and devotional works, while the secular prose books he reads reflectively, on his own. His journals show a marked pattern of reading religious material on Sunday evenings, both solo and with others. This includes Hervey's *Meditations*, a new edition of *The Whole Duty of Man*, *The Whole Duty of Woman*, Burkitt on the New Testament, and sermons by Sherlock, Sterne, Sharp, and Hervey. He read many sermons to individual friends and family throughout the week, and these habits of sermon reading seem to provide the cement in his friendships, a mode of mutual self-improvement and spiritual focus. Turner reads more or less every night to his friend Thomas Davy, the local shoemaker, who he describes as his "best friend" in the early years of the diary.[55] Sometimes they combine work and leisure: "In the evening T. Davy brought a pair of shoes for my nephew, and stayed and supped with us. I read to him the 47th of Tillotson's sermons."[56] Tillotson is the author Turner most commonly reads to Davy. Sometimes they only get through one or two sermons, perhaps in combination with another work such as Young's *Night Thoughts*. But on other occasions Turner reads out up to eight sermons in one sitting.

This principle of communal self-improvement through reading together—and presumably, discussing the books read—also typifies Turner and Davy's other nonfictional reading. Turner seems to have taken on some kind of responsibility for educating his friend—it is always Turner who reads, and the diary suggests that it is also he who provides the venue and the books. His record of their joint reading suggests a mutual interest in using reading to learn more about the world, and in particular, other religions: "Thomas Davy came in after supper and stayed with us about 2½ hours. He and I looked over Gordon's *Geographical Grammar*, and in particular the religions of all nations." On other occasions the texts perused have a scientific application: "In the evening Thomas Davy at our house to whom I read part of Euclid's *Elements of Geometry*."[57] Reading this educational, religious, and secular material to Thomas Davy may also have been part of Turner's long battle against his drinking, for which he berates himself constantly: "A sad unpleasant day. Oh! The reflection on yesterday intolerable";[58] "How should such instances as these teach mankind to shun that hateful vice of drunkenness, a crime almost productive of all other vices."[59]

Perhaps the fortifying sociability of evenings with Davy was an antidote to the many other times when he drank excessively on his own or with other neighbours. Reading and drinking are often connected for Turner. This is evident in what he chooses to read: "Thomas Davy sat with us a while in the evening, to whom I read Bishop Gibson's sermon against intemperance in meats and drink."[60] He also remarks: "In the evening read part of the 4th volume of *The Tatler,* which I think the oftener I read the better I like it. I think I never found the vice of drinking so well exploded in my life as in one of the numbers."[61] But Turner's drinking habits are also plain in the way he talks about his addiction to reading: indeed, so pervasive an influence was alcohol in his life that even his reading was articulated in the same language: "As I am mortal, so I have my faults and failings common with other mortals. I believe by a too eager thirst after knowledge I have oftentimes to gratify that insatiable humor [*sic*] at too great an expense in buying books and spent rather too much time in reading, for it seems to be the only diversion that I have any appetite for."[62]

Turner is not the only reader who forges a connection between reading and drinking. Henry Prescott, the clerk from Chester we encountered previously, is never happier than when enjoying books along with "a domestic pint"—in his case, reading and the discussion of books are done alongside drinking, often in one of the many local inns.

To Talk Better of It

Thomas Turner's account of his reading shows us a man earnestly striving to use books to make himself a finer person, drawing his friends and neighbours into his programme. For him, the social aspect of reading is not about performance, but about moral and educational betterment. But for others reading factual or religious books could help to provide conversational gloss. Dudley Ryder believed that people read sermons to improve their conversational skills: "The general view of most people seems to be either because it would be disreputable not to go to church or . . . so as to be able to give a better account of their religion and talk better of it."[63] Ryder's cynical perspective would have been deplored by contemporary moralists—but his emphasis on reading as providing a basis for social exchange is undoubtedly an important aspect of the domestic consumption of nonfictional material, from religion to history and popular science. As we have seen, the culture of visiting and the role of discursive skills within it became increasingly prominent over the course of the eighteenth century. Thomas Turner aspired to become a more informed person, but many others, particularly from the newly affluent and leisured middling classes, also aspired to *seem* more informed. What we find in the eighteenth century is both kinds of readers deploying their knowledge of the world in social situations, alongside a significant output of printed works enabling them to do so.

The increasing socialization of knowledge is manifest in the reading and print culture of historiography. During the eighteenth century, historical knowledge became an ever more desirable asset, for both men and women. As the study of the past moved beyond the realm of monastic chroniclers and civic officials, it evolved into a more popular and accessible genre that straddled the worlds of scholarship and literary culture. The reading aloud of historical works shifted away from court, great households, and the marketplace, to the more intimate setting of the private home, thanks to increasing literacy and greater access to books.[64] History was no longer the preserve of the lone scholar, but was a topic on which the polite could deploy their newfound knowledge.[65] Writers across the century advocated the advantages of a grasp of history, particularly for young women. In an essay from the early eighteenth century, "Of Academies" (1702), Defoe observed that women should "be brought to read Books, and especially History" because it would grant them "the necessary air of Conversation" as well as enabling them to understand the world.[66] It was a view echoed by Mary Wray in *The Ladies Library* (1714): "No Reading better qualifies a Person to converse well in the World than that of *History*."[67] In her 1773 *Letters on the Improvement of the Mind*, the conduct book author Hester Chapone advised young women: "The principal study I would recommend, is *history*. I know of nothing equally proper to entertain and improve at the same time [. . .] more materials for conversation are supplied by this kind of knowledge, than by almost any other."[68] Chapone went on to assert that "a woman makes a poor figure who affects, as I have heard some ladies do, to disclaim all knowledge of times and dates."[69] These and other guides to feminine conduct presented historical knowledge as part of the suite of feminine accomplishments that would render a young woman fit for company, without making her overly learned. Although Chapone was more severe in her condemnation of superficial learning merely for show, she was a keen advocate of history as a basis for conversation.

Much of the scholarship on early modern readers of history has focussed on the dedicated note-taking of individual scholars, the historiographical seriousness of a Gabriel Harvey or John Dee.[70] But for the polite readers envisaged in the conduct books cited above, history could also be enjoyed more informally, pace Chapone, as the acquisition of piecemeal knowledge about historical characters, or random entertaining facts, or the reading of a narrative. There were, of course, as many different ways of consuming history as there were printed histories, and the period is dotted with examples of serious solitary students who made notes in margins, read each work cover to cover, and compared historical accounts. But people probably used their texts in different ways if they were reading for social gain or entertainment.

For some, the reading of a specific historical passage was related to the celebration or commemoration of a particular event. Henry Prescott read to mark royalist anniversaries such as the execution of Charles I or the Restoration of Charles II. He spent 29 May 1718 with his son: "Over my pint supper, proper parts are read, by my son, in Clarendon."[71] Talk of books might be mixed with the discussion of antiquities or specialist collections. Prescott was a keen collector of Roman artefacts and coins, and like many of his contemporaries, enjoyed showing his friends historical objects and talking about them, sharing areas of amateur enthusiasm. A remarkably sociable man, well connected in local political, social, and ecclesiastical circles, Prescott notes on various occasions that books are part of an evening's discussion: "In the Evening at the Fountain with Mr. Maul a ClergyMan of Ireland, Mr. Bowyer and Mr. Rhode, wee have much of Books and variety of Learning, till near 12";[72] "with Dean Sterne at his Quarters the Golden Talbot, where over 3 pints we discourse on Books and our collegiate acquaintances past 10";[73] "After late dinner and supper the Ale circulates, Jack returns with a good Account of his Excursion. Mr. Jones . . . joins our company, wee have much of Books and learning and no little Ale continuing till 11";[74] "After E. prayers Mr. Medlicot is with us in the study, I entertain him with my Coins, and Books of Antiquity, myself supping on my smal pint."[75] Nicholas Blundell recorded similar occasions (although these are usually less alcoholically charged): "Edward Pourtor was here after dinner, he brought Mr. James a Writing-Master of Leverpoole along with him, I shewed him some of my Droughts and some Curiosityes."[76]

Local and familial history was often at the forefront of these amateur historical enthusiasms. John Wilson, of Broomfield Hall, outside Sheffield, compiled a substantial manuscript collection during his lifetime, collecting from diverse sources materials relating to the local area and historical documents concerning neighboring families. Extracts from many of these were collected in the commonplace book, for sharing amongst other members of his own family. The oddest kinds of historical documents could be enjoyed as a social pastime. Anne Lister records "having myself proposed making it a rule to have the pedigree [family tree] brought down & read aloud the 21st days of every June & December, began the thing this evening."[77]

The recreational reading of history was a way of both improving the reader or auditor's understanding of historical events and giving practice in recitation. Writing from Edinburgh to his son Henry in Plymouth, William Woollcombe urged him to read history in the evenings to his mother and sisters, and in doing so, to be mindful that "the history of the past affords sufficient grounds of rational conjecture concerning the future, & enables us to apply the experience of ages to the establishment of rules for the regula-tion of our own conduct & opinions."[78] And in reading aloud, William was also getting good preparation for later life in public:

> You employ your evenings in reading the History of England to my mother & sisters & you are not perhaps aware of the many advan-tages you may derive from this. To read well requires good sense & good taste, & many defects can be corrected only by attending to the observations of those to whom we read & who must be much better judges of what is wanting, than we can be ourselves. In the writings of Hume, you have a specimen of correct, elegant & pure stile, superior perhaps to that of any of our Historians. I have known many men of good Education, who have felt distressed and indeed I have experienced it myself on being called upon to read a passage even to a small circle.[79]

Henry took his father's advice to heart. As we have seen, his journal, which he began in 1797 and kept for the next twenty years, documents his endeavours both to keep reading for self-education and to practice reading aloud—even when no one else was present. His comments on what he has read are invariably related to both the entertainment and the profit he has received from them:

> Much entertainment & much benefit I hope I receive from the perusal of Clarendon's History of the Rebellion. He has there laid open the characters of the enthusiastic Puritans in such a light, that will deter me from falling into their Hypocrisy.

Saturday evening Janry the 12th. Read the Life of Lord Littleton . . . and very much pleased with it, particularly that part where Johnson has transcribed an account of his last Illness published by his Physician. I earnestly wished that my last Conversation might be like his.[80]

Henry Woollcombe was a single man who generally preferred reflective solitary reading—although as discussed earlier, this was not entirely without reference to others. He tended to try to read the whole of a work rather than browse. But there are also lots of other examples suggesting that the use of historical anecdote in social situations encouraged the same reading and publishing practices that we have seen elsewhere in the communal enjoyment of imaginative works.

Social uses of history fostered habits of reading histories for the elements that could be taken out of context, and the culling of the example, the isolated episode, and the portable story were features of historical as well as literary reading. This was not a new phenomenon; Tudor chronicles were full of portable tales, often involving very minor or domestic events rather than the great deeds that were normally expected from historians, and they filled a conversational role.[81] The tendency towards excerpting also meant that some historians were more popular than others—there was an increasing vogue for tersely quotable Tacitus over languorous Livy.[82] The abridgement and serialization of histories, like that of novels, was a mainstay of the emergent periodical and magazine market, satisfying the same demand for accessible extracts of prose.

Commonplace books were another repository of appealing excerpts. The Sheffield tailor George Hoyland mixes up his poetic extracts with random historical information. For example, he follows a comic poem on Quakers with the note, "In the year 1815 in the Russian Empire there Died 160 Persons at the age of 100 Years, 233 of 105, 106 of 110, 53 of 115; 20 of 120; 5 of 125; 4 of 130 and 1 of 160."[83] The commonplace books of John Wilson or Mary Madan, both discussed earlier, reveal a similarly magpie-like collection of remarkable historical facts or accounts, Wilson collecting everything from local archeological information to transcribed passages "On the Great Wall of China" to "Some of the Many Outrages upon the Church in the Rebellion."[84] Other readers produced their own summaries or abridgements of factual works they had enjoyed, for the benefit of friends and family.

Sarah Cowper digested William Howell's *An Institution of General History* for her daughter-in-law Judith.[85] The schoolmaster Walter Gale notes: "I delivered to him [means 'them,' that is, Mr. Kent and Mr. Edwards, the schoolmasters] the abstract I had made of the *Christian Schoolmaster Instructed;* he promised to return it to me in a little time."[86]

And, as with the recycling of prose and verse extracts in print culture that we previously read about, the type of excerpts cut out or transcribed in commonplace books also found their way into printed collections. Comic stories and tales of jestbook culture were often based on historical figures. *The Merry Jester* (1773) contains short stories about Diogenes, Charles II, Henry IV of France, Prince Maurice of Nassau, Philip II of Spain, William Penn, Sir Nicholas Bacon, Sir Robert Howard, Purcell, Caesar, Sir Robert Walpole, and Pope Sixtus V, all within the first twenty pages.[87] Such mingling of modern and classical history in these comic anecdotes, which are found throughout the hundreds of jestbooks of the time, suggests that much of what was lifted from the pages of histories and then floated as conversation was amusing rather than serious discussion. There were also character pieces, potted accounts of the lives of interesting figures, found in the collections of prose extracts for recitation that proliferated in the second half of the century. *The English Reader* (1799) includes both classical and modern history as types of prose, and within that, the pieces are designated according to their genre. Hume's characters of Queen Elizabeth and King Alfred are "Descriptive pieces." The account of Lady Jane Grey's fate is a "Narrative piece." The trial of the Earl of Strafford, taken from Goldsmith, is classed as "Pathetic."

Volume 4 of Vicesimus Knox's hugely influential *Elegant Extracts* is also made up of historical extracts. This volume was a kind of historical primer—offering an introduction to basic historical concepts, as well as extracts for recitation. It began with a short essay from Voltaire on the ages of history, followed by mini-essays on the feudal system, the Crusades, and a whole series of characters from Epaminondas to Chatham and Townshend, the contents drawn from the works of Hume, Robertson, Smollett, and Burke.

Again, the prose "character" was central to the packaging of history for new readers, and as we shall see, it was often history as character that people responded to when they read for entertainment. Compilations of historical extracts mingled fictional and factual sources. *Beautiful Extracts of Prosaic Writers* (1795) moves swiftly from "The Character of Martin Luther" by Robertson to "The Story of Le Fevre" by Sterne, and then on to the resignation of the Emperor Charles V (Robertson). Sterne's story of Obadiah is followed by Voltaire on "the Great historical ages," and in the second volume, "Romulus to the People of Rome" from Hooke comes straight after "Julia; or, the Adventures of a Curate's Daughter" by Macmillan.

This mixing of factual and nonfactual narratives offers an insight into the distinction between the two forms. Many critics have assumed that the reason prose fictions were called "histories" in the eighteenth century was because their authors or publishers were trying to seem authentic. When they have found evidence of readers who have confused fictional histories with the real thing, they have attributed this to a public unsure about the new genre of the novel.[88] But in fact, the term "history" was so broad in its usage in the seventeenth and eighteenth centuries that it could quite easily encompass a whole range of writing, from a chapbook to a semihistorical fiction, to the works of Thucydides.

Readers commonly saw histories as the histories of lives, just like novels—only better, because they were true. The compiler of the Ernst family commonplace book, dating from the beginning of the nineteenth century, observes that biographical accounts of past individuals were a much better way of learning about the world.

> Well chosen & well written lives would form a valuable substitute for no small portion of those works of imagination which steal away the hearts & time of our Youth. Novels, were there no other objection to them, however ingeniously they may be written, as they exhibit only fictitious characters, acting in fictitious scenes, on fictitious occasions & being sometimes the work of writers who rather guess what the world is rather than describe it from their own knowledge, can never give so vivid a picture of life & manners, as is to be found in the Memoirs of Men who were actual performers on the great stage of the World.[89]

History could provide the same insights into human nature as the novel, but without its ethical complications. Mary Delany writes to her friend Mrs. Port: "Encourage your young pupil to read history, particularly of England, and to give you an account every day of what she reads. No novels, but don't seem to *forbid* them, only in speaking of them disapprove generally of their falsehood and insignificancy."[90] History, for Delany, was a form of narrative that could be used to wean the vulnerable off novels and towards a more improving kind of narrative. What is fascinating about Delany's attitude regarding the history she reads with her friends is that she shows much less critical distance from, and more identification with, historical figures than she would be tempted to venture with a fictional character:

> Our everyday reading is still Carte's History of the old Duke of Ormonde: he is one of the greatest heroes I ever read of, such courage, prudence, loyalty, humanity, and virtues of every kind make up his character, but the sufferings of King Charles the First, though there but in part related, *break one's heart!* . . .[91]
>
> We are now reading Cart's History of England, which they say is the best which has yet been published: we are still fighting with the Romans—Agricola is the present hero.[92]
>
> We are now reading the lives of Pope Alexander and Caesar Borgia [by Alexander Gordon]—two execrable villains; I am tired of their company.[93]

Delany's embrace of the historical person and his or her story is not unique. One of the consequences of the ferocious moral debates around novel reading was that educated readers like Delany were cautious in their approach to fiction but seemingly less so in relation to historical narrative. Anna Larpent was another copious reader who, like Delany, disapproved in general of novel reading (despite devouring a lot of novels herself). The assessing voice that she brings to her evaluation of imaginative works is much less present in her discussions of history, society, or politics, in which she shows a sense of herself as more of a receptacle for information.[94] This may be because she didn't feel qualified to evaluate these genres in the same way, or because she perceived them to serve a different purpose, as a source of documentation of current and past affairs.[95] Amelia Steuart of Dalguise, in Perthshire, a devout Episcopalian, records regular communal reading of historical works, from which she notes allegories, anecdotes, and bon mots. Her recollections of what has been read tend towards pen portraits of characters: "French in the evening & the following Anecdote a Great Prince whose name I have forgot"; "The following charming anecdote of Charles 12 of Sweden was read."[96] Steuart also dismisses novels as "unprofitable," but her accounts of the histories being read convey an immersion in the factual narrative account. Often her records are in the present tense: "Edward is engaged in a war with France w^t various success."[97] Elsewhere historical writing is discussed by the group in terms similar to those used about literary works.[98] Frances Hamilton, reflecting on the items she'd borrowed from the Taunton book club in the 1780s and 1790s, was likewise drawn to character as opposed to societal or political narrative. She records Henry IV's portrait of Sully: "his temper harsh, impatient, obstinate, too enterprising, presuming too much upon his own opinions, exaggerating the worth of his own actions."[99] Her attachment to history is partly informed by her personal interest in medicine: "Abdiah Cole, a Physician of Note, flourished in this reign"; "I have met wth nothing written by Dr. Cole; but he & Culpepper translated several books in conjunction."[100]

Polite Science

The terms in which Steuart, Delany, and others describe the works they read are not part of scholarly discourse. Theirs is a generalised vocabulary focussing on affect and narrative style. Such a nonspecialist approach to the acquisition of knowledge is an important part of shared reading. There was a distinction between genteel familiarity with a subject and an inelegant parade of expertise. Mixed company was a crucial part of this socializing of knowledge. Instructing his son on the rudiments of sociability, the Somerset merchant Jonathan Chubb noted: "Politeness is more easily obtained amongst the Fair: not that in general they are more polite."[101] In a manuscript essay, "Conversation," the Gloucestershire student Samuel Gwinnett declared that "there is nothing which gives a man a more agreable Turn, than a frequent Resort to Female Assemblies; for by a blending the Softness & Delicacy, so peculiar to that Sex, does Conversation receive it's Finishing Stroke."[102] Mixed company should enjoy general conversation about a range of topics. Over and over again conduct writers emphasised the dangers of too much learning; it was important to acquire a smattering of knowledge, but not so much as to become an unattractive pedant. Being able to talk about modern or classical history as if it were a matter of everyday anecdotal interest was a covetable skill. Sounding like a bookish expert was not. In a guide to conversation for gentleman, John Constable describes the unacceptable face of historical reference: "I remember a Gentleman once, when the Discourse was upon a great Prince, mentioned very properly the Character of *Theodoric*. Had he been content to have stopt there, we should have been much pleased. But he ruined all by immediately hurrying away into wild Excursions of the

Goths and *Vandals*, the *Quadi, Heruli*, and *Huns;* and frighted us almost as much with their Names, as the World was formerly with their Arms."[103]

One of the virtues of history was that it was a relatively accessible branch of knowledge. The author of *The Ladies Library* recommended history 'because most of the other Parts of Learning are clogg'd with Terms that are not easily intelligible."[104] This aversion to books or conversations "clogg'd" with incomprehensible words and ideas is important in understanding the social culture of reading. The widespread domestication of learning, for both men and women, that we see in the eighteenth century is part of a bigger historical picture, a shift in attitudes towards the display of knowledge.[105] By the beginning of the century, the scientific virtuoso or the professional scholar was increasingly parodied by the social and literary elite for his obsession with arcane detail and his self-important incomprehensibility; the Royal Society had promoted the use of ordinary language in scientific discussion, and remote and overly specialised discourse was no longer a marker of excellence.[106] Satires like Gay's *Three Hours After Marriage* or Pope's *Dunciad* mercilessly mocked the specialist scholar as a desiccated obsessive, the type who was "in the true spirit of a whimsical Pedant, strangely impolite in his Language, Manners, Dress, and every thing else."[107] The contemplative sequestration that had in the Middle Ages been celebrated as a mark of true knowledge was now associated with pedantry. Alternative models of gentlemanly learning, and experimental philosophy, often associated with the Royal Society, instead emphasised politeness, sociability, and flexibility, virtues that were in themselves seen as vital for the production of reliable knowledge.[108] In this model, scientific enquiry was more likely to succeed if those pursuing it were open to others' ideas, and prepared to debate their own.

In a world in which polite discourse was the sine qua non of cultural life, and the narrow acquisition of knowledge for its own sake was deeply unsociable, to favour the life of the mind over all other considerations was not a good thing. Elizabeth Hamilton strove to hide her intellectual pursuits beneath a veneer of communal reading:

> without literary pretensions, Mrs Marshall had a genuine love of reading, and when no other engagement intervened, it was one of her domestic regulations, that a book should be read aloud in the evening for general amusement; the office of reader commonly devolved on Miss Hamilton . . . These social studies were far from

satisfying her avidity for information; and she constantly perused many books by stealth. Mrs Marshall, on discovering what had been her private occupation, expressed neither praise nor blame, but quietly advised her to avoid any display of superior knowledge by which she might be subjected to the imputation of pedantry. This admonition produced the desired effect, since, as she herself informs us, she once hid a volume of Lord Kames's Elements of Criticism under the cushion of a chair lest she should be detected in a study which prejudice and ignorance might pronounce unfeminine."[109]

In the context of these negative stereotypes of asocial learning, the promotion of science to a wider public involved repackaging knowledge to fit a polite and sociable readership—or at least, a readership aiming for those attributes. It is in the eighteenth century that we see the beginning of a shift from Latin as the language of learning to the vernacular, and most eighteenth-century medical and scientific works followed this trend by appearing in English. At the beginning of the eighteenth century the most accessible forms of scientific reading were English translations of continental works, such as Bernard de Fontenelle's *Conversations on the Plurality of Worlds* (1697 in English, new edition 1715) or Voltaire's *Elements of Sir Isaac Newton's Philosophy* (English translation 1738). But in the latter half of the period, along with the miscellanies, primers, and other learning aids directed at a gentry and middling-sort market, a new strain of English popular science emerged, aimed specifically at the domestic sphere. At the same time that public scientific lectures became a fashionable forum for public engagement with new ideas, scientific knowledge was promoted as a component of polite exchange. Various commodities, including books, pamphlets, and instruments, were made to appeal to interested amateurs who wanted a taste of the world in their own homes.[110] Benjamin Martin's *Young Gentleman and Lady's Philosophy* (1755), *The Newtonian System of Philosophy* (1761), and James Ferguson's *Young Gentlemen and Lady's Astronomy* (1768) all repositioned natural philosophy as an activity for the whole family.

Newtonian science was a bit of a problem, however. Newton was widely lauded as a national hero, and his role in advancing the scientific revolution something to boast about. But how could ordinary readers understand him? In both his own time and for later biographers, Newton was known as an antisocial autodidact, not a natural communicator.[111] His works did not easily speak to his would-be followers; even after the *Principia* became available in English, Newton's audience still faced the task of wading through the mathematics to conquer the natural philosophy. The fact that very few managed this inspired perhaps the most significant trend in the marketing of eighteenth-century books in the physical sciences: works on contemporary advances in natural philosophy presented without the difficult mathematics.[112] Benjamin Martin's *A Plain and Familiar Introduction to the Newtonian Experimental Philosophy* was subtitled "Designed for the Use of such Gentlemen and Ladies as would acquire a Competent Knowledge of this Subject without Mathematical Learning."[113] One of the consequences of this popularization of Newton was that pretty much all aspects of natural knowledge became subsumed under the idea of Newtonianism. The seventeenth-century scientist's name was exploited mercilessly in the marketing of

Fig. 52. *Isaac Newton*, by Bickham sen. (engraver), published by Robert Sayer, 1787 (© Ashmolean Museum, University of Oxford)

popular science books, regardless of the precise relationship between their content and his original publications (fig. 52).[114]

Astronomy was a popular focus for domestic science (fig. 53). Closely linked to geography, long included as an element of a genteel, liberal education, it could be pursued at home both through print publications, such as those listed above, and through instruments such as the orrery, a clockwork device designed to demonstrate the motions of the earth, sun and moon, and thus enable one to understand phenomena such as the seasons, eclipses, and the phases of the moon. While the most expensive orreries were elaborate constructions in silver and ebony, by the middle of the century they had dropped to a price point affordable to the middling sort.

Thomas Turner bought a "modern microcosm," with which he entertained his sister and sister-in-law. In a 1714 essay advocating the orrery (at a time when such a device was still expensive), Richard Steele attempted to "Incite any numerous Family of Distinction to have an *Orrery* as necessarily as they would have a Clock. This one Engine would open a new Scene to their Imaginations; and a whole Train of useful Inferences concerning the Weather and the Seasons, which are now from Stupidity the Subjects of

ASTRONOMY.

Fig. 53. *Astronomy,* after Richard Houston, published by Robert Sayer, c. 1750 (Private Collection / The Stapleton Collection / Bridgeman Images)

Discourse, would raise a pleasing, an obvious, an useful, and an elegant Conversation."[115]

As Steele's essay suggests, the use of the orrery was a communal one— it was designed to feed conversation, like the globes, mini-telescopes, and other devices promoted as the centrepiece of elegant entertaining. Many scientific publications in the eighteenth century were associated with the products of the London scientific instrument trade.[116] Texts "on the use of the globes," which offered brief introductions to astronomy and geography illustrated by these popular pieces of library furniture, constitute one of the largest genres of scientific books published in the eighteenth century, with a new or republished title on the subject appearing almost yearly between 1750 and 1820. A few members of the instrument trade also wrote and published books illustrating and advertising their products, including perhaps the most prolific scientific author of the eighteenth century, lecturer and instrument retailer Benjamin Martin. Martin produced over eighty works ranging from single-sheet explanations of astronomical phenomena to multivolume popularizations of Newtonian natural philosophy. And there were many other ways in which the wide worlds of astronomy or geography were introduced through more everyday domestic objects. William Greatbatch's Staffordshire pottery produced creamware teapots with enameled illustrations of "The World with Sun, Moon, and Stars" on one side, or "The XII Houses of Heaven" (fig. 54).[117]

Dissected puzzles tested young geographers on their knowledge of national boundaries (fig. 55).[118] These early jigsaws were hand-coloured maps, printed from copper plates, mounted on thin sheets of mahogany and cut into pieces along the borders of the region mapped. Some were sold "without the sea" to make them cheaper.[119] Such puzzles were frequently offered by the same publishers who sold maps and books for children, and the acquisition of a broad knowledge of the countries of the world was promoted as part of a desirable set of social skills. In 1758 John Newbery published an elegant atlas for children, *The Atlas Minimus,* which contained "a New set of Pocket Maps of the Several Empires, Kingdoms and States of the Known World, With Historical Extracts Relative to Each." In his prefatory material, he declared: "Nothing need be said in Favour of this Study; almost every one is acquainted with its usefulness and excellency, and sees how essential it is, towards forming the Character of the fine Gentleman and agreeable Companion."[120]

Fig. 54. Teapot depicting the sun, moon, and stars, made at the factory of William Greatbatch, Fenton, c. 1770–82, lead-glazed earthenware, transfer printed and painted in enamel colours (Victoria and Albert Museum, C.11&A-1937; © Victoria and Albert Museum, London)

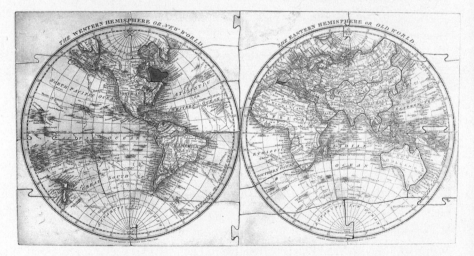

Fig. 55. Puzzle, *The World Dissected upon the Best Principles to Teach Youth Geography*, published in England by William Darton, 1820, hand-coloured engraving on wood (Victoria and Albert Museum, E.3229&A-1938; © Victoria and Albert Museum, London)

Hester Chapone also recommended a knowledge of geography for young women, offering tips on how to remember national boundaries: "Perhaps annexing to any country the idea of some particular form which it most resembles may at first assist you . . . thus Italy has been called a *boot*—and Europe compared to a *woman sitting*."[121] The reinforcing of domestic learning of geography is also found in the late-eighteenth-century tradition of embroidering geographical samplers (fig. 56). Such needlework projects, which also depicted mathematical tables, spellings, and illustrations of the solar system, provided a way of locating knowledge within the appropriate spheres of female accomplishment.[122]

Maps found their way on to various household objects in the eighteenth century. On handkerchiefs, for example, ladies could combine instruction in both needlework and geography.[123] And their sewing could be combined with a woman's current reading: *The Lady's Magazine* of 1786 carried a series of articles on Cook's voyages, as well as an article on the geography of

Fig. 56. Sampler of a map of Europe made by Elizabeth Hawkins, Plymouth, England, dated 1797, wool embroidered with coloured silk (Victoria and Albert Museum, T.165–1959; © Victoria and Albert Museum, London)

Africa accompanied by a map pattern for embroidery.[124] These geographical materials also enabled readers curious about the world to see it without travelling.

One of the features of domestic science books was that they encouraged their readers to understand physical phenomena through the behaviour of everyday objects in their homes. Fans, teacups, or patches could be used to illustrate the way the world worked. A letter from Polly Stevenson, a young woman being educated by Benjamin Franklin, shows the way in which she used a tea set to understand the key tenets of laws of motion:

> I have often remark'd as I sat at the Tea Table, that when a Cup has been turn'd down, and there has been some Tea in the Saucer, the Cup would be lifted up, and the Bubbles would rise in the Tea. I think I can discover the Cause of this to be the Heat rarefying the Air within the Cup, which endeavouring to expand itself lifts up the Cup, and forces its way out at the Bottom where the Tea rises in Bubbles. To confirm the Truth of this suggestion I try'd the Experiment with cold Water, and then the Effect ceas'd.[125]

John Newbery's *The Newtonian System of Philosophy, adapted to the capacities of Young Gentlemen and Ladies* (1761), subtitled "A Philosophy of Tops and Balls," ingeniously turned scientific education into a form of play, using the kinds of objects and toys lying around in an eighteenth-century home.[126] The work seems to have been designed not for private study but to be read aloud by a parent or guardian to an eager group of budding natural philosophers. At the heart of the book is the idea that we can see the workings of natural laws all around us—so a candle, a cricket ball and a fives ball are used to demonstrate the phenomenon of an eclipse, while the double rotation of the Earth is explained by reference to a carriage wheel circling on a nearby drive.

Conversational Knowledge

Like the material goods, print publications that promoted popular science were designed to encourage discussion rather than solitary study. When the *Guardian* in 1713 recommended improving ways for women to spend time at home, it suggested that they read aloud to one another, and discuss their reading, while undertaking chores: "It was very entertaining to me to see them dividing their Speculations between Jellies and Stars, and making a sudden Transition from the Sun to an Apricot, or from the Copernican System to the figure of a Cheese-cake."[127]

Popular science guides often took the form of conversations, which modelled both the rudiments of generalist knowledge and the appropriate ways of discussing it in company. The dialogue, with its roots in classical rhetoric, was well established as a form suitable for embedding instruction within a domestic environment. Titles such as Althea Fanshawe's *Easter Holidays: or Domestic Conversations, Designed for the Instruction, and it is Hoped for the Amusement of Young People* (1797) not only embodied instruction within a dialogue form, but also expressly aimed to teach young people to "find their pleasure and satisfaction at home" rather than in the giddy world of public assemblies.[128] *The Polite Lady; or, a Course of Female Education* encouraged its readers to deploy their reading in conversation as a way of testing out their newly acquired knowledge: "It would be a good maxim, to make what you have been lately reading the subject of conversation, as often as you decently can, without the imputation of pedantry . . . By this means you will not only have your doubts removed, but, by considering and examining the same thing in a variety of lights, you will even understand more distinctly what you thought you understood sufficiently before."[129]

Authors and editors of these conversation guides modelled the way in which books might be read and used together—not just read aloud, but also discussed by interested friends and family members. They promoted the communal discussion of natural science, and in particular, of botany, as superior to solitary study. Charlotte Smith's *Rural Walks* and *Conversations introducing Poetry*, two conversationally formatted conduct books for young women, presented dialogues about a range of improving subjects, and claimed that the solitary pleasure of botany was less valuable than using botany in a family or social context. In these works, Smith also drew on the natural world to show examples of social behaviour, and the way it could inform debates about poverty and charity.[130] Not everyone approved of the dialogue form as a way of conveying information. Henry Woollcombe comments in one diary entry:

> Saturday Even. I finished Fontenelle's Plurality of Worlds; from which I received much entertainment & much instruction, for tho I was not ignorant of the Subjects he there treats of I had never considered it so fully as it is still given to us. The Stile I should suppose may have suffered by the Translation but it is not a mode of

writing I am perfectly reconciled to, it may be very well for the vola-
tile Frenchman but does not suit my Phlegm. I was not at all pleased
at being brought down to this little spot by the occurrence of some
Compt to the Marchioness when I was soaring aloft, & trying as far
as the limits of a finite understanding.[131]

But despite Woollcombe's particular dislike of the awkward transitions
between intellectual content and pseudo-conversational padding, by the end of
the eighteenth century there was a whole host of conversation-style introductions to various aspects of knowledge, including natural science: for example,
*Lilliputian Spectacle de la nature: or, Nature Delineated, in conversations and
letters passing between the children of a family* (1779–89); *An Introduction to
Botany in a Series of Familiar Letters* (1796); *Mentoria: or the Young ladies
instructor, in familiar conversations on moral and entertaining subjects* (1779);
Roman Conversations (1792); and *Conversations on Chemistry* (1806). *Conversations
on Botany* (1817) was typical in staging a dialogue between a mother and her
son: "Mother: You must now hold the flower in your hand, and look at every
part very attentively, while I read to you the descriptions of a few genera in the
second class, Diandra . . . Look at your calyx, and see if it is like this."[132]

The *New Lady's Magazine* of 1786 included an utterly implausible
"Botanical Conversation" between two women, who demonstrated the ways
in which their aesthetic appreciation of a plant might be combined with a new
understanding of Linnaean principles of plant classification.

> INGEANA: How charming these snow-drops still look;
> notwithstanding the late frost, and the depth of the snow, with
> whose whiteness they seem to vie.
> FLORA: The snow, my dear, has preserved both their beauty and
> life; otherwise they must have fallen a sacrifice to the severity of
> the weather.
> INGEANA: What elegant simplicity and innocence in this flower! It
> belongs, I believe, to the sixth class of the Linnaean system, called
> Hexandria, and by our botanical society Six Males, and to the first
> order of that class: but it seems to me to be two flowers, a less
> within a greater.[133]

Conversation and familiar letters framed the act of learning as an
exchange between a nonspecialist enthusiast—sometimes a mother, sometimes a slightly flirtatious tutor or suitor—and one who sought to learn from

them. They enabled authors to expose a body of knowledge from the bottom up. In their fictionalised encounters, they permitted the most ignorant of questions to be asked, and to receive reasonable answers. Highly unlikely as actual conversations, they were nonetheless crucial to the evolution of the print culture of popular science.

Language was also crucial in this repositioning of knowledge. How was one to discourse about science if the main ideas were fossilised in obscure terminology? Eighteenth-century guides to conversation demonised scholarly enthusiasts who were intent on using words no one understood to discuss things that no one was interested in. In John Constable's guide *The Conversation of Gentlemen*, one of the speakers describes his experiences with a garrulous chemist, who was "Always for inviting, nay forcing one into *Spagyric* and *Pyrotechnic* Wonders. He must teach you to *Amalgame* and *Fulminate*. You may tell him, you neither fully understand those Terms, nor have any Curiosity that Way. Still he will force you along to his *Terra damnata*, and will not cease, till he has left you nothing but his *Caput mortuum*."[134]

In order to succeed, the literature of polite science needed to develop a language of scientific discourse that was free of the jargon associated with learned debate. Books designed for the domestic market advertised themselves as "easy and familiar," and redescribed scientific principles in terms accessible to their readers, offering Newton without mathematics, or botany without the classical languages. Botany became a hugely fashionable pursuit for women in the late decades of the eighteenth century—as a topic of study, and as an impetus to engage in amateur crafts. Specimens were collected and pressed by women across the country. Intricate crafts of flower cutting and shell sticking flourished in homes (fig. 57).[135] Eleanor Butler's diary is full of references to botanical craftwork produced by various friends: "Very polite sentimental note from Mrs. Scanlan with a present of the most beautiful Tree in Seaweed elegantly arranged"; "Dr. Hamilton brought his Portefeuille, his and his daughters' most admirable drawings. One copy of a lily which he saw growing in a flowerbed in Exmouth."[136]

Botany was not uncontroversial. One speaker in Althea Fanshawe's instructional guide *Easter Holidays, or Domestic Conversations* (1797) declares: "Considered as a science, botany is a study which may be useful to many people, but very seldom to women; and as a mere smattering at science is really an absurdity, I do not like to see every Miss, who buys a botanical fan, fancy she has as much knowledge on the subject as the ingenious contriver of it must possess."[137] Even more worrying than the idea that women were

Fig. 57. *Acanthus Spinosus (Dydinamia Angospermia)*, by
Mary Delany, from an album (Vol. I, 1), Bear's Breech,
1778, collage of coloured papers, with bodycolour and
watercolour, on black ink background (British Museum,
1897, 0505.1; © The Trustees of the British Museum)

merely dabbling, was what they were dabbling in. Botany was full of sex.
The moralist and antifeminist Richard Polwhele parodied the lascivious
botanical interests of young women:

> With bliss botanic as their bosoms heave,
> [they] still pluck forbidden fruit, with mother Eve,
> For puberty in sighing florets pant,
> Or point the prostitution of a plant;
> Dissect its organ of unhallow'd lust,
> And fondly gaze the titillating dust.

He added in a footnote: "Botany has lately become a fashionable amusement
with the ladies. But how the study of the sexual system of plants can accord

with female modesty, I am not able to comprehend."[138] With all its organs and sexual difference, the study of the working of plants was full of dangers. Concerns over how to introduce plant classification and reproduction to innocent young women are manifest in the controversy in the late eighteenth century over how to present botany to the uninitiated. The physician William Withering, a member of the Lunar Society, set out to write a popular manual, and his *Botanical Arrangement of All the Vegetables Naturally Growing in Great Britain* (1776) was intended as a primer in plant classification and the Linnaean system. Because he was trying to make this system accessible to readers, especially women, who had little Latin, he translated the Latin terms of Linnaeus into English. But in making plant classification fit for consumption, he also had to confront plant sexuality, and because he had conservative tastes and was writing in part for his daughter, he made the decision to leave out sexual references. So despite the fact that male and female sexual parts were the key to Linnaean plant classification, they were not to be found in his guide, as he explained in the preface to the first edition: "From an apprehension that Botany in an English dress would become a favourite amusement with the Ladies . . . it was thought proper to drop the sexual distinctions in the titles in Classes and Orders . . . every System yet invented, undoubtedly may glory in its peculiar beauties, and with no less reason, blush for its particular defects."[139]

Like Thomas Bowdler and his *Family Shakspeare*, for Withering, reading at home meant censoring material that might threaten chaste femininity. His editorial decisions were met with some derision by fellow botanists, particularly the Botanical Society of Lichfield, who issued their own translation of Linnaeus, authored by Erasmus Darwin, as a primer called *A System of Vegetables* (1783), which was intended to bridge the gap between the original taxonomy and new readers.[140] They complained that Withering had not only cut out the sexual distinctions, but also turned words into English that were better left in Latin. They won the day, and their approach was to set the course for later treatments of botany. By the third revised edition of *Botanical Arrangement*, Withering had bowed to public demand and restored both sex and Latin names to the world of plants. His primer was to continue to be a mainstay of domestic botanical knowledge, offering not just a way of classifying types of plants but also a way of thinking about the world. For Amelia Steuart of Dalguise, the descriptions of plant life found within its pages became metaphors for her own existence:

I was thinking before I got up this morning of one of the species of grapes mentioned in Witheridge's Botany—the seed of it is kept in a sort of continual agitation by a singular process of Nature—till the removal of the higher plants in the neighbourhood suffer it to get away. If that were not the case, it would sink & rot in its own habitation. Such are we—if we have not our minds kept above the habitation of ours by some agitating fear as distress—we are very ready to look no further. Our natural Weight pulls us down—but Heavenly Grace is mercifully imployed to keep us up.[141]

One way of communicating science, and of contextualizing it within the sphere of domestic accomplishment, was by larding it with references to the world of letters, a world much more obviously part of the domain of genteel converse. John Harris, the author of *Astronomical Dialogues*, combined scientific information with extracts from other, more familiar fields of interest: he advertises in his preface his use of "Digressions, Reflexions, Poetry, and Turns of Wit," which are used to make agreeable notions that "without such a kind of Dress, would appear too crabbed and abstracted."[142] The book, which claimed to present astronomy and geography in a "pleasant, easy, and familiar way," took the form of a dialogue between a young woman and a more knowledgeable man. Modelled on Fontenelle's *Dialogues of the Dead*, the exchanges between the couple showed them quoting passages of Dryden, Butler, and Milton in explication of the unfolding solar system. So, as the man attempts to explain the solar system, Lady C interjects:

> Well, said she, as for your Greek, I know nothing of the matter; but now I begin to find out the Justness of those Lines, in *Hudibras;* wherein he describes *Sydrophil*'s Surprize at the Discovery of his new Star, occasion'd by a Lanthorn at the Tail of a School-boy's Kite:
>
> > 'Tis not among that mighty Scrowl,
> > Of Birds, and Beasts, and Fish, and Fowl,
> > With which like Indian Plantations
> > The Learnd stock the Constellations.

As this passage suggests, the volume educates through comparison—the pupil is encouraged through analogies from worlds she already knows about. The whole was designed to make the world of science closer to everyday polite conversation, and to suggest that to learn about the shape and movements of the planets one could use a familiar cultural vocabulary. And for many eighteenth-century readers, the combination of poetic illustration and scientific information would not have seemed so strange. Since both poetry and natural philosophy could be seen as ways of expressing the wonderment of God's creation, they were commonly thought to have an affinity. It was the role of both the poet and the scientist to expose the astonishing glories of God's creation, as the author of *The Microscopical Theatre of Seeds* (1745) explained: "The Design of this Work is . . . to demonstrate the surprising Appearances of the minute Parts contained in the Seeds of Vegetables . . . the Examination of which will not only entertain the Reader, but raise in his Mind the highest Notions of the Power and Wisdom of the Divine Creator."[143]

Others were engaged in a similar task. Richard Blackmore's heavily excerpted poem *Creation*, and the many other physico-theological poems that followed in its wake, attempted to convey the detail and the scale of Newtonian revelation for an amateur readership. James Thomson's *Seasons*, perhaps the most popular poem of the whole century, was a blank verse encomium to the natural world, hymning God's grandeur through the description of phenomena ranging from rainbows to the microscopic structure of matter, and to the nature of gravity. Popular science in the eighteenth century involved a fusion of rational and imaginative ways of reading the world. Poets used Newtonian science to celebrate the marvels of nature, while popular introductions to the study of natural philosophy championed scientific discovery by drawing on literary parallels, again forging links between the detail of natural process and the heavenly design behind it.

꧁꧂

The eighteenth-century home was shaped by the spiritual and intellectual worlds outside it. Its occupants practiced their religion, taught themselves and their children, and learnt about the world through the texts they encountered together within in their domestic spaces. Forms of knowledge previously confined to universities and libraries became accessible to an ever wider public, as publishers and authors sought to capitalise on the popular zeal for understanding the visible and invisible world. Although science, history, and religion provoked their own distinctive debates about what was and wasn't appropriate, we can discern an ongoing concern about show and performance that is also characteristic of the discussion of plays, poems, and novels. There were tensions between external forms of authority and their manifestation in domestic form. Might the reading of sermons at home supplant the role of the preacher or vicar? Was it appropriate for women to do it? And in the case of secular knowledge, the amateur appetite for history, geography, or natural science was of no social benefit if it lapsed into mere pedantry. Easy, well-informed conversation was a very different thing from mere showing off.

Afterword

This book offers a series of vignettes of reading lives and practices. It has presented a cluster of historical figures, and a range of historical books, and used them to try to reconstruct what literature has meant and what it has been used for. It is a partial story, but as a way of examining the history of books and reading in the round, it has some important implications.

Although I have been concerned primarily with how people used the books they read, these uses are closely bound up with other aspects of amateur, domestic culture. Looking at the evidence of manuscript albums, notebooks, letters, and diaries of enthusiastic readers, one is aware of the way in which reading was embedded in, and often inseparable from, other areas of life: visits and conversations, embroidery and jigsaws, trips to the theatre, concerns about one's children. We cannot exclude all these aspects of human experience from our understanding of what books have meant. But equally, it is difficult to know what then is the appropriate "context" within which to locate literary texts—should we think about all of these areas of life? How do we decide which are most significant? It also seems important to acknowledge that there were various prompts for reading: entertainment, self-improvement, social aspiration, utility, and application mattered differently between one reader and another.

Everyday sociable literary culture does not always fit well with the ways we conventionally analyse or read texts. Many of the traditional questions at the heart of literary criticism, such as the source for a particular textual borrowing, are unanswerable when faced with the swirling movements of words and lines that formed habits of amateur reading. Few of the readers I have looked at here explain why they quoted what they quoted; a lot of the time, they don't even acknowledge that they are using another writer's words. And if we want to look at the broader cultural afterlife of literary works, and consider the other forms books assumed in the home, it can be difficult to "read" material objects in the same ways that we might read textual adaptations. Why did middling-sort homeowners acquire an earthenware figurine of Sterne's "Poor Maria"? Had they actually read the novel she came from? Did owning the figure speak to their emotional engagement with a sentimental fictional episode, or their desire to deploy their cultural prowess amongst friends?

The increasing availability of literary works and characters in alternative formats also highlights the question of access. Much recent work on the history of reading has focussed on the high prices of new books, and the extent to which those costs limited the availability of literature. But as we have seen, reading was not dependent on ownership, and recently published single-author editions were far from the only way in which readers gained access to literature. Eighteenth-century society offered numerous points of entry: libraries, book groups, and reading clubs reshaped the literary landscape; and they sat alongside older forms of exchange, such as lending and borrowing. A house with a decent book collection could be a resource for an extended community. Moreover, the emergence of new formats, such as part books, serial publication, abridgements, magazines, and collections of extracts drastically reduced the initial outlay for those keen to read without a gentleman's income. While all these variables make it hard to quantify how many people in eighteenth-century Britain had access to texts, they show us that the spread of readers extended far beyond the circle of those wealthy enough to buy new books on a regular basis.

The stories and examples contained in this book also force us to question the movement of text between print and manuscript. It was once assumed that the eighteenth century saw the completion of a shift from the scribal circulation of text to professional authorship in print. Yet looking at the rich archives of amateur literary culture we can see the way in which habits of personalizing text, through commonplacing and copying out into manuscript volumes, flourished throughout this period. Often these habits of compilation sat alongside creative writing. Existing texts were remodelled; old poems given new meaning as gifts, tributes, or jokes. And at the same time, print mimicked manuscript forms: collections of poetic aphorisms or flowery descriptions, miscellanies pretended to be taken from a collection of letters broken open. Sometimes the exchange was wholly circular: pieces came out of manuscript, appeared in print, and then were copied back down again by pleased readers.

We see a similarly complex dynamic between oral and written forms. The history of Western literature has long been characterised as a transition from oral to literate culture. This is a paradigm that has tended to downplay, for example, the importance of rhetoric in early modern society, or the extent to which texts were read out loud in an era of minimal literacy.[1] And the vocalizing of text in the eighteenth century, often in domestic social situations, shows us that the exchange between the written and the spoken continued to move backwards and forwards. Works were shaped by the demands of vocalised reading—they had to be clear, dramatic, appropriate, excerptable, or useful. We find print moving back into spoken media, as, for example, jestbook collections provided stories to be read aloud as if they were personal anecdotes. Elocution primers and guides for clergymen offered passages marked up for emphatic delivery. Natural philosophy was made palatable by presenting it in the form of domestic conversations. There is a feedback loop in all these processes that elides transmission and creation.

The Social Life of Books focusses on the eighteenth century, but it also speaks to the longer history of books in company. There are many directions in which one might pursue this story onwards: in Britain, educational initiatives currently promote "poetry by heart." Where once children were encouraged to recite verse out loud for social and moral improvement, the orality of literature is now seen as crucial to establishing literacy. Amongst adults, the informal social functions of literature are evident in the continuing rise of book groups. Works aimed at this readership now come accompanied by their own questions for discussion—as was true of our eighteenth-century forebears, the enjoyment of reading is coupled with the pleasure of conversations around a book. New technologies enable us to mark up and share digitally our favourite passages in a book, as we might once have transcribed them into a journal. Short-form fiction has flourished because it is so well suited to both small mobile devices and time-poor readers. Such habits, like the older reading patterns described in this book, offer moments of imaginative engagement rather than lengthy immersion. We are apt to describe our own age as uniquely distracted, a time in which attention spans diminish and texts are perpetually in competition with other stimuli.[2] But as we have seen, anxieties about forms of reading are not new.[3]

Eighteenth-century commentators worried about learning bought too easily and readers who could no longer engage with whole texts. Families encouraged reading together because they feared that young people were losing their sense of reality through their immersion in addictive imaginative fictions. The world of eighteenth-century reading was a very different land, but in some ways, perhaps not so far from our own as we like to think.

Notes

Introduction

1. Thursday 15th April, 1802, *The Grasmere Journals*, ed. Pamela Woof (Oxford: Clarendon, 1991), 84–86.

2. Steven Shapin, "'The Mind Is Its Own Place': Science and Solitude in Seventeenth-Century England," first published in *Science in Context* 4 (1991), 191–218, reprinted in Shapin, *Never Pure: Historical Studies of Science* (Baltimore: Johns Hopkins University Press, 2010), 119–41, 120.

3. Robert Darnton, "First Steps Towards a History of Reading," *Australian Journal of French Studies* 23 (1986), 14.

4. Elizabeth Hamilton, *Memoirs of the Late Mrs Elizabeth Hamilton with a Selection from Her Correspondence*, ed. Miss Benger (London, 1819), 49–50.

5. Harriet Martineau and Maria Weston Chapman, *Harriet Martineau's Autobiography*, 3 vols. (London: Smith Elder, 1877), 1:430.

6. For a discussion of the middling sort in this period, see Margaret Hunt, *The Middling Sort: Commerce, Gender, and the Family in England, 1680–1780* (Berkeley: University of California Press, 1996).

7. Brean Hammond, *Professional Imaginative Writing in England, 1670–1740: "Hackney for Bread"* (Oxford: Clarendon, 1997); *The Cambridge History of the Book in Britain, 1695–1830*, ed. Michael Suarez and Michael Turner (Cambridge: Cambridge University Press, 2014); John Feather, *The English Provincial Book Trade Eighteenth-Century England* (Cambridge: Cambridge University Press, 1985); R. M. Wiles, "The Relish for Reading in Provincial England Two Centuries Ago," in *The Widening Circle: Essays on the Circulation of Literature in Eighteenth-Century Europe*, ed. J. Korshin (Philadelphia: University of Pennsylvania Press, 1976).

8. Influential works include Alberto Manguel, *A History of Reading* (London: HarperCollins, 1996); Roger Chartier and Guglielmo Cavallo, eds., *A History of Reading in the West* (Oxford: Polity, 1999); Steven Roger Fischer, *A History*

of Reading (London: Reaktion, 2004); Robert Darnton, "First Steps Towards a History of Reading," *Australian Journal of French Studies* 23 (1986), 5–30; for a collection of influential contributions, see *The History of Reading: A Reader,* ed. Shafquat Towheed, Rosalind Crone, and Katie Halsey (London: Routledge, 2010). Major works focussing on the eighteenth century include David Allan, *Commonplace Books and Reading in Georgian England* (Cambridge: Cambridge University Press, 2010); Stephen Colclough, *Consuming Texts: Readers and Reading Communities, 1695–1860* (London: Palgrave, 2007); Jan Fergus, *Provincial Readers in Eighteenth-Century England* (Oxford: Oxford University Press, 2006); Isabel Rivers, *Books and Their Readers in Eighteenth-Century England* (Leicester: Leicester University Press, 1982 and 2001); William St Clair, *The Reading Nation in the Romantic Period* (Cambridge: Cambridge University Press, 2004); Mark Towsey, *Reading the Scottish Enlightenment: Books and Their Readers in Provincial Scotland, 1750– 1820* (Leiden: Brill, 2010). Important work has been done on Jane Austen and sociable reading, notably by Patricia Michaelson in *Speaking Volumes: Women, Reading, and Speech in the Age of Austen* (Stanford: Stanford University Press, 2002). The present study does not focus on Austen because of the wealth of discussion of her reading practices in this and other secondary criticism.

9. Rolf Engelsing, *Der Bürger als Leser: Lesergeschichte in Deutschland, 1500– 1800* (Stuttgart: Metzler, 1974); Roger Chartier, "The Practical Impact of Writing," in *A History of Private Life: Passions of the Renaissance,* ed. Roger Chartier, trans. Arthur Goldhammer (Cambridge: Harvard University Press, 1989). See also Reinhard Wittman, "Was There a Reading Revolution at the End of the Eighteenth Century?," in *The History of Reading in the West,* ed. Cavallo and Chartier, 284–312.

10. For a sense of the European dimensions of this shift in reading habits, see Wittman, "Was There a Reading Revolution?"

11. Elspeth Jajdelska, *Silent Reading and the Birth of the Narrator* (Toronto: University of Toronto Press, 2007).

12. 29 June 1786, *Betsy Sheridan's Journal: Letters from Sheridan's Sister, 1784–1786 and 1788–1790,* ed. William LeFanu (New Brunswick: Rutgers University Press, 1960), 88.

13. William Cowper, "The Task," book 3, ll. 389–96, *The Poems of William Cowper,* ed. John D. Baird and Douglas Ryskamp, 3 vols. (Oxford: Clarendon, 1995), 2:172–73.

14. 24 October 1729, Gertrude Savile, *Secret Comment: The Diaries of Gertrude Savile, 1721–1757,* ed. Alan Saville (Devon: Kingsbridge History Society, 1997), 191.

15. 17 March 1788, Diary of George Sandy, Apprentice in *The Book of the Old Edinburgh Club* (Edinburgh, 1942, printed by the club), 24:1–69, 16.

16. Lambeth Palace Library, MS 1697 Wye Book Club Papers, Minutes and Accounts 1812–1860, accounts for 1814–15.

17. *A Catalogue of Books in the Macclesfield Circulating Library* (Macclesfield, 1779), 10; *A Catalogue of the Books in the Circulating Library at Halifax* (Halifax, 1786), 27; *A Catalogue of the Present Collection of Books, in the Manchester Circulating Library* (Manchester, 1794), 59; *A Catalogue of R. Fisher's Circulating Library, in the High-Bridge, Newcastle* . . . (Newcastle-upon-Tyne, 1791), 71; *A Catalogue of the Circulating Library opened by R. Bliss, Bookseller and Stationer, High Street, Oxford* . . . (Oxford, 1785), 55; *A New Catalogue of Bell's Circulating Library* . . . (London, 1778), 74; *A Catalogue of Meyler's Circulating Library* . . . (Bath, 1790), 53.

18. Nancy Woodforde, diary entries for 16, 18, 20, 23, 25 February 1792, in *Woodforde Papers and Diaries*, ed. Dorothy Heighes Woodforde (Bungay: Morrow, 1990), 45–46. The original *Devil Upon Two Sticks* is not listed in the inventory of books left at her death.

19. *Dr Last; or, the Devil Upon Two Sticks* (London, 1771, published by H. Roberts), Bodleian Library Vet. A5 e.892 (1).

20. *Spectator* 10, 12 March 1711, *The Spectator*, ed. Donald F. Bond, 5 vols. (Oxford: Clarendon, 1965), 1:44.

21. Amanda Vickery, *Behind Closed Doors: At Home in Georgian England* (New Haven: Yale University Press, 2009); Vickery, *The Gentleman's Daughter: Women's Lives in Georgian England* (New Haven: Yale University Press, 1998); Benjamin Heller, "Leisure and the Use of Domestic Space in Georgian London," *Historical Journal* 53 (2010), 623–34; Michael McKeon, *The Secret History of Domesticity: Public, Private, and the Division of Knowledge* (Baltimore: Johns Hopkins University Press, 2005); Charles Saumarez Smith, *Eighteenth-Century Decoration: Design and the Domestic Interior in England* (London: Weidenfeld and Nicolson, 1993); Karen Lipsedge, *Domestic Space in Eighteenth-Century British Novels* (Basingstoke: Palgrave, 2012).

22. William Cowper, *The Task*, book 3, ll. 41–42, 48, *Poems of William Cowper*, 2:164. According to Hall and Davidoff's study of middle-class society in the late eighteenth century, Cowper is the poet most commonly quoted by their middle-class readers, a popularity partly based on his celebration of the quiet pleasures of domestic life. Leonore Davidoff and Catherine Hall, *Family Fortunes: Men and Women of the English Middle Class, 1780–1850* (Chicago: University of Chicago Press, 1987), 157.

23. Davidoff and Hall, *Family Fortunes*, 149–82.

1. *How to Read*

Epigraph: Diary entry of 29 September 1785, *The Hamwood Papers of the Ladies of Llangollen and Caroline Hamilton*, ed. G. H. Bell (London: Macmillan, 1930), 56.

1. *Ben Jonson's Timber or Discoveries*, ed. Ralph S. Walker (Syracuse, N.Y.: Syracuse University Press, 1953).

2. Jonathan Hope, *Shakespeare and Language: Reason, Eloquence, and Artifice in the Renaissance* (London: Arden Shakespeare, 2010), 30.

3. There are also seventeenth-century texts endorsing rhetoric as a form of self-advancement, such as, for example, *The Academy of Complements* (1640).

4. For a thorough investigation of the changing relationship between speech, class, and text in this period, see Elspeth Jajdelska, *Speech, Print, and Decorum in Britain, 1600–1750* (London: Routledge, 2016).

5. On the ways in which listening to and taking notes on sermons influenced habits in listening to dramatic performance, see Tiffany Stern, "Sermons, Plays, and Note-Takers: *Hamlet* Q1 as a 'Noted' Text," in *Shakespeare Survey*, vol. 66, ed. Peter Holland (Cambridge: Cambridge University Press, 2013), 1–23.

6. 10 September 1727, in Gertrude Savile, *Secret Comment: The Diaries of Gertrude Savile, 1721–1757*, ed. Alan Saville (Devon: Kingsbridge History Society, 1997), 60. The sermon was *Of Preparation for Death and Judgment* (1695).

7. 26 February 1728, in Savile, *Secret Comment*, 106. She is referring to Edward Young's essay on the role of the emotions in devotion in *A Vindication of Providence; or, a True Estimate of Human Life* (1728).

8. 26 May 1728, in Savile, *Secret Comment*, 116.

9. On the coexistence of poor delivery alongside verbal eloquence within early modern culture, see Carla Mazzio, *The Inarticulate Renaissance: Language Trouble in an Age of Eloquence* (Philadelphia: University of Pennsylvania Press, 2008).

10. For more examples of his sermon shopping, see Dudley Ryder, *Diary of Dudley Ryder: 1715–1716*, ed. William Matthews (London: Methuen, 1939), 43, 50, 157, 372.

11. 12 June 1715, in Ryder, *Diary*, 33.

12. Ibid.

13. 10 July 1715, in Ryder, *Diary*, 50.

14. December 1715, in Ryder, *Diary*, 157.

15. December 1716, in Ryder, *Diary*, 372.

16. 8 April 1716, in Ryder, *Diary*, 216.

17. For excellent accounts of the rise of oratory in this period, see Paul Goring, *The Rhetoric of Sensibility in Eighteenth-Century Culture* (Cambridge: Cambridge University Press, 2005), esp. 2–40; and Patricia Michaelson, *Speaking Volumes: Women, Reading, and Speech in the Age of Austen* (Stanford: Stanford University Press, 2002); Jacqueline George, "Public Reading and Lyric Pleasure: Eighteenth-Century Elocutionary Debates and Poetic Practices," *ELH* 76 (2009), 371–97.

18. Francis Gentleman, *The Orator or English Assistant: Being an Essay on Reading and Declamation* (Edinburgh, 1771), 31.

19. *Some Rules for Speaking and Action; To be Observed at the Bar, in the Pulpit, and the Senate* (London, 1716), 14–15.

20. 18 April 1783, in James Boswell, *Life of Johnson*, ed. R. W. Chapman (Oxford: Oxford University Press, 1980), 1224.

21. James Fordyce, *An Essay on the Action Proper for the Pulpit* (London, 1753), 73.

22. Ibid., 73.

23. See Dana Harrington, "Remembering the Body: Eighteenth-Century Elocution and the Oral Tradition," *Rhetorica* 28 (2010), 67–95, 71–75.

24. 18 February 1763, in Adam Smith, *Lectures on Rhetoric and Belles Lettres, Delivered in the University of Glasgow by Adam Smith, Reported by a Student in 1762–63*, ed. John M. Lothian (London: Thomas Nelson and Sons, 1963), 192.

25. Gilbert Austin, *Chironomia; or, a Treatise on Rhetorical Delivery* (London, 1806), xi.

26. See also the Protestant clergyman Michel Le Faucheur, whose treatise on bodily eloquence was first published in English under the title of *An Essay upon the Action of an Orator* in 1702, and subsequently appeared in various editions and selections over the course of the eighteenth century.

27. Charles Le Brun, *A Method to Learn to Design the Passions* (London, 1734), 20–21.

28. Ibid., 30.

29. Jennifer Montagu, *The Expression of the Passions: The Origin and Influence of Charles Le Brun's Conférence sur l'expression générale et particulière* (New Haven: Yale University Press, 1994); Alistair Smart, "Dramatic Gesture and Expression in the Age of Hogarth and Reynolds," *Apollo* 82 (1965), 90–97.

30. On gesture on the early modern stage, see Andrew Gurr, *The Shakespearean Stage, 1574–1642*, 3rd ed. (Cambridge: Cambridge University Press, 1992),

95–103. Gurr cites John Bulwer's *Chirologia; or, the Naturall Language of the Hand* (1644), which describes how emotional states are communicated through the hands.

31. Thomas Sheridan, *A Course of Lectures on Elocution* (London, 1762), 102.

32. See Michaelson, *Speaking Volumes*, 107–8.

33. *The Thespian Oracle; or, a New Key to Theatrical Amusements* (London, 1791), xvi.

34. See Murray Cohen, *Sensible Words: Linguistic Practice in England, 1640–1785* (London: Johns Hopkins University Press, 1977), 115–19.

35. James Buchanan, *The British Grammar; or, an Essay, in Four Parts, towards Speaking and Writing the English Language Grammatically, and Inditing Elegantly* (London, 1762), 49.

36. See Alicia Rodriguez-Alvarez, "Teaching Punctuation in Early Modern England," *Studia Anglia Posnaniensia* 46 (2010), 35–49; Park Honan, "Eighteenth and Nineteenth Century English Punctuation Theory," *English Studies* 41 (1960), 92–102.

37. Henry Care, *The Tutor to True English* (London, 1687), 59.

38. See Cohen, *Sensible Words*, 115–19.

39. Thomas Sheridan, *A General Dictionary of the English Language*, 2 vols. (London, 1780), 1:8.

40. Betty Rizzo, "Male Oratory and Female Prate: 'Then Hush and Be an Angel Quite,'" *Eighteenth-Century Life* 29 (2005), 23–49, 27.

41. 14 November 1768, in Sylas Neville, *The Diary of Sylas Neville*, ed. Basil Cozens-Hardy (Oxford: Oxford University Press, 1950), 51.

42. "To the Printer of the St. James's Chronicle," *St James's Chronicle, or the British Evening Post*, 13 May 1762.

43. "London," *Public Advertiser*, 5 September 1764.

44. John Taylor, *Records of My Life*, 2 vols. (London, 1832), 2:27.

45. Graham Midgley, *The Life of Orator Henley* (Oxford: Clarendon, 1973).

46. "At the Lecture Room," *Public Advertiser*, 24 December 1754.

47. See Gerald Kahan, *George Alexander Stevens and the Lecture on Heads* (Athens: University of Georgia Press, 1984), 18.

48. James Burgh, *The Art of Speaking in Two Parts*, 2nd ed. (Dublin, 1763), 3.

49. See Michaelson, *Speaking Volumes*, 43–46.

50. James Fordyce, *Sermons to Young Women in Two Volumes*, rev. 2nd ed. (London, 1766), 1:294.

51. John Drummond, *A Collection of Poems for Reading and Repetition* (Edinburgh, 1762), vi.

52. Unknown annotator, *A Key to Spelling and Introduction to the English Grammar, Designed for the Use of Charity and Sunday-Schools* (1788), BL 12983.b.6, facing 31.

53. On the potential for female involvement in public oratory, see Rizzo, "Male Oratory and Female Prate."

54. "A Hint to Female Orators," *Morning Post*, 28 November 1780.

55. Likely collections of extracts are *The Lady's Poetical Magazine*, 2 vols. (London, 1791); *The Most Agreeable Companion*, 2 vols. (Leeds, 1782); *The English Lyceum*, 3 vols. (Hamburg, 1787); *The Sky-Lark; or, the lady and gentleman's harmonious companion* (Edinburgh, 1785).

56. "To the Printer of the St. James's Chronicle," *St. James's Chronicle*, 13 May 1762.

57. 1 December 1807, in *The Diary of the Revd William Jones, 1777–1821*, ed. O. F. Christie (London: Brentano's, 1929), 221–22.

58. Burgh, *The Art of Speaking*, title page.

59. John Drummond, *The Art of Reading and Speaking in Public* (Edinburgh, 1780), title page.

60. Ibid., 114.

61. John Walker, *Elements of Elocution: Being the Substance of a Course of Lectures on the Art of Reading*, 2 vols. (London, 1781), 2:266–67.

62. In his influential history of the mass reading public, Richard D. Altick argued that the popularity of elocution courses was greatly responsible for the development of a wider audience for polite literature. Richard D. Altick, *The English Common Reader: A Social History of the Mass Reading Public, 1800–1900* (Chicago: University of Chicago Press, 1957), 43.

63. *The Reader or Reciter: by the Assistance of which any Person may teach himself to read or recite English Prose* (London, 1799), iv.

64. Ibid., 10.

65. Ibid., 2.

66. For commentary on Johnson's "distinctive style," see *The Reader*, 36.

67. On the reading choices of later working-class readers, and the idea of a time lag in the canon, see Jonathan Rose, "A Conservative Canon: Cultural Lag in British Working-Class Reading Habits," *Libraries and Culture* 33 (1998): 98–104.

68. Thomas Sheridan, *Lectures on the Art of Reading*, 2 vols. (London, 1775), 1:107–8.

69. On the class element of speech and elocution in this period, see Jajdelska, *Speech, Print, and Decorum in Britain*, 146–95.

70. *Beauties of Eminent Writers: Selected and Arranged for the Instruction of Youth [. . .] for the Use of Schools and Private Classes,* 2 vols., 2nd ed. (Edinburgh, 1794), 1:1.

71. See, for example, François Fénelon, *Instructions for the Education of a Daughter* (London, 1707), 230.

72. Fordyce, *Sermons to Young Women,* 1:291.

73. Ibid., 2:294–95.

74. *The Reader,* 142.

75. *Sheridan's and Henderson's Practical Method of Reading and Reciting English Poetry* (London, 1796), ix.

76. Elspeth Jajdelska, " 'The very defective and erroneous method': Reading Instruction and Social Identity in Elite Eighteenth-Century Learners," *Oxford Review of Education* 36, no. 2 (2010), 141–56, 143–48.

77. 6 Nov 1716, in Ryder, *Diary,* 360.

78. James Fordyce, *Dialogues Concerning Education,* 2 vols. (London, 1745), 2:297.

79. *The Art of Delivering Written Language; or, an Essay on Reading* (London, 1775), ix.

80. Undated nineteenth-century memorandum, Chubb correspondence, Somerset Heritage Centre, A/CSC 2/3.

81. Commonplace book/notebook of Jonathan Chubb, Somerset Heritage Centre, A/CSC 1/1, fol. 26.

82. Undated letter from Jonathan Chubb to Jack [John] Chubb, December 1759. Addressed "To Mr Charles La Roche Cheapside for Master Chubb, London." Chubb correspondence A/CSC 2/3.

83. John Chubb to Jonathan Chubb, 15 January 1760, Chubb correspondence A/CSC 2/3.

84. Undated letter, John Chubb to Jonathan Chubb, Chubb correspondence A/CSC 2/3.

85. Chubb's paintings are now at the Bridgwater Blake Museum, in Bridgwater. See Mark Girouard, "Country-Town Portfolio: John Chubb's Bridgwater Drawings," *Country Life* 183, no. 49 (7 December 1989), 154–59.

86. John Chubb's commonplace books, Somerset Heritage Centre, A/CSC 1/2 and A/CSC 1/3 and A/CSC 1/.

87. John Chubb, letter to Morley Chubb, 1798, Somerset Heritage Centre, A/CSC 2/4.

2. *Reading and Sociability*

Epigraph: Diary entry of 19 March, 1790, Diary of William Hugh Burgess, London Metropolitan Archives, F/WHB/2, volume 1.

1. On the commercialisation of culture and the rise of new public entertainments, see John Brewer, *The Pleasures of the Imagination: English Culture in the Eighteenth Century* (New York: Farrar, Straus and Giroux, 1997); J. H. Plumb, *The Commercialisation of Leisure in the Eighteenth Century* (Reading: University of Reading, 1973); David Solkin, *Painting for Money: The Visual Arts and the Public Sphere in Eighteenth-Century England* (New Haven: Yale University Press, 1993). On evolving notions of sociability and politeness, see Lawrence E. Klein, *Shaftesbury and the Culture of Politeness: Moral Discourse and Cultural Politics in Early Eighteenth-Century England* (Cambridge: Cambridge University Press, 1994); Philip Carter, *Men and the Emergence of Polite Society, Britain, 1660–1800* (Harlow: Longman, 2001); Paul Langford, *A Polite and Commercial People: England, 1727–1783* (Oxford: Oxford University Press, 1998); Langford, "The Uses of Eighteenth-Century Politeness," *Transactions of the Royal Historical Society* 12 (2002), 311–31.

2. Recent accounts of the period have emphasised that the home was far from an exclusively female space. See Benjamin Heller, "Leisure and the Use of Domestic Space in Georgian London," *Historical Journal* 53 (2010), 623–45; Karen Harvey, *The Little Republic: Masculinity and Domestic Authority in Eighteenth-Century Britain* (Oxford: Oxford University Press, 2012).

3. 29 July 1714, in Nicholas Blundell, *Blundell's Diary and Letter Book 1702–1728*, ed. Margaret Blundell (Liverpool: Liverpool University Press, 1952), 85.

4. Ibid., 86.

5. "Appendix I," in Blundell, *Blundell's Diary and Letter Book*, 252.

6. See Heller, "Leisure and the Use of Domestic Space in Georgian London.'

7. 7 September 1769, in Sylas Neville, *The Diary of Sylas Neville*, ed. Basil Cozens-Hardy (Oxford: Oxford University Press, 1950), 79.

8. See Henry Prescott, *The Diary of Henry Prescott, LL.B., Deputy Registrar of Chester Diocese*, ed. John Addy, 3 vols. (Chester: Record Society of Lancashire and Cheshire, 1987–97).

9. James Fordyce, Sermon VI, *Sermons to Young Women in two volumes*, rev. 2nd ed., 2 vols. (London, 1766), 1:191.

10. *A New Tea-Table Miscellany; or, Bagatelles for the Amusement of the Fair Sex* (London, 1750), ii–iv.

11. Ibid., vii.

12. Ibid., iii.

13. See Carter, *Men and the Emergence of Polite Society*, 66–70. On the importance of men mingling with women, see Joseph Addison, *Spectator* 57,

5 May 1711, in *Spectator*, 1:242; James Forrester, *The Polite Philosopher; or, an Essay on that Art which makes a Man happy in Himself* (Edinburgh, 1734), 49.

14. See Kate Retford, "From Interior to Interiority: The Conversation Piece in Georgian England," *Journal of Design History* 20 (2007), 291–307.

15. See Susan Whyman, *Sociability and Power in Late Stuart England: The Cultural Worlds of the Verneys, 1660–1720* (Oxford: Oxford University Press, 1999), 91–99.

16. See Amanda Vickery, *The Gentleman's Daughter: Women's Lives in Georgian England* (London: Yale University Press, 1998), 205–9; Whyman, *Sociability and Power in Late Stuart England*, 91–99.

17. Diary of Elizabeth Tyrrell, 4 August 1809, London Metropolitan Archives, CLC/510.

18. 4 November 1776, "Miss Mary Curzon to Miss Heber," in *Dear Miss Heber, An Eighteenth-Century Correspondence*, ed. Francis Bamford (London: Constable, 1936), 4.

19. 25 October 1758, in Elizabeth Raper, *The Receipt Book of Elizabeth Raper* (Soho: Nonesuch Press, 1924), 19.

20. Thomas Turner, *The Diary of Thomas Turner, 1754–1765*, ed. David Vaisey (Oxford: Oxford University Press, 1984), 137–39.

21. John Evelyn, *A Character of England* (London: 1659), 70.

22. 24 July 1785, "Miss Iremonger to Miss Heber: At Weston, Towcester, Northamptonshire," in *Dear Miss Heber*, 17.

23. Diary of Elizabeth Watkins 1771, written in a memorandum/pocket book, Gloucester Archives, D2685/23.

24. James Hervey, *Sermons and Miscellaneous Tracts, by James Hervey* (London, 1764), 122.

25. For a detailed consideration of one family's visiting habits, see Whyman, *Sociability and Power in Late Stuart England*, 97–98.

26. Patrick Boyle, "Preliminary Address," in *The Ladies' Complete Visiting Guide Containing Directions for Footmen and Porters* (London: 1800), vi. See Emma Walshe, "Paper Politeness: The Currency of the Visiting Card in the Long Eighteenth Century," in *The Materiality of Writing in the Long Eighteenth Century*, ed. Eve Rosenhaft and Helga Müllneritsch (Liverpool: Liverpool University Press, 2016).

27. Fordyce, *Sermons to Young Women*, 243.

28. Ibid., 231.

29. Ibid., 240.

30. Ibid., 251–52.

31. October 1785, Mary Delany, "The Hon. Mrs. Boscawen to Mrs. Delany," in *The Autobiography and Correspondence of Mary, Mrs Delany,* ed. The Right Honourable Lady Llanover, 2nd series, 3 vols. (London: Richard Bentley, 1862), 3:296; see *The Hamwood Papers of the Ladies of Llangollen and Caroline Hamilton,* ed. G. H. Bell (London: Macmillan, 1930), 58, 61, 66.

32. 20 June 1826, in *The Diary of Robert Sharp of South Cave: Life in a Yorkshire Village, 1812–1837,* ed. Janice E. Crowther and Peter A. Crowther (Oxford: Oxford University Press, 1997), 42.

33. 9 March 1708, in Nicholas Blundell, *The Great Diurnal of Nicholas Blundell of Little Crosby, Lancashire,* ed. J. J. Bagley, 3 vols. (Chester: Record Society of Lancashire and Cheshire, 1968–72), 1:165.

34. James Lackington, *Memoirs of the First Forty-Five Years of the Life of James Lackington* (London, 1793), 165.

35. Hugh Miller, *My Schools and Schoolmasters: or, the Story of My Education* (1852), ed. James Robertson (Edinburgh: B & W, 1993), 33–34.

36. David Vincent, *Bread, Knowledge, and Freedom: A Study of Nineteenth-Century Working-Class Autobiography* (London: Methuen, 1981), 123–24. Vincent notes that industrialization made it far more difficult to read while at work, confining nearly all self-education to after working hours and the home (124).

37. John Jones, "Some Account of the Writer, Written by Himself," in John Jones and Robert Southey, *Attempts in Verse* (London, 1831), 173.

38. *Reminiscences of a Stonemason: By a Working Man* (London: 1908), 50–51.

39. See R. C. Richardson, *Household Servants in Early Modern England* (Manchester: Manchester University Press, 2010); on the transgressive nature of servants listening in on their employers, see Alison Light, *Mrs Woolf and the Servants* (London: Fig Tree, 2007).

40. Hester Piozzi, *Thraliana: The Diary of Mrs. Hester Lynch Thrale (Later Mrs. Piozzi), 1776–1809,* ed. Katharine C. Balderston, 2nd ed., 2 vols. (Oxford: Clarendon, 1951), 1:534.

41. "Hints on Reading," *Lady's Magazine,* April 1789, 177–78.

42. Ibid., 178.

43. See Amanda Vickery, *Behind Closed Doors: At Home in Georgian England* (New Haven: Yale University Press, 2009), 274–76, 294–95.

44. See Maxine Berg, *Luxury and Pleasure in Eighteenth-Century Britain* (Oxford: Oxford University Press, 2005), 197–325.

45. *The Lady's Companion; or, an Infallible Guide to the Fair Sex* (1740), 62.

46. Abbé d'Ancourt, *The Lady's Preceptor; or, a Letter to a Young Lady of Distinction upon Politeness: Taken from the French of the Abbé D'Ancourt, and adapted to the Religion, Customs, and Manners of the English Nation* (London, 1743), 49.

47. Charles Allen, *The Polite Lady; or, a Course of Female Education* (London, 1760), 154.

48. Ernst Family notebook (undated, early 19th century), Somerset Heritage Centre, DD/SWD/16, fol. 1r.

49. For a longer discussion of Ryder's reading habits, see Stephen Colclough, *Consuming Texts: Readers and Reading Communities, 1695–1870* (Basingstoke: Palgrave Macmillan, 2007), 68–74.

50. 11 July 1715, in Ryder, *Diary*, 51.

51. 16 August 1715, in Ryder, *Diary*, 78.

52. 18 June 1715, in Ryder, *Diary*, 38.

53. 7 January 1616, in Ryder, *Diary*, 164.

54. For a fuller discussion of books as the basis for conversation in the romantic period, see Heather Jackson, *Romantic Readers: The Evidence of Marginalia* (New Haven: Yale University Press, 2005), 121–97.

55. Fordyce, *Sermons to Young Women*, 269.

56. Amy Cruse, *The Englishman and His Books in the Early Nineteenth Century* (London: George G. Harrap, 1930), quoted in Steven Roger Fischer, *A History of Reading* (London: Reaktion, 2003), 273.

57. Cf. William Beatty Warner, "Staging Readers Reading," *Eighteenth-Century Fiction* 12 (2000), 391–416.

58. Richard Brinsley Sheridan, *The Rivals, a Comedy*, in *The Dramatic Works of Richard Brinsley Sheridan*, ed. Cecil Price, 2 vols. (Oxford: Clarendon, 1973), 1:84.), 25.

59. *The Theatre of Wit; or, a Banquet of the Muses, a Collection of Pieces in Verse and Prose, Selected from the Most Eminent Authors* (London, 1746), 39–40.

60. See Clive Wainwright, "The Library as Living Room," in *Property of a Gentleman: The Formation, Organisation and Dispersal of the Private Library, 1620–1920*, ed. Robin Myers and Michael Harris (Winchester: St Paul's Bibliographies, 1991), 15–24.

61. See David Pearson, "The English Private Library in the Seventeenth Century," *The Library* 13 (2012), 379–99, 383.

62. See ibid., 387.

63. James Raven, "From Promotion to Prescription: Arrangements for Reading and Eighteenth-Century Libraries," *The Practice and Representation of*

Reading in England, ed. James Raven, Helen Small, and Naomi Tadmor (Cambridge: Cambridge University Press, 1995), 175–201, 188–90.

64. "Memorandum for making a distinct catalogue of a library," Edinburgh 1759 National Library of Scotland, MS 2975 f.39.

65. Ibid., f.40v.

66. Mark Girouard, *Life in the English Country House: A Social and Architectural History* (New Haven: Yale University Press, 1978), 234.

67. *Passages from the Diaries of Mrs Philip Lybbe Powys of Hardwick House, Oxon* (London, 1899), 197.

68. William Parkes, *Domestic Duties; or, Instructions to Young Married Ladies* (New York, 1829), 99.

69. Wainwright, "The Library as Living Room," 16.

70. Jacqueline Pearson, *Women's Reading in Britain, 1750–1835: A Dangerous Recreation* (Cambridge: Cambridge University Press, 1999), 170.

71. The sofa appears in this guise in Frances Jacson's *Plain Sense*, 3 vols. (London, 1799); Catharine Selden's *The English Nun* (London, 1797); and Selden's *Serena*, 3 vols. (London, 1800).

72. A. Hepplewhite and Company, *The Cabinet-Maker and Upholsterer's Guide; or, Repository of Designs for Every Article of Household Furniture*, 3rd ed. (London, 1794), 17.

73. See *Upwards of One Hundred New and Genteel Designs [. . .] of Houshold Furniture in the present Taste* (London), reproduced in facsimile as *Genteel Houshold Furniture in the Present Taste*, ed. Christopher Gilbert (Wakefield: EP, 1978), 51–70.

74. "John Weskett, James Cooper, Theft theft from a specified place, Theft receiving, 12th December 1764," *Old Bailey Proceedings Online* (www.oldbaileyonline.org) Ref. t17641212-52.

75. On the challenges of reading the history of books in this sample of inventory evidence, see Hannah Fleming, "At Home with Books: Resuscitating the History of Eighteenth-Century Reading and Readers at the Geffrye Museum," *Art Libraries Journal* 39/3 (2014), 5–9.

76. Nicholas Browning Baker, 3 June 1800, St Giles Cripplegate, London, NA: PROB/31/921/736.

77. On the inventory evidence of books in middling-sort homes in the eighteenth century, see Fleming, "At Home with Books."

78. John Cornforth, *Early Georgian Interiors* (New Haven: Yale University Press, 2004), 53. In the late 1740s and early 1750s, greater length was needed in drawing rooms for upholstered seating, particularly pairs of long settees flanking a chimney piece.

79. "West Humble, [1] September 1801 To Doctor Burney," in Fanny Burney, *The Journals and Letters of Fanny Burney*, ed. Joyce Hemlow, 11 vols. (Oxford: Oxford University Press, 1973), 4:501.

80. "420: West Hamble, 6 September 1801 To Doctor Burney," in Burney, *The Journals and Letters of Fanny Burney*, 504.

81. Humphrey Repton, "A Modern Living Room," in *Fragments on the Theory and Practice of Landscape Gardening* (London, 1816), 57.

82. On the decline of the circle, see Girouard, *Country House*, 238.

83. Leonore Davidoff and Catherine Hall, *Family Fortunes: Men and Women of the English Middle Class, 1780–1850* (London: Hutchinson, 1987), 165–67.

84. For an excellent discussion of Lister's reading, see Stephen Colclough, "Do you not know the quotation? Reading Anne Lister, Anne Lister Reading," in *Lesbian Dames: Sapphism in the Long Eighteenth Century*, ed. John C. Beynon and Caroline Gonda (London: Ashgate, 2010), 159–72.

85. 20 July 1823, in Anne Lister, *I Know My Own Heart: The Diaries of Anne Lister, 1791–1840*, ed. Helena Whitbread (London: Virago, 1988), 265–66.

86. 17 July 1823, in Lister, *I Know My Own Heart*, 263.

87. 19 June 1824, in Lister, *I Know My Own Heart*, 347.

88. Maureen Dillon, *Artificial Sunshine: A Social History of Domestic Lighting* (London: National Trust, 2002), 12.

89. Library catalogue for Carmichael House, NLS, MS 3528, fols. 19v–24r.

90. Richard Twining, *Recreations and Studies of a Country Clergyman of the Eighteenth Century Being Selections from the Correspondence of the Rev. Thomas Twining* (London: John Murray, 1882), 32fn.

91. "The Task," in William Cowper, *Poems, by William Cowper*, 2 vols. (London, 1799), 2:108–9.

92. Diary of Eliza Tyrrel, 12 July 1818, London Metropolitan Archives, CLC/510.

93. *Hamwood Papers*, 55.

94. Ibid., 58.

95. James Lackington, *Memoirs of the First Forty-Five Years of the Life of James Lackington* (London, 1793), 256.

96. *Memoirs of Richard Lovell Edgeworth*, 2 vols. (London, 1820), 1:352.

97. See Jon Mee, *Conversable Worlds: Literature, Contention, and Community, 1762–1830* (Oxford: Oxford University Press, 2011).

98. 5 July 1775, "The Hon. Mrs Boscawen to Mrs. Delany," in Delany, *Autobiography and Correspondence*, 2nd series (1862), 2:144.

99. 3 November 1774, "Mrs. Delany to the Right Hon. Viscountess Andover," in Delany, *Autobiography and Correspondence*, 2nd series (1862), 2:54.

100. 28th November 1774, "Mrs. Delany to Bernard Granville, Esq.," in Delany, *Autobiography and Correspondence*, 2nd series (1862), 2:74.

101. Sarah Jordan, *The Anxieties of Idleness: Idleness in Eighteenth-Century British Literature and Culture* (London: Associated University Presses, 2003), 84–122.

102. Ibid., 86.

103. Ibid., 20.

104. Thomas Gisborne, *An Enquiry into the Duties of the Female Sex* (London 1797), 220.

105. Ibid., 224.

106. Nicolas Venette, *The Pleasures of Conjugal-Love Explain'd: In an Essay Concerning Human Generation* (London, 1740), 26.

107. Hester Chapone, *A Letter to a New-Married Lady* (London, 1777), 16.

108. Ibid., 17.

109. Jane Collier, *An Essay on the Art of Ingeniously Tormenting* (London, 1753), 123.

110. On the depiction of the text as conjugal obstacle, see Leah Price, *How to Do Things with Books in Victorian Britain* (Princeton: Princeton University Press, 2012), 51–67.

111. For a good discussion of unhappy marriages in this period, see Vickery, *Behind Closed Doors*.

112. "Hannah White, Theft other, 14th January 1743," *Old Bailey Proceedings Online* (www.oldbaileyonline.org), Ref. t17430114-48. See also "Edward Parker, Mary Hull, Theft grand larceny, 16th April 1729," Ref. 17290416-11.

113. Karen Lipsedge, "A Place of Refuge, Seduction or Danger?: The Representation of the Ivy Summer-House in Samuel Richardson's *Clarissa*," *Journal of Design History* (2006), 185–96, 188–89.

114. 15 June 1790, *Reynolds-Rathbone Diaries and Letters, 1753–1839*, ed. Eustace Greg (Edinburgh, 1905), 54; see also 8 June 1786, 39, and 29 November 1785, 32.

115. 23 August 1776, "The Duchess of Portland to Mrs. Delany," in Delany, *Autobiography and Correspondence*, 2nd series (1862) II, 254.

116. Gertrude Savile, *Secret Comment: The Diaries of Gertrude Savile, 1721–1757*, ed. Alan Saville (Devon: Kingsbridge History Society, 1997), 55.

117. "The Preface," *The Aviary; or, Magazine of British Melody* (London, 1765), n.p.

118. *The Companion, Being a Choice Collection of the most Admired Pieces from the Best Authors, in Verse and Prose* (Edinburgh, 1790), I, vi–vii.

119. John Chubb to Jonathan Chubb, 23 October 1759, Chubb correspondence, Somerset Heritage Centre, A/CSC 2/3.

120. 18 October 1760, "Mrs. Delany to Mrs. Dewes," in *The Autobiography and Correspondence of Mary Granville, Mrs. Delany,* ed. Lady Llanover, 3 vols. (London, 1861) 3:604–5.

121. 12 June 1754, "Mrs Delany to Mrs. Dewes," in *The Autobiography and Correspondence of Mary Granville,* 276.

3. *Using Books*

Epigraph: Abbé d'Ancourt, *The Lady's Preceptor; or, a letter to a young lady of distinction upon politeness: Taken from the French of the Abbé D'Ancourt, and adapted to the Religion, Customs, and Manners of the English Nation* (London, 1743), 62.

1. The evolution of reading practices may have involved a shift in the way time was spent and conceived. Reinhard Wittman, "Was There a Reading Revolution in the Eighteenth Century?," in *A History of Reading in the West,* ed. Roger Chartier and Guglielmo Cavallo (Oxford: Polity, 1999), 284–312, 299.

2. 21 March 1763, in James Boswell, *Boswell's London Journal, 1762–1763,* ed. Frederick A. Pottle (London: McGraw-Hill, 1950), 224.

3. For a full history of domestic lighting in this period, see Maureen Dillon, *Artificial Sunshine: A Social History of Domestic Lighting* (London: National Trust Publications, 2002) 12–67.

4. Ibid., 48.

5. John Cornforth, *Early Georgian Interiors* (New Haven: Yale University Press, 2004), 129.

6. James Lackington, *Memoirs of the First Forty-Five Years of the Life of James Lackington* (London, 1793), 100.

7. Alexander Somerville, *The Autobiography of a Working Man* (London, 1848), 3. See David Vincent, *Bread, Knowledge, and Freedom: A Study of Nineteenth-Century Working-Class Autobiography* (London: Methuen, 1981), 122–23; Marjorie Plant, *The Domestic Life of Scotland in the Eighteenth Century* (Edinburgh: Edinburgh University Press, 1952), 35–36.

8. 30 May 1741, "To the Same," in *The Letters of Mrs. Elizabeth Montagu, with Some of the Letters of Her Correspondents,* 3 vols. (London, 1809), 1:210–11.

9. 31 October 1774, "Mrs. Delany to Bernard Granville, Esq.," in *The Autobiography and Correspondence of Mary Granville, Mrs Delany*, ed. The Right Honourable Lady Llanover, 2nd series, 3 vols. (London: Richard Bentley, 1862), 2:50.

10. William Hugh Burgess, MS Diaries from January 1788 to October 1790, vol 1 F/WHB/, London Metropolitan Archive.

11. By the late nineteenth century, this had developed into a more concrete set of beliefs about how to read healthily: one should not read lying down, with the book too close to the eyes, while riding in carriages or trains, or too late into the night. Chris Otter, *The Victorian Eye: A Political History of Light and Vision in Britain, 1800–1910* (Chicago: University of Chicago Press, 2008), 41.

12. 5 February 1818, in Anne Lister, *I Know My Own Heart: The Diaries of Anne Lister, 1791–1840*, ed. Helena Whitbread (London: Virago, 1988), 38.

13. "Hints on Reading," *Lady's Magazine*, April 1789, 177.

14. 17 January 1710, in Nicholas Blundell, *Blundell's Diary and Letter Book, 1702–1728*, ed. Margaret Blundell (Liverpool: Liverpool University Press, 1952), 67.

15. 30 June 1710, in Blundell, *Blundell's Diary and Letter Book*, 67.

16. 20 July 1710, in Blundell, *Blundell's Diary and Letter Book*, 67.

17. David Brewster, "The Sight and How to See," *North British Review* 36 (1856), 176.

18. Daniel Gunston, *Jemmy Twitcher's Jests; collected by a member of the Beef-Steak-Club* (Glasgow, 1798), 21; Giovanni Paolo Marana, *The Eight Volumes of Letters Writ by a Turkish Spy*, 23rd ed., 8 vols. (Dublin, 1736), 8:80; "Report of an Adjudged Case, not to be Found in any of the Books," in William Cowper, *Poems by William Cowper, of the Inner Temple, Esq* (London, 1782), 315.

19. Otter, *The Victorian Eye*, 40.

20. Robert Isaac Wilberforce and Samuel Wilberforce, *The Life of William Wilberforce*, 5 vols. (London, 1838), 4:312.

21. Ibid., 79.

22. 8 September 1818, "William Wilberforce, Esq to H. Bankes, Esq," in *The Correspondence of William Wilberforce*, ed. Robert Isaac and Samuel Wilberforce, 2 vols. (London, 1840), 2:410.

23. 27 July 1826, "William Wilberforce, Esq. to Z. Macaulay, Esq," in *Correspondence of William Wilberforce*, 2:501.

24. George Adams, *An Essay on Vision, briefly Explaining the Fabric of the Eye and the Nature of Vision: Intended for the Service of those Whose Eyes are Weak or Impaired* (London, 1789), 72.

25. "Register of Books Published in July, 1736," *Gentleman's Magazine*, July 1736, 427.

26. Advertisement, "This Day publish'd," in *Westminster Journal or New Weekly Miscellany*, 2 March 1745.

27. Advertisement for "Books Printed, and Sold by the Bible-Sellers of London," in *The Whole Duty of Man, Laid Down in a Plain and Familiar Way* (London, 1753), end paper.

28. Letter cited in Alexander Pringle, *Prayer for the Revival of Religion in All the Protestant Churches* (Edinburgh 1796), 144.

29. Many of the early works for children, issued by John Newbery, were in very small, compacted formats. It does not seem to be until the publication of Anna Laetitia Barbauld's *Lessons for Children of Three Years Old* in 1779 that the now familiar practice of formatting books for those learning to read with wide margins and clear, simple text was established.

30. Samuel Richardson to Lady Barbara Montagu, October 15 1759, Cornell University Library, Rare Books and Manuscripts Collection, 4600, box 48. I am grateful to Dr. Linda Bree for this source.

31. Preface to *Beauties in Prose and Verse, Selected from the Most Celebrated Authors* (Stockton, 1783), vi.

32. *A Memoir of Maria Edgeworth, with a Selection from Her Letters*, 3 vols. (London, 1867), 1:189.

33. 1 January 1820, Maria Edgeworth to Miss Ruxton, *A Memoir*, 2: 45.

34. "Letter IX," in Mary Delany, *The Autobiography and Correspondence of Mary Granville, Mrs Delany*, ed. The Right Honourable Lady Llanover, 1st series, 3 vols. (London: Richard Bentley, 1861), 1:63.

35. 5 April 1716, in Dudley Ryder, *The Diary of Dudley Ryder, 1715–16*, ed. William Matthews (London: Methuen, 1939), 214.

36. *The Life of William Hutton, Stationer, of Birmingham: and the History of His Family, Written by Himself* (London, 1841), 93.

37. 27 November 1807, *Reynolds–Rathbone Diaries and Letters, 1753–1839*, ed. Eustace Greg (Edinburgh, 1905), 123.

38. *The Private Journal and Literary Remains of John Byrom*, ed. Richard Parkinson, 2 vols. (Manchester: Chetham Society, 1854–57), 1 (1854): 46.

39. 31 July 1794, "Letter XCVII. Mrs Jackson," in *Letters of Anna Seward, written between the years 1784 and 1807*, 6 vols. (London, 1811), 3:384–85.

40. Elspeth Jajdelska, *Silent Reading and the Birth of the Narrator* (Toronto: University of Toronto Press, 2007), 8.

41. See Garrett Stewart, *The Look of Reading: Book, Painting, Text* (Chicago: University of Chicago Press, 2006), 231–73.

42. Leah Price, *How to Do Things with Books in Victorian Britain* (Princeton: Princeton University Press, 2012), 47.

43. Peter Stallybrass, "Books and Scrolls: Navigating the Bible," in *Material Texts: Books and Readers in Early Modern England*, ed. Jennifer Andersen, Elizabeth Sauer, and Stephen Orgel (Philadelphia: University of Pennsylvania Press, 2001), 42–79, 45.

44. On the longer history of anxiety about distracted reading and short attention spans, see Frank Furedi, *Power of Reading: Socrates to Twitter* (London: Bloomsbury, 2015), 143–47.

45. "Interchange of Criticisms.—A Good-Natured Man.—Plans for the Future. To his Brother," 6 November 1778, in *Recreations and Studies of a Country Clergyman of the Eighteenth Century: Being Selections from the Correspondence of the Rev. Thomas Twining* (London: John Murray, 1882), 57.

46. "Hints on Reading," *Lady's Magazine*, February 1789, 80.

47. 10 April 1820, in Lister, *I Know My Own Heart*, 120.

48. 14 February 1821, in Lister, *I Know My Own Heart*, 146.

49. 19 August 1817, in Lister, *I Know My Own Heart*, 12.

50. 8 March 1802, "Miss S. More to Dr. Whalley, 22 Devonshire Shreet, London," in *Journals and Correspondence of Thomas Sedgwick Whalley*, ed. Rev. Hill Wickham, 2 vols. (London: Richard Bentley, 1863), 2:215–16. The pamphlet was Whalley's own *Animadversions on the Curate of Blagdon's Three Publications* (London, 1802).

51. Pierre Bayard, *How to Talk About Books You Haven't Read* (London: Granta, 2007), 15.

52. Paul Valéry, *Masters and Friends*, trans. Martin Turnell (Princeton: Princeton University Press, 1968), 295; quoted by Bayard, *Books You Haven't Read*, 17.

53. Valery, *Masters and Friends*, 298; cited in Bayard, 20.

54. Jan Fergus, *Provincial Readers in Eighteenth-Century England* (Oxford: Oxford University Press, 2007), 108–17.

55. 6 June 1831, in *The Diary of Robert Sharp of South Cave: Life in a Yorkshire Village, 1812–1837*, ed. Janice E. Crowther and Peter A. Crowther (Oxford: Oxford University Press, 1997), 314.

56. Eliza Pierce to Thomas Taylor, "To Thomas Taylor Esq. This—," in *The Letters of Eliza Pierce, 1751–1775* (London: Frederick Etchells and Hugh Macdonald, 1927), 57.

57. See, for example, Giovanni Bona, *A Guide to Eternity, Extracted out of the Writings of the Holy Fathers*, translated by Sir Roger L'Estrange, 5th ed. (London, 1709), 192.

58. Samuel Johnson, *Idler* 85, 1 December 1759, *The Idler and The Adventurer*, ed. W. J. Bate, J. M. Bullitt, and L. F. Powell (New Haven: Yale University Press, 1963), 264–66.

59. See Robert de Maria, *Samuel Johnson and the Life of Reading* (Baltimore: Johns Hopkins University Press, 1997), 138–78.

60. For a discussion of the value of "surface" reading, see Stephen Best and Sharon Marcus, "Surface Reading: An Introduction," *Representations* 108, no. 1 (2009), 1–21.

61. On Woollcombe's feelings about his bachelor status, see David Hussey and Margaret Ponsonby, *The Single Homemaker and Material Culture in the Long Eighteenth Century* (Farnham: Ashgate, 2012), 8–10.

62. "An Account of the Antiquarian and Archeological Manuscripts of Henry Woollcombe FSA, c.1839," Plymouth and West Devon Record Office, 2395.

63. 31 January 1796, Henry Woollcombe II Diary 1796–1803, Plymouth and West Devon Record Office, Ref 710/391, fol. 1.

64. Woollcombe Diary for 1797, fol. 3.

65. Woollcombe Diary for 1797, fol. 8.

66. Woollcombe Diary for 1797, fol. 41.

67. Woollcombe Diary for 1797, fol. 8.

68. Letter from William Woollcombe at Edinburgh to Henry Woollcombe at Britonside, Plymouth, 28 October 1794, Plymouth and West Devon Record Office, 710/406.

69. Ibid.

70. Woollcombe Diary for 1797, fol. 42.

71. Woollcombe Diary for 1797, fol. 135.

72. Woollcombe Diary for 1797, fol. 4.

73. 25 November 1785, in *Reynolds–Rathbone Diaries*, 32.

74. 12 April 1786, in *Reynolds Rathbone Diaries*, 36.

75. 8 June 1785, in *Reynolds Rathbone Diaries*, 39.

76. Journal A, 1749–50, "Ralph Jackson's diaries (Book A). Newcastle, October 1749–June 1750. Journal Letter A–began October 16th 1749," in "Ralph Jackson's Diaries" (http://greatayton.wikidot.com/ralph-jackson-diaries). (This and later references accessed 27 July 2015 from online transcript of diaries.)

77. See chap. 4 of Barbara Crosbie, "The Rising Generations: A Northern Perspective on Age Relations and the Contours of Cultural Change, England c. 1740–1785" (unpublished doctoral thesis, University of Durham, 2011), 122–51.

78. Journal C 1750, in "Ralph Jackson's Diaries," 21 January 1752.

79. Journal E 1752, in "Ralph Jackson's Diaries," 4 June 1753.

80. Journal E 1752, in "Ralph Jackson's Diaries," 27 July 1753.

81. Journal E 1752, in "Ralph Jackson's Diaries," 28 July 1753.

82. See Vincent, *Bread, Knowledge, and Freedom*, 120–22. For an example, see John Clare, *Sketches in the Life of John Clare*, ed. Edmund Blunden (London, 1931), 48–49.

83. See Vincent, *Bread, Knowledge, and Freedom*, 125–27.

84. *Boswell's Life of Johnson*, ed. G. B. Hill, rev. L. F. Powell, 2nd ed., 6 vols. (Oxford: Clarendon, 1934–64), 2:36 4n3.

85. DeMaria, *Samuel Johnson and the Life of Reading*, 27.

86. On reading as a social barrier in nineteenth-century fiction, see Leah Price, *How to Do Things with Books*, 45–71.

87. Mary Berry, *Extracts from the Journals and Correspondence of Miss Berry, from the Year 1783 to 1852*, ed. Lady Theresa Lewis, 2nd ed., 3 vols. (London, 1866), 1:7.

88. Anna Seward, Letter to Mrs Childers, September 19, 1798, in *Letters of Anna Seward, Written Between the Years 1784 and 1807*, 6 vols. (Edinburgh, 1811), 5:151–52.

89. *Memoirs of Richard Cumberland, Written by Himself* (London, 1806), 256.

90. Anne Fisher, *A Practical New Grammar; or, An Easy Guide to Speaking and Reading the English Language Properly* (London, 1767), 154.

91. Berry, *Extracts*, I, 437.

92. *Memoirs of Richard Cumberland, Written by Himself* (London, 1806), 82.

93. Richard Brinsley Sheridan, *Memoirs of the Colman Family*, 2 vols. (London, 1841), 2:327.

94. John Taylor, *Records of My Life. In Two Volumes* (London, 1832), 1:240.

95. See Dr Thomas Sedgwick Whalley, *Journals and Correspondence*, 2 vols. (London, 1863), 1:321; Joseph Cradock, *Literary and Miscellaneous Memoirs* (London, 1826), 77–78.

96. *The Life and Times of Frederick Reynolds*, 2 vols. (Philadelphia, 1826), 1:97–98.

97. James Fordyce, *Sermons to Young Women in Two Volumes*, rev. 2nd ed., 2 vols. (London, 1766), 1:295.

98. *Memoirs of Richard Lovell Edgeworth, Esq. Begun by Himself and Concluded by His Daughter, Maria Edgeworth*, 2 vols. (London, 1820), 2:125–26.

99. Philip MacDermott, annotation to *Childe Harold's Pilgrimage: A Romaunt* (London, 1827), BL 11642.a.51, 105. Quoted by Heather Jackson in *Romantic Readers: The Evidence of Marginalia* (New Haven: Yale University Press, 2005), 73.

100. See Patrick Spedding, "A Reading of Gay's Fables," *Script and Print* 30 (2006), 181–85.

101. Thomas Gisborne, *An Enquiry into the Duties of the Female Sex* (London, 1797), 218.

102. See David Allan, *Commonplace Books and Reading in Georgian England* (Cambridge: Cambridge University Press, 2010), 144–49.

103. 9 May 1818, Lister, *I Know My Own Heart*, 124.

104. Simon Dickie, *Cruelty and Laughter: Forgotten Comic Literature and the Unsentimental Eighteenth Century* (Chicago: University of Chicago Press, 2011), 4.

105. 26 March 1809, Diary of Elizabeth Tyrrell, London Metropolitan Archives, CLC/510.

106. 15 December 1791, "Miss Drake to Miss Heber: At Weston, Towcester, Northamptonshire," in *Dear Miss Heber, An Eighteenth Century Correspondence,* ed. Francis Bamford (London: Constable, 1936), 117.

107. 29 May 1716, in Ryder, *Diary,* 247.

108. 18 September 1716, in Ryder, *Diary,* 332.

109. 22 October 1781, in Sylas Neville, *The Diary of Sylas Neville,* ed. Basil Cozens-Hardy (Oxford: Oxford University Press, 1950), 275.

110. 13 November 1774, "The following Rules were written by Mrs. Delany," in Delany, *Autobiography and Correspondence,* 2nd series (1862) 2:55–56.

111. 24 January 1732–33, "Mrs. Pendarves to Mrs. Ann Granville," in Delany, *Autobiography and Correspondence,* 1:397.

112. *The Literary Works of Matthew Prior,* 2nd ed., 2 vols. (Oxford: Clarendon, 1971) 1:188.

113. Samuel Johnson, *The Works of Samuel Johnson, LL.D.,* 12 vols. (London, 1810), 10:175.

114. *Sir John Fielding's Jests; or, New Fun for the Parlour and Kitchen* (London, 1781), title page.

115. Ibid., iii.

116. On this theme, see Keith Thomas, "Bodily Control and Social Unease: The Fart in Seventeenth-Century England," in *The Extraordinary and the Everyday in Early Modern England,* ed. Garthine Walker and Angela McShane (Basingstoke: Palgrave, 2010), 9–30.

117. *Memoirs of the Late Thomas Holcroft, Written by Himself* (London: Longman, Brown, Green, and Longmans, 1852), 105–6.

118. *Memoirs of Richard Lovell Edgeworth*, 2:136.

119. James Boswell, *Life of Johnson*, ed. R. W. Chapman (Oxford: Oxford University Press, 1980), 743.

120. Hannah More, *Strictures on the Modern System of Female Education* (London, 1799), 2nd edition, I, 173.

121. Ibid., 174.

4. *Access to Reading*

Epigraph: Egerton 3702 B fol. 72, The Barrett Collection of Burney Papers, The British Library, "Fol. 60–75 Charlotte Barrett, d. 1870 née Francis; wife of H. Barrett: Miscellaneous notes: n.d."

1. James Raven, "The Book as a Commodity," in *The Cambridge History of the Book in Britain*, ed. Michael F. Suarez and Michael L. Turner, 6 vols. (Cambridge: Cambridge University Press, 1999), 5:83–117, 92.

2. Ibid., 85ff.

3. On the decrease of access to literary texts by the lower end of the reading market, see William St Clair, *The Reading Nation in the Romantic Period* (Cambridge: Cambridge University Press, 2004). St Clair's arguments and methodology have since been questioned. For a critical rebuttal, see Thomas F. Bonnell, "When Book History Neglects Bibliography: Trouble with the 'Old Canon' in *The Reading Nation*," *Studies in Bibliography* 57 (2005–6), 243–61. See also Robert D. Hume, "The Economics of Culture in London, 1660–1740," *Huntington Library Quarterly* 69 (2006), 487–533, 497, 524.

4. See John Brewer, *Pleasures of the Imagination: English Culture in the Eighteenth Century* (London: HarperCollins, 1997), 167; R. S. Schofield, "Dimensions of Illiteracy, 1750–1850," *Explorations in Economic History* 10 (1973), 437–54; Margaret R. Hunt, *The Middling Sort: Commerce, Gender, and the Family in England, 1680–1780* (Berkeley: University of California Press, 1996), 84–89.

5. See Lorna Weatherill, *Consumer Behaviour and Material Culture in Britain, 1660–1760* (London: Routledge, 1996), 49.

6. October 1726, in *The Monthly Catalogue: Being an Exact Account of all Books and Pamphlets Published* (London, 1723–), 111.

7. "This Day is publish'd, (beautifully printed) Price 6 d.," *Evening Post*, 22–24 November 1726.

8. "To Mr. Read," *Weekly Journal or British Gazetteer*, 26 November 1726.

9. Margaret Lambert and Enid Marx, *English Popular Art* (London: Batsford, 1951; new ed., London: Merlin, 1989), 41, 58. On the literary themes of children's chinaware, the most common sources are *Robinson Crusoe*, Bernardin de Saint-Pierre's *Paul and Virginia*, and *Uncle Tom's Cabin*, see Noel Riley, *Gifts for Good Children: The History of Children's China, 1790–1890*, 2 vols. (Somerset: Richard Dennis, 1991), 1:86–114.

10. National Archives, C113/11, Inventory of John of Bow, 1740. Sourced and transcribed for the Geffrye Museum by Jane Hamlett and Laurie Lindey. See also National Archives, C108/285 Inventory of Mr Webb, 1792.

11. See Jennifer Batt and Abigail Williams, "Poetry and Popularity," special edition of *Eighteenth-Century Life*, 2016.

12. See Thomas F. Bonnell, *Most Disreputable Trade: Publishing the Classics of English Poetry, 1765–1810* (Oxford: Oxford University Press, 2008). On the effect of these compilations on less affluent readers, see Richard D. Altick, *The English Common Reader: A Social History of the Mass Reading Public, 1800–1900* (Chicago: University of Chicago Press, 1957), 55–60.

13. See Hume, "The Economics of Culture.'

14. Jacob Vanderlint, *Money Answers All Things; or, an Essay to Make Money Plentiful among All Ranks of People* (London, 1734), 76, 141–42.

15. Ibid., 19.

16. See Hume, "The Economics of Culture." On costs of housing and food, see Kirsten Olsen, *Daily Life in Eighteenth-Century England* (Westport: Greenwood Press, 1999). On relative prices in this era, see St Clair, *The Reading Nation*, 24.

17. At the beginning of the century, in 1709, evidence from the publishers' catalogues shows that of the 152 titles advertised, half cost no more than a shilling, and the most common price, that of a quarter of all titles, was sixpence. Fifty-eight of the advertised works cost less than this. At the top end of the market, a smaller number of titles cost between three and five shillings. By the end of the century, Fanny Burney's *Camilla* cost seven shillings for three volumes in 1785, and *The Mysteries of Udolpho* one pound for four volumes. On the economics of the trade in printed books, see St Clair, *The Reading Nation*, 19–42. See also Hume, "The Economics of Culture," 509.

18. See Raven, "The Book as Commodity," 85–91.

19. National Archives, C113/11, Inventory of John Mitford of Bow, 1740; National Archives, PROB 3/45/17, inventory of Francis Gibson, 1745/6; National Archives, PROB/31/921/736, inventory of Nicholas Browning, 1800. Sourced and transcribed for the Geffrye Museum by Jane Hamlett and Laurie Lindey.

20. Stephen Colclough, " 'R. R. A Remarkable Thing or Action': John Dawson (1692–1765) as Reader and Annotator," *Variants,* Reading Notes 2/3 (2004), 61–78.

21. 6 August 1751, in Samuel Johnson, *The Yale Edition of the Works of Samuel Johnson,* ed. W. J. Bate and Albrecht B. Strauss, 23 vols. (New Haven: Yale University Press, 1969), vol. 5, *The Rambler,* 11–12.

22. Cyprian Blagden, "The Distribution of Almanacks in the Second Half of the Seventeenth Century," *Studies in Bibliography,* 11 (1958), 107–16.

23. On the definition of chapbooks and their relationship to children's literature, see Jan Fergus, *Provincial Readers in Eighteenth-Century England* (Oxford: Oxford University Press, 2006), 161–75. On the history of chapbooks, see Margaret Spufford, *Small Books and Pleasant Histories: Popular Fiction and Its Readership in Seventeenth-Century England* (Cambridge: Cambridge University Press, 1981).

24. See Michael J. Preston, "Rethinking Folklore, Rethinking Literature," in *The Other Print Tradition: Essays on Chapbooks, Broadsides, and Related Ephemera,* ed. Cathy Lynn Preston and Michael J. Preston (London: Garland, 1995); Pat Rogers, *Literature and Popular Culture in Eighteenth-Century England* (Brighton: Harvester, 1985), 162–82, 183–197.

25. See Jonathan Barry, "Literacy and Literature in Popular Culture: Reading and Writing in Historical Perspective," in *Popular Culture in England, c. 1500–1850,* ed. Tim Harris (London: Macmillan, 1995), 84. See also James Raven, "New Reading Histories, Print Culture and the Identification of Change: The Case of Eighteenth-Century England," *Social History* 23 (1998), 268–87, 287; Anna Bayman, "Printing, Learning and the Unlearned," *The Oxford History of Popular Print Culture,* vol. 1, *Cheap Print in Britain and Ireland to 1660,* ed. Joad Raymond (Oxford: Oxford University Press, 2011), 76–87.

26. John Dunton, *The Life and Errors of John Dunton* (London, 1705), 56.

27. Preface to Thomas Cox, *The Life and Strange Surprizing Adventures of Robinson Crusoe . . . now faithfully abridged* (London, 1719), A2r–v.

28. See Lois E. Bueler, ed., *Clarissa: The Eighteenth-Century Response, 1747–1804,* 2 vols. (New York: AMS, 2010).

29. See Leah Price, *The Anthology and the Rise of the Novel: From Richardson to George Eliot* (Cambridge: Cambridge University Press, 2000), 15.

30. *The Companion, Being a Choice Collection of the most Admired Pieces from the Best Authors, in Verse and Prose,* 3 vols. (Edinburgh, 1790), 1:v.

31. Ibid., vi.

32. Ibid., vii.

33. Antonia Forster, "Review Journals and the Reading Public," in *Books and Their Readers in the Eighteenth-Century England*, ed. Isabel Rivers, 2 vols. (London: Continuum, 2003), 2:178; quoted in Fergus, *Provincial Readers*, 7.

34. See Nicholas Seager, "Serialization of Defoe's *Tour* in *All Alive and Merry*," *Notes and Queries*, 62 (2015), 295–97.

35. "Friday, May 16th," in Rev. John Penrose, *Letters from Bath, 1766–1767, by the Rev. John Penrose* (Gloucester: Alan Sutton, 1983), 119.

36. Reginald Heber vol of Miscellaneous Verse Ms Engl Poet e.111 dated 1788 by Bod. fol. 42 verso.

37. Eliza Chapman's poetry notebook, Bodleian MS Montagu e.14.

38. R. M. Wiles, *Serial Publication in England Before 1750* (Cambridge: Cambridge University Press, 1957), 6.

39. George Crabbe, *The Library: A Poem* (London, 1781), 8.

40. See Wiles, *Serial Publication*, 8–9.

41. "Mr Bavius," *Grub Street Journal*, 19 September 1734.

42. Titles include *Proposals for Printing, by Subscription, Harleian Miscellany a Collection of Scarce Tracts and Pamphlets, Found in the Late Earl of Oxford's Library* and *An Appendix to the Greek Thesaurus of H. Stephens, and the Greek Lexicons of Constantine and Scapula*. See "List of books publish'd periodically, January 1745," *Gentleman's Magazine*, 1744.

43. For full discussion of the evidence and development of literacy across the period, see David Cressy, *Literacy and the Social Order: Reading and Writing in Tudor and Stuart England* (Cambridge: Cambridge University Press, 1980), 176–77; Schofield, "Dimensions of Illiteracy," 442–43, 445–46; Peter Earle, "The Female Labour Market in London," *Economic History Review* 43 (1989), 328–53, 333–36, 343–44; Hunt, *Middling Sort*, 85.

44. "Mr. Bavius." *The Grub Street Journal*, 19 September 1734.

45. Sarah Trimmer, prospectus for *The Family Magazine; or, a repository of Religious Instruction and rational amusement* (1788), 1.

46. Ibid., 2.

47. The 1778 inventory of Richard Davies lists "Gullivers Travals 2 Voll 3 Books & some pamphlets" in the maid's room. National Archives, C110/187.

48. See J. Jean Hecht, *The Domestic Servant Class in Eighteenth-Century England* (London: Routledge and Kegan Paul, 1956), 99–100.

49. Collection of chapbooks Bodleian, Vet. A5 e.6858. For another example of a servants' library, see Owen McKnight, "Reading for Servants," *Worcester College Record* (2013), 96–100.

50. Jan Fergus, "Provincial Servants' Reading in the Late Eighteenth Century," in *The Practice and Representation of Reading in England*, ed. James Raven, Helen Small, and Naomi Tadmor (Cambridge: Cambridge University Press, 1996), 202–25, 205.

51. Ibid., 215–25.

52. For an excellent discussion of the book-related tensions between servants and employers (or "dusters and readers") in the nineteenth century, see Leah Price, *How to Do Things with Books in Victorian Britain* (Princeton: Princeton University Press, 2012), 175–218.

53. "Eleanor Clark, Theft grand larceny, 21st October 1761," *Old Bailey Proceedings Online* (www.oldbaileyonline.org) Ref. t17611021-24. For other examples of servants stealing, see "John Frank, Theft burglary, 12th January 1780," *Old Bailey Proceedings Online* (www.oldbaileyonline.org) Ref. t17800112-2.

54. "William Francis, Theft grand larceny, 14th December 1785," *Old Bailey Proceedings Online* (www.oldbaileyonline.org) Ref. t17851214-46.

55. For a survey of servants' literary self-representation in this period, see R. C. Richardson, *Household Servants in Early Modern England* (Manchester: Manchester University Press, 2010), 38–62.

56. David Vincent, *Bread, Knowledge, and Freedom: A Study of Nineteenth-Century Working Class Autobiography* (London: Methuen, 1981), 110–11.

57. John Clare, *Sketches in the Life of John Clare*, ed. Edmund Blunden (London, 1931), 51.

58. See, for example, "Letters from Miss Heartfree," *Lady's Magazine*, March 1776, 141.

59. Daniel Defoe, *The Compleat English Gentleman*, ed. Karl D. Bulbring (London, 1890) 135. See also *The Eccho, or Edinburgh Weekly Journal*, 8 July 1730.

60. See Mark Purcell's discussion of the library and reading of Edward Leigh, an eighteenth-century aristocrat. "'A Lunatick of Unsound Mind': Edward, Lord Leigh (1742–86) and the Refounding of Oriel College Library," *Bodleian Library Record*, 17 (2001), 246–60, 257.

61. Raven, "The Book as Commodity," 95.

62. Ibid., 88; B. R. Mitchell, *British Historical Statistics* (Cambridge: Cambridge University Press, 1988), 25, 77, 89, 102.

63. See Peter Borsay, *The English Urban Renaissance: Culture and Society in the Provincial Town, 1660–1770* (Oxford: Clarendon, 1989).

64. "Milton," in *Samuel Johnson: The Lives of the Poets, a Selection*, ed. Roger Lonsdale and John Mullan (Oxford: Clarendon, 2006), 86.

65. Borsay, *The English Urban Renaissance*, 131.

66. Leonore Davidoff and Catherine Hall, *Family Fortunes: Men and Women of the English Middle Class, 1780–1850* (London: Hutchinson, 1987), 156.

67. Borsay, *The English Urban Renaissance*, 135–36.

68. See table 4.2, "Circulating Libraries: Some Subscription Costs," in David Allan, *A Nation of Readers: The Lending Library in Georgian England* (London: British Library, 2008), 148. For more evidence on prices of circulating libraries, see also St Clair, *The Reading Nation in the Romantic Period*, appendix 10, 665–75.

69. On resort libraries, see Colclough, *Consuming Readers*, 91–96.

70. *Travels in Georgian Devon: The Illustrated Journals of the Reverend John Swete, 1789–1800*, ed. Todd Gray (Tiverton: Devon), 2:139.

71. "Repertory for News," *Times*, 4 July 1789.

72. On circulating libraries and communities of readers, see Colclough, *Consuming Texts*, 88–117.

73. Paul Kaufman, "The Community Library: A Chapter in English Social History," *Transactions of the American Philosophical Society* 57 (1967), 11–13; Charlotte A. Stewart-Murphy, *A History of British Circulating Libraries: The Book Labels and Ephemera of the Papantonio Collection* (Newtown, Pa.: Bird and Bull, 1992).

74. Stewart-Murphy, *A History of British Circulating Libraries*, 69.

75. Allan, *A Nation of Readers*, 138.

76. See, for example, BL 1430.b.19, "Hargrove's Circulating Library," in *The History of the Castle and Town of Knaresborough* (Knaresborough, 1769), final folio verso.

77. Kaufman, "The Community Library," 3–67.

78. Fergus, *Provincial Readers*, 7.

79. " 'Inlets of Vice and Debauchery': The Circulating Libraries," in Allan, *A Nation of Readers*, 119.

80. Edward Mangin, *An Essay on Light Reading: As It May Be Supposed to Influence Moral Conduct and Literary Taste* (London, 1808), 2.

81. Ibid., 3.

82. Ibid., 10.

83. Ibid., 12.

84. Thomas Gisborne, *An Enquiry into the Duties of the Female Sex* (London, 1798), 229.

85. See Jacqueline Pearson, *Women's Reading in Britain, 1750–1835* (Cambridge: Cambridge University Press, 1999), 160–61.

86. *The Use of Circulating Libraries Considered; With Instructions for Opening and Conducting a Library* (London, 1797), 9–10.
87. *The Tunbridge Wells Guide; or, an Account of the Ancient and Present State of that Place* (Tunbridge Wells, 1786), 103–4.
88. *Bath: A Poem* (London, 1748), 21.
89. For a model of this kind of library, see *A Catalogue of the Circulating Library Opened by R Bliss, Bookseller [. . .] High Street Oxford* (Oxford, 1785?), iv.
90. Colclough, *Consuming Texts*, 96–111.
91. Allan, *A Nation of Readers*, 29.
92. See table 3.3, "Subscription Libraries: Some Membership Costs," in Allan, *A Nation of Readers*, 92.
93. Boston Literary Society Rules fols 1r–2r, cited in Allan, *A Nation of Readers*, 53.
94. Although see, too, Keith Manley's study of the Hull Subscription Library, which illustrates the element of contention and censorship in subscription libraries, and the fights in annual meetings over the place of "controversial" material. Keith Manley, "Jeremy Bentham has been Banned': Contention and Censorship in Private Subscription Libraries Before 1825," *Library and Information History* 29 (2013), 170–81.
95. Allan, *A Nation of Readers*, 53–54.
96. Charles Shillito, *The Country Book Club: A Poem* (London, 1788), 38.
97. Memorandum book for Frances Hamilton, Somerset Heritage Centre, DD\FS 5/2.1–5/2.2.
98. Frances Hamilton, Account and Day Books, Somerset Heritage Centre, DD\FS/7, fols. 368–7 (the back of the notebook is used).
99. Frances Hamilton, Memorandum Book, Somerset Heritage Centre, DD\FS 5/2.1–5/2.2.
100. For a detailed case study of borrowings from a subscription library, see Paul Kaufman, *Borrowings from the Bristol Library, 1773–1784: A Unique Record of Reading Vogues* (Charlottesville: Bibliographical Society of the University of Virginia, 1960).
101. Rebecca Bowd, "Useful Knowledge or Polite Learning?: A Reappraisal of Approaches to Subscription Library History," *Library and Information History* 29 (2013), 182–95.
102. On the wider Scottish context of access to reading, see V. Dunstan, "Reading Habits in Scotland circa 1750–1820" (unpublished Ph.D. dissertation, University of Dundee, 2010).

103. Richard Polwhele, *The Language, Literature, and Literary Character of Cornwall* (London: T. Cadell and W. Davies, 1806), 98.

104. See K. A. Manley, "Lounging Places and Frivolous Literature: Subscription and Circulating Libraries in the West Country to 1825," in *Printing Places: Locations of Book Production and Distribution Since 1500*, ed. John Hinks and Catherine Armstrong (London: Oak Knoll, 2005), 107–20.

105. August or September 1791, "469. To Sir John Sinclair of Ulbster, Bart," in *The Letters of Robert Burns*, 2nd ed., ed. G. Ross Roy, 2 vols. (Oxford: Clarendon, 1985), 2:107.

106. 17 Jan 1791, "430. (9) [Peter Hill]," in *The Letters of Robert Burns*, 2:66.

107. "Diary of George Sandy, Apprentice W.S., 1788," in *The Book of the Old Edinburgh Club*, 45 vols. (Edinburgh: Printed by T. A. Constable, 1908–), 24 (1942), 1–69.

108. "Diary of George Sandy, Apprentice W.S., 1788," 16.

109. Ibid., 19.

110. Ibid., 26.

111. Ibid., 55–56.

112. "Monday, Apr. 28," Penrose, *Letters from Bath*, 63.

113. 17 April 1766, Penrose, *Letters from Bath*, 38.

114. 13 May 1766, Penrose, *Letters from Bath*, 108.

115. 29 May 1766, Penrose, *Letters from Bath*, 150.

116. 22 April 1767, Penrose, *Letters from Bath*, 171.

117. 13 April 1767, Penrose, *Letters from Bath*, 167.

118. 29 May 1766, Penrose, *Letters from Bath*, 150.

119. "A Catalogue of Books in Quires and Copies" (1740), John Johnson Collection, Bodleian Library, Trade Sale Catalogues vol. (80).

120. Raven, "The Book as a Commodity," 108.

121. See ibid., 90, 96.

122. Hume, "The Economics of Culture," 500.

123. Nicholas Blundell, *Blundell's Diary and Letter Book, 1702–1728*, ed. Margaret Blundell (Liverpool: Liverpool University Press, 1952), 50.

124. September 1725, in Nicholas Blundell, *The Great Diurnal of Nicholas Blundell of Little Crosby, Lancashire*, ed. J. J. Bagley, 3 vols. (Chester: Record Society of Lancashire and Cheshire, 1968–72), 3:166. See, for example, "A Catalogue of Books in the possession of Henry Falshaw of Buckden taken 1747," Commonplace Book of Wilson family of Broomhead Hall, Sheffield Record Office, MD145, fol. 265.

125. 20 February 1827, in *The Diary of Robert Sharp of South Cave: Life in a Yorkshire Village, 1812–1837*, ed. Janice E. Crowther and Peter A. Crowther (Oxford: Oxford University Press, 1997), 109.

126. 19 March 1790, 2 August 1792, 1 January 1788, in *The Diary of a Country Parson, the Reverend James Woodforde*, ed. John Beresford, 5 vols. (London: H. Milford, Oxford University Press, 1924–31), 3:179–80, 3:367, 3:1.

127. 25 July 1798, "Miss Iremonger To Miss Heber: At Weston, Towcester, Northamptonshire," in *Dear Miss Heber, An Eighteenth Century Correspondence*, ed. Francis Bamford (London: Constable, 1936), 180.

128. 29 Jan 1766, "To Thomas Taylor Esqr: at Mrs Collins's in The Church Yard Bath," in *The Letters of Eliza Pierce, 1751–1775* (London: Frederick Etchells and Hugh Macdonald, 1927), 97.

129. 20 November 1753, Mary Delany, *The Autobiography and Correspondence of Mary Granville, Mrs Delany*, ed. The Right Honourable Lady Llanover, 1st series, 3 vols. (London: Richard Bentley, 1861), 3:242.

130. "Mr George Ballad to Mrs Dewes," in Delany, *Autobiography and Correspondence*, 1st series, 3:323–24.

131. See Mark Towsey, " 'I can't resist sending you the book': Private Libraries, Elite Women, and Shared Reading Practices in Georgian Britain," *Library and Information History* 29 (September 2013), 210–22.

132. Ibid., 212.

133. Ibid., 214–16.

134. Norna Labouchere, *Ladies' Book Plates: An Illustrated Handbook for Collectors and Book-lovers* (London: George Bell and Sons, 1895), viii.

135. "Extracts from the Journal of Walter Gale, Schoolmaster at Mayfield, 1750, Edited by R. W. Blencowe, Esq," in *Sussex Archaeological Collections, Relating to the History and Antiquities of the County* (London: The Sussex Archaeological Society, 1857), vol. 9.

136. 6 January 1750, in "Extracts from the Journal of Walter Gale," 188.

137. 30 November 1792, Nancy Woodforde, "Nancy Woodforde: A Diary for the Year 1792," in *Woodforde Papers and Diaries*, ed. Dorothy Heighes Woodforde (Bungay: Morrow, 1990), 81.

138. March 1792, Mary Woodforde, "Mary Woodforde's Book, 1684–1690," in *Woodforde Papers and Diaries*, 47–48.

5. *Verse at Home*

1. On the evolution of copyright in this period, and its implications for the ownership of literary texts, see Mark Rose, *Authors and Owners: The Invention of Copyright* (Cambridge: Harvard University Press, 1993).

2. Anna Seward to George Hardinge, 25 March, 1787, *Letters: Written Between the Years 1784 and 1807; in Six Volumes* (Edinburgh and London, 1811), 2:275–76.

3. For a short history of the classical origins of commonplacing, see David Allan, *Commonplace Books and Reading in Georgian England* (Cambridge: Cambridge University Press, 2010), 35–45. On the commonplace book as a form of life writing, see Adam Smyth, *Autobiography in Early Modern England* (Cambridge: Cambridge University Press, 2010), 123–58. On the changing nature of the commonplace book in the seventeenth century, see Ann Moss, *Printed Commonplace-Books and the Structuring of Renaissance Thought* (Oxford: Oxford University Press, 1996).

4. Allan, *Commonplace Books and Reading in Georgian England*, 71–73.

5. The history of the transition from print to manuscript is also complicated by Peter Stallybrass, who has argued that printing was not a clear break from manuscript culture, but rather an incitement to write more by hand. See Stallybrass, "Little Jobs: Broadsides and the Printing Revolution," in *Agents of Change: Print Culture Studies After Elizabeth Eisenstein*, ed. Sabrina Alcorn Baron et al. (Amherst: University of Massachusetts Press, 2007), 340–67.

6. Harold Love, *Scribal Publication in Seventeenth-Century England* (Oxford: Clarendon, 1993), 177–230.

7. See Margaret Ezell, *Social Authorship and the Advent of Print* (Baltimore: Johns Hopkins University Press, 1999).

8. Order book of G. W. R. Hoyland, draper and tailor, 22 West Barr, Sheffield, Sheffield Record Office, MD1191.

9. Joseph Hunter, *Hallamshire: The History and Geography of the Parish of Sheffield* (London: Lackington, Hughes, Harding, Mavor, and Jones, 1819), 276.

10. Ibid., 276.

11. Commonplace Book of Wilson family of Broomhead Hall, Sheffield Record Office, MD145, fol. 7, fols. 14–15.

12. Ibid., fols. 121–22.

13. Ibid. fol. 229.

14. Hunter, *Hallamshire*, 277.

15. "Lusus Seniles; or, Trifles to Kill Time in Confinement and Old Age," Bodleian Library, Oxford, Ms Eng poet d.47.

16. Given the title of the first poem, it is possible that the group formed some sort of amicable society, but there is no documentary evidence to support this.

17. "Lusus Seniles," fol. 1 verso.

18. Ibid., fol. 86r, fol. 83r.

19. Verse notebook of Mary Allanson, Bodleian Library, Ms Eng Poet f.28.

20. MS Harding b.41, fol 9 v.

21. See David Allan, *Commonplace Books and Reading in Georgian England*, 215–25.

22. Mary Madan, Verse scrapbook, Bodleian Library MS Eng. Poet c. 51.

23. Diary of Paul Ourry Treby, at Eton College, 1798, Plymouth and West Devon Record Office, 2607/4.

24. Ibid.

25. Ibid.

26. Commonplace book of John Chubb, Somerset Heritage Centre, A/CSC 1/2, fol. 3.

27. Ibid., fol. 155.

28. Undated 1773 letter from C Gardiner to John Chubb, Chubb Correspondence, Somerset Heritage Centre, A/CSC 2/4.

29. Commonplace book of John Chubb, Somerset Heritage Centre, A/CSC 1/3.

30. Ibid., A/CSC 1/4.

31. On earlier printed commonplace books, many dating from around 1600, see Zachary Lesser and Peter Stallybrass, "The First Literary *Hamlet* and the Commonplacing of Professional Plays," *Shakespeare Quarterly* 59 (2008): 371–420.

32. The compilation was first issued in octavo in 1702; it reappeared in duodecimo in 1714, and was republished in 1718, 1724, 1737, and 1762, along with reissues. *The Art of Poetry* exists in four different stages of enlargement represented by the editions of 1702, 1705, 1708, and 1718. In the first form it consisted of 1,452 quotations from forty-eight different authors; in the second, which is nearly half again as large, of 2,123; and in the third and fourth revisions of 2,517 and 2,693 respectively. On the evolution of the various volumes from 1702 onwards, see A. Dwight Culler, "Edward Bysshe and the Poet's Handbook," *PMLA* 63 (1948), 858–85, 861–62.

33. Edward Bysshe, *The Art of Poetry* (London, 1702), 201–2.

34. See Peter Dixon, "Edward Bysshe and Pope's 'Shakespear,'" *Notes and Queries* 11 (1964), 292–93; Michael E. Connaughton, "Richardson's Familiar Quotations: 'Clarissa' and Bysshe's 'Art of English Poetry,'" *Philological Quarterly* 60 (1981), 183–95.

35. Bysshe, *The Art of English Poetry*, dedication, n.p.

36. Diary and memorandum book of John Andrews of Modbury, 1772, Plymouth and West Devon Record Office, 535/11.

37. On the history of scrapbooks, see Ellen Gruber Garvey, *Writing with Scissors: American Scrapbooks from the Civil War to the Harlem Renaissance* (Oxford: Oxford University Press, 2013); on the earlier cutting and pasting of texts, see Juliet Fleming, William Sherman and Adam Smyth, special issue entitled "Renaissance Collage: Towards a New History of Reading," *Journal of Medieval and Early Modern Studies* 45 (September 2015).

38. Mary Madan, Verse scrapbook, Bodleian Library MS Eng. Poet c.51.

39. Eliza Chapman's poetry notebook, dating from 1788 and 1789, entitled "Poetry, Selected and Original, 1788 & 1789." Bodleian MS Montagu e.14.

40. Ibid., fols. 31, 46, 79.

41. Ibid., fol. 49.

42. Ibid., fol. 56.

43. Ibid., fol. 28, fol. 41.

44. Ibid., fols. 71–72.

45. Elizabeth Carter, *Poems on Several Occasions*, 4th ed. (Dublin, 1777), 32.

46. *Memoirs of Richard Lovell Edgeworth, Esq, Begun by Himself, and Concluded by his Daughter*, 2 vols. (London, 1820), 2:334.

47. *The Complete Essays of Montaigne*, trans. Donald Frame (Stanford: Stanford University Press, 1957), 296. On the nature of forgetting books that one has read, see Pierre Bayard, *How to Talk About Books You Haven't Read* (London: Granta, 2006), 47–57.

48. *Sheridan and Henderson's Practical Method of Reading and Reciting English Poetry* (London, 1796), 6.

49. Ibid., 25–26.

50. Ibid., 82.

51. Ibid., 106.

52. Ibid., 202.

53. Christopher N. Phillips, "Cotton Mather Brings Isaac Watts's Hymns to America; or, How to Perform a Hymn Without Singing It," *New England Quarterly* 85 (June 2012), 203–21.

54. John Walker, *Exercises for Improvement in Elocution, Being Select Extracts from the Best Authors, for the Use of Those Who Study the Art of Reading and Speaking in Public* (London, 1777).

55. On Walker's influence as an elocutionist, see Jack Hall Lamb, "John Walker and Joshua Steele," *Speech Monographs* 32 (1965), 411–19; E. K. Sheldon, "Walker's Influence on the Pronunciation of English," *PMLA* 62 (1947), 130–46.

56. Walker, *Exercises*, Advertisement, n.p.

57. Joseph Addison, *The Spectator*, 19 June 1712.

58. Walker, *Exercises for Improvement*, 67.

59. Selections of lines from the poem appear unattributed under the titles "Fishing," "Fowling," and "Pheasant," in *A Collection of Poems for Reading and Repetition Selected from the Most Celebrated British Poets*, 2 vols. (1762), 1:34, 35–36, 85.

60. Image and transcription in David Drakard, *Printed English Pottery: History and Humour in the Reign of George III, 1760–1820* (London: Jonathan Horne, 1992), 105. I have been unable to trace this item. The lines frequently appeared in books discussing field sports, from John Boreham, *A Description of More Than Three Hundred Animals, Interspersed with Entertaining Anecdotes* (London, 1829), to *Time's Telescope for 1817: Or a Complete Guide to the Almanack* (London, 1817).

61. *A Collection of Poems for Reading and Repetition; Selected from the Most Celebrated British Poets*, ed. John Drummond (Edinburgh, 1762).

62. Ibid., v.

63. In this sense, it is comparable with early-eighteenth-century commonplace miscellanies such as Edward Bysshe's *Art of English Poetry*, which offered selections of very short quotations from poems, organised thematically, resembling a manuscript commonplace book in printed form. The difference is that the selections in the *Collection of Poems for Reading and Repetition* are much longer, up to thirty lines, and none of those in the first, alphabetical section of the collection are attributed to their authors.

64. On the printing of the poem in the eighteenth century, see Sandro Jung, "Visual Interpretations, Print and Illustrations of Thomson's *The Seasons*, 1730–1797," *Eighteenth-Century Life* 34 (2010), 23–64.

65. On *The Seasons'* republication in American almanacs, see Louise Stevenson, "The Transatlantic Travels of James Thomson's *The Seasons* and Its Baggage of Material Culture, 1730–1870," *American Antiquarian Society* 116 (2006), 121–65, 125.

66. On the shift in emphasis from allegorical depictions of the seasons to these sentimental episodes, see Jung, "Visual Interpretations," 42–44.

67. Stevenson, "Transatlantic Travels," 121–65. On middling-sort ownership of fine ceramics in this period, see Sarah Richards, *Eighteenth-Century Ceramics: Products for a Civilised Society* (Manchester: Manchester University Press, 1999), 104–26.

68. For images of Lavinia and Palemon transfer-printed jugs, see Drakard, *Printed English Pottery*, 64; Frank Hurlbutt, *Old Derby Porcelain and Its Artist-Workmen* (London: Werner Laurie, 1925), 42.

69. See John Sekora, *Luxury: The Concept in Western Thought, Eden to Smollett* (Baltimore: Johns Hopkins University Press, 1977).

70. See Mary Weightman's collection *Poems on Various Subjects Selected to Enforce the Practice of Virtue*, ed. Thomas Tomkins (London, 1780), 8 editions before 1800.

71. Thomas Gisborne, *An Enquiry into the Duties of the Female Sex* (London 1797), 230–31.

72. Ibid., 232.

73. Thomas Dyche, *A Guide to the English Tongue: in Two Parts*, 2nd ed. (London, 1710).

74. For a selection, see Clare Browne and Jennifer Wearden, *Samplers from the Victoria and Albert Museum* (London: V&A Publications, 1999).

75. Notebook containing poems, essays, sermons, and hymns written and collected together by Elizabeth Warner and dedicated to her mother, Warwickshire Record Office, CR4141/7/45.

76. Ibid., fol. 1r.

77. Ibid., fol. 17.

78. Ibid., fol. 78.

79. For a discussion of the commonplace book as a form of female self-display, see Susan Stabile, "Female Curiosities: The Transatlantic Female Commonplace Book," in *Reading Women: Literacy, Authorship, and Culture in the Atlantic World, 1500–1800*, ed. Heidi Brayman Hackel and Catherine E. Kelly (Philadelphia: University of Pennsylvania Press, 2008), 217–44.

80. James Woolley, "Swift's Most Popular Poems" in *Reading Swift: Papers from the Sixth Münster Symposium on Jonathan Swift*, ed. Kirsten Juhas, Hermann J. Real, and Sandra Simon (Munich: Wilhelm Fink, 2013), 367–82.

81. *The Laugher's Delight; or the Alive-and-Merry-Fellow, Containing, the True Art of Jesting* (London, 1765), title page.

82. On the role of seventeenth century jestbooks, see Adam Smyth, "Divines into Dry Vines: Forms of Jesting in Early Modern England," in *Formal Matters: Reading the Forms of Early Modern Texts*, ed. Allison Deutermann and András Kiséry (Manchester: Manchester University Press, 2013), 56–72; and Smyth, " 'Ha, ha, ha': Shakespeare and the Edge of Laughter," in *Staged Transgression*, ed. Rory Loughnane and Edel Semple (Palgrave Macmillan, 2013), 49–62.

83. Robert Burton, *The Anatomy of Melancholy, What it is, With all the Kinds, Causes, Symptomes, Prognostickes, & Severall Cures of it . . . By Democritus Junior*, 6th ed. (Oxford, 1651), 305.

84. Sir Richard Blackmore, *A Treatise of the Spleen and Vapours: or, Hypocondriacal and Hysterical Affections* (London, 1725), 164.

85. Johan Verberckmoes, *Laughter, Jestbooks, and Society in the Spanish Netherlands* (London: Macmillan, 1999), 60.

86. Ibid., 60–61.

87. Medical opinion in the eighteenth century continued to assert the role of the blood: Richard Blackmore explained that the disorder stemmed from "the want of rich and generous Qualities in the Blood." Blackmore, *A Treatise of the Spleen*, 155.

88. Blackmore, *A Treatise of the Spleen*, 174.

89. Verberckmoes, *Laughter, Jestbooks, and Society*, 62–63.

90. Heyman Iacobi, *Het Schat der armen, oft een medecijn boecxken dienstelijck voor alle menschen, inhoudende hoemen sijn ghesontheyt onderhouden sal* (Amsterdam, 1626), 7. Quoted in Verberckmoes, *Laughter, Jestbooks, and Society*, 65.

91. Ibid., 303.

92. Ibid., 305.

93. Timothy Rogers, "Mr. Timothy Rogers Advices to the Relations and Friends of These under Religious Melancholy," in *Counsels and Comforts to Troubled Christians: In Eight Sermons by James Robe* (Glasgow, 1749), 276.

94. On the use of such frontispieces in miscellanies, see Abigail Williams, "How to Read a Book: Eighteenth-Century Frontispieces and Popular Collections," *Anglistik* 25 (2014), 91–102, 99–100.

95. On the illustration of drinking bowls, cups, and jugs, see Drakard, *Printed English Pottery*, 84–89.

96. On the transition of humour from the popular to the elite, see introduction to *A Cultural History of Humour: From Antiquity to the Present Day*, ed. Jan Bremmer and Herman Roodenburg (Cambridge: Polity, 1997), 5.

97. Historians of humour often note the changing social profile of joke tellers. After the Middle Ages, the collecting and telling of jokes spread over the social spectrum, and it is clear that the telling of jokes even became part and parcel of the art of conversation amongst gentlemen. See Derek Brewer, "Prose Jest-Books Mainly in the Sixteenth to Eighteenth Centuries in England," in *A Cultural History of Humour*, ed. Bremmer and Roodenburg, 90–111, 91–92.

98. *Fun for the Parlour; or, All Merry Above Stairs* (London, 1771), 84.

99. "The Flats and Sharps of the Nation," in *Hilaria; or, the Festive Board* (London, 1798), 25.

100. See Tim Reinke-Williams, "Misogyny, Jest-Books, and Male Youth Culture in Seventeenth-Century England," *Gender and History* 21 (2009), 324–39.

101. See Stanley J. Kahrl, "The Medieval Origins of the Sixteenth-Century English Jest-Books," *Studies in the Renaissance* 13 (1966), 166–83; F. Wilson, "The English Jest-Books of the Sixteenth and Early Seventeenth Centuries," in *Shakespearian and Other Studies,* ed. Helen Gardner (Oxford: Clarendon, 1969), 285–324; Derek Brewer, "Prose Jest-Books Mainly in the Sixteenth to Eighteenth Centuries in England," 90–111.

102. Simon Dickie, "Hilarity and Pitilessness in the Mid-Eighteenth Century: English Jestbook Humor," *Eighteenth-Century Studies* 37 (2003), 1–22, 5.

103. As Mary Anne Lund has argued, this dual perspective is characteristic of Burton's approach to reading: "Tensions between therapeutic and dangerous reading are not continuously in evidence; occasional remarks about reading as potentially disquieting or unhealthy are not enough to destroy his presentation of reading as a healing activity, though they do present a challenge to it." Mary Ann Lund, *Melancholy, Medicine, and Religion in Early Modern England: Reading "The Anatomy of Melancholy"* (Cambridge: Cambridge University Press, 2010), 98.

104. Burton, *Anatomy of Melancholy,* 285.

105. Anne Vernon to Catherine Collingwood, 27 August 1734, Letters written to Catherine Collingwood, Warwickshire County Record Office, Throckmorton papers, Tribune, CR 1998/CD/Folder 49.

106. Margaret Portland to Catherine Collingwood, 16 September 1733, WRO, Throckmorton papers, Tribune, CR 1998/CD/Folder 49.

107. Margaret Portland to Catherine Collingwood, 16 September 1734, WRO, Throckmorton papers, Tribune, CR 1998/CD/Folder 49.

108. Margaret Portland to Catherine Collingwood, 20 October 1734, WRO, Throckmorton papers, Tribune, CR 1998/CD/Folder 49.

109. Diary entry 26 March 1809, Diaries of Elizabeth Tyrrell, 1769–1835, and her daughter Elizabeth, London Metropolitan Archives, GB 0074 CLC/510.

110. MSS Verses of Elizabeth Countess of Harcourt, 1750–1804, Bodleian Library Mss Eng. D. 3887, fol. 168.

111. Sarah Jordan, *The Anxieties of Idleness: Idleness in Eighteenth-Century British Literature and Culture* (London: Associated University Presses, 2003), 84–122. Diane Buie, "Melancholy and the Idle Lifestyle in the Eighteenth Century" (doctoral thesis, Northumbria University, 2010), 86–97.

112. Samuel Johnson, *The Idler* 80, 27 October 1759, in *The Idler and The Adventurer*, ed. W. J. Bate, J. M. Bullitt, and L. F. Powell (New Haven: Yale University Press, 1963), 250.

113. Gisborne, *An Enquiry into the Duties of the Female Sex*, 216.

114. Anna Vernon to Margaret Portland, 24 May 1734, WRO, Throckmorton papers, Tribune, CR 1998/CD/Folder 49.

115. Anna Vernon to Margaret Portland, 17 June 1736, 1 August 1737, WRO, Throckmorton papers, Tribune, CR 1998/CD/Folder 49.

6. *Drama and Recital*

Epigraph: Mary Clarke to Edward Clarke, April 1700, in "Correspondence of Edward Clarke of Chipley," transcribed by Bridget Clarke. Correspondence to Edward from wife Mary, 1675–1704, Somerset Heritage Centre, DD\SF/7/13.

1. Jane Austen, *Mansfield Park*, ed. John Wiltshire (Cambridge: Cambridge University Press, 2005), 213.

2. For discussion of the episode, and the wider depiction of reading in the novel, see Patricia Michaelson, *Speaking Volumes: Women, Reading, and Speech in the Age of Austen* (Stanford: Stanford University Press, 2002), 127–34.

3. Austen, *Mansfield Park*, 149.

4. The disapproval might additionally be related to the presence of Mr. Yates, who is not a member of the family, but who is performing in the play. A similar instance involving a private theatrical occurs in Fanny Burney's *The Wanderer*.

5. See Margaret Weedon, "Jane Austen and William Enfield's The Speaker," *Journal for Eighteenth-Century Studies* 11 (1988), 159–62.

6. William Enfield, *The Speaker; or, Miscellaneous Pieces, Selected from the Best English Writers, and Disposed Under Proper Heads* (London, 1774), iii.

7. Weedon, "Jane Austen and William Enfield's The Speaker," 159–62.

8. William Enfield, "An Essay on Elocution," prefixed to *The Speaker; or, Miscellaneous Pieces, Selected from the Best English Writers, and Disposed Under Proper Heads* (London, 1774), iii–xxviii, xxviii.

9. *Sheridan's and Henderson's Practical Method of Reading and Reciting English Poetry* (London, 1796), v and vii.

10. Ibid.

11. Ibid., 42.

12. Ibid., 14–15.

13. Ibid., 4.

14. Ibid., 14.

15. Gilbert Austin, *Chironomia; or, a Treatise on Rhetorical Delivery* (London, 1806), 202.

16. John Rice, *An Introduction to the Art of Reading with Energy and Propriety* (London, 1765), 291.

17. See Michael Dobson, *The Making of the National Poet: Shakespeare, Adaptation and Authorship, 1660–1769* (Oxford: Oxford University Press, 1994); Fiona Ritchie and Peter Sabor, eds., *Shakespeare in the Eighteenth Century* (Cambridge: Cambridge University Press, 2012).

18. Pat Halfpenny, *English Earthenware Figures, 1740–1840* (Woodbridge: Antique Collectors Club, 1991), 181, 143, 148, 177, 178, 166, 179, 188, 190.

19. Bernard M. Watney, *Liverpool Porcelain of the Eighteenth Century* (Shepton Beauchamp: Richard Dennis, 1997), 118–19.

20. The direct source for the figure was probably a reduced-sized plaster of the sculpture sold in London by John Cheere (http://collections.vam.ac.uk/item/O108792/figurine-derby-porcelain-factory).

21. The editor, Nicholas Rowe, regularised and modernised Shakespeare's spelling, wrote lists of dramatis personae for the more than thirty plays that did not possess them, and standardised, corrected, and completed those lists for plays that did. He added a note at the end of each list of dramatis personae describing where the action of that play takes place, and in more than half the plays, Rowe also indicated at the beginning of each scene where the action of that scene takes place, a feature not found in any of the folios. For an excellent discussion of Tonson's remarketing of Shakespeare, see Don-John Dugas, *Marketing the Bard: Shakespeare in Performance and Print, 1660–1740* (Columbia: University of Missouri Press, 2006).

22. See ibid., 145.

23. Ibid., 179.

24. Colin Franklin, *Shakespeare Domesticated: The Eighteenth-Century Editions* (Aldershot: Scolar, 1991), 137; Kalman Burnim and Philip Highfill, *John Bell, Patron of British Theatrical Portraiture* (Carbondale: Southern Illinois University Press, 1998), 10.

25. Stuart Sillars "Seeing, Studying, Performing: Bell's Edition of Shakespeare and Performative Reading," *Performance Research: A Journal of the Performing Arts,* 10 (2005), 18–27, 19.

26. Advertisement in William Shakespeare, *Bell's Edition of Shakespeare's Plays,* 2nd ed., 5 vols. (London, 1774), 9.

27. For a fuller discussion of Bell's edition as a performance text, see Sillars "Seeing, Studying, Performing," 18–27.

28. Ibid., 53.

29. *Bell's Edition of Shakespeare's Plays*, 3:3.

30. *Bell's Edition of Shakespeare's Plays*, 5:295.

31. On Bell's edition and its utility for performance, see Lois Potter, "Humor Out of Breath: Francis Gentleman and the Henry IV Plays," in *Shakespeare, Text, and Theater: Essays in Honor of Jay L. Halio*, ed. Lois Potter and Arthur F. Kinney (London: Associated University Presses, 1999), 285–97; Linda McJannet, "'The Scene Changes'? Stage Directions in Eighteenth-Century Acting Editions of Shakespeare," in *Reading Readings: Essays on Shakespeare Editing in the Eighteenth Century*, ed. Joanna Gondris (London: Associated University Presses, 1998), 86–99.

32. *Bell's Edition of Shakespeare's Plays*, 1:65.

33. Ibid., 68.

34. Ibid., 70.

35. Ibid., 6.

36. Ibid., 8.

37. *Bell's Edition of Shakespeare's Plays*, 2:123.

38. *Bell's edition of Shakespeare's Plays*, 1:215.

39. Thomas Bowdler, *The Family Shakspeare in One Volume; in Which Nothing Is Added to the Original Text but Those Words and Expressions Are Omitted Which Cannot with Propriety be Read Aloud in a Family*, ed. Thomas Bowdler, 8th ed. (London: Longman, Brown, Green and Longmans, 1843), title page.

40. Noel Perrin, *Dr. Bowdler's Legacy: A History of Expurgated Books in England and America* (London: Macmillan, 1969), xii.

41. *The Family Shakespeare: In Four Volumes*, 4 vols. (London: J. Hatchard, 1807), 1:xi.

42. Bowdler, *The Family Shakspeare in One Volume*, viii fn.

43. Ibid., viii.

44. August 1773, in Frances Burney, *The Early Diary of Frances Burney, 1768–1778*, ed. Annie Raine Ellis, 2 vols. (London: George Bell and Sons, 1889), 1:252.

45. 13 March 1807, in Frances Burney, *The Journals and Letters of Fanny Burney*, ed. Joyce Hemlow et al., 12 vols. (Oxford: Clarendon, 1972–84), 6:801.

46. Bowdler, *The Family Shakspeare in One Volume*, 880.

47. Ibid.

48. "On the Lives of Actors," in *Blackwood's Edinburgh Magazine, Vol. VIII. October–March, 1820–21* (Edinburgh, T. Cadell and W. Davies, 1821), 512.

49. "Art. III. The Family Shakespeare," *Edinburgh Review,* October 1821, 53, quoted in Perrin, *Dr. Bowdler's Legacy,* 84.

50. Thomas Gisborne, *An Enquiry into the Duties of the Female Sex* (London, 1798), 225.

51. See Perrin, *Dr. Bowdler's Legacy,* 5.

52. Algernon Swinburne, "Social Verse," *The Forum,* October 1891, 178.

53. *A Second and Last Collection of the Most Celebrated Prologues and Epilogues Spoken at the Theatres of Drury-Lane and Lincolns-Inn* (London, 1727).

54. *The Court of Thespis; Being a Collection of the Most Admired Prologues and Epilogues* (London, 1769).

55. *The British Spouter; or, Stage Assistant* (London, 1773).

56. Ibid., i.

57. Diary of Elizabeth Tyrrell, 25 June 1818, London Metropolitan Archives, CLC/510.

58. William Dunlap, *Memoirs of the Life of George Frederick Cooke,* 2 vols. (New York, 1813), 1:324–25.

59. *Thesaurus Dramaticus: Containing All the Celebrated Passages, Soliloquies, Similes, Descriptions, and Other Poetical Beauties,* 2 vols. (London, 1724).

60. Charles Lamb, "On the Tragedies of Shakespeare," in *Miscellaneous Prose by Charles and Mary Lamb,* ed. E. V. Lucas (London: Methuen, 1912), 115. This essay was originally published in 1811.

61. Preface to *The Miniature Library,* Volume the Sixth, Duncombe: 19 Little Queen Street, Holborn.

62. The series seems to have been seasonally dependent, since its publisher states on the frontispiece to the new series that "During the Summer Months this Work will be published once a Fortnight."

63. Duncombe's Miniature Library, Dramatic Tales and Romances, 7 vols., 24mo., J. Duncombe & Co. [1831–32?], *Love's Labours Lost,* 240.

64. Advertisement to *Duncombe's Acting Edition of the British Theatre Comprising the Best Pieces As performed at all the London Theatres.*

65. See Simon Eliot, "A Prehistory for Penguins," in *Reading Penguin: A Critical Anthology,* ed. William Wootten and George Donaldson (Newcastle upon Tyne: Cambridge Scholars Publishing, 2013), 1–26.

66. *An Accurate Description of the Spectacle of Cinderella, Illustrated with Engravings* (London: John Fairburn, 1804), Bodleian Library Harding Collection, Uncat A, Box 143.

67. Ibid.

68. *Dramas for the Use of Young Ladies* (Birmingham: Swinney & Walker, 1792).

69. Ibid., 3.

70. Ibid. 21.

71. Samuel B. Morse, *School Dialogues [. . .] Calculated to Promote an Easy and Elegant Mode of Conversation Among the Young Masters and Misses of the United States* (Boston: Manning & Loring, 1797), iii.

72. See Michaelson, *Speaking Volumes,* 188–89.

73. January 1728, in Gertrude Savile, *Secret Comment: The Diaries of Gertrude Savile, 1721–1757,* ed. Alan Saville (Devon: Kingsbridge History Society, 1997), 100. On Savile's reading habits, see Colclough, *Consuming Texts,* 48–63.

74. 15 February 1728, in Savile, *Secret Comment,* 103.

75. 26 February 1728, in Savile, *Secret Comment,* 106.

76. 19 March 1728, in Savile, *Secret Comment,* 109.

77. March 1767, in Sylas Neville, *The Diary of Sylas Neville,* ed. Basil Cozens-Hardy (Oxford: Oxford University Press, 1950), 5.

78. 5 August 1767, in Neville, *Diary,* 22.

79. 29 March 1769, in Neville, *Diary,* 66.

80. Richard Bagshawe, Commonplace Book, Sheffield Record Office, OD/1396, fols. 36r–39r.

81. *Dr Last; or, the Devil Upon Two Sticks* (London: H. Roberts, 1771), Bodleian Library Vet. A5 e.892 (1).

82. Heather McPherson, "Theatrical Celebrity and the Commodification of the Actor," in *The Oxford Handbook of the Georgian Theatre, 1737–1832,* ed. Julia Swindells and David Francis Taylor (Oxford: Oxford University Press, 2014), 192–212, 199–206. On ceramic figures of Garrick, see Watney, *Liverpool Porcelain of the Eighteenth Century,* 39, 43.

83. The fullest account of these elite productions is Sybil Rosenfeld, *Temples of Thespis: Some Private Theatres and Theatricals in England and Wales, 1700–1820* (London: The Society for Theatre Research, 1978).

84. "London," *St James' Chronicle; or, The British Evening Post,* 2 November 1776.

85. For a discussion of the relationship between public and private theatricals, see Helen E. M. Brooks, "'One Entire Nation of Actors and Actresses': Reconsidering the Relationship of Public and Private Theatricals," *Nineteenth Century Theatre and Film* 38 (2011), 1–13.

86. The fullest collection of documents relating to private theatre in this period is the scrapbook of playbills, printed programmes, newspaper clippings, and tickets assembled by Charles Burney and Sarah Sophia Banks. British Library, *A Collection of Playbills, Notices, and Press Cuttings Dealing with Private Theatricals, 1750–1808*.

87. "Blenheim Theatricals," *World*, 3 December 1789, in *Collection of Playbills*, fol. 10.

88. "Blenheim Theatricals," *Diary*, Dec 7th 1789, in *Collection of Playbills*, fol. 10.

89. Heber family MS play, "Britain Triumphant or the Spaniards foild. A Tragedy. occasion'd by the Success of the British Arms in the West Indies." Bodleian Library, MS Eng misc e.577.

90. Bodleian Library, MS Rawl Poet 22a, fol. 89v.

91. 31 December 1768, Elizabeth Harris, Salisbury, to James Harris in Madrid, in *Music and Theatre in Handel's World: The Family Papers of James Harris, 1732–1780*, ed. Donald Burrows and Rosemary Dunhill (Oxford: Oxford University Press, 2002), 531.

92. 6 January 1770, Elizabeth Harris, Salisbury, to James Harris jr, [Madrid], in *Music and Theatre in Handel's World*, 575.

93. 20 January 1770, Elizabeth Harris to James Harris, in *Music and Theatre in Handel's World*, 577.

94. For a fuller discussion of the Harris production of a Shakespeare adaptation, see Michael Dobson, *Shakespeare and Amateur Performance: A Cultural History* (Cambridge: Cambridge University Press, 2011), 37–45.

95. "Bath Journal, November 24th 1774. On the Ladies of the Close of S[alisbur]y now acting Elvira," in *Music and Theatre in Handel's World*, 783–84. See also 4 December 1774. Elizabeth Harris, Salisbury, to James Harris jr, in *Music and Theatre in Handel's World*, 783: she sends JH some "vile verses" from the *Bath Journal*.

96. 31 December 1768, Elizabeth Harris, Salisbury, to James Harris, jr, Madrid, in *Music and Theatre in Handel's World*, 531.

97. 20 January 1770, Elizabeth Harris, Salisbury, to James Harris jr, Madrid, in *Music and Theatre in Handel's World*, 577.

98. Ibid.

99. Mary Clarke to Edward Clarke, November 1, 1699, in "Correspondence of Edward Clarke of Chipley," transcribed by Bridget Clarke, Correspondence to Edward from wife Mary, 1675–1704, Somerset Heritage Centre, DD\SF/7/13. I am very grateful to Bridget Clarke for access to these transcriptions and further information about the Clarke family.

100. See, for example, Thomas Jordan's "A Prologue to Introduce the First Woman that came to Act on the Stage in the Tragedy, call'd the Moor of Venice," in *A Loyal Arbor of Royal Poesie* (1663), 21–22.

101. John Corye, *The Generous Enemies; or, The Ridiculous Lovers a Comedy* (London, 1672), A4v.

102. Vicesimus Knox, "Of the Prevailing Practice of acting Plays by private Gentlemen and Ladies," in *Winter Evenings: or Lucubrations on Life and Letters,* 3 vols. (London, 1788), 3:33.

103. Ibid., 35.

104. Ibid., 37.

105. For a discussion of the gendering of the debate about amateur theatricals, see Michaelson, *Speaking Volumes,* 127–34.

106. Knox, "Of the Prevailing Practice," 38.

107. *The Oracle*, 9 March 1798; see also Rosenfeld, *Temples of Thespis,* 12–15.

108. Richard Cumberland, "Remarks upon the Present Taste for Acting Private Plays," in *The Observer, Being a Collection of Moral, Literary and Familiar Essays,* 5 vols. (London 1786), 4:289.

109. Ibid., 291.

110. Bodleian Library, Oxford Ms Pigott d. 22 "Letters & Jeux d'Esprits at the Epoch of the Salop Private Theatricals. Sketches made of the parties by Sir W Gell & other Wits 1811 & later." Bodleian Library Oxford, MS Pigott c. 2, "Pic Nic" Vol I Miss H Pigott.

111. Ms Pigott d. 22, fol 17.

112. Ibid., fol. 63r.

113. Ibid., fol. 157.

114. Ibid., fol. 8.

115. Ibid., fol. 73.

116. Ibid., fols. 87v, 88r.

117. Cumberland, "Remarks upon the Present Taste," 287.

118. Epilogues and prologues were not unique to the Pigott group—they are, for example, also part of the much more decorous dramatic entertainment created by the Heber family, the Harris family, and the group who acted "Eumenes," discussed earlier in this chapter.

119. Ms Pigott d. 22, fol. 133 r.

7. *Fictional Worlds*

1. Michael Suarez puts the fraction of novels in relation to other printed output at no more than 3.5 percent at its peak. See Michael F. Suarez, "Towards a

Bibliometric Analysis of the Surviving Record, 1701–1800," *Cambridge History of the Book in Britain 1685–1830*, ed. Michael Suarez and Michael Turner (Cambridge: Cambridge University Press, 2009), 37–65, 48. On recent questioning of the "rise of the novel," see J. Alan Downie, "Literature and Drama," *A Companion to Eighteenth-Century Britain*, ed. H. T. Dickinson (Oxford: Blackwell, 2002), 329–43, 340.

2. On the relationship between history and fictional narrative, see Robert Mayer, *History and the Early English Novel: Matters of Fact from Bacon to Defoe* (Cambridge: Cambridge University Press, 1997); Lennard Davis, *Factual Fictions: The Origins of The English Novel* (Philadelphia: University of Pennsylvania Press, 1997).

3. Ian Watt, *The Rise of the Novel: Studies in Defoe, Richardson, and Fielding* (Berkeley: University of California Press, 1957). For a more recent account of the changing nature of individual identity in this period, see Dror Wahrman, *The Making of the Modern Self: Identity and Modern Culture in Eighteenth-Century England* (New Haven: Yale University Press, 2004).

4. J. Paul Hunter, *Before Novels: The Cultural Contexts of Eighteenth-Century English Fiction* (London: W. W. Norton, 1990), 42.

5. See J. Paul Hunter, "The Loneliness of the Long Distance Reader," *Genre* 10 (1977), 455–85. John Sitter, *Literary Loneliness in Eighteenth-Century England* (Ithaca: Cornell University Press, 1982).

6. For a sense of the range of debate about the novel over the century, see Ioan Williams, ed., *Novel and Romance, 1700–1800: A Documentary Record* (London: Routledge and Kegan Paul, 1970).

7. Vicessimus Knox, " 'On Novel Reading,' No. XIV, Essays Moral and Literary, 1778," in *Novel and Romance, 1700–1800: A Documentary Record*, ed. Williams, 304–7.

8. Jane Spencer, *The Rise of the Woman Novelist* (Oxford: Blackwell, 1986); Dale Spender, *Mothers of the Novel* (London: Pandora, 1986); Janet Todd, *The Sign of Angellica* (London: Virago, 1989); Ros Ballaster, *Seductive Forms* (Oxford: Clarendon, 1992); Catherine Gallagher, *Nobody's Story: The Vanishing Acts of Women Writers from the Marketplace, 1670–1820* (Berkeley: University of California Press, 1994); Cheryl Turner, *Living by the Pen: Women Writers in the Eighteenth Century* (London: Routledge, 1992).

9. Jan Fergus, *Provincial Readers in Eighteenth-Century England* (Oxford: Oxford University Press, 2006), 40–47.

10. Mark Towsey, *Reading the Scottish Enlightenment: Books and Their Readers in Provincial Scotland, 1750–1820* (Leiden: Brill, 2010); David Allan, *A Nation of*

Readers: The Lending Library in Georgian England (London: British Library, 2008).

11. Allan, *A Nation of Readers*, 105. As discussed in Chapter 4, there was massive variation in the degrees to which they specialised or not in fashionable modern novels.

12. 17 April 1818, in *The Diary of the Revd William Jones, 1777–1821*, ed. O. F. Christie (London: Brentano's, 1929), 275–76. "Gatty Aubrey" refers to a character in Laetitia Hawkins's novel *The Countess and Gertrude* (1811).

13. Quoted in Allan, *A Nation of Readers*, 105.

14. Jacqueline Pearson, *Women's Reading in Britain, 1750–1835: A Dangerous Recreation* (Cambridge: Cambridge University Press, 1999), 197. She cites *Ladies Magazine* 11 (1780), 693; 4 (1773), 293, 531; 11 (1780), 275; 18 (1787), 596; 22 (1791), 59–61. On the authors perceived to be above the bar in libraries, see Allan, *A Nation of Readers*, 105.

15. Thomas Gisborne, *An Enquiry into the Duties of the Female Sex*, 3 ed., corrected (London, 1798), 228–29.

16. Vicessimus Knox, "'On Novel Reading,' No. XIV, Essays Moral and Literary, 1778," in *Novel and Romance, 1700–1800*, ed. Ioan Williams (London: Routledge and Kegan Paul, 1970), 306.

17. 22 October 1728, in Gertrude Savile, *Secret Comment: The Diaries of Gertrude Savile, 1721–1757*, ed. Alan Saville (Devon: Kingsbridge History Society, 1997), 144.

18. 20 October 1727, in Savile, *Secret Comment*, 71. Savile here refers to Eliza's Haywood's *Memoirs of the Baron de Brosse*.

19. See William Beatty Warner, "Staging Readers Reading," *Eighteenth-Century Fiction*, 12 (2000), 391–416.

20. Ibid., 393.

21. Robert Folkenflik, "Reading Richardson/Richardson Reading," in *Representation, Heterodoxy, and Aesthetics: Essays in Honor of Ronald Paulson*, ed. Ashley Marshall (Newark: University of Delaware Press, 2015), 41–59, 43. See also Roger Chartier's discussion of Chardin's painting *The Amusements of Private Life* (1745), in "The Practical Impact of Writing," in *A History of Private Life: Passions of the Renaissance*, ed. Philippe Aries and Georges Duby (Cambridge: Harvard University Press, 2003), 111–60. Chartier calls it "a pictorial synecdoche: the part (reading) stands for the whole (private life). A single practice, that of reading, stands for the whole range of private pleasures in the time left free after family chores and obligations," 144.

22. Elizabeth Mure, National Library of Scotland, Ms 5003, "Essay on the Change of Manners in my Own Time," fol. 8r.

23. *The Critical Review; or, Annals of Literature* (London, 1764), 18:480.

24. On the importance of communal domestic reading in contemporary novels, see Pearson, *Women's Reading in Britain*, 17–175.

25. Gisborne, *An Enquiry into the Duties of the Female Sex*, 225.

26. Mary Wollstonecraft, *Vindication of the Rights of Woman* (London, 1782), 431.

27. "Mr Urban," *Gentleman's Magazine*, December 1767, 580.

28. See Cynthia Richards, "'The Pleasures of Complicity': Sympathetic Identification and the Female Reader in Early Eighteenth-Century Women's Amatory Fiction," *Eighteenth Century* 36 (1995), 220–33.

29. James Fordyce, *Sermons to Young Women*, 2 vols. (London, 1766), 2:167, quoted in Kathryn L. Steele, "Hester Mulso Chapone and the Problem of the Individual Reader," *Eighteenth Century* 53 (2012), 473–91.

30. Frances Burney, *Evelina, or, The History of a Young Lady's Entrance into the World*, ed. Edward A. Bloom (London: Oxford University Press, 1968), 296.

31. "Letter VI. From Lady Davers to Mrs. B," Samuel Richardson, *Pamela in her Exalted Condition*, ed. Albert J. Rivero (Cambridge: Cambridge University Press, 2012), 24.

32. Ann Radcliffe, *The Mysteries of Udolpho: A Romance*, 2nd ed., 4 vols. (London, 1794), 4:195.

33. See Joe Bray, *The Female Reader in the English Novel: From Burney to Austen* (London: Routledge, 2009), 35–38.

34. For fuller discussion, see Folkenflik, "Reading Richardson/Richardson Reading," 41–59.

35. 1 February 1741, "Richardson to Aaron Hill," in *The Correspondence of Samuel Richardson: With Aaron Hill and the Hill Family*, ed. Christine Gerrard (Cambridge: Cambridge University Press, 2013), 90.

36. Samuel Richardson, *Pamela; or, Virtue Rewarded: In a Series of Familiar Letters, The Second Edition, To which are prefixed, extracts from several curious letters written to the Editor on the Subject* (London: 1741), 1:xvi.

37. Ibid., xxviii.

38. Ibid., xxxii–xxxiii.

39. On the rise of sensibility and sentiment, see Ann Jessie Van Sant, *Eighteenth-Century Sensibility and the Novel: The Senses in Social Context* (Cambridge: Cambridge University Press, 1993); Janet Todd, *Sensibility: An Introduction* (London: Methuen, 1986).

40. "Number V. Tuesday, October 6, 1795," in *The Sylph* (Deptford, 1796), 36–37.

41. See Paul Goring, *The Rhetoric of Sensibility in Eighteenth-Century Culture* (Cambridge: Cambridge University Press, 2005).

42. 18 September 1782, "Miss Burney's 'Cecilia.' To Dr. Burney," in *Recreations and Studies of a Country Clergyman of the Eighteenth Century: Being Selections from the Correspondence of the Rev. Thomas Twining, M.A.* (London: John Murray, 1882), 111.

43. 16 December 1749, Letter from Lady Bradshaigh to Samuel Richardson, quoted in T. C. Duncan Eaves and Ben D. Kimpel, *Samuel Richardson: A Biography* (Oxford: Clarendon, 1971), 287.

44. On the cultural history of crying in this period, see Thomas Dixon, *Weeping Britannia: Portrait of a Nation in Tears* (Oxford: Oxford University Press, 2015).

45. Harriet Martineau, *Harriet Martineau's Autobiography: With Memorials by Maria Weston Chapman*, 3rd ed., 3 vols. (London: Smith, Elder, 1877), 3:430.

46. Preface to *Beauties in Prose and Verse Selected from the Most Celebrated Authors* (Stockton, 1783), vii.

47. 4 September 1826, Lady Louisa Stewart to Sir Walter Scott, in *The Private Letter-Books of Sir Walter Scott*, ed. Wilfred Partington (London: Hodder and Stoughton, 1930), 273. Stewart also records a changed response to the novel a few decades later, describing her friends reading aloud *The Man of Feeling*, when "the effect altogether failed. Nobody cried, and at some of the passages, the touches that I used to think so exquisite—Oh Dear! They laughed" (ibid., 273).

48. On the earthenware Maria, see Pat Halfpenny, *English Earthenware Figures, 1740–1840* (Woodbridge: Antique Collectors Club, 1991), 149. For a list of the various Maria products available, see William Blake Gerard, *Laurence Sterne and the Visual Imagination* (Aldershot: Ashgate, 2006), 227–31. On Maria in decorative pottery, see W. B. Gerard, "Sterne in Wedgewood: 'Poor Maria' and the 'Bourbonnaise Shepherd,'" *Shandean* 12 (2001), 78–88.

49. Hester Piozzi, *Thraliana: The Diary of Mrs. Hester Lynch Thrale (Later Mrs. Piozzi), 1776–1809*, ed. Katharine C. Balderston, 2nd ed., 2 vols. (Oxford: Clarendon, 1951), 2:823.

50. *The Reader or Reciter: By the Assistance of which any Person may teach himself to read or recite English Prose* (London, 1799), 75.

51. Ibid., 77.

52. On the differences between French and English punctuation of prose fiction in this period, see Vivienne Mylne, "The Punctuation of Dialogue in

Eighteenth-Century French and English Fiction," *The Library*, 1 (1979), 43–61.

53. *The Reader or Reciter*, 77.

54. Ibid., 78.

55. Ibid., 80.

56. Ibid.

57. David Steel, *Elements of Punctuation* (London, 1786), 58 note a.

58. M. B. Parkes, *Pause and Effect: An Introduction to the History of Punctuation in the West* (Aldershot: Scolar, 1992), 92. Critics disagree on the aurality of Sterne's dashes, and whether or not they enable reading aloud. See Michael Vande Berg, "Pictures of Pronunciation: Typographical Travels Through *Tristram Shandy* and *Jacques le Fataliste*," *Eighteenth-Century Studies* 21 (1987), 23–24; Roger B. Moss, "Sterne's Punctuation," *Eighteenth-Century Studies* 15 (1981–82), 180–81. On the design of Sterne's pages, see Janine Barchas, *Graphic Design, Print Culture, and the Eighteenth-Century Novel* (Cambridge: Cambridge University Press, 2003).

59. *The Reader or Reciter*, 82–87.

60. Ibid., 92.

61. Ibid., 94.

62. John Rice, *Introduction to the Art of Reading with Energy and Propriety* (London, 1765), 291.

63. John Wilson, *Principles of Elocution* (Edinburgh, 1798), 64.

64. See Mylne, "The Punctuation of Dialogue," 58.

65. See Catherine Gallagher, *Nobody's Story: The Vanishing Acts of Women Writers in the Marketplace, 1670–1820* (California: University of California Press, 1995), 279.

66. Gilbert Austin, *Chironomia; or, a Treatise on Rhetorical Delivery* (London, 1806), 206.

67. Caroline Austen, *My Aunt Jane Austen, a Memoir* (London: Spottiswoode, 1952), 10.

68. Patricia Michaelson, *Speaking Volumes: Women, Reading, and Speech in the Age of Austen* (Stanford: Stanford University Press, 2002), 178.

69. "Susan to Frances Burney," in Frances Burney, *The Early Diary of Frances Burney, 1768–1778*, ed. Annie Raine Ellis, 2 vols. (London: George Bell and Sons, 1889), 2:230.

70. 16 July 1778, "Susan to Frances Burney, at Chesington," in Burney, *The Early Diary*, 2:246.

71. 5 July 1778, "Susan to Frances Burney," in Burney, *The Early Diary*, 2:239.

72. "Susan to Frances Burney," in Burney, *The Early Diary*, 2:230.

73. Carolyn Steedman, *Master and Servant: Love and Labour in the English Industrial Age* (Cambridge: Cambridge University Press, 2007), 63.

74. Commonplace Book of John Chubb, Somerset Heritage Centre, A/CSC 1/4, fols. 48v, 49r.

75. 1–23 January 1722, in Savile, *Secret Comment*, 23.

76. 21 June 1732, "Mrs. Pendarves to Mrs. Ann Granville," in Mary Delany, *The Autobiography and Correspondence of Mary Granville, Mrs Delany*, ed. The Right Honourable Lady Llanover, 1st series, 3 vols. (London: Richard Bentley, 1861), 1:356.

77. 28 June 1732, "Mrs. Pendarves to her sister Mrs. Ann Granville," in Delany, *Autobiography and Correspondence*, 1st series (1861), 1:362.

78. 13 August 1732, "Mrs Pendarves to Mrs. Ann Granville," in Delany, *Autobiography and Correspondence*, 1st series (1861), 1:372–73.

79. August 1750, "Mrs Delany to Mrs. Dewes," in Delany, *Autobiography and Correspondence*, 1st series (1861), 2:582.

80. For a fuller discussion of Larpent's reading, see John Brewer, "Reconstructing the Reader: Prescriptions, Texts, and Strategies in Anna Larpent's Reading," in *The Practice and Representation of Reading in England*, ed. James Raven, Helen Small, and Naomi Tadmor (Cambridge: Cambridge University Press, 1996), 226–45. See also an excellent discussion of Larpent's reading in Polly Bull, "The Reading Lives of English Men and Women" (Ph.D. thesis, Royal Holloway, University of London, 2012), 236–76. Bull challenges Brewer's claim that Larpent was less confident in evaluating historical texts.

81. Quoted by John Brewer, *Pleasures of the Imagination: English Culture in the Eighteenth Century* (London: HarperCollins, 1997), 197.

82. 10 January 1818, Larpent Diaries on microfilm, British Library microfilm 1016/4.

83. "Strictures on the Modern System of Female Education," in Hannah More, *The Works of Hannah More*, 2 vols. (New York: Harper and Brothers, 1835), 1:348.

84. Brewer, "Reconstructing the Reader," 242.

85. See Goring, *The Rhetoric of Sensibility*, 168.

86. Anna Laetitia Barbauld, *The Correspondence of Samuel Richardson, Author of Pamela, Clarissa, and Sir Charles Grandison*, 6 vols. (London: Richard Phillips, 1804), 1:lviii.

87. See Jennie Batchelor, "Reinstating the 'Pamela Vogue,' " in *Women and Material Culture, 1660–1830*, ed. Jennie Batchelor and Cora Kaplan (Basingstoke: Palgrave, 2007), 163–75; T. C. Duncan Eaves, "Graphic Illustration of the Novels of Samuel Richardson," *Huntington Library Quarterly* 14 (1950), 349–83.

88. On the social role of fine ceramics in this period, see Sarah Richards, *Eighteenth-Century Ceramics: Products for a Civilised Society* (Manchester: Manchester University Press, 1999), 127–51.

89. *The Norfolk Ladies Memorandum Book; or, Fashionable Pocket Repository, for the Year 1787* (Bury St Edmunds, 1787), in the Berg Collection, New York Public Library. Image in Catherine M. Parisian, *Frances Burney's Cecilia: A Publishing History* (London: Ashgate, 2012), 123.

90. For other images of the episode, see Parisian, *Frances Burney's Cecilia*, 139, 164, 180.

91. On the material afterlife of the Lorenzo episode, see W. G. Day, "Sternean Material Culture: Lorenzo's Snuff-Box and His Graves," in *The Reception of Laurence Sterne in Europe*, ed. Peter de Voogd and John Neubauer (London: Continuum, 2004), 247–58. None of the Lorenzo snuffboxes have survived. For a fuller discussion of the episode and the ideology of sentimental exchange, see Lynn Festa, *Sentimental Figures of Empire in Eighteenth-Century Britain and France* (Baltimore: Johns Hopkins University Press, 2006), 69–81.

92. See Batchelor, "Reinstating the 'Pamela Vogue,' " 166–68.

93. David Drakard, *Printed English Pottery: History and Humour in the Reign of George II, 1760–1820* (London: Jonathan Horne, 1992), 65, plate 147.

94. Advertisement in the *Daily Advertiser*, 28 April 1741.

95. Hunter, *Before Novels*, 42.

96. Review of *The Mysteries of Udolpho*, in *Critical Review*, 2nd series, 11 (1794), 361.

97. See Patricia Meyer Spacks, *Novel Beginnings: Experiments in Eighteenth-Century English Fiction* (New Haven: Yale University Press, 2006), 26.

98. Ibid., 129.

99. Thomas Clay records, NRO D7938, quoted in Fergus, *Provincial Readers*, 188.

100. Diary of Elizabeth Tyrrell, August 18, 1818, London Metropolitan Archives, CLC/510.

101. Brewer, "Reconstructing the Reader," 242.

102. Fergus, *Provincial Readers*, 108–17.

103. Ibid., 109.

104. Ibid., 112.

105. "Diary of George Sandy, Apprentice W.S., 1788," in *The Book of the Old Edinburgh Club*, 45 vols. (Edinburgh: Printed By T. A. Constable, 1908–), 24 (1942), 1–69, 16.

106. Ibid., 43.

107. Ibid., 47.

108. 13 April 1767, *Letters from Bath, 1766–1767, by the Rev. John Penrose* (Gloucester: Alan Sutton, 1983), 166.

109. For a comprehensive study, see Robert Mayo, *The English Novel in the Magazines, 1740–1815* (London: Oxford University Press, 1962).

110. Ibid., 2.

111. "Hints on Reading," *Lady's Magazine*, February 1789, 80–81.

112. Richard C. Taylor, "James Harrison, *The Novelist's Magazine*, and the Early Canonizing of the English Novel," *Studies in English Literature, 1500–1900* 33 (1993), 629–43, 636–37.

113. Simon Fisher, *Fisher's Cheerful Companion to Promote Laughter* (London, 1800).

114. *The Merry Medley for Gay Gallants and Good Companions* (Dublin, 1748).

115. Ibid., 5.

116. Ibid., 9.

117. This emphasis on the metropolitan or elite origin of the quip can be traced back to the first jestbook proper, which is normally reckoned to be the *Facetiae*, a collection of jests made by Poggio Bracciolini, the great humanist scholar. His collection of scabrous, sometimes ancient, anecdotes was said to have arisen from the gossip of papal secretaries in Rome. Poggio claimed that the jests were written by named persons about others—witty, malicious gossip—but they had received literary polish. The jokes were written in Latin in 1450, circulated widely in Europe, and were printed in 1477. They were immensely popular, and other writers adopted individual items, as similar books began to be published in Europe.

118. *Baron Munchausen's Narrative of his Marvellous Travels and Campaigns in Russia* (Oxford, 1786), title page.

119. The 1780s and '90s saw the publication of over twenty editions and reworkings of the Munchausen collection, many of them subtitled "Gulliver revived."

120. W. Carew Hazlitt, *Studies in Jocular Literature* (London: Elliot Stock, 1890), 12.

121. See Michaelson, *Speaking Volumes*.

122. Simon Dickie, "Hilarity and Pitilessness in the Mid–Eighteenth Century: English Jestbook Humor," *Eighteenth-Century Studies* 37 (2003), 1–22, 9.

123. Some collections were prefaced with advertisements for other instructional works: *Sir John Fielding's Jests*, for example, included a puff for *The New Universal Story-Teller*, which consisted of "a greater *Variety* of valuable Matter calculated for the *Pleasures* and *Improvements* of *Readers of every Class*." *Sir John Fielding's Jests; or New Fun for the Parlour and Kitchen* (London, 1781), ii.

124. *Fun for the Parlour; or, All Merry Above Stairs* (London, 1771), title page.

8. *Piety and Knowledge*

Epigraph: William Woollcombe at Edinburgh to Henry Woollcombe at Britonside, Plymouth, 17 November 1793, Plymouth and West Devon Record Office, ref. 710/406.

1. R. M. Wiles, *Serial Publication in England Before 1750* (Cambridge: Cambridge University Press, 1957), 246.

2. 19 May 1778, in *The Diary of the Revd William Jones, 1777–1821*, ed. O. F. Christie (London: Brentano's, 1929) 21.

3. 2 April 1779, in *The Diary of the Revd William Jones*, 51.

4. See Arnold Hunt, *The Art of Hearing: English Preachers and Their Audiences, 1590–1640* (Cambridge: Cambridge University Press, 2010), 117–86.

5. MS quoted in David D. Brown, "The Text of John Tillotson's Sermons," *The Library*, 5th ser., 13 (1958), 18–36, 27. On the most popular sermons of the period, see Ian Green, *Print and Protestantism in Early Modern England* (Oxford: Oxford University Press, 2000), 194–216.

6. See William Gibson, "John Trusler and the Culture of Sermons in Late Eighteenth-Century England," *Journal of Ecclesiastical History* 66 (2015), 302–19.

7. John Trusler, *A List of Books, published by the Rev. Dr. Trusler* (London, 1790), 10.

8. On the differences in sermon style between denominations, see Jennifer Farooq, *Preaching in Eighteenth-Century London* (Woodbridge: Boydell, 2013), 8.

9. Trusler MS, 192–93, cited in Gibson, "John Trusler and the Culture of Sermons," 316.

10. John Trusler, Advertisement to second edition of *The Sublime Reader; or, the Evening and Morning Service of the Church* (London, 1784), iii.

11. See Farooq, *Preaching in Eighteenth-Century London.*

12. The topicality of sermons and their absorption into wider print culture is evidenced by fact that a number of sermon readers transcribed newspaper articles relating to the sermons; ibid., 122.

13. Ibid., 74.

14. Samuel Hilliard, *A Sermon Preach'd at the Cathedral Church of St Paul . . . Oct the 9th, 1709* (London, 1709), 7.

15. See Henry Prescott, *The Diary of Henry Prescott, LL.B., Deputy Registrar of Chester Diocese,* ed. John Addy, 3 vols. (Chester: Record Society of Lancashire and Cheshire, 1987–97), 1:260–61.

16. 28 May 1820, in Anne Lister, *I Know My Own Heart: The Diaries of Anne Lister, 1791–1840,* ed. Helena Whitbread (London: Virago, 1988), 128.

17. August 1797, Diary of Henry Woollcombe II, 1796–1803, Plymouth and West Devon Record Office, Ref 710/391, 90.

18. *Woodforde Papers and Diaries,* ed. Dorothy Heighes Woodforde (London: Peter Davies, 1932).

19. 21 July 1759, Diary of Elizabeth Prowse, Gloucester Archives, D3549/14/1/2, fol. 27.

20. Mrs Amelia Ann Sophia Steuart of Dalguise, Gask Journals, March 1789–1792, NLS MS 983, fol. 30v, fol. 31v.

21. W. M. Jacob, *Lay People and Religion in the Early Eighteenth Century* (Cambridge: Cambridge University Press, 1996), 103.

22. Margaret Spufford, *Small Books and Pleasant Histories: Popular Fiction and Its Readership in Seventeenth-Century England* (Cambridge: Cambridge University Press, 1981), 211.

23. The Bible was the prime example. Ever since Henry VIII first decreed that the vernacular Scriptures were to be read in churches, those who were able to read would often read for those who could not. In Chelmsford around 1540, "divers poor men in the town" could be found on Sundays "reading in [the] lower end of the church, and many would flock about them to hear their reading." Cited by David D. Hall, *Cultures of Print: Essays in the History of the Book* (Amherst: University of Massachusetts Press, 1996), 52. See also Adam Fox, *Oral and Literate Culture in England, 1500–1700* (Oxford: Clarendon, 2000), 39–40. Also Keith Thomas, *Religion and the Decline of Magic: Studies in Popular Beliefs in Sixteenth- and Seventeenth-Century England* (New York: Scribner, 1971).

24. *The Reverend Richard Baxter's Last Treatise,* ed. Frederick J. Powicke (Manchester: The University Press, 1926) 190, quoted in Fox, *Oral and Literate Culture,* 38.

25. Ian Green, *The Christian's ABC: Catechisms and Catechizing in England, c. 1530–1740* (Oxford: Clarendon, 1996).

26. Jacob, *Lay People and Religion*, 95.

27. 25 November 1720, in Nicholas Blundell, *The Great Diurnal of Nicholas Blundell of Little Crosby, Lancashire*, ed. J. J. Bagley, 3 vols. (Chester: Record Society of Lancashire and Cheshire, 1968–72), 3:31.

28. 3 April 1720, in Blundell, *The Great Diurnal*, 3:9.

29. December 1703, in Blundell, *The Great Diurnal*, 1:25.

30. 6 February 1709, in Blundell, *Great Diurnal*, 1:202.

31. 23 September 1711, in Blundell, *Great Diurnal*, 1:301.

32. Edward Chandler, *A Sermon Preached to the Societies for Reformation of Manners, at St Mary-le-Bow, on Monday January the 4th, 1724* (London, 1724 [1725]), 13.

33. Richard Allestree, *The Whole Duty of Man, Laid Down in a Plain and Familiar Way for the Use of All, but Especially the Meanest Reader* (London, 1719), 108.

34. Jacob, *Lay People and Religion*, 106.

35. James Lackington, *Memoirs of the First Forty-Five Years of the Life of James Lackington* (London, 1793), 420.

36. Richard D. Altick, *The English Common Reader: A Social History of the Mass Reading Public, 1800–1900* (Chicago: University of Chicago Press, 1957), 39–40.

37. Martha More, *Mendip Annals; or, A Narrative of the Charitable Labours of Hannah and Martha More*, ed. Arthur Roberts, 3rd ed. (London, 1859), 236.

38. "Not only was the teaching of writing discouraged, but very many Sunday school scholars left the schools unable to read, and in view of the parts of Old Testament thought most edifying this at least was a blessing." E. P. Thompson, *The Making of the Working Class* (London: Victor Gollancz, 1980), 414–15.

39. *A Memoir of Thomas Bewick, Written by Himself* (Newcastle-on-Tyne: Ward, 1862), 55.

40. May 13, 1758, Transcript of Thomas Turner's Diaries, East Sussex Record Office, AMS 6532/3, 720. Wake's Catechism is William Wake's *The Principles of the Christian Religion Explained: in a brief commentary upon the church-catechism*. It was first published in 1699, with seven editions over the next half-century.

41. Trusler MS, 192, cited in Gibson, "John Trusler and the Culture of Sermons," 315.

42. 22 March 1765, Thomas Turner Diaries, AMS 6532/5, 1476–77.

43. 28 February 1756, Thomas Turner Diaries, AMS 6532/1, 168.

44. 2 August 1758, Thomas Turner Diaries, AMS 6532/3, 616.

45. 8 July 1758, Thomas Turner Diaries, AMS 6532/3, 610.

46. 1 March 1755, Thomas Turner Diaries, AMS 6532/1, 33.

47. 16 December 1756, Thomas Turner Diaries, AMS 6532/1, 364.

48. 14 June 1758, Thomas Turner Diaries, AMS 6532/3, 740.

49. 26 March 1757, Thomas Turner Diaries, AMS 6532/2, 440.

50. 25 September 1755, Thomas Turner Diaries, AMS 6532/1, 87–88.

51. 3 August 1764, Thomas Turner Diaries, AMS 6532/5, 1362–63.

52. 1 December 1762, in James Boswell, *Boswell's London Journal, 1762–1763*, ed. Frederick A. Pottle, 2nd ed. (New Haven: Yale University Press, 2004), 62.

53. 18 June 1715, in Dudley Ryder, *The Diary of Dudley Ryder, 1715–16*, ed. William Matthews (London: Methuen, 1939), 38.

54. 23 March 1771, in Sylas Neville, *The Diary of Sylas Neville*, ed. Basil Cozens-Hardy (Oxford: Oxford University Press, 1950), 96.

55. Naomi Tadmor, *Family and Friends in Eighteenth-Century England: Household, Kinship, and Patronage* (Cambridge: Cambridge University Press, 2001), 172–73. Turner and Davy's interest in devotional works was not unusual in their artisan class. Study of subscription lists for practical devotional works amongst craftsmen in both rural and urban areas shows significant inclusion of weavers, shoemakers, butchers, grocers, and tanners. Geraint H. Jenkins, *Literature, Religion, and Society in Wales, 1660–1730* (Cardiff: University of Wales Press, 1978), 274.

56. 18 September 1756, Thomas Turner Diaries, AMS 6532/1, 309.

57. 9 April 1756, Thomas Turner Diaries, AMS 6532/1, 192; 21 August 1756, Thomas Turner Diaries, AMS 6532/1, 513; 16 May 1758, Thomas Turner Diaries, AMS 6532/3, 721.

58. 10 February 1757, Thomas Turner Diaries, AMS 6532/2, 403.

59. 11 January 1763, Thomas Turner, Diaries, AMS 6532/5, 1259.

60. 20 October 1760, Thomas Turner, Diaries, AMS 6532/4, 856.

61. 28 August 1754, Thomas Turner, Diaries, AMS 6532/1, 78.

62. 23 March 1758, Thomas Turner Diaries, AMS 6532/3, 686.

63. 7 September 1716, in Ryder, *Diary*, 311.

64. Daniel R. Woolf, *Reading History in Early Modern England* (Cambridge: Cambridge University Press, 2000), 80–81.

65. D. R. Woolf, "A Feminine Past? Gender, Genre, and Historical Knowledge in England, 1500–1800," *American Historical Review* 102, 3 (June 1997), 645–79.

66. "Of Academies," in Daniel Defoe, *Essays Upon Several Projects* (London 1702), 292.

67. Richard Steele [Mary Wray], *The Ladies Library*, 3 vols. (London, 1714), 1:22.

68. Hester Chapone, *Letters on the Improvement of the Mind*, 2 vols. (London: J. Walter, 1773), 2:125.

69. Ibid., 178–79.

70. William Sherman, *John Dee: The Politics of Reading and Writing in the English Renaissance* (Amherst: University of Massachusetts Press, 1995); Lisa Jardine and Anthony Grafton, "How Gabriel Harvey Read His Livy," *Past and Present* 129 (1990), 30–78.

71. 29 May 1718, in Prescott, *Diary of Henry Prescott*, 2:636.

72. 20 July 1704, in Prescott, *Diary of Henry Prescott*, 1:62.

73. 9 September 1704, in Prescott, *Diary of Henry Prescott*, 1:70.

74. 26 September 1705, in Prescott, *Diary of Henry Prescott*, 1:116.

75. 20 May 1719, in Prescott, *Diary of Henry Prescott*, 2:695.

76. 19 March 1710, in Blundell, *The Great Diurnal*, 1:248.

77. 21 June 1818, in Lister, *I Know My Own Heart*, 48.

78. William Woollcombe at Edinburgh to Henry Woollcombe at Britonside, Plymouth, 28 October 1794, Plymouth and West Devon Record Office, ref. 710/406.

79. William Woollcombe at Edinburgh to Henry Woollcombe at Britonside, Plymouth, 17 November 1793, Plymouth and West Devon Record Office, ref. 710/406.

80. Diary of Henry Woollcombe II, 1796–1803, Ref 710/391, 2, 3.

81. Annabel Patterson *Reading Holinshed's Chronicles* (Chicago: University of Chicago Press, 1994); Annabel Patterson, "Foul, his Wife, the Mayor, and Foul's Mare: the Power of Anecdote in Tudor Historiography," in *The Historical Imagination in Early Modern Britain: History, Rhetoric, and Fiction, 1500–1800*, ed. Donald R. Kelley and David Harris Sacks (Cambridge: Cambridge University Press, 1997), 159–78.

82. Woolf, *Reading History*, 106.

83. G. W. R. Hoyland, draper and tailor, 22 West Barr, Sheffield Order book. Sheffield Record Office, MD1191, fol 2 v.

84. Commonplace Book of Wilson family of Broomhead Hall, 18th century, Sheffield Record Office, MD145, fol. 112.

85. Woolf, *Reading History*, 100.

86. 14 December 1758, "Extracts from the Journal of Walter Gale, Schoolmaster at Mayfield, 1750: Edited By R. W. Blencowe, Esq.," in *Sussex Archaeological*

Collections: Relating to the History and Antiquities of the County, 152 vols. (London: John Russel Smith, 1857), 9:201.

87. Robert Baker, *The Merry Jester, Containing a Great Variety of Comical Jests, Keen Waggeries, Smart Repartees* (London, 1773).

88. For an example of such readerly confusion, see 22 May 1719, in Prescott, *Diary of Henry Prescott*, 2:695.

89. Ernst Family Notebook, Somerset Heritage Centre, DD/SWD 15.

90. 18 November 1774, "Mrs. Delany to Mrs. Port, of Ilam," in Mary Delany, *The Autobiography and Correspondence of Mary, Mrs Delany*, ed. The Right Honourable Lady Llanover, 2nd series, 3 vols. (London: Richard Bentley, 1862), 2:67.

91. 28 December, 1750, "Mrs. Delany to Mrs. Dewes," in Mary Delany, *The Autobiography and Correspondence of Mary Granville, Mrs Delany*, ed. The Right Honourable Lady Llanover, 1st series, 3 vols. (London: Richard Bentley, 1861), 2:633.

92. 16 November 1751, "Mrs. Delany to Mrs. Dewes," in Delany, *Autobiography and Correspondence*, 1st series, 3:59–60.

93. 2 February 1760, "Mrs Delany to Mrs. Dewes," in Delany, *Autobiography and Correspondence*, 1st series, 3:584.

94. For a fuller discussion of Larpent's reading, see John Brewer, "Reconstructing the Reader: Prescriptions, Texts and Strategies in Anna Larpent's Reading," in *The Practice and Representation of Reading in England*, ed. James Raven, Helen Small, and Naomi Tadmor (Cambridge: Cambridge University Press, 1996), 226–45. On her disapproval of novels, see 223–34.

95. See ibid., 236, and for a slightly different interpretation, Polly Bull, "The Reading Lives of English Men and Women, 1695–1830" (unpublished doctoral thesis, Royal Holloway, University of London, 2012), 253–60.

96. Mrs Amelia Ann Sophia Steuart of Dalguise, Gask Journals, March 1789–1792, National Library of Scotland MS 983, fol. 1 r, fol. 3v.

97. April 7th, Gask Journals, fol. 10r.

98. Weds 20th, Gask Diaries, fol. 20 r.

99. Frances Hamilton, Account and Day Book, Somerset Heritage Centre, DD/FS/7, fol. 349.

100. Frances Hamilton, Account and Day Book, fols. 344, 348.

101. Undated letter from Jonathan Chubb to Jack [John] Chubb, December 1759. Addressed to "To Mr Charles La Roche Cheapside for Master Chubb, London." Chubb correspondence A/CSC 2/3.

102. Samuel Gwinnett, "On Conversation," in "Lusus Pueriles; or, Essays in Prose and Verse," Gloucestershire Archives, D9125/1/5344, Fol 102.

103. John Constable, *The Conversation of Gentlemen Considered in Most of the Ways That Make Their Mutual Company Agreeable* (London, 1738), 44.

104. Steele, *Ladies Library*, 1:22.

105. See Adrian Johns, *The Nature of the Book: Print and Knowledge in the Making* (Chicago: University of Chicago Press, 1998), 470, on reading and sociability.

106. Steven Shapin, " 'A Scholar and a Gentleman': The Problematic Identity of the Scientific Practitioner in Early Modern England," *History of Science* 29 (1991), 279–327, reprinted in Shapin, *Never Pure: Historical Studies of Science* (Baltimore: Johns Hopkins University Press, 2010), 142–81.

107. Constable, *The Conversation of Gentlemen*, 235.

108. See Shapin, *Never Pure*, 161.

109. Elizabeth Hamilton, *Memoirs of the Late Mrs Elizabeth Hamilton with a Selection from her Correspondence*, ed. Miss Benger (London, 1819), 49–50.

110. See Alice N. Walters, "Conversation Pieces: Science and Politeness in Eighteenth-Century England," *History of Science* 35 (1997), 121–54.

111. Steven Shapin, " 'The Mind Is Its Own Place': Science and Solitude in Seventeenth-Century England," *Science in Context* 4 (1991), 191–218, reprinted in Shapin, *Never Pure: Historical Studies of Science* (Baltimore: Johns Hopkins University Press, 2010), 119–41, 134.

112. See Alice Walters, "Scientific and Medical Books, 1695–1780," in *The Cambridge History of the Book in Britain, 1695–1830*, ed. Michael Suarez and Michael Turner (Cambridge: Cambridge University Press, 2009), 818–26, 820.

113. Benjamin Martin, *A Plain and Familiar Introduction to the Newtonian Experimental Philosophy* (London, 1765).

114. James A. Secord, "Newton in the Nursery: Tom Telescope and the Philosophy of Tops and Balls, 1761–1838," *History of Science* 23 (1985), 127–151, 132.

115. *The Englishman*, no. 11, October 1713, in Richard Steele, *The Englishman: Being the Sequel of the Guardian* (London, 1714), 72–73.

116. See Walters, "Scientific and Medical Books," 823–24.

117. David Barker, *William Greatbatch: A Staffordshire Potter* (London: Jonathan Horne, 1990), plate 19, plate 148, 149.

118. Jill Shefrin, *Neatly Dissected for the Instruction of Young Ladies and Gentlemen in the Knowledge of Geography: John Spilsbury and Early Dissected Puzzles* (Los Angeles: Cotsen Occasional Press, 1999).

119. Ibid., 7.

120. "Preface," in *Atlas Minimus, or a New Set of Pocket Maps of the Several Empires* (London, 1758), n.p.

121. Chapone, *Letters on the Improvement of the Mind*, 2:152.

122. Judith A. Tyner, *Stitching the World: Embroidered Maps and Women's Geographical Education* (Farnham: Ashgate, 2015). For illustrations of solar system maps, almanacs, and mathematical tables, see Clare Browne and Jennifer Wearden, *Samplers from the Victoria and Albert Museum* (London: V&A Publications, 1999).

123. Tyner, *Stitching the World*, 18.

124. Ibid., 10.

125. 13 January 1761, Polly Stevenson to Benjamin Franklin, in *The Papers of Benjamin Franklin*, ed. Leonard W. Labaree et al., 41 vols. (New Haven: Yale University Press, 1959–), 9:270; cited in Walters, "Conversation Pieces," 136.

126. A precursor to this volume is Francesco Algarotti's *Newtonianism for Ladies* (Italian version 1737, trans. 1742), a series of lively dialogues that introduced accessible elements of Newtonian optics. See Massimo Mazzotti, "Newton for Ladies: Gentility, Gender, and Radical Culture," *British Journal for the History of Science* 37 (2004), 119–46.

127. *Guardian*, 155, 8 September 1713.

128. Althea Fanshawe, *Easter Holidays, or Domestic Conversations* (Bath, 1797), 3.

129. Charles Allen, *The Polite Lady; or, a Course in Female Education: In a Series of Letters from a Mother to her Daughter* (Dublin, 1763), 153–54.

130. Ann B. Shteir, *Cultivating Women, Cultivating Science: Flora's Daughters and Botany in England, 1760 to 1860* (Baltimore: Johns Hopkins University Press, 1996), 72. See also Samantha George, *Botany, Sexuality, and Women's Writing* (Manchester: Manchester University Press, 2007).

131. January 1797, Diary of Henry Woollcombe II, 1796–1803, Plymouth and West Devon Record Office, reference Ref 710/391, 6.

132. Elizabeth Fitton, *Conversations on Botany* (London, 1817), 22.

133. *New Lady's Magazine, or Polite and Entertaining Companion for the Fair Sex*, May 1786, 177.

134. Constable, *The Conversation of Gentlemen*, 141.

135. See Theresa Kelley, *Clandestine Marriage: Botany and Romantic Culture* (Baltimore: Johns Hopkins University Press, 2012); Amanda Vickery, *Behind Closed Doors: At Home in Georgian England* (New Haven: Yale University Press, 2009), 240–45.

136. *The Hamwood Papers of the Ladies of Llangollen and Caroline Hamilton,* ed. G. H. Bell (London: Macmillan, 1930), 206, 204.

137. Fanshawe, *Easter Holidays,* 148.

138. Richard Polewhele, *The Unsex'd Females, A Poem* (New-York, 1800), 10–11.

139. William Withering, *A Botanical Arrangement of all the Vegetables naturally growing in Great Britain,* 2 vols. (Birmingham, 1776), 1:v.

140. D. G. King-Hele, "Erasmus Darwin: Man of Ideas and Inventor of Words," *Notes and Records of the Royal Society of London* 42 (1988), 149–80.

141. Amelia Ann Sophia Steuart of Dalguise, Gask Journals, March 1789–1792, NLS MS 983 fol. 99r.

142. John Harris, *Astronomical Dialogues Between a Gentleman and a Lady* (London, 1719), v.

143. Advertisement for *The Microscopical Theatre of Seeds* (London, 1745), 1:n.p.

Afterword

1. Jennifer Richards's forthcoming study, *Voices and Books in the English Renaissance,* will offer an important corrective to our limited sense of early modern orality.

2. See, for example Maggie Jackson, *Distracted: The Erosion of Attention and the Coming Dark Age* (Amherst, N.Y.: Prometheus, 2008), or David L. Ulin, *The Lost Art of Reading: Why Books Matter in a Distracted Age* (Seattle: Sasquatch, 2010).

3. On the longer history of controversy and apprehension surrounding habits of reading, see Frank Furedi, *Power of Reading: From Socrates to Twitter* (London: Bloomsbury, 2015).

Index

Page numbers in *italics* refer to illustrations